A M E R I C A N
G O V E R N M E N T

THE
CORE

AMERICAN
GOVERNMENT

Second Edition

PETER WOLL
Brandeis University

SIDNEY E. ZIMMERMAN

McGraw-Hill, Inc.
New York St. Louis San Francisco Auckland Bogotá
Caracas Lisbon London Madrid Mexico City Milan
Montreal New Delhi San Juan Singapore
Sydney Tokyo Toronto

This book is printed on acid-free paper.

AMERICAN GOVERNMENT
The Core

4 5 6 7 8 9 0 DOC DOC 9 0 9 8 7 6 5 4

ISBN 0-07-071672-2

This book was set in Times Roman by General Graphic Services, Inc.
The editors were Bertrand W. Lummus and Fred H. Burns.
The cover was designed by Albert M. Cetta.
The photo editor was Anne Manning;
the photo researcher was Elyse Rieder.
R. R. Donnelley & Sons Company was printer and binder.

Chapter Opening Photo Credits
Chapter 1: Fredrik D. Bodin/Stock, Boston; Chapter 2: Carlin/The Picture Cube; Chapter 3: Peter Gridley/FPG International; Chapter 4: Craig Aurness/ Woodfin Camp & Associates; Chapter 5: UPI/Bettmann Newsphotos; Chapter 6: Lionel Delevingne/Stock, Boston; Chapter 7: J. L. Atlan/Sygma; Chapter 8: Paul Conklin/Monkmeyer; Chapter 9: UPI/Bettmann Newsphotos; Chapter 10: Bill Leissner/TexaStock; Chapter 11: Reuters/Bettmann Newsphotos; Chapter 12: Reuters/Bettmann Newsphotos.
Page 136: Chenet/Newsweek; page 137: Copyright © 1991 by The New York Times Company. Reprinted with permission. The New York Post.

Library of Congress Cataloging-in-Publication Data

Woll, Peter, (date).
    American government: the core / Peter Woll and Sidney E. Zimmerman.
        p.   cm.
    Includes bibliographical references and index.
    ISBN 0-07-071672-2
        1. United States—Politics and government.   I. Zimmerman, Sidney E.   II. Title.
JK274.W725   1992
320.973—dc20
                                                            91-17962

ABOUT THE AUTHORS

Peter Woll is Professor of Politics at Brandeis University, where his courses include an introduction to American government. He has also taught at the University of California at Los Angeles. Among his many books on government and politics are *Behind the Scenes in American Government, American Bureaucracy, The Private World of Congress*, with Rochelle Jones, and *America's Political System*, with Robert H. Binstock.

Sidney E. Zimmerman is a writer and editor living in New York.

For Mary, Cindy, and Bob

CONTENTS

PREFACE

T his brief text for the introductory course in U.S. government covers the nuts and bolts of American politics. Written in a style we believe will hold student interest. *American Government: The Core* was created as an alternative to the conventional textbook. Such textbooks may well be over 700 pages long and cost students as much as three times the price of our book. Moreover, our book's brevity permits professors assigning *The Core* to use a variety of supplements—readers, monographs, articles—that enrich and expand their courses as desired.

Although our purpose in writing a brief text was to keep the subject within manageable limits for students, we also wanted them to grasp the dynamics of American politics. To that end we placed our discussions of political institutions and processes within appropriate historical contexts. We also stressed the constitutional framework within which political action takes place. Students are thus able to see changes that have taken place within our political structures and yet sense the restraints on those changes that stem from the Constitution.

But a purely institutional approach to politics may be too abstract and forbidding for most students. We have therefore illustrated the text with short anecdotes drawn from the past, some of which is very recent. These little stories not only lighten the text, they also give it a human dimension and help students understand how political principles operate in the real world.

American Government: The Core takes the normal instructional route of introductory courses. The opening chapter provides the background and context for the study of American politics and democracy. It is followed by chapters devoted to the Constitution, civil liberties and civil rights, federalism, political parties, interest groups, the media, Congress, the presidency, the bureaucracy, the judiciary, and policies and politics. Each of the chapters following the first opens with a brief and very general discussion of its subject, then provides background—for the most part historical—on the subject, goes on to discuss the essentials of the subject, and ends with a summary and conclusion.

The text introduces students to both the formal and informal forces that have shaped our governmental institutions and political processes. Chapter 1 discusses the nature of government, politics, and democracy as they developed within history. The chapter also presents very short comparisons of American democracy with other democratic systems and briefly introduces students to some of the central concepts that have shaped our politics.

The second chapter presents the Constitution. Here the debates and political maneuvering at the Constitutional Convention of 1787 are portrayed. After treating the battle for ratification, the essentials of the Constitution are discussed. This discussion covers the electoral process, the impact of constituencies, checks and balances, and the structure of federalism. The chapter then continues with a brief discussion of the role of the Bill of Rights and a slightly longer treatment of the amendment process.

Next, Chapter 3 covers civil liberties and civil rights, tracing their origin and development throughout history. The political dimensions of civil liberties and rights are treated at some length. Each of the first ten amendments is analyzed and its broader significance discussed. A substantial part of the chapter is devoted to the nationalization of most of the Bill of Rights under the due process clause of the Fourteenth Amendment.

Having covered the origins and constitution of the national government, the text turns to a discussion of state governments and the essentials of federalism in Chapter 4. The structure of state and local governments is covered, as is the relationship between them and the national government. State experiments with public policy, one of the chief reasons usually given to buttress state and local governments, are discussed.

The text proceeds to the essentials of political parties and interest groups in chapters 5 and 6, respectively. The constitutional context of each is analyzed, and the important role that parties and interest groups play is stressed. Chapter 5 discusses the two-party system, party organization, national nominating conventions, and a variety of factors affecting voters and elections. Chapter 6 portrays lobbying and how lobbyists operate, and includes the important topic of political action committees and their role in the democratic process. Students are introduced here to different types of interest groups: business, labor, agricultural, professional, ideological, and public. The effort to influence public opinion is further pursued in Chapter 7, ''Public Opinion and the Media.'' In this chapter, the relationship of the media to public opinion is treated. Students are introduced to methods of measuring public opinion, the formation of attitudes and values, and agenda-setting function of the media, the impact of the media on public opinion, problems of truth and objectivity, the way the media operates, and sources of news stories.

The text turns next to an analysis of governmental institutions. First, Chapter 8 depicts the ''keystone of the Washington political establishment''—Congress. Included in the analysis are the constitutional structures of Congress, committee organization, congressional parties, and how a bill becomes law. In addition, the political environment of Congress and the power relationship of the president and the legislature are discussed.

The president and the bureaucracy are respectively covered in chapters 9 and 10. The ninth chapter analyzes the origin and nature of presidential power, and the complex role of the chief executive. This chapter includes a discussion of problems of succession and transition. Turning from the White House to the bureaucracy, Chapter 10 notes the growth of the American bureaucracy and its ambiguous role in our constitutional system. The structure and functions of the bureaucracy are next presented, including a discussion of the cabinet and its relationship to the Executive Office of the President. Other topics include rule making and adjudication of the bureaucracy, congressional oversight, and the development of the civil service.

The judiciary and particularly the Supreme Court occupy a unique position in the American political system. This is discussed in Chapter 11, which covers the origins of the judiciary and its role in contemporary politics. While the focus of the chapter is the Supreme Court, the organization and role of the lower federal judiciary is also discussed.

Each of the chapters on Congress, the presidency, the bureaucracy, and the judiciary presents a separate case study on policy-making to give students concrete examples of the important connection between government and the policies that rule them. While short illustrative examples of policy-making are given throughout the text where relevant, these unique case studies give students a more in-depth look at how public policy is actually made.

Finally, Chapter 11 gives an overview of policies and politics. Issues of legitimacy in making policy are addressed, and the ways in which policy-making and the political process interact are analyzed. The chapter concludes with a look at democracy in America—past, present, and future—and restates one of the basic themes of the book, first proposed in Chapter 1, that American democracy is a dynamic process undergoing continuous change.

PEDAGOGICAL AIDS

Subheadings guide the student throughout the text. Each chapter begins with a background discussion of its topic, and a conclusion and summary help give the reader perspective. Each chapter but the first contains an essentials section, with subheadings that pinpoint the major topics of the chapter. Important terms are set in italics and defined in the text. At the back of the book, students will also find a glossary that provides them with the vocabulary of current political discourse. Tables, charts, and diagrams containing important information on American political institutions and processes are furnished throughout the text and in appendices in the back of the book. The appendices also contain the Declaration of Independence and the Constitution for the interested student's easy reference.

A separate instructors' manual, prepared by Martin Sutton of Bucks County Community College in Pennsylvania, contains multiple choice, true/false, and essay questions as well as learning objectives and bibliographies for each chapter.

ACKNOWLEDGMENTS

We would like to take this opportunity to thank the following reviewers: Christopher Berkeley, Framingham State College; James R. Bowers, St. John Fisher College; Larry Elowitz, Georgia College; Robert Keele, University of the South; Richard W. Lacy, J. Sargeant Reynolds Community College; Sam W. McKinstry, East Tennessee State University; David Nice, University of Washington; Ronald W. Reinighaus, Valencia Community College; Jan P. Vermeer, Nebraska Wesleyan University; John Wallenfang, Lake Michigan College; and Herbert Weisberg, Ohio State University, Columbus. Their criticisms and suggestions were always helpful and have influenced this revised edition. However, final responsibility for all of the content remains with us.

Bertrand Lummus, our McGraw-Hill editor, conceived of the project and skillfully guided it to completion. The authors greatly appreciate his generous spirit, which was comforting and stress-reducing but not at the expense of being properly demanding. William Barter and Fred Burns of McGraw-Hill greatly contributed to the book, guiding its development and production with an expert eye and an understanding of the needs of introductory students.

Finally, the book could not have been completed without the dedication and hard work of Elaine Herrmann, who took time out of a busy schedule to word-process the manuscript. She was a calm and important kingpin of the project.

Peter Woll

Sidney E. Zimmerman

A WORD TO THE STUDENT

I n the last several years, democracy seemed to have triumphed around the globe. Or, at least, so crowed the American press. "Communism Collapsed" was shouted from TV tubes and in banner headlines. There was an almost audible sigh of relief: "Democracy is safe at last."

Well, not so fast. Democracy is always in danger. And the danger is not necessarily external. It may very well come from within itself. As the ancient Greek philosopher Aristotle pointed out about 2,500 years ago, democracy is vulnerable to demogoguery. We can see the truth of his statement in our own history. Just recall the widespread persecution of Catholics and immigrants by the Know-Nothings of the 1840s and 1850s; the popularly backed witch hunt of political dissidents by the U.S. Attorney General during the Red Scare of the early 1920's; and the often mean-spirited and brutal hounding of those suspected of Communist sympathies by Senator Joseph McCarthy and the rest of the country during the early to mid 1950s. In each of these instances, Constitutionally guaranteed freedoms were violated, with the approval of the majority of people. In each case, American democracy stumbled because of risks inherent in the democratic process.

For over 200 years, the United States has survived the dangers inherent in democracy. We have managed to do so because of the way government is structured and power distributed in our society. To assure the continued existence of democracy in this country, it is necessary for all of us to know and understand how our system of government works. It is toward this end that *American Government: The Core* is directed.

This book was written with students such as yourselves in mind. Its central purpose is to explain how government works in the United States today and how democracy in America developed over time. The text, therefore, approaches its dual purpose from three vantage points. It looks at the constitutionally mandated government and the realities involved in actually governing. The text also examines the dynamic and changing character of democracy, especially as it is affected by the realities of governance. And third, the text places our notions of democracy within a broad historical context so that you can get some idea of the rich past from within which those notions evolved. As Franklin D. Roosevelt observed some little while ago: "The democratic aspiration is no mere recent phase of human history. It *is* human history."

Several themes run through the text. A major one is that the American system of government is based on conflict. Related to this is the theme that the presidency has been growing in power throughout our history. A second theme is that respect for minorities—political, religious, and racial—is central to American democracy. Related to this is the constant struggle to maintain this central feature of our democratic system. A third major theme is that American democracy is dynamic and in a process of constant change. Related to this is that rights and liberties for most groups have increased over time, but have also been continually threatened with restrictions.

When you complete this text you should have some notion of the essential features of the American government. You should also be able to describe the nature of American democracy. And finally, you should have some sense of where our notions of democracy came from. You might also be able to guess where they are headed.

AMERICAN
GOVERNMENT

chapter
1

BACKGROUND and CONTEXT: POLITICS and AMERICAN DEMOCRACY

The polis exists to assure the good life.

Aristotle

The American political system is the end product of a long development. The process started in antiquity, reached a culmination in the eighteenth century, and has continued into our own age. Values that the ancient Greeks promoted more than 2,500 years ago still command the allegiance of some Americans today. Socrates, for example, refused to escape prison and certain death because as a good citizen he felt he had to obey the authorities of ancient Athens. During the Iran-contra affair, three American military men—Admiral John Poindexter, General Richard Secord, and Lieutenant Colonel Oliver North—grudgingly accepted disgrace, a kind of professional death, because they felt that they had to carry out the wishes of the top authorities in the United States government. In both instances, the state was considered "prior to the individual," to quote another ancient Greek.

But, for the most part, the American political system does not stress the "priority" of the state. Indeed, the American tradition instead places a strong emphasis on individual rights and government as the servant—rather than the master—of that collection of individuals known as *the people*. However, the American tradition is not monolithic, as we can see from our brief review of the individual and the state.

Clearly, several perspectives influence the American way of politics. Some views, such as the priority of the state, are of ancient vintage; some, such as the emphasis on individual rights, stem from the seventeenth and eighteenth centuries; and some, such as the notion that government should guarantee the well-being of all the people, became prominent in the twentieth century. Central to each of these ways of looking at politics is the relationship of government to the individuals who are governed. This then raises the question: What do we mean by government?

WHAT IS GOVERNMENT?

Any attempt to answer the question of what government is must first deal with the issue of how government came to be. This is a very difficult problem to solve. The earliest written records that we have were produced about 5,500 years ago by the priestly rulers of the city-state of Ur between the Tigris and Euphrates rivers in present-day Iraq. It is clear from these records that government—and bureaucracy—had already been in existence for a long time. We know from other archeological remains that there were cities in the Middle East almost 10,000 years ago. Cities require social organization, and social organization implies the presence of government, however rudimentary.

Any social grouping that lasts, however small, possesses a kind of governmental structure. We can take the family as an example. A family is usually headed by a father or mother who, within the family, generally exercises the highest authority (i.e., legitimate power). Nevertheless, he or she is usually bound by family custom—a set of unwritten laws—and according to those customs arbitrates family disputes. A prime responsibility of the family head is thus to keep the peace within the family. One aspect of keeping the peace is to make certain that all family members receive their due. This does not necessarily mean that everyone receives the same amount of something, but rather that they all accept as just the amounts they do receive. On the basis of this description, we can say that the family customarily has a system of authority, a tradition of justice, and an acceptable distribution of family rewards. The parental figure who assures the smooth functioning of this arrangement we can reasonably consider a government.

Larger political structures, such as the nation-state, serve much the same purpose as the family. *States* are societies seen from within a political perspective. They are organized communities that occupy large territories and provide authority, security, laws, justice, and rewards. Perhaps a short digression is in order here. The term ''state'' is used not only with reference to the large political entity just described; it is also often used to mean ''government.'' We shall try to keep these terms distinct, although it may not always be possible, as when quoting Louis XIV, the seventeenth-century king of France, who said ''I am the state,'' meaning quite correctly that he was the government.

In any case, we can tentatively define *government* as that organ of the state which exercises the highest authority so as to provide security and justice according to laws or customs that allow the rewards of society to be distributed peacefully. But, of course, the government does not stand alone in society. It interacts with the populace it governs, in some instances to accommodate the popular will, in some instances to suppress it.

POLITICS AND GOVERNMENT

For the purposes of our discussion, we might say that *politics* is the process by means of which government and the people who are governed interact. One of the prime considerations in this interactive relationship is the available methods for peaceful change. The ability to change government policies or practices peacefully is crucial to national stability, and stability is essential to the economic well-being of a nation. As Edmund Burke, the great eighteenth-century English political thinker, put it: "A state without the means of some change is without the means of its conservation."

"It's true, Dave, that I have an unsavory past, but if elected to public office I hope to hold myself up to a higher standard."

CHANGE AND STABILITY

In the American system, the relationship between the people and the government is complex and based on the possibility of constant change. This arrangement can create instability in some areas of society. We have so many elections that governmental policies can and often do change in midstream. An example of this is the recently altered course of affirmative action programs (programs to offset the negative effects of past discrimination against blacks and women). During the years between the presidency of Lyndon B. Johnson and the election of President Ronald Reagan, the government pursued a vigorous affirmative action policy. Since Reagan's election, the government has moderated its pursuit of that policy and has even at times opposed affirmative action in the courts. Another potential cause of instability is the shifting alliances within the electorate, as when large numbers of workers joined with their traditional adversaries, small-business people, to vote for Ronald Reagan in 1980 and for George Bush in 1988. These changing alliances often have a profound effect on both legislation and elections.

Authoritarian regimes do not face the same problem, although they, like democracies, must have a "positive" relationship with the majority of those they govern. A positive relationship does not necessarily require popular approval. It can come about as a result of fear, indifference, cynicism, or overwhelming despair. In any case, authoritarians provide absolute stability, at least for the period they are in power, and are often enthusiastically supported by a significant portion of their populace for this very reason, as evidenced by the sweeping victory of the former communist leaders in Romania's first free election, held in 1990.

The American system, despite its penchant for change, is sufficiently stable to have continued and grown for some 200 years. In a sense, both American stability and changeableness were built into the system from the start. The very constitutional system that makes change frequent also makes for stability and continuity. Members of the House of Representatives are elected for two-year terms, senators are elected for six-year terms, and presidents for four-year terms. Moreover, one-third of the Senate is up for election every two years. This complex electoral requirement makes for an uneven rotation of individuals, hence of political beliefs, in two of the formal centers of power, the presidency, or executive, and the Congress, or legislature. In the other power center, the federal judiciary headed by the Supreme Court, judges are appointed for life and generally sit through several changes in the executive and legislative branches. The constitutional provision for continuity in the midst of change serves to restrain any extreme innovations on the part of the government.

Thus, continuity tends to be the norm in the United States, and major changes in social policy, such as the civil rights act of the 1960s, require massive support from various interest groups. However, radical change in governmental behavior or policy can also come about through other means. This can occur when a president and a significant part of the legislature are newly elected and are in basic agreement, as happened, for example, during President Reagan's first term. But for the most part, the Constitution tends to inhibit radical change.

Formal Constraints: Checks and Balances.   The constitutional inhibition of governmental radicalism derives from the Founding Fathers' anxiety about strong government and majority control. As James Madison wrote Thomas Jefferson: "Wherever the real power in the Government lies, there is the danger of oppression. In our Government the real power lies in the majority of the Community, and the invasion of private rights is chiefly to be apprehended ... from acts in which the Government is the mere instrument of the major number of the constituents." To allay their fears, the Framers of the Constitution designed a government based on a conflict model.

Often citing the arguments in *The Spirit of the Laws,* written by the eighteenth-century French political theorist Baron Charles de Montesquieu, the Framers divided the authority of the state between the executive, legislative, and judicial branches of government. Through this *separation of powers* the Framers felt that "ambition [was] made to counteract ambition ... in such a manner as that each may be a check on the other," to quote James Madison again, this time from *The Federalist,* No. 51.[1]

The system of checks and balances devised by the Framers extends into all areas of governmental relations. Congress is divided into two chambers—the Senate and the House of Representatives—so as to serve as a further check on excessive legislative power. In this instance the Framers shared with Thomas Jefferson his abhorrence of legislative tyranny when he said "One hundred and seventy-three despots would surely be as oppressive as one." Beyond the checks and balances within the national government, federalism was intended to provide a system of mutual checks on federal, state, and local governments. Through this intricate system of countervailing forces, the Framers hoped to tame the black beast of their nightmares, strong government.

But the Framers of the Constitution were not all of one mind. Within the leadership of the Constitutional Convention itself there was disagreement over the nature of government. Both George Washington and Alexander Hamilton, for example, were advocates of strong central governments. During the convention, Washington expressed his sentiments bluntly in a letter to Hamilton: "The Men who oppose a strong & energetic government are, in my opinion, narrow minded politicians." Hamilton, for his part, had proposed a plan to the convention in which a strong central government would be supreme over the states. In *The Federalist,* No. 70, he argued for a strong executive, saying "a feeble executive implies a feeble ... government [which] must be in practice a bad government." Madison and his mentor Jefferson were, as we have seen, equally strong advocates of limited government restrained by a system of checks and balances. Both also firmly believed that in a republic "the legislative authority necessarily predominates," and of course also needed to be checked.

The tension visible among the founders has continued to our own day. At different times in our history, the Madisonian or Hamiltonian models of government have prevailed. During periods of extreme crisis, such as the Civil War or the First World War, the presidency has been ascendant. Otherwise, the Madi-

---

[1] *The Federalist,* ed. Clinton Rossiter (New York: Mentor, 1961). *The Federalist* was a series of newspaper articles written by Alexander Hamilton, James Madison, and John Jay. Appearing under the name Publius, the articles were written to persuade New York State's voters and ratifying convention to adopt the new Constitution signed in Philadelphia on September 17, 1787. *The Federalist* has since become almost as sacred as the Constitution that it defended and explained.

sonian model of checks and balances with an occasionally dominant Congress characterized the political system until the presidency of Franklin D. Roosevelt. For a variety of reasons—the double crises of the Great Depression and World War II, the electoral majority of the president's party in Congress for his four terms, and his charismatic personality—the Roosevelt administration inaugurated a prolonged period in which presidents dominated the political scene. With the near impeachment of President Richard Nixon in the mid-1970s, there was a short hiatus during which Congress reasserted its authority. When Ronald Reagan was elected in 1980 with a majority of his party in the Senate, the so-called imperial presidency was resumed. In the middle of his second term, and as a result of his administration's blatant disregard of certain restrictive laws, Congress had once again asserted its authority. The constitutional adjustments available through the separation of powers tends so far to provide a kind of self-correcting and stabilizing mechanism when the system gets too far out of balance.

Nonformal Pressures.   In addition to formal, institutional mechanisms that make for stability within change, nonformal relationships also do the same. Representative governments are very sensitive to the demands of organized segments of the electorate, or *interest groups,* as they are often called. As a consequence, elected or appointed members of the government will respond at times to interest-group pressure by changing policies or laws.

Interest groups differ from political parties in structure and objectives. American political parties are large, loosely knit, decentralized organizations primarily concerned with placing their candidates in public office. By contrast, interest groups are small, centralized organizations that focus on a single issue. Their prime objective is to influence those within government regardless of party affiliation.

The influence an interest group has on an elected or appointed official stems in part from the group's ability to mobilize a part of the electorate around its issue. Environmental and senior citizen organizations are examples of this sort of interest group. Another source of interest-group influence is money. Many large corporations have political action committees (PACs) that buy influence by contributing to the campaigns for elective office of candidates who are opposing one another. Of course there are other kinds of PACs as well. There are PACs representing professional organizations, such as the American Medical Association, unions, such as the AFL-CIO, and ideological positions, such as conservative and liberal views. Very often the PACs and other kinds of interest groups provide specialized knowledge to lawmakers and bureaucrats. This service is an invaluable aid to legislators in drawing up bills and to government officials in formulating or revising regulations, and hence is a third major source of interest-group influence.

Collectively, interest groups reflect most of the political concerns of the nation. This very broad representation tends also to provide a system of checks and balances, as was anticipated by James Madison in *The Federalist,* No. 51. Often, powerful interest groups are in conflict with each other, thereby neutralizing one another's influence. One result of this neutralizing process is the continuation of earlier policies, which may not always be beneficial. For example, gun-control groups have been unable to persuade Congress to pass a law requiring federal registration of small handguns because of the opposition of gun-owning groups. Of course, the continuation of earlier policies despite strong opposition can also be very beneficial, as in providing government support to the sick and elderly poor.

But interest groups are not the only influential forces in politics, whether in the United States or elsewhere.

POLITICS AND POWER

Political pressure to influence representative governments is most often brought to bear by *political parties,* which are formal organizations seeking to win or retain public office. Although there are a fairly large number of political parties in the United States, only two are dominant and able to put people in national office— the Democratic and Republican parties. Great Britain, a parliamentary democracy in which the legislature chooses the executive, also has two dominant parties, although recently a third one has gained some prominence. In Europe, by contrast, the parliamentary democracies of West Germany, France, Italy, and Spain have a multitude of parties. Political parties outside the United States tend to be highly centralized national organizations having a top-downward direction, or what Americans consider an authoritarian party structure. The national leadership generally formulates party policy and tactics for the entire country, however democratic the political system itself may be.

In parliamentary democracies, the executive is formed from among the leaders of the dominant party or parties in the legislature. When there is a multiplicity of parties, as in Italy or Israel, the executive is formed by tenuous, ephemeral coalitions that can break down at any moment. To assure itself of enough votes in the legislature to govern, the executive often gives way to tiny minority parties that in this fashion wield power out of all proportion to their numbers.

Power, as we know, is the ability to influence or compel others to act in a particular, desired way. Most often we think of power as if it were identical with physical force, but obviously, as in the case of the multiparty state, this is not necessarily so. When a tiny minority party can force a much larger party to do its will, its power derives from its ability to withhold something, parliamentary votes in our example, that is needed to govern. In other instances, power stems from persuasive ability, as in the case of Martin Luther King, Jr., who was able to convince the elite white power structure of the United States that it should try to improve the condition of black people. And, of course, we all know that power also comes out of the barrel of a gun.

In one-party states, such as the Soviet Union, political pressure tends to build below the surface and to be exerted by informal groups within the party elite. Since the elevation of Mikhail S. Gorbachev to the top leadership within the Communist Party, subterranean pressures have reached the surface and become quite visible. These pressures have proven explosive and have resulted in the breakdown of the Soviet system. We do not yet know the consequences of this breakdown. From a system that permitted no deviation from a rigid party line, the Soviet Union has changed to a system that seems to allow a multitude of contending figures to struggle for power.

IDEOLOGY AND POLITICS

Democratic leaders, of course, also vie for power. Their competition is usually cast in ideological terms. *Ideology*[2] is a group of related ideas, values, assumptions, and prejudices that constitute the basic political beliefs of groups of individuals. The term *political philosophy* is often used as a synonym. Very often, an ideology is unsystematic, and sometimes, it is self-contradictory. Nevertheless, it can be emotionally compelling and move people to action. For example, the official American ideology of "democracy" is that government—the executive—is subject to the "will of the people" as expressed by the legislature, Congress. Yet, the members of the executive branch have sometimes been willing to violate basic American principles and act counter to laws passed by Congress, as happened in the Iran-contra affair.

Holding contradictory ideological views simultaneously is not unusual. Most Americans, as most citizens of most countries, do not have strong political beliefs. They can thus hold at the same time two ideological views that are diametrically opposed, as, let us say, the belief that *everyone* should earn an income on his own without government help and that the government should make sure no one starves. But this is not true of those who are politically active. Individuals who are actively involved in politics, whether within established parties or not, generally espouse ideologically consistent views. These people are usually vocal and articulate about their beliefs. Periodically, they tend to move the inconsistent part of the electorate in one or another ideological direction. In the United States, the direction is often determined by one of two main contending ideologies: *liberalism* and *conservatism*.

Liberalism.   Often applied to the beliefs of the late eighteenth century, the term *liberalism* was originally used in the nineteenth century with reference to an ideology stressing an elected government having very limited powers. Minimal government was the ideal. In essence, this view raised the individual above the state and government. As long as individuals did not harm one another, they should be free of all social restraints and live in a laissez-faire society.

Gradually over time, laissez-faire liberalism shifted toward an activist belief that government ought to intervene to improve social and economic conditions, but still respect the privacy of individuals as a supreme value. In the United States, interventionist liberalism can be thought to have started with William Lloyd Garrison's abolitionist writings in the early nineteenth century and Abraham Lincoln's Emancipation Proclamation in 1863 outlawing slavery. The anti-trust laws, beginning with the Sherman Act of 1890, which were intended to protect small business and labor from the excessive power of giant corporations, continued the interventionist style of liberalism. At this point, liberalism entered the twentieth century. Modern liberalism gained an internationalist component when Woodrow

---

[2]The term was invented by the French political thinker Destutt de Tracy (1758–1836) to describe a systematic arrangement of ideas, among which were concepts of government, religion, ethics, etc. The German philosopher Karl Marx (1818–1883) applied the term to society and assigned it a specifically political meaning.

Wilson brought the United States into World War I in 1917 "to save democracy" and advocated entry into the League of Nations in 1919 after the war had ended. Liberalism reached its final form during the administration of Franklin D. Roosevelt and his New Deal. Roosevelt initiated a program of active government intervention to stimulate the economy, assist the poor and weak, and equalize the bargaining power of labor and management. Toward the end of his tenure, FDR publicly espoused Wilson's internationalism.

In the years following FDR's death, liberalism completed its ideological move from advocacy of minimal government without regard for the poor and weak to advocacy of an activist government engaged in aiding those who are vulnerable socially or economically, such as women, minorities, the poor, the elderly, the sick, and others. But liberalism has continued its earlier adherence to the view that one's private life and personal beliefs are inviolable and must not be interfered with or regulated by government. Basically, the goal of modern liberalism is a "just" society that respects personal freedom. However, it also favors the suppression of an individual's freedom to be unjust—as in refusing to hire a black person—even though this suppression contradicts one of its basic principles.

Conservatism. Like the term *liberal,* the word *conservative* arose in the nineteenth century and was applied retroactively to the political beliefs of tradition-

DRAWING BY HANDELSMAN; © 1984 THE NEW YORKER MAGAZINE, INC.

"Hutchins, what on earth gave you the notion that we want the rich to get poorer and the poor to get richer?"

alists in the late eighteenth century. At that time, conservatism held that a central government must have absolute authority, every citizen owed unquestioning obedience to the state, individual freedom must be restrained for the good of the state, religious values furnished by an established church should govern personal behavior and should be enforced by the state, and an aristocracy or other elite should provide the leadership of the state. In the United States, conservatism also argued that the country should not be involved with international affairs. Thus, in the late eighteenth and nineteenth centuries, the principles of conservatism were diametrically opposed to those of laissez-faire liberalism.

But because of its identification with elites, and as liberal governments began to restrict the privileges of the upper classes, conservatism started to shift ground. Conservatives started to argue for individual rights and nonintervention by government in economic matters. With the increasing effort by liberal governments to protect the rights of workers and enforce racial equality, conservatives came out in support of minimum government and the freedom of individuals from government "interference." Finally, as communist power grew around the world, conservatives began to advocate an aggressive international policy to combat what they saw as "international communism." In short, modern conservatism has selectively adopted many of the arguments of laissez-faire liberalism for nonliberal purposes.

Most present-day conservatives also hold to some earlier conservative beliefs, especially on social issues. They still argue, for example, that the government must regulate private behavior, as in the case of a woman's right to an abortion or a person's right to read any kind of literature he or she wishes. They still hold that religious values are essential to the moral fabric of our society and ought to be taught in school. Many conservatives in the "Religious Right" maintain that Darwin's theory of evolution should not be presented in schools because it is counter to religious doctrine.

Among both conservatives and liberals there are, of course, many shadings of gray. Neither ideology is entirely monolithic, and both have been influenced by other ideologies on their fringes. Although the adherents of our two belief systems tend to come from certain strata of society, social class does not predict political beliefs. For example, many conservatives live in rural America, especially in the Midwest, yet the Progressive movement—one of the influences on mainstream liberalism—was very strong in agricultural states like Wisconsin. Workers, to choose another example, were a bulwark of New Deal liberalism, yet they voted in droves for conservative presidents in the 1972, 1980, and 1988 elections.

It is clear that our two main competing ideologies are in constant flux, continually adapting to changing circumstances and appealing to varying constituencies. Both liberalism and conservatism, at different times, also influence our conception of "democracy." The American notion of *democracy* is not a rigidly fixed set of principles. It is, and has been throughout our history, a dynamic set of beliefs that is constantly changing. It has on many occasions been called upon to explain the actions of both liberal and conservative administrations in Washington, D.C. American governments have used imagined threats to democracy to justify the suspension of basic democratic principles such as the right to express one's opinion freely, as in the wholesale arrest of socialists, pacifists, and labor leaders made by the liberal administration of Woodrow Wilson during the Red Scare of 1919 and 1920.

Many strands went into the theory of democratic government, and it took many centuries for them to get woven into a single, if many-colored, fabric. We will now take a fast look at the weaving.

PRELUDES TO THE AMERICAN SYSTEM

THEORIES OF GOVERNMENT

In ancient Greece, Plato and Aristotle believed that the successful state provides an orderly system in which all the citizens accept their place in society. Plato argued that this would be best achieved by having wise rulers—philosopher-kings or sage "guardians"—who would possess *absolute authority* (unrestrained and unquestioned power accepted as legitimate). Aristotle, by contrast, stated that there were basically three kinds of government: monarchy; aristocracy; and "polity," government by the citizenry as a whole in the public interest. Each type was legitimate and could, if properly run, meet the needs of its citizens. If a government was not properly run and did not meet all its citizens' needs, then rebellion by those who were not satisfied was justified.

The ancient Roman jurist Cicero accepted Plato's notion of the need for absolute authority, but he also suggested the existence of a primeval equality. In the earliest times, Cicero posited, individuals living together as equals in a state of nature agreed to form a republic. Although he did not use the term, Cicero first suggested in *De Republica* that a social contract was the basis of the state. The term *social contract* refers to a presumed agreement made in earliest times to form a government for certain purposes. To Cicero, the purpose of the government is to secure property rights. About 1,500 years after his death, Cicero's writings greatly influenced Renaissance writers and thinkers.

Contract theories similar to Cicero's came to the fore in seventeenth-century England, a period of extraordinary political turmoil. The central conflict of the time was between the kings of England and Parliament. The kings claimed on religious grounds that they ruled by divine right and possessed absolute authority. Parliament contended that it should be the sole lawmaking body, that the king's authority should be limited, and that he should be accountable under the law.

In 1651, Thomas Hobbes published *Leviathan,* an entirely secular, rationalistic defense of absolute authority. He based his argument on the social contract produced in some primordial time, a time he called the *state of nature*. In the state of nature, he argued, all individuals are completely free and equal. Their natural inclination is to acquire as much power over others as they can, which puts them all "in that condition called war, and such a war as is every man against every man." Therefore, "the life of man [in the state of nature is] solitary, poor, nasty, brutish, and short." To protect their lives and improve their condition, individuals enter into a "covenant," or social contract, with one another in which they surrender their personal liberty and submit totally to the absolute authority of "one man, or one assembly of men.''[3] Hobbes's theory could serve equally well to defend the autocratic monarchies of the past and the totalitarian regimes of the present.

Diametrically opposed to Hobbes, John Locke worked out a theory of representative government that has become the basis of what we now call *democracy*. In 1690, Locke published his *Second Treatise of Civil Government* as a defense of limited monarchy and parliamentary supremacy. He too based his argument on man in a state of nature agreeing to a social contract. Locke's state of nature, however, is very different from Hobbes's nasty, brutish condition. For Locke, as for Cicero, individuals in a state of nature enjoyed complete equality, freedom, peace, and the satisfaction of working together for mutual benefit. But, Locke further argued, this harmonious condition was fragile and easily destroyed by the unjust use of force, as when a prince takes away a citizen's rights or a thief steals a person's property. To protect themselves against injustice, individuals enter into a ''compact,'' or social contract, in which they give up a portion of the ''equality, liberty, and executive power they had in the state of nature.'' By this contract they form a ''commonwealth,'' or state, and place their trust in a legislative authority. If this authority violates its trust, then the people have the right to rebel and change their government.

Locke's theory of government directly influenced the making of the United States Constitution. He proposed a three-part division of government in which the legislative division was supreme. He asserted that ''there remains still in the people a supreme power'' after vesting authority in what he called ''constitutional government.'' He argued that government can justly govern only with the consent of the governed. He called for an electoral system that would provide equal representation of all the people in the state. Finally, he said that the ability of the people to peacefully change their representatives is essential to a just society. Later generations of Americans took Locke's prescription—he was a medical doctor—and, combining it with other ideas, developed a viable democratic system.

THE COLONIAL EXPERIENCE

Although Locke and other thinkers had a profound influence on our Founding Fathers, other factors also influenced them. Chief among these was their own history in the Americas. By the time of the American Revolution and the Constitutional Convention, the people on these shores had evolved a past and tradition of their own. That tradition was a complex one and still influences our attitudes and political behavior today.

The early settlers on the eastern coast of North America came for a wide variety of reasons. Many were merchants, artisans, tradesmen, and small farmers who came mainly in the hope of making their fortunes in a ''new and open'' society. The ''old country,'' mainly England, was very much a closed society in the seventeenth and eighteenth centuries. There were few opportunities for either social or economic advancement, especially for the lower classes, from which

---

[3]Thomas Hobbes, *Leviathan, or the Matter, Forme, and Power of a Commonwealth Ecclesiastical and Civil*, ed. Michael Oakeshott (New York: Macmillan, 1973), p. 100.

most early settlers were drawn. When they arrived, they settled mainly in the northern and middle colonies, such as Massachusetts, New York, and Pennsylvania.

Others, also arriving in America for economic reasons, came essentially as investors with capital to buy and develop land or as indentured servants bound to the investors for a period of time in return for their passage. These indentured servants worked mainly as sort of short-term serfs on the investors' land; while their hope was that they would be able to earn some money after working off their debt so that they could buy a little land of their own, most died before completing their service. Both investors and indentured servants settled chiefly in colonies having fertile land, such as Virginia or the Carolinas, where they developed the plantation system of the South. As their holdings prospered and since their indentured servants were not a permanent work force, either because they died early or departed, the plantation owners began to import slaves from Africa to work their lands.

Still others came for religious reasons. Religion, like politics, generates a great deal of emotion that tends to affect many areas of life. Moreover, the distinction we normally make between politics and religion was virtually inconceivable to most people in the seventeenth century. Back then, people fused religious, political, and economic interests into a single ideological amalgam much as they do now in the Middle East.

The first religious migrants—the Pilgrims and Puritans—settled in the Northeast on Cape Cod and around Massachusetts Bay. Although they were fleeing religious intolerance, the governments they set up here did not tolerate divergent religious views. For example, Anne Hutchinson, whose views on the role of the Bible and the clergy differed from those of established Puritan beliefs, was banished in the seventeenth century from Massachusetts as a heretic. Deeply interested in educating the young, the Puritans founded the first public schools so that "the knowledge of the Scriptures ... may not be buried in the grave of our fathers...."[4] Our present-day conflicts over the separation of church and state in such matters as school prayer or teaching evolution to children have their origins in the Puritans' view that all life must conform to religious doctrine.

The Puritans' intolerance gave rise, early on within their own community, to highly vocal dissent, as we saw with Anne Hutchinson. Even before Hutchinson was banished, Roger Williams was evicted from Massachusetts. He had called for the separation of church and state, which was bad enough. But he also demanded religious freedom for all, and argued persuasively for government by consent of all without regard to religious affiliation. Banished by the theocratic government of Massachusetts, Williams left with a fairly large following and established his own colony in Providence, Rhode Island, in 1644.

Others besides the Puritans came to America seeking some degree of religious freedom. Lord Baltimore founded Maryland as a haven for Catholics, but eventually established freedom of worship for all Christians (non-Christians faced the

---

[4]From the Massachusetts school law of November 11, 1647, reprinted in *Living American Documents*, ed. Isidore Starr et al. (New York: Harcourt Brace Jovanovich, 1971), p. 13.

possibility of being "punished with death"). Somewhat later, William Penn established a representative government in Pennsylvania granting religious freedom to all believers in God but restricting political office to Christians. Obviously, atheists could not find a home in either Pennsylvania or Maryland, and neither Jews nor Turks, to borrow Roger Williams's categories, could hold office in Pennsylvania or survive in Maryland. The road to complete freedom of religion was a bumpy one indeed.

The Judeo-Christian faith posits a contract with God, and as deeply religious folk, seventeenth-century Englishmen were inveterate contract writers. They wrote charters for corporations, indentures for servants, and various contractual agreements with their monarchs, such as the Petition of Right of 1628 and the English Bill of Rights of 1689. When Englishmen came to America they did the same. Shortly before landing at Plymouth on Cape Cod, the Pilgrims composed the Mayflower Compact. After they migrated to Connecticut from Massachusetts, a group of Puritans wrote the first constitution in America, which they called *The Fundamental Orders*.

All colonies were founded by charters, some of which were essentially business contracts, as in the case of the Massachusetts Bay Company or the Virginia Company that founded Jamestown; others were royal grants of land as if to feudal lords, as in the case of Maryland or Pennsylvania; and still others were constitutions written by the colonists themselves and accepted by the crown, as in the case of Connecticut or Rhode Island. Each of these "contracts" established systems of government. Some vested ultimate authority in a proprietor, such as Lord Baltimore or William Penn; others in an elected or appointed governor; and still others in an assembly elected by all "freemen," as in Massachusetts. In those colonies that did not at first have representative governments to make their laws, so many problems arose that, as in New York and Virginia, the colonies finally received royal charters granting such governments. By the mid-eighteenth century, social contracts granting a high degree of self-government were the norm in the American colonies.

Despite extensive self-government, many colonists chafed under English rule. For about 100 years prior to the Revolution, there was antagonism between the American colonists and the English government. The colonists felt their rights were being violated by an increasingly oppressive central government that was in London and far removed from the local scene. In an effort to correct this situation, many colonists agreed with John Adams when he called for a "federal system" in which colonial governments and Parliament would be separate and equal authorities under the king. But that was not to be. While Adams called for equality under the king, others called for freedom from all kings. For a large number of colonists, the monarchical system as such had lost all legitimacy. As the Revolution started, they and an increasing number of colonists responded enthusiastically to Tom Paine's call for "the free and independent states of America."

LEGITIMACY AND DEMOCRACY

When the former colonists got together after the Revolution to frame a new government, they were concerned that it be strong enough to protect the people, but not so strong as to oppress them. To this end, they devised the American Constitution. From the Framers' point of view, power should flow, within certain limits, from the will of the people. But in reality, power flows from that which has the most influence, and almost everywhere, governments have the most influence. The acceptance of this influence by the people means that they have granted legitimacy to their government. When governments lose legitimacy, as Britain did here in 1775, they face revolution.

The term *legitimate* comes from the Latin *legitimus*, meaning "lawful," "just," "equitable," and "proper," and was often used with reference to the right to inherit property. *Legitimacy* is the noun form of legitimate. During the period when monarchy was virtually the sole form of government, "legitimacy" applied to the lawful heir to the throne and hence to the legal right to rule. In this sense, the prince or king had legitimacy. Over time, as more and more people felt that legally constituted royal governments were "unjust" or "inequitable," some additional meanings of legitimacy came to the fore. More than simply the legal right to rule was demanded of the ruler. When the actions of an oppressive, despotic ruler were considered "unjust" or "improper," many of his subjects then felt that he lost legitimacy—the right to rule. At this point the word acquired considerable moral force.

In early monarchical and aristocratic states, the source of legitimacy was a relatively simple matter. A king, prince, noble, or other heir was granted legitimacy

"We'd better tone this down or George III will sue us for libel. . ."

DRAWING BY ED FISHER; © 1984 THE NEW YORKER MAGAZINE, INC.

"Well, that ends all discussion of the 'electability' question."

by the parents' marriage contract. Over time, the marriage contract was by itself not enough to confer legitimacy on a ruler. In response, kings began to claim they were specially ordained by God and thus ruled by divine right. In this instance, legitimacy derived from the will of God. In time, this claim was also challenged and divine rule was toppled by revolution. Today, where kings remain on the throne, they are "constitutional monarchs," and legitimacy is conferred on their governments by the social contracts they have with those who are governed.

Although governments can rule by force for relatively short periods, this is an extremely inefficient method. Those that rely solely on coercion encounter so much resistance from so many elements of the society on so many levels that they eventually collapse, as happened with the military dictatorships in Spain, Portugal, and Argentina in the twentieth century. Rather than face this difficulty, all governments desire to have their use of power accepted by the majority of people as "morally right and proper," in short, as legitimate. Legitimate power is, as we noted earlier, the definition of *authority,* and authority is the grease that makes government run smoothly. If the government's authority is not accepted and internalized by the citizenry, people would not voluntarily pay taxes, serve on juries, stop at red lights, and carry out any number of other actions that governments cannot oversee. We willingly abide by many rules because we accept the government's right to make those rules.

In the last half of the twentieth century, democracy has been perceived generally as the most legitimate form of government. Even communist states had the trappings, albeit not the substance, of democratic government. When students in Beijing, China, called for further "democratic" reforms, for example, the communist government, which had allowed some liberalization in their regime, crushed the student demonstrations with extraordinary ferocity. Government leaders were afraid that the entire communist system would collapse if they yielded to student demands. This indeed has seemed to occur in the Soviet empire.

When Mikhail S. Gorbachev, the President of the Soviet Union, eased the restrictions on the Soviets' satellite countries in Eastern Europe and promised not to intervene in their internal affairs, several of these countries almost immediately overthrew their communist regimes. It remains to be seen whether these newly noncommunist nations will also be recognizably democratic in our terms, with tolerance for minority views.

Within the Soviet Union itself, Gorbachev's permissive approach to political and economic matters had resulted in turmoil and division. As an apparent consequence of the introduction of some democratic reforms, ancient ethnic animosities erupted and threatened to tear apart the Soviet Union. After all, Russia—stretching across the eastern half of Europe and all of northern Asia to the Pacific Ocean—finished cobbling together its vast empire from a melange of often mutually hostile nations less than 150 years ago. The communists never quite eliminated the old hatreds that continued to seethe beneath the surface. Democratic practices in the Soviet Union, defined only as the will of the people, proved in several instances to be extremely undemocratic and intolerant of minority opinions and peoples.

This danger, which is inherent in democracy, is precisely what the Framers tried to prevent by chopping up government power and spreading it among a number of institutions, not all of which are equally dependent on the "will of the people." As we saw earlier, our system of checks and balances sets up centers of countervailing power within the national government. Federalism continues the arrangement between the national and state governments. This intricate diffusion of power among several centers was carefully contrived by the Framers of the Constitution to avoid precisely what has happened in the Soviet state.

Even though the American system was contrived so that the government's exercise of power did not last long without some strong indication of popular sentiment, that sentiment can sometimes be complex and ambivalent, as in the case of President Ronald Reagan. Although the voting public continued to be fond of Reagan, returning him to office in the landslide victory of 1984, a significant minority had serious doubts about his policies. Thus, in the congressional elections of 1986, voters reduced his majority support in the Senate and increased the number of his opponents in the House, thereby enabling Congress to return to its traditional role and serve as a brake on what many voters thought a runaway presidency. The striking feature of the American system is that it allows minority views to find expression, and, through the electoral process, to often act as a corrective to the majority. In the final analysis, government cannot long function without sanction from the electorate, and the Constitution defines that electorate. Its definition, however, has changed over time. The next chapter will look more closely at the Constitution of the United States.

Suggested Readings

Louis Hartz. *The Liberal Tradition in America*. New York: Harcourt Brace, 1955.

John Locke. *Second Treatise On Civil Government* (1690). Many editions are available in paperback for this classic work.

Robert Nisbet. *History of the Idea of Progress*. New York: Basic Books, 1980.

Clinton Rossiter, ed. *The Federalist Papers* (1788). New York: Mentor, 1961.

Alexis de Tocqueville. *Democracy in America,* Phillips Bradley edition. New York: Knopf, 1945.

chapter

2

THE CONSTITUTION

The blessings of society depend entirely on the constitutions of government.

John Adams

As we saw in the last chapter, the founders came from a tradition of contract writers. Their English ancestors wrote contracts for all sorts of business purposes and for as many political situations as they could. Even as far back as the thirteenth century, Englishmen tried to limit the power of their king by forcing him to sign a contract, the Magna Carta. In the seventeenth and eighteenth centuries, political contracts seemed perfectly natural to many colonists. There was good reason for this. All colonies together with their forms of government were established by charter, which is a type of contract. Moreover, the most advanced theories of government, especially those of John Locke, were based on the concept of a social contract between rulers and those whom they ruled.

Thus, when it came time to form a government, it seemed "right and proper" to the founders to do so by writing a social contract. They overcame their ideological doubts and differences enough to come together in Philadelphia during the hot summer of 1787. There they sat from May to September and hammered out a written constitution for an entire nation, the first of its kind. The Framers of the Constitution took up the challenge of "establishing good government from reflection and choice," to borrow Alexander Hamilton's phrase. The form of government outlined by the Constitution that they produced has lasted over 200 years.

BACKGROUND

Needless to say, there are many reasons the constitutional government produced that summer has lasted as long as it has. One of these may be the reason the Constitutional Convention was called in the first place. The alternatives were not very attractive. Many of the founders felt that the choice was between anarchy or absolutism. They had fought a war to free themselves from the evils of absolutism, and they were currently living, many felt, in a state of anarchy.

GOVERNMENT UNDER THE ARTICLES OF CONFEDERATION

Each of the colonies that rebelled against Great Britain in 1776 had different origins and traditions. In some instances, a colony had been formed as a result of dissatisfaction with the practices and policies of another colony, as in the case of Rhode Island. Most colonies differed from one another on important issues such as religion. Therefore, as the colonies declared their independence from Britain, they became separate sovereign states—political communities that jealously guarded their newly asserted independence. After all, they had not gone through a bloody revolution to become subservient once again to a powerful central government.

When the First Continental Congress met in 1774, it gave each colony one vote, establishing a principle of equality among states that has lasted to the present time. This principle was confirmed in the Articles of Confederation that were unanimously adopted by the sovereign states in 1781.

The Articles created a weak, almost nonexistent national government that was completely controlled by the states. The newly formed Confederation had neither an executive nor a judicial branch, which meant it lacked enforcement powers. National authority was vested solely in a weak Congress in which each state had one vote, regardless of its size. Because major national policy decisions required unanimous approval, one state alone could veto action desired by the other twelve. And, whatever authority Congress did have was subordinate to that of the states. Article II of the Confederation made this clear: "Each state retains its sovereignty, freedom and independence, and every power, jurisdiction, and right. . . ."

The Confederation was essentially an alliance of states to fight the Revolutionary War. No serious thought was given to establishing a national government. Furthermore, Congress was not given the powers essential to any effective government, those of taxation and the regulation of commerce. Nor did Congress have the legislative authority to pass laws that would be binding on individual citizens of the states. It could only pass laws binding on states, but even in that instance, it lacked enforcement powers.

THE NEED FOR A NATIONAL GOVERNMENT

Several pressing needs pushed the sovereign states toward submitting to a national government. Chief among these was the need to reduce rivalry and regulate commerce among the individual states. Just as pressing was the growing demand for a stronger national defense as a result of territorial encroachments by Britain and Spain. Still a third was the wish to compromise as much as possible the differing interests of the northern and southern states.

Despite the pressures to form a stronger national government, many citizens of the independent states disliked the idea. A good many of them feared that a strong national government would become aristocratic or monarchical. Others feared that a republic without safeguards would turn into a tyranny of the majority. And still others feared that universal suffrage would allow those who have no stake in "good government"—the poor and propertyless—to vote. Yet the mounting pressures, especially the threat of interstate conflict and the possible dissolution of the union, led to a call by Virginia's leaders for a convention of all states to deal with the problems of interstate commerce.

PRELUDE TO PHILADELPHIA

The convention met in Annapolis, Maryland, in 1786. Among the first delegates to arrive were Alexander Hamilton and James Madison. Both argued forcefully that the present convention could not deal adequately with the problems of the Confederation. They urged that the meeting be dissolved and that a new convention be called for the following year in Philadelphia. Those delegates present agreed, dissolved the Annapolis convention, and relayed the Hamilton-Madison proposal to the states.

As luck would have it, while the states were considering this new proposal they were frightened by an event in Massachusetts. In the western part of the state, a large number of Continental Army veterans—most of them small farmers—were faced with bankruptcy. Unable to pay their debts with the paper money issued by the Continental Congress, they lost their lands. The state and local governments, which refused to accept congressional paper as valid, sided with the merchants and moneylenders who were foreclosing on the farms. Led by Daniel Shays, also a veteran of the Revolutionary War, the farmers rose in massive rebellion against the state government and prevented the foreclosures. The rebellion was quashed easily enough, but it scared the daylights out of the propertied and moneyed people. When the call for a new convention reached them, they prevailed on the state governments to grasp this "golden opportunity of rescuing the American empire from disunion, anarchy and misery," to quote from Alexander Hamilton's letter to George Washington.

Every state but Rhode Island endorsed the call, and in May 1787 the Constitutional Convention began in Philadelphia.

FRAMING THE CONSTITUTION

Practical politics as much as political theory shaped the Constitution. The majority of the fifty-five delegates to the Convention were committed *nationalists,* people favoring a strong national government in place of the weak Confederation. All the delegates were among the most respected members of their communities. The states had sent men such as James Madison, George Washington, Edmund Randolph, and George Mason of Virginia; Alexander Hamilton of New York; and Benjamin Franklin and Gouverneur Morris of Pennsylvania. Thomas Jefferson and John Adams would certainly have been present if they were not serving the Confederation overseas. Of those present in Philadelphia, both Madison and Hamilton had been instrumental in getting the Convention to meet in the first place, and both, particularly Madison, strongly influenced the outcome. The entire assembly was presided over by Washington, who, together with Franklin, gave it national stature and prestige.

POLITICS AND THE CONVENTION

Those delegates who favored a stronger national government than before knew that they would have an uphill struggle. The forces arrayed against them were dispersed but potentially powerful at the time. In at least six states, including New York and Virginia, opponents of a new national government, called Antifederalists, appeared to outnumber the Federalists, those favoring a strong central government. Among those who were opposed were men of the stature of Patrick Henry of Virginia and Governor George Clinton of New York.

The nationalists knew that they would have to deal delicately with a number of issues, chief among which was that of state sovereignty. The Constitution had

DRAWING BY STEINER; © 1982 THE NEW YORKER MAGAZINE, INC.

"Remember, gentlemen, we aren't here just to draft a constitution. We're here to draft the best damned constitution in the world."

to appear to preserve the sovereignty of the states while at the same time granting the new national government the power to make and enforce laws for the entire country. The nationalists' determination to have a new social contract led them to maneuver around their opponents and work out a number of difficult and long-lasting compromises.

CONTROVERSIES AND COMPROMISES

On many occasions the Constitutional Convention seemed doomed to failure. In a letter, Washington observed that the Convention was more than once "upon the point of dissolving without agreeing on any system." Not only did the delegates have difficulty agreeing among themselves, they did not all support the final outcome. Elbridge Gerry of Massachusetts, for example, refused to endorse the Constitution that he worked on because he found it "ambiguous, indefinite, and dangerous."

There were many conflicting views of what the new government should be like. Hamilton, for example, wanted a strong central government. He presented a plan in which a senate and executive were chosen for life by indirect (not popular) election. In effect, this would have created an aristocratic government. It was because of this very possibility that George Mason objected to the final document. He argued that the government created by the Constitution "will commence in a moderate Aristocracy [and will go on to produce either] a Monarchy, or a corrupt oppressive Aristocracy."[1] Furthermore, Mason continued, "there is no Declaration of Rights" and the "Legislature [cannot prohibit] the further Importation of Slaves," which he felt was destructive of the country's moral fiber.

By contrast, James Madison felt that a separate Declaration of Rights was unnecessary. The enumerated powers of the separate branches served to limit the national government, he believed, and thus alone protected the rights of individuals and states. As to slavery, both he and Franklin were willing to see it continue so that the Constitution would not fail passage. Elbridge Gerry, on the other hand, objected to the Constitution precisely because "the liberties of America were not secured by the system." In his view, too much power was vested in what he called a "national government." "The Constitution proposed," he argued, "has few, if any *federal* features. . . ."

And indeed, the lack of "federal features"—that is, an explicit guarantee of state sovereignty—was a serious sticking point for many. In addition, the different states had varying perspectives on representation in the new legislature. The small states, such as New Jersey and Delaware, wanted equality with the large states, such as New York and Virginia. The large states, especially Virginia, wanted representation according to population. In an effort to satisfy both small and large states, the delegates worked out what has come to be called the *Great Compromise*. This was an arrangement by which the small states had an equal vote to the large states in the Senate, and all states had a vote proportionate to their population in the House of Representatives.

---

[1]This and following quotes from the constitutional convention are taken from *The Records of the Constitutional Convention, 1787*, 4 vols., ed. Max Farrand (New Haven: Yale University Press, 1966).

Among many of the delegates there was a profound fear of the general public. Once again, Hamilton expressed most forcefully the view held by most conservatives of his day. ''The people are turbulent and changing; they seldom judge or determine right.'' Shays' Rebellion confirmed this opinion for many. Thus, the delegates wrote into the Constitution constraints on popular government. Neither senators nor presidents were to be elected directly by the people. Senators were to be chosen by state legislatures and presidents by an electoral college, the members of which were to be appointed by the states. Finally, the concluding statement of Article IV of the Constitution says, with Shays's Rebellion in mind, that the federal government shall ''protect [every State in this Union] against domestic violence.'' Other people's revolutions were not to be tolerated.

THE BATTLE FOR RATIFICATION

The Framers knew that regardless of their compromises, the Constitution they had drafted would be highly controversial. The lines were quickly drawn between those who favored the Constitution, the Federalists, and those who opposed it, the Antifederalists. The debate between these two camps soon began in every state of the union.

In New York, where it seemed the opponents of the Constitution might be a majority, Alexander Hamilton persuaded John Jay and James Madison to join him in writing a series of polemical articles known as *The Federalist* papers. Very early on these articles gained a reputation for brilliance.[2] They were opposed by equally brilliant essays written by someone known as the *Federal Farmer* in one instance and *Brutus* in another. Both Antifederalist writers were concerned that the people would not be adequately represented in the national government. They foresaw an unresponsive and eventually despotic central government under which the people lost their freedom. Ideological conflict was thus bred into the American system by the fight for ratification of the Constitution and later guaranteed by the First Amendment to the Bill of Rights.

During the course of the ratification debates, both Federalists and Antifederalists agreed that the new Constitution needed a bill of rights, which the Framers had not included because of lack of time and a feeling that it was unnecessary. As a result of the struggle for ratification, Madison and the other Federalists, to gain support, promised that a bill of rights would be added after the Constitution was ratified. Elected to the first Congress, Madison carried through on this promise and led the drive for the Bill of Rights we now have.

ESSENTIALS OF THE CONSTITUTION

Limited government is the central idea of the Constitution. The charter limits government by creating a system of checks and balances through the separation

---

[2]In 1788, Washington wrote Hamilton, ''. . . the *Production* of your *Triumvirate* . . . will merit the notice of Posterity.'' About a half century later, Alexis de Tocqueville wrote, ''*The Federalist* . . . should be familiar to statesmen of all countries.''

of powers. It also does so by diffusing the authority of the national government and reserving rights to the states.

SEPARATION OF POWERS

Separation of powers means that legislative, executive, and judicial authority is placed in separate branches of government—Congress, the president, and the courts. *Legislative power* is the authority of Congress to make laws for the community as a whole or for any group within it. *Executive power* refers to the president's authority to enforce the laws, carrying them out through the various agencies of government. The way executive agencies implement the law often shapes public policy and can lead to conflicts with Congress. For example, if the Environmental Protection Agency does not vigorously enforce environmental legislation, it in effect alters a policy established through law by Congress. Constitutionally, Congress, not the executive, is the policy-making branch of government. Finally, *judicial power* is the authority of the courts to judge specific cases and controversies arising under law. Unless a law is challenged, it cannot go to court for judgment.

The constitutional powers progress logically from legislation to enforcement to judgment. As Congress makes the laws on Capitol Hill, the president, his aides, and the executive bureaucracy implement them in the White House and elsewhere. East of the Capitol, the Supreme Court hears appeals from lower federal and state courts on laws having major constitutional import. Clearly, each branch is involved somewhat with the others.

The mutual involvement of the coordinate branches raises the dangerous possibility of cooperation instead of conflict. If cooperation did occur, it would undermine the balance of powers the Framers thought necessary to the preservation of limited government and individual liberties. Therefore, they devised a system in which each branch is constitutionally motivated to resist encroachments on its power from the other branches of government. This motivation was supplied by having different electorates choose the members of each branch.

SPLITTING THE ELECTORATE

The Framers of the Constitution were anxious to "oblige [government] to control itself," Madison wrote in *The Federalist*. They were also very suspicious of the mass of people. Classically educated, most agreed with Aristotle, who viewed democracy as a dangerous and degenerate form of government. Hence, the Framers took the precaution of limiting popular influence on government as they worked out the separation of powers.

Choosing the President.   According to the Constitution, the president—that is, the individual in command of the coercive power and executive machinery of the United States—is not directly elected by the people. Rather the president is chosen by the electoral college. The members of the "college" are selected by the states so that "the immediate election [of the president] should be made by men most capable of analyzing the qualities" needed for that office, as Hamilton expressed

it in *The Federalist*, No. 68. Hamilton also observed a bit further on in the same article that having "an intermediate body of electors will be much less apt to convulse the community" than direct election by the people, who might choose someone possessing "talents for low intrigue, and the little arts of popularity."

State legislatures determine how electors are chosen. In the early years of the country, state legislators chose the electors. Today, state party leaders choose the electors—both parties run a full slate of electors equal to the number of state senators and representatives in Congress. Voters choose electors—who are hardly ever named on the ballot—by pulling the lever for president. The prevailing system today works on a "winner-take-all" basis. The electors from the political party that wins a plurality (the most, but not a majority) of votes in the state cast their ballots for president. As a rule, they vote unanimously for the candidate of their party, but not always. In 1976, a Republican elector voted for Ronald Reagan rather than Gerald Ford, the candidate of his party, and in 1988 a Democratic elector voted for Lloyd Bentsen, the vice-presidential candidate, rather than Michael Dukakis, the party's presidential contender.

Choosing Legislators.   The government was further insulated from direct popular pressure by the method of choosing senators. At the beginning, and for more than 100 years afterward, members of the Senate were chosen by state legislatures. This method of choosing senators was seen, in James Madison's words, "as a defense to the people against their own temporary errors and delusions."

In 1913, after many years of struggle, three-fourths of the states ratified the Seventeenth Amendment requiring that senators be elected directly by the voters. Senators, however, represent an entire state, which means that they often have to balance conflicting interests from different constituencies. For example, in many states there are opposing demands made by rural people for highway funds, let's say, and by city dwellers for public transportation funds. Generally, a senator will come down on the side that has the most votes, which means that some portion of his or her state is not adequately represented.

Members of the House of Representatives are elected directly by the people. Initially, however, the "people" were mostly property-owning white males, although the amount of property required to vote was often insignificant. By contrast, most states required that a candidate for public office own a fairly large amount of property to be eligible for election. Therefore, representatives were generally not from the lower classes and rarely represented the unpropertied residents of their states or districts. Property qualifications for voters were finally removed in 1852, although a species of property qualification—the poll tax—remained in effect until 1964, when the Twenty-fourth Amendment outlawed it.

Choosing the Supreme Court.   It is only in the choice of justices for the Supreme Court that all pretense of a popular mandate is dropped from the Constitution. Supreme Court justices are nominated by the president, usually at the recommendation of leading members of the legal profession, and approved by the Senate for lifetime positions. Justices, however, also have several constituencies, inside and outside the power structure, to which they are beholden. First among these is the legal profession from which they come. Most nominees to the Court are part of the elite within their profession. Second, most justices came from the upper levels of society, attended the best schools, and enjoyed the privileges of success. None of this means that they are necessarily conservative. Indeed, many since Franklin D. Roosevelt's tenure have been liberal. But liberalism is sometimes the ruling ideology of American elites, and Supreme Court justices tend to be especially sensitive to elite opinion.

Favorable elite opinion may be the only support the Court has as it passes judgment on the actions of the president, Congress, state legislatures, and the lower judiciary. Although the Constitution does not specifically grant the Supreme Court authority to review the acts of federal and state governments, the Court has since 1803 claimed the right to do just that. Known as *judicial review,* the Federalists had presented this right as a constitutional necessity as early as 1788. The prime example is Hamilton's argument for the high court in *The Federalist,* No. 78.

> The complete independence of the courts of justice is . . . essential in a limited Constitution. Limitations . . . can be preserved in practice no other way than through the medium of courts of justice, whose duty it must be to declare all acts contrary to the . . . Constitution void. Without this, all the reservations of particular rights or privileges would amount to nothing.

> The interpretation of the laws is the proper . . . province of the courts. A constitution is, in fact, and must be regarded by the judges as, a fundamental law. It therefore

belongs to them to ascertain its meaning as well as the meaning of any particular act proceeding from the legislative body.

Not only does the Supreme Court judge the laws made by Congress, it also judges actions and claims made by presidents. In 1952, the Court ruled that President Harry Truman did not have the authority to order the seizure of steel mills faced with a strike even though we were in the middle of the Korean War. In 1974, the Court ruled that President Nixon could not use the claim of executive privilege to withhold evidence in a criminal case. The evidence consisted of tapes he made of conversations that implicated himself and his aides in the burglary of Democratic party headquarters in Washington that came to be known as the Watergate scandal.

The Supreme Court's authority to pass on state laws was established by the Judiciary Act of 1789. Although the Court has rarely reversed a decision by a president or a law of Congress, it has frequently ruled against state laws. In 1987, to cite a recent example, the Court struck down a Louisiana state law requiring that the biblical account of creation be taught as a scientific theory if the theory of evolution was taught in a school classroom. School integration, protection of the rights of those arrested, and fairer voting practices are among the changes that have resulted from Supreme Court rulings on state laws.

Generally, the Court's rulings, almost always on controversial issues, are accepted by all levels of political society. During the 1950s, however, the Court's decision on school integration had to be enforced by federal troops. That is the central feature of the Supreme Court. It has only moral authority and must depend on others to enforce its rulings. This means that the power elite must accept the Court's role as chief arbiter of legitimacy. Its moral authority must be sufficiently compelling so that even when a Court decision goes against a particular member of the elite, as in the case of President Nixon, the person voluntarily complies with the ruling.

THE IMPACT OF CONSTITUENCIES

The Framers of the Constitution relied on the different electorates to bolster the separation of powers. Electorates are constituencies. The term *constituency* refers to a legislator's election district. It also refers to the body of voters in that election district. After a while, the term's meaning was extended to cover all supporters of a public official in any area of government. Today, the word also refers to that group, class, or other collectivity that a public official feels identified with and accountable to.

The constituency of a member of the House of Representatives is the district from which he or she is elected and the voters in that district. Those who support the representative, either financially or ideologically, are also part of his or her constituency. A senator's constituency was at first the members of his state's legislature. Today, it consists of the voters in the state as well as those who contribute, time, money, or ideology to his or her support. The constituency of the president consists of the members of the electoral college, the political leaders of his party, the voters of the entire nation, and his ideological supporters. The constituencies for each of these political figures clearly overlap but are not identical.

Although members of the Supreme Court are not elected by popular vote, they too have a constituency. Theirs consists of the president and the Senate, who through the nominating and confirmation process in effect *elect* justices to office. As we have seen with the nomination of William Rehnquist in 1986 to be Chief Justice, nominees to the high court often behave like any other candidate for public office. They campaign for votes from their constituency, the U.S. Senate. Of course, Supreme Court justices also have their ideological supporters as part of their constituency as well as members of the legal profession.

Constituencies function simultaneously as sources of pressure and as constraints on political action. For example, a representative from a district with a large Ukrainian population is likely to be very interested in America's foreign policy toward the Soviet Union. But the Ukrainian community is split over how best to deal with Soviet Russia. Some Ukrainians want the province to be an independent nation and would like the United States to cut off all relations with Russia. Others, having family in the old country, wish to continue relations with Russia, even though they too are strong nationalists. The representative has to balance both sentiments so as to satisfy the divided constituency and stay in office.

Members of Congress—senators and representatives—generally have relatively small constituencies with fairly narrow interests that may bring them into conflict. Senators from the South and Midwest, for example, represent large agrarian interests that are very much against what they call "protectionism." Opposed to the agricultural sections of the country are the industrial states of the Great Lakes region. These states have suffered economically as a result of the easy access foreign manufacturers have to the American market. Thus, senators from the north central states generally favor using some means—presidential or legislative action—to restrict imports and offer protection to American industry from overseas competitors. The conflict over protectionism is as old as the country itself. Under the banner of "tariffs," this regional conflict contributed to the dissolution of the Confederation, to the establishment of the present federal system, and to the Civil War.

But the members of Congress are not always in conflict. Indeed, there is a good deal more cooperation than there is confrontation. For example, a senator from the Southwest may try to get funding for water projects in his or her state, while a senator from the Northeast might want federal subsidies for low-cost housing. These two might strike a deal in which they each vote for the other's project and thereby help themselves and their constituencies to greater satisfaction.

Sometimes the deals worked out by the members of Congress will bring them into conflict with the president. He may have his own set of priorities, and they may differ radically from those of Congress. In that case, he may veto the legislation Congress has passed, and, if he has enough support in the Senate and

House, he will be able to sustain his veto. But if enough members of both houses favor the legislation, they can override the president's veto with at least a two-thirds majority.

On major issues of national policy, modern presidents, taking their cue from Franklin D. Roosevelt, often appeal directly to their national constituency in an effort to force Congress into compliance. Sometimes they are effective, and sometimes they are not. Even the most persuasive, FDR, occasionally failed to garner support for his goal. After Roosevelt, the most effective shaper of national opinion has been Ronald Reagan, who earned the epithet the "Great Communicator" for his skill in moving his listeners to action. On one occasion, finding Congress unwilling to spend money on the weapons he wanted, Reagan went on national television and asked his audience to write their congresspersons saying they backed him. That night and the following days, Congress was inundated with phone calls and mail.

Congress, through selected individuals, has increasingly tried to offset the president's influence by also using the national media to address the voting public. But members of Congress are at a distinct disadvantage in this exchange unless they have the charisma to match either Roosevelt or Reagan. Because individual congresspeople represent local constituencies, their national appeal tends to be very limited. By contrast, the investigative function of Congress, conducted in televised committee hearings, has proven a powerful weapon in countering presidential overreach. Both Presidents Reagan and Nixon, for example, were taken down several notches at the height of their popularity by televised hearings of joint committees of Congress. Working jointly, the members of Congress represent a national constituency that can balance the one represented by the president.

CHECKS AND BALANCES

The ability to appeal to the same constituency from different vantage points enhances the checks and balances aspect of the constitutional separation of powers. The high regard with which the Supreme Court is held by almost all constituencies has enabled it to play its part in the game of checks and balances envisioned by the Framers. But the game takes place mainly between the executive and legislative branches of government.

Shared powers are what enables the president and Congress to check and balance each other. Both branches participate in making the laws and thus can interfere with the exercise of power by the other. The president can veto congressional legislation, which is often enough to kill a bill. With great effort, and usually only after strong popular backing, Congress can override a presidential veto. Moreover, the president can, and often does, propose legislation to Congress. He thereby participates positively in lawmaking and policy setting rather than just negatively through the veto. In this instance, Congress has the direct power to approve, disapprove, or modify the president's program.

In addition to having the power to enact or not the president's program, Congress has direct oversight of certain presidential actions. Through its constitutional power to advise and consent, the Senate has the authority to approve or disapprove presidential appointments of public officials, such as cabinet officers, ambassadors, Supreme Court justices, and the like. While the president has the authority to make treaties, those treaties cannot go into effect until they are approved by the Senate in a two-thirds vote. For example, President Reagan and Soviet leader Mikhail Gorbachev signed the important INF (intermediate-range nuclear force) treaty on December 8, 1987, but it did not take effect until six months later when the Senate ratified it on June 1, 1988. Congress has a further check on the executive branch through its authority to appropriate money for the White House and executive agencies. Congress alone has the authority to create executive agencies and determine their tasks. Some of this power may be delegated to the president, but Congress always retains control over how it will be exercised.

Constitutionally, the major source of legitimate power lies in Congress, but the president has considerable influence and has a number of checks on the abuse of congressional power. Unbridled political power can be very dangerous. Checks and balances seem the natural way to prevent governmental abuse of power. Therefore, the Framers extended checks and balances to the all-powerful legislature as well. Concerned about uncontrolled majority rule, the Framers created a bicameral (two-chamber) legislature in which the Senate can check popular "errors and delusions" in the House. The House in turn can check some of the "aristocratical" impulses some Framers saw in the Senate. Both houses have to agree on a piece of legislation before it can become law. A further check on both houses is provided by presidential authority. As John Adams put it in his *Defense of the American Constitutions:* "Each of the three branches, executive, upper house and lower house, acts as a check on the other. There can be no stability or freedom without balance, and there can be no balance without three separate powers."

FEDERALISM

In addition to the system of checks and balances within the national government, the Framers reserved certain powers to the states. Those reserved powers enable the states to counter the authority of the central government and are part of the system of checks and balances. The "reserved powers" are made explicit in the tenth amendment, the last of the Bill of Rights, and are the basis for claims to "states' rights" and the recent upsurge of support for "federalism."

The term *federalism* has an interesting history in American politics. Technically, the word *federal* refers to a league of fully independent, sovereign states. Traditionally, such leagues did not have any central government whatever, although they may have had deliberative, nonlegislating assemblies. It was in this sense that defenders of the Articles of Confederation used the term. When Elbridge Gerry wrote to the Massachusetts General Court explaining his objections to the new government, he observed, "The Constitution proposed has few, if any *federal* features, but is rather a system of *national* government." The Federal Farmer who wrote in defense of the Articles of Confederation also used the same sense of the word.

Our object has been all along to reform our federal system and to strengthen our governments.... The plan of government now proposed is evidently calculated totally to change, in time, our condition as a people. Instead of being thirteen republics, under a federal head, it is clearly designed to make us one consolidated government.

As the debate over ratification heated up, those who favored the "consolidated," "national" government shrewdly took the word *federal* for themselves. In the process, of course, they changed the meaning of the word. At first, in *The Federalist,* No. 1, Hamilton uses "federal" as his opponents do, to refer to the Confederation. Later, in *The Federalist,* No. 9, he continues this identification, treating "federal" and "confederate" as synonyms. But here he starts to shift the meaning of both terms so as to have them refer to what Elbridge Gerry had called a "national government." Hamilton says:

> The definition of a *confederate republic* seems simply to be "an assemblage of societies," or an association of two or more states into one state. The extent . . . of the federal authority are matters of discretion. So long as the separate organization of the members be not abolished; so long as it exists, by a constitutional necessity, for local purposes; though it should be in perfect subordination to the general authority of the union, it would still be, in fact and in theory, an association of states, or a confederacy. The proposed Constitution, so far from implying an abolition of the State governments, makes them constituent parts of the national sovereignty, by allowing them a direct representation in the Senate, and leaves in their possession certain exclusive and very important portions of sovereign power. This fully corresponds, in every rational import of the terms, with the idea of a federal government.

By *The Federalist,* No. 23, where Hamilton argues for a strong central government, the term *federal* refers entirely and solely to the national government created by the new Constitution. Hamilton's side won the debate, and the word *federal* has taken on the meanings he gave it. Today, the term is generally accepted to refer to a system of government in which authority is divided between a national government and state or provincial governments. Article I, Section 10, and Article VI of the United States Constitution clearly establish between them the supremacy of the national government over the states.

The tenth amendment to some degree qualifies the constitutional grant of supremacy to the national government, but it does not do so unambiguously. As a result, we have had a Civil War and 200 years of controversy over the respective powers of the federal and state governments. Since the FDR era especially, the federal government has asserted its dominance over the states, particularly on social issues such as discrimination, civil rights, abortion, prayer in the schools, and so forth. Under the banner of "federalism," the Reagan administration advocated turning back to the states the power to decide such issues for themselves. Over the course of American history, federalism and the reserved powers of the states have expanded and contracted in accordianlike fashion with the changes in political ideologies.

BILL OF RIGHTS

It is important to realize that the twenty-six amendments, including the Bill of Rights, are an integral part of the Constitution. The rights detailed in the amendments were intended by the Framers and later lawmakers to protect each of us individually from abuse by government power. These rights are at the core of what we mean by American democracy. The first ten amendments are the Bill of Rights, without which the Constitution produced in Philadelphia would not have been ratified.

The federal government, especially the Supreme Court, has used the first eight amendments of the Bill of Rights to force state and local governments to accept more liberal social policies than they would have on their own. For example, on the basis of the first amendment's clause regarding an "establishment of religion," the Supreme Court has ruled that prayer in public schools is unconstitutional. It was for this as well as a number of other rulings that the Reagan administration tried to change the character of the Supreme Court and, through the advocacy of former Attorney General Edwin Meese, to restrict the scope of judicial review.

Amendments I to VIII broadly define the freedoms and rights of individual citizens. These amendments were originally intended only to limit the national government. It was not until very recently that they were applied to the states. This came about as the result of a long, case-by-case judicial process that "nationalized" each of the amendments' provisions. That extension of the Bill of Rights was made possible by the due process clause of the Fourteenth Amendment. (See Chapter 3 for a discussion of the nationalization of the Bill of Rights.)

The First Amendment is at the center of the democratic process as we understand it. It guarantees those freedoms of expression without which most Americans would think democracy a hollow shell. Contained in the First Amendment are protections of freedom of speech, press, religion, and the right to peacefully assemble and petition government for a redress of grievances. Neither the First Amendment freedoms nor the other provisions of the Bill of Rights are absolute, however. Under certain circumstances, the federal government may suspend those rights if it believes the national interest requires it. This suspension has occurred several times in the past, usually during wartime or in the military forces.

CHANGING THE CONSTITUTION

As we saw in the first chapter, an essential function of all governments is to provide stability, for stability contributes to the well-being of society. One of the major causes of unstable governments is the inability to change those governments by legitimate means. Rigidity breeds revolution. The Framers accepted this maxim and built into the American system the possibility of change within continuity.

THROUGH THE AMENDMENT PROCESS

Recognizing that political pressures might force changes in the Constitution, the Framers carefully provided a mechanism for change. That mechanism is the constitutional amendment. But changing the structure of government too easily can itself be a cause of instability. Political life can then seem to take place within a revolving door. To prevent this from occurring, the Framers made the process of amending the Constitution a difficult one.

The process requires a two-thirds congressional vote to recommend amend-ments to the states. Approval by three-fourths of the state legislatures or by special state ratifying conventions is needed for the adoption of amendments. Twenty-five of the twenty-six amendments have been adopted by the state-legislature method. Only the Twenty-first Amendment repealing prohibition was adopted by state ratifying conventions.

THROUGH JUDICIAL INTERPRETATION

The Constitution was so broadly written that from its beginnings it needed to be interpreted. Supreme Court interpretations have shaped the Constitution as much as, if not more than, the amendments have. The Court has made many important decisions that helped define the character of federalism, the concept of separation of powers, the extent of civil liberties, and the nature of personal rights.

In relation to federalism, the Supreme Court led by Chief Justice John Marshall from 1801 to 1835 adopted a viewpoint that promoted the clear-cut supremacy of the national government over the states. Marshall's doctrines were modified some-what as the Court stressed for the next 100 years the importance of the reserved powers of the states. Under pressure from the Roosevelt administration in 1936–1937, the Court returned to a position that is more favorable to national supremacy. This again changed somewhat as a result of President Reagan's appointments to the bench.

In other areas, the Court has helped expand presidential authority to make foreign policy, has curbed congressional attempts to control the executive branch, and has extended the Bill of Rights to state laws. It has also redefined basic rights, as when it ruled that there is a constitutional right to privacy that prohibits federal and state governments from banning abortion, although what has been dubbed the "Reagan Court" has begun to retreat from this position.

THROUGH CUSTOM

Informal constitutional changes may take place without amendments or judicial decisions. For example, the executive departments and agencies have spawned a federal bureaucracy that is in effect a fourth branch of government. Abuses of power, economic or otherwise, have generated enormous pressures to regulate large segments of society. The tremendous growth in population has also produced a greater need for government services. And increasing social sensitivity has engendered ever more pressing calls for government aid to the helpless and in-secure. All this has resulted in a bureaucracy employing nearly 3 million people. The rules and regulations produced by this vast apparatus affect every area of our lives and have as much impact on us as the constitutionally sanctioned laws.

The crises of depression and war in the twentieth century have given rise to political pressures originating outside the formal framework set up by the Con-stitution. Political parties and interest groups have been highly influential in the making of laws and the devising of regulations. For example, in the 1960s political pressures, from new and established groups, created alliances that forced on political parties and all branches of government a greater awareness than in the past of the demand for civil rights.

It is important to recognize that alongside the formal, constitutionally sanc-tioned power of government is a highly potent informal force that acts on the American political system. This informal force can, and sometimes does, alter the system and our understanding of the Constitution.

In Conclusion

The Framers of the Constitution were primarily concerned with the preservation of liberty. They therefore created a national government of limited powers. To ensure that the government would continue to be limited, they divided its powers among three equal branches. In effect, they created a conflict model of government so as to secure the maximum personal freedom.

Remarkably, the government established by the Constitution has lasted for two centuries, longer than any other similarly established government. Perhaps be-cause it was admittedly imperfect—George Washington kept apologizing for its imperfections—the Constitution had built into it explicit and implicit means of change. As a consequence, the government and its charter have been able to adapt to the changing circumstances of the nation.

Suggested Readings

W. B. Allen and Gordon Lloyd, ed. *The Essential Antifederalist*. New York: University Press of America, 1985.

Edward S. Corwin. *The "Higher Law" Background of American Constitutional Law*. Chicago: University of Chicago Press, 1953.

J. W. Peltason. *Understanding the Constitution,* 11th ed. New York: Holt, Rinehart and Winston, 1988.

Clinton Rossiter, ed. *The Federalist Papers* (1788). New York: Mentor, 1961.

Garry Wills. *Explaining America*. New York: Doubleday, 1981.

chapter

3

CIVIL LIBERTIES
and
CIVIL RIGHTS

Justice is the constant and permanent intention of giving each man his due.

Justinian's Institutions of Roman Law

The desire for "liberty and justice for all" is at the center of the American struggle for democracy. That desire motivated our revolutionary founders as much as our civil rights marchers. The problem for Americans then and now is that we cannot always agree on the meaning of liberty and justice, and over time we have changed our ideas of whom to include in our meaning of "all." For example, in the early parts of the civil rights movement, several of its leaders objected strenuously to the demand of some women for their "liberation" from sexual servitude. In the case of blacks, it is doubtful that anyone intended to include them in the word "all" when the Pledge of Allegiance was adopted in 1892.

We should keep in mind that "liberty" is not available in an absolute way. None of us is free to shout "fire" in a crowded theater just because we feel like it. Nor are we free to take the life or property of someone for whatever reason. Most Americans would agree to these and a few other restrictions on their freedom. But most of us also believe that, in a just society, all restrictions of liberty should apply equally to everyone. Essential to the American belief system is that no one is above the law and that no one, especially a person in power, has the freedom to break the law.

Although we have never settled on a clear, uniform definition of liberty, justice, and equality, we have talked about these concepts since before the founding of the nation. Some people, for example, think of "liberty" as referring exclusively to the freedom of groups or classes of people from tyranny or oppression, as in the case of women's liberation or national liberation movements. Many think of "liberty" as meaning only the freedom to participate in the political process. Others think of "liberty" as the freedom to do whatever one wishes. And still others think of "liberty" as freedom of thought or belief, as in religion, politics, art, and the like. Related to the freedom of thought is the concept of "liberty" as freedom of choice. Of course, for many of us these various definitions are not mutually exclusive at all.

We can, however, reduce these different meanings of "liberty" to essentially two distinct types. One refers to individual liberties, such as the freedom to act, believe, or choose as one wishes. The other refers to group liberties, as the freedom of blacks to sit wherever they choose on a bus, the freedom of India from British colonial rule, or the freedom of Jews to worship in Soviet Russia. Both types or broad meanings of liberty overlap. For example, to restrict the choice of a broad class, such as blacks, is to deprive each member of his or her individual freedom. The reverse is also true. For example, to devise tests of physical strength so that almost all individual female applicants fail is to effectively deprive women as a class of their freedom of choice.

Today, many Americans would consider such deprivations unjust. Our ideas of liberty and justice are involved in each other. Justice itself has essentially two meanings. One refers to the punishment of wrongdoing, as when we say "the criminal has been brought to justice." This is called retributive justice, and this type of justice requires absolute equality before the law. The other meaning of justice refers to having a proper share of the highest rewards of society. In the United States those rewards are liberty, wealth, and social status. This is called distributive justice. For this type of justice we generally think of equality as relative rather than as absolute. Our most intense political and social conflicts arise over issues connected with distributive justice. For example, most of us claim equal access to the rewards of our society, and when we are deprived of that access we generally feel that an injustice has been done.

For most of us, liberty, equality, and justice are closely linked. Whatever meanings we may assign these terms, we now feel they are rights belonging to each of us in some fundamental way. In the Western tradition, those rights are either granted or recognized by civil societies. For this reason, they are called civil rights and liberties. Although our civil rights and liberties are relatively recent, the concepts underlying them are very ancient.

BACKGROUND: LIBERTY AND AUTHORITY

In the mid-nineteenth century, the great English philosopher John Stuart Mill wrote in his major essay, *On Liberty:* "The struggle between liberty and authority is the most conspicuous feature . . . of history. . . .'' If we take the Old Testament story of the expulsion from Eden as a political parable, we can see the struggle is indeed very old. In our secular version, the supreme authority in Eden had prohibited a certain action, but his subjects exercised their freedom of choice and acted contrary to his command. The supreme authority was furious at this disobedience. He therefore ordered his subjects expelled from his realm. This is the classic conflict between liberty and authority.

That conflict is also reflected in the great philosophers of ancient Greece and Rome. Both Plato and Aristotle agreed that justice is central to the well-ordered society. They disagreed, however, on the place of liberty in that society. Plato, holding that absolute authority was essential, looked upon liberty with contempt. To him the word was synonymous with self-indulgence. Aristotle, who linked liberty, equality, and justice, argued that freedom is worthwhile as long as it is kept within the bounds of law. The Roman lawyer Cicero was influenced by both Aristotle and Plato. Although he may have borrowed his notion of natural law from Aristotle's concept of natural right or justice, he was not much concerned with the question of liberty. The role of authority was far more important to him and later Roman writers.

For more than a thousand years, during the Middle Ages, liberty had little meaning. The prime value was placed on authority because it was conceived as participating in the divine. In Romans 13:1–2, St. Paul stated what was to become the prevailing medieval view: "Let every soul be subject unto the highest powers. For there is no power but of God: the powers that be are ordained of God. Whosoever therefore resisteth the power, resisteth the ordinance of God: and they that resist shall receive to themselves damnation." As for liberty, most medieval thinkers believed that true liberty consisted in unquestioning obedience to God and to His representatives on earth, whether prince, king, or pope.

With the Renaissance came a revival of the classical habit of closely questioning accepted beliefs. Although this questioning was applied somewhat in politics, it reached its most complete expression in religion. From the fourteenth century onward there were efforts, over the objections of the Catholic Church, to translate the Bible into the several languages of the common people, such as English or German. During the Protestant Reformation, these efforts merged with the Protestants' assertion that all true believers, whether priests or not, are capable of interpreting the Scriptures for themselves. Even John Calvin, who was an extreme authoritarian, held that "the consciences of believers . . . should raise themselves above the law. . . ." The logical extension of this view is that all individuals should be free to think for themselves. Although Calvin, Martin Luther, and other Protestant leaders were outraged at such "free-thinking" notions, these ideas achieved a vibrant underground life in the sixteenth century.

At the time of the Puritan Revolution of the seventeenth century, free-thinking ideas came above ground, to the great distress of the parliamentary rulers of England. Parliament's move to repress the free exchange of ideas prompted one of England's greatest poets, John Milton, to write the first brilliant defense of free expression in Western civilization. In *Areopagitica*, Milton stated the basic creed of all free thinkers: "Give me the liberty to know, to utter, and to argue freely according to conscience, above all liberties." There is no reason to fear the free expression of ideas, Milton contended, for "Let [Truth] and Falsehood grapple; who ever knew Truth put to the worse in a free and open encounter?" Although Milton was arguing within a religious context, *Areopagitica* is one of the major statements of modern political thought. It argues for freedom from government interference in the exchange of ideas, in the publication of those ideas, and in the practice of those ideas whether in the realm of politics or religion.

Milton's polemics had a great impact on the creators of the American system. As a result, freedom of speech, press, and religion constitute the first article of our Bill of Rights. As early as 1776, Thomas Jefferson may have had Milton as well as Roger Williams in mind when he wrote into the draft of the Virginia Constitution: "All persons shall have full and free liberty of religious opinion; nor shall any be compelled to frequent or maintain any religious institution." And for freedom of the press, Jefferson wrote: "Printing presses shall be free, except so far [as they commit libel against private individuals and therefore can be sued for damages]." In a later letter, Jefferson virtually quotes Milton: ". . . man may be governed by reason and truth. Our first object should therefore be, to leave open to him all the avenues to truth. The most effectual . . . is the freedom of the press." Jefferson's views greatly influenced James Madison, and Madison in large part composed the Bill of Rights.

Although the desire for liberty motivated almost all the leaders of the American Revolution, they did not all agree on how much freedom is permissible and in which areas one can be free. To get a sense of this difference, it is instructive to compare Jefferson's draft constitution with the draft for the Constitution of Massachusetts, written by John Adams. Adams's draft opens with a "Declaration of Rights." The second of these rights deals with religion and says: "It is the duty of all men in society, publicly, and at stated seasons, to worship the SUPREME BEING, the great Creator and Preserver of the universe." The article goes on to allow for freedom of worship, but it does not allow one to refuse to worship a "supreme being." There is in Adams's draft no provision for independence of thought on religious matters as there is in Jefferson's. Nor did Adams make any provision for freedom of the press as Jefferson did. To Adams, liberty referred mainly to the right of "acquiring, possessing, and protecting property," as he asserted in the first of his declared rights. Indeed, property rights were so important to Adams that he said in his *Discourses on Davila:* "Property must be secured, or liberty cannot exist."

POLITICS AND CIVIL RIGHTS

In the great drama of America's struggle for civil rights, Jefferson and Adams are the heroic antagonists. Jefferson's devotion to freedom of expression was so famous that it became the subject of a widely circulated story at the time. While he was president he was visited by a noted traveler from Europe. The visitor noticed a newspaper that had published a vicious attack on Jefferson lying on the presidential desk. "Why is this vile rag not suppressed and its editor not imprisoned?" asked the traveler. Jefferson, handing the paper to his visitor, said: "Keep this newspaper with you. In the future, if you hear our liberty questioned or our freedom of the press doubted, show your questioner this paper and tell him it was given you by the president of the United States, who is the subject of the attack.''

Although Jefferson complained of the "falsehoods, the misrepresentations, the calumnies and the insults resorted to by a faction" in the press, he also believed that the people "may safely be trusted to hear everything true and false, and to form a correct judgment between them." John Adams, in contrast, was not so confident in the judgment of ordinary folk. In a letter to a quarrelsome friend, Adams noted: "Knowledge is applied to bad purposes as well as to good ones. Knaves and hypocrites can acquire it. . . . It is employed as an engine and a vehicle to propagate error and falsehood, treason and vice. . . ."[1] In the same letter, Adams also observed that "many newspapers have been directed by vagabonds, fugitives from a [sheriff, a prison, or a hangman's noose]. . . ."[2] And indeed, the American press at the time tended to publish vehement attacks in which no holds were barred. President Adams and the Federalists were so angry at the newspapers and other journals opposing them that they passed the Sedition Act of 1798. Under this law, it was treasonable to publish criticism of the government. Several Jeffersonian publications were closed and their editors imprisoned. In an official letter to his secretary of state, Adams wrote: "I really think . . . that learned academics, not under the immediate inspection and control of government, have disorganized the world, and are incompatible with social order." Here Adams expressed the essential justification for authoritarian control.

The tension that existed between Jefferson and Adams over civil liberties has been a constant in American history.

RIGHTS DENIED

As was to happen so often in the future, the Sedition Act of 1798 was passed in a fit of antiradical hysteria. Adams and the Federalists were frightened by the French Revolution, which indeed was rather chaotic in the mid-nineties. They were afraid the same chaos—anarchy, Hamilton called it—would take root in the United States, and they saw Jefferson and his supporters sponsoring the "natural turbulence of the people." With his signature to the Sedition Act, Adams in effect suspended the First Amendment guarantees of free expression: the several rights of free speech, of free press, of assembly, and of petitioning for change of public policy.

Such suppression has occurred with some frequency in American history. One might be able to explain such suppression in the midst of war, but it is difficult to justify its occurrence in times of peace. Most often it was offbeat ideas that were suppressed because in some way they were presumed to threaten public safety. In the early nineteenth century, the Freemasons, a secretive fraternal organization devoted to democratic principles, was persecuted by local commu-

---

[1]From *The Political Writings of John Adams*, ed. George A. Peek, Jr. (New York: Bobbs-Merrill, 1954), p. 208.
[2]Ibid, p. 207.

nities as a secret, murderous, and unpatriotic society. Another group that was denied its first amendment rights in the early nineteenth century was the Mormon church. Their members were persecuted for their religious beliefs and social practices. Closer to home, after the end of World War II the United States government required an oath of loyalty from all its employees. They had to swear that they were not members of the Communist party, which at that time in this country was tiny. Many state governments followed suit and an "anti-red witch hunt" was underway during most of the 1950s. Throughout our history, we have had to be on guard to protect the right to hold minority views and to belong to minority groups. Unfortunately, we have let our guard down too often.

As we noted in Chapter 2, the First Amendment contains the basic components of American liberty. Without it we would not have a free society. Therefore, government violation of First Amendment guarantees can be seen as more directly threatening to the American way than the minuscule Communist party or other fringe groups. But First Amendment rights were not the only ones denied to many Americans. Workers, for example, were not given the *constitutional* right to form unions and bargain collectively until the mid-1930s; women were denied the right to vote until 1920, blacks until 1870. Each of these rights were denied on constitutional grounds and required intensive campaigns, with the general public, in the legislatures, and in the courts, before they were granted.

THE ROLE OF THE COURTS

Because we are a nation of laws, the courts are enormously powerful. In large measure they determine the rights we have and their applicability to the real-life situations in which we may find ourselves. Judges have been called upon to decide on the constitutionality of laws passed by Congress and state legislatures. They have also had to make decisions regarding executive actions. The Supreme Court ruled in 1952 that President Harry Truman could not seize the steel mills in order to prevent a strike in wartime. In 1954, the Court overturned a state law that required segregation in school systems and thereby changed race relations in the country. In 1986, the high court struck down a portion of the Gramm-Rudman law passed by Congress as a deficit-controlling measure. In each instance, the Supreme Court relied on voluntary compliance from these other centers of power. The authority of the Court stems from the great respect and affection with which it is held by the general public. Much of this respect derives from the belief that federal judges, who have lifetime appointments, are above politics. But, as we saw in Chapter 2, the federal judiciary is a creature of the political branches of government and as such is deeply implicated in politics. The federal judiciary is involved in politics in another way also. Often the cases brought before federal judges have political as well as constitutional importance. The right of individuals to express themselves freely and openly is both a political and constitutional issue. So is the right of a person to be free of racial discrimination, to make private sexual decisions, or to have the same opportunities for advancement at work as others.

We usually think of the Supreme Court as the chief protector of the rights of the "little guy" against abuses by more powerful forces, such as big government or big business. But the Court did not always play this role. For most of the nineteenth century and the first third of the twentieth, the Supreme Court helped make a weak federal government and a small industrial economy into almost irresistibly powerful giants. And this was often done at the expense of the pro-verbial "little guy," the underpaid and overworked laborer, the struggling small farmer, the highly vulnerable small businessman, and the needy consumer. And indeed, when government sided with the weak and powerless against giant cor-porations, the Court generally protected the interests of big business. The Supreme Court changed its view of social issues under political pressure from President Franklin D. Roosevelt. Only after he threatened to "pack" the Supreme Court with six extra justices of his choosing did the Court shift its stance on the social and economic inequities of the American system.[3]

The courts can deal with social or political issues only when cases are brought before them. Lawsuits involve time and expense, which makes it difficult for most private persons to use the judicial system to protect or assert their rights. Large organizations, such as giant corporations, state and federal governments, or trade associations, have the personnel and money to engage in lawsuits. To correct this imbalance in the area of civil rights, special interest groups, such as the American Civil Liberties Union (ACLU), the National Association for the Advancement of Colored People (NAACP), and the National Organization of Women (NOW), have arisen. They have provided free lawyers and advice on individual cases involving civil rights violations. These organizations are not only effective in the legal area, but they also conduct very impressive educational and lobbying programs. By building public support and thereby influencing the executive and legislative branches, these civil rights organizations bring political pressure on the Court.

THE ROLE OF THE PRESIDENT AND CONGRESS

Advances in civil rights were often brought about by actions of executives and legislatures on the state and federal levels of government well before the Supreme Court took action. In 1840, for example, President Martin Van Buren ordered a ten-hour day for all federal workers. The average workday at the time was twelve to sixteen hours, and in private companies this practice continued until the laws changed. It was not until 1847 that a state legislature—that of New Hampshire—took up Van Buren's lead and passed a law limiting the workday to ten hours for everyone in the state. By the late 1860s, most states had passed laws limiting the workday to ten hours. In 1905, however, the Supreme Court ruled that ten-hour laws were unconstitutional and that government did not have the authority to restrict private business.

---

[3]In 1935 and 1936 the Supreme Court ruled against New Deal laws designed to aid recovery from the Great Depression as well as to establish economic and social justice. To combat the Court's negative stance, FDR threatened in 1937 to change its ideological complexion by naming additional justices to the bench. Chief Justice Charles Evans Hughes had already shifted in favor of Roosevelt's programs by the end of the 1936 term, but still another judge was needed to gain a majority. By "chance," Associate Justice Owen Roberts changed his position to favor New Deal legislation in what has come to be called "the switch in time that saved nine."

Presidents and legislators are sometimes more responsive to public pressure than the Court chiefly because they are elected officials and the justices are not. When large numbers of voters, such as workers, share a common interest and are united in their demands, elected officials generally pay very close attention to what is being said. Although in many instances this responsiveness has been a boon for civil liberties and rights, it is also sometimes a danger. It is this very responsiveness that James Madison had in mind when he complained of the "tyranny of the majority." And we have had ample evidence of that "tyranny" in our history. The antiforeign hysteria that led to the Sedition Acts of 1798 and 1918 and the anticommunist hysteria that resulted in the persecutions of the 1920s and 1950s can serve as examples. In those instances, the courts have sometimes provided safeguards for our civil liberties.

RIGHTS IN CONFLICT

Often, though, the resistance is little and late, and for good reason. Usually, when national security interests are involved, as in the examples we just gave, two rights are in serious conflict. In our examples, the right of the majority to be protected from danger is in conflict with the right of an individual to his or her beliefs. But not all conflicts involve national security. Some concern only conflicting desires, as in the ongoing school prayer controversy; others involve differing notions of propriety, as in attempts to define and suppress "pornographic" material. But, however trivial or amusing the conflict may seem, serious issues concerning our concepts of freedom are at stake. In the case of school prayer, the issue is whether Jefferson's "wall of separation between church and state" will be maintained so as to assure freedom of religion. As to pornographic material, however it is defined, the question always is whether a community has the moral right to dictate what the permissible limits of an individual's private desires should be.

Conflicts over rights are almost always fought out in the political arena. Groups of people favoring one or another position in a conflict join together in hopefully massive rallies, contribute time and money to their "cause," and badger their representatives to pass laws supporting their program. Battles in court are part of the same process. The decisions made regarding our rights—laws passed, laws judged—shape the culture and society in which we live. Without the continuous process of redefining our rights brought about by our conflicts, the Bill of Rights would be a dead letter. Fortunately for us, the founders did not carve the first ten amendments in stone.

ESSENTIALS OF THE BILL OF RIGHTS

The first ten amendments were conceived by the founders as protecting the individual from a possibly oppressive national government. If it were not for the promise of such protection, the Constitution would not have been ratified in 1789 by the states. In the beginning, the Bill of Rights was thought of as restraining only the federal government. Much later, some of those restraints were extended to the state governments by the Fourteenth Amendment. From a political and cultural point of view, the most significant of our rights are contained in the First Amendment.

THE FIRST AMENDMENT: FREEDOM OF SPEECH AND PRESS

In essence, the First Amendment guarantees us freedom of expression, belief, and political action. But the guarantee is limited. In times of crisis, the Constitution permits the temporary suspension of the First Amendment guarantees. This seems reasonable enough. The nation in a time of crisis may be vulnerable. Under these conditions, free political speech and action may threaten its survival. But there may be problems with this seemingly clear situation. The government may claim a threat to national security as a mask covering its suppression of dissent or criticism. During World War I, the United States government used the presumed threat to national security to imprison socialists, union organizers, and others who were critical of the American system. One may justify this action by arguing that criticism in a time of war might cause resistance to governmental authority. If sufficiently widespread, this situation can present a "clear and present danger" to the nation. Democracies, one may argue, cannot allow the very freedoms they cherish to bring about their destruction.

The highly specific words "freedom of speech, or of the press" have been interpreted by the Supreme Court to cover almost all forms of expression. Not only can you say, write, and publish anything you wish within reason, but you may also express your views by wearing buttons, armbands, or T-shirts. You can also convey your opinions by handing out leaflets, carrying signs, making films, or using any other method of communication. Even burning the American flag is protected "speech." In *Texas v. Johnson* (1989) the "conservative" Rehnquist Court held that burning the flag in a political protest is protected by the First Amendment. A year later the Court confirmed its earlier opinion. In *United States v. Eichman* (1990), the Rehnquist Court held that the National Flag Protection Act, which Congress had passed to overturn *Texas v. Johnson* and make flag burning a federal crime, also violated the First Amendment's free speech guarantees. These freedoms extend as well to art and literature, as long as they contain "serious literary, artistic, political . . . value."

As essential to free expression as the speech and press clauses is the First Amendment's guarantee of the "right of the people peaceably to assemble, and to petition the government for a redress of grievances." These clauses permit you to march, demonstrate, hold mass meetings, and otherwise join with others to express your views on political or other matters. For example, during the early 1960s, groups of college students in the South held "sit-in" demonstrations at lunch counters and other public places to express their opposition to segregation. When students were arrested by the local authorities, the Supreme Court held that the students' rights of free speech and free assembly were violated.

But as with every other right, the freedom of expression is not absolute. We have already seen that it can be restricted in a national security context. There are also other restraints as well.

Libel.   You cannot knowingly write, publish, or broadcast any false information about someone that would injure that person. Such action is known as *libel*. If you libel someone you can be sued. A private individual has only to prove that the statement is false and harmful to win the case and have you pay damages. The situation is a little different with political figures and celebrities. They also have to prove "malicious intent," that you meant to harm them. This charge is extremely difficult to prove, as was the case when General William Westmoreland, the former commander of American forces in Vietnam, sued CBS's *Sixty Minutes*. He claimed that the television show had shown him purposely misleading President Lyndon B. Johnson during the Vietnam War. Unable to prove malicious intent, Westmoreland settled with CBS out of court.

Obscenity.   This is one of the more difficult restraints. One person may see a piece of writing as "obscene," while another person sees the same work as having the highest literary merit, as indeed happened with James Joyce's *Ulysses,* a major literary work of the early twentieth century. Most definitions of obscenity are religiously based and reflect the often-puritanical biases of a majority of the residents in a state or local area. State and local governments, reflecting these majority views, have often passed laws forbidding the publication or sale of "obscene" material. Various forms of censorship were common until the Supreme Court, responding to the changing mores of the 1960s, largely put an end to them. Although obscenity laws are still on the books in most states, they must pass some pretty strict constitutional requirements to be enforceable. Of course, this may change since the composition of the Supreme Court has changed.

FREEDOM OF RELIGION

As important as freedom of expression is the freedom of belief guaranteed by the First Amendment. Because of the world's long history of religious bigotry and violence, the Framers of the Bill of Rights cast their desire for "freedom of conscience" in terms of freedom of religion. They wanted to separate church and state. For about 200 years prior to the American Revolution, each state in Europe chose one or another of the competing Christian churches as its official religion and did its best to wipe out all other sects. Many American colonies continued the same attitudes here. For example, James Madison complained in a letter to Jefferson: "One of the objections in New England was that the Constitution by prohibiting religious tests opened a door for Jews, Turks & infidels." To Madison, New England's attitude was a violation of what he called "freedom of conscience." But not all the colonies felt as New England did. In his autobiography, Jefferson describes the passage of his bill on the same subject through Virginia's General Assembly: "The bill establishing religious freedom ... passed ... in proof that they [the Virginia legislators] meant to comprehend, within the mantle of its protection, the Jew and the Gentile, the Christian and the Mahometan, the Hindoo, and infidel of every denomination."[4]

---

[4]Thomas Jefferson, "Autobiography," in *Writings,* ed. Merrill D. Peterson (New York: Library of America, 1984), p. 40.

Since there were so many different positions regarding religious belief, the founders decided that if they wanted to hold together the thirteen states they had best keep the national government out of religion altogether. They therefore restricted Congress from making any "law respecting an establishment of religion, or prohibiting the free exercise thereof." Since the establishment and exercise clauses of the First Amendment restrain the federal government only, religious persecution and discrimination were practiced in many states during the nineteenth and early twentieth centuries. In the 1840s and 1850s, for example, intensive anti-Catholic campaigns were carried out by groups we today call nativists. The Ku Klux Klan has carried this earlier hatred of Catholics as well as of Jews and blacks into our own age. Many states made little or no effort to restrain the excesses of religious bigotry and indeed often cooperated with it. Starting in the mid-1940s, the Supreme Court began to apply the freedom of religion clauses to the states. It did so by asserting that the First Amendment was *incorporated,* that is, included within, the due process clause of the Fourteenth Amendment, which applies to the states.

Since the mid-1940s, the courts have been called upon to resolve many controversial cases arising from the freedom of religion clauses of the First Amendment. State governments have provided aid to religious institutions in a number of ways. One example is the use of public funds to reimburse all or part of the textbook expenses of private school, including parochial school, pupils. Two other examples are the loan of public school buses to transport parochial school students and the release time granted public school students to get religious instruction at another location during school hours. All are still permitted by the Supreme Court, all are still controversial. The latest example of the high court's permissiveness in this area is *Board of Education v. Mergens* (1990). In this case, the Court ruled that a student bible club could meet on the grounds of a high school without breaching Jefferson's "wall of separation between church and State." Here too controversy surrounds the Court's decision.

But perhaps the most controversial of all the church-state issues is prayer in the public schools. In 1962, the Court declared school prayers unconstitutional in a case known as *Engel v. Vitale*. The opinion stated that the establishment clause of the First Amendment "must at least mean that it is no part of the business of government to compose official prayers for any group of the American people to recite as part of a religious program carried on by government." Public schools are part of the government, hence prayers composed by school officials entangle the government in religion. The Supreme Court has held consistently that the government must maintain neutrality toward religion. Neither state nor federal governments may take action that will advance or inhibit religious interests. As Justice Robert H. Jackson wrote for the Court in 1943: "If there is any fixed star in our constitutional constellation, it is that no official, high or petty, can prescribe what shall be orthodox in politics, nationalism, religion. . . ."

In the same statement in which he raised the wall between church and state, Jefferson also said, the "powers of government reach actions only, and not opinions."[5] In large measure, the courts have followed Jefferson's injunction. You can generally believe what you will in the area of religion, but you cannot always act on the basis of that belief. When a state claims a "compelling interest," the Supreme Court has often allowed it to suspend the free exercise clause of the First Amendment. This decision has been made in a number of cases involving Christian Science parents whose free exercise rights have been denied because they endangered the lives of their children. But the Rehnquist Court seems to be breaking new ground. The traditional "compelling interest" requirement had been dropped in a recent decision involving the free exercise clause. The Supreme Court held in *Employment Division of Oregon v. Alfred L. Smith* (1990) that the state could prohibit the use of peyote without regard to the drug's religious significance to some groups and without claiming a compelling state interest in overriding the free exercise clause of the First Amendment. As Associate Justice Harry A. Blackmun observed in his dissent, the Court's decision is in effect "a wholesale overturning of settled law concerning the Religion Clauses of our Constitution."

AMENDMENTS GRANTING THE RIGHT TO PRIVACY

Implicit within the First Amendment is the right to the privacy of one's beliefs about politics, religion, or any other matter. The right to privacy is also implicit in the fourth, fifth, and ninth amendments. In Amendment IV, the opening clause carries strong connotations of privacy when it declares: "The right of the people to be secure in their persons, houses, papers, and effects against unreasonable searches and seizures, shall not be violated." Some courts have used this clause

---

[5]From "To Messrs Nehemiah Dodge and Others, A Committee of the Danbury Baptist Association, in the State of Connecticut," in Thomas Jefferson, *Writings*, p. 510.

to rule against government wire taps and drug tests, and some have not. The issue is not yet fully resolved. The clause in the Fifth Amendment stating that no person "shall be compelled in any criminal case to be a witness against himself" also has overtones of a right to privacy.

The Ninth Amendment's declaration that the people have rights even though they may not be named in the Constitution has been interpreted by the Supreme Court as including a "natural right" or "fundamental right" of privacy. In 1965, the Court used the privacy implications of the Ninth Amendment together with the Fourteenth Amendment's due process clause to strike down a state law against contraception. In 1973, the same combination was used by the Supreme Court in *Roe v. Wade,* the case that legalized abortion throughout the country. Few cases in American history have roused as much emotion over as prolonged a period as the abortion issue. Advocates of both sides have used all legal means of persuasion, and a few antiabortion activists have resorted to illegal means, such as bombing abortion clinics. The Court's reasoning was basically that there is no "compelling public purpose" served by depriving a woman of her fundamental right to choose freely whether or not to give birth. The majority on the Court also held that this choice is a private matter and that constitutional precedent establishes a fundamental right of privacy. More recently, the Court's stance on abortion and the right to privacy has been modified. In *Webster v. Reproductive Health Services* (1989), a majority of the high court held that states may restrict abortions because they have a countervailing "interest in protecting potential human life." In *Hodgson v. Minnesota* (1990), the Court held that if a teen-age girl can get permission for an abortion from a judge, she must tell both parents of her intention even if she knows they will disapprove. This exposure places a heavy psychological burden on many young girls and may serve to discourage their seeking an abortion. Slowly, the right to privacy represented by *Roe* is being chipped away.

The Ninth Amendment was written to take care of Hamilton's objection that a list of specific rights is necessarily limited and suggests that the people do not have any other rights than those named. Therefore, the Framers thought of this amendment as a kind of catch-all. It would take care of all those rights the Framers did not think necessary to name because they were part of the natural rights all people are born with. The amendment would also suit Jefferson's demand that the future not be bound by the past. Later generations could create rights to meet their new circumstances. As Jefferson wrote to Madison: "The earth belongs to the living generation. They manage it then, . . . exercising in fact the power of repeal [which] leaves them as free as if the constitution or law had been expressly limited to nineteen years only."[6]

AMENDMENTS PROTECTING THE ACCUSED

In addition to implying the right of privacy, the Fourth and Fifth Amendments were designed to protect persons accused of crime. Several other amendments also afford protection to the accused. The following is a brief description of them.

---

[6]From letter of September 6, 1789, in Thomas Jefferson, *Writings,* p. 963.

Fourth Amendment.   As we had seen, this amendment prohibits unreasonable search and seizure methods for collecting evidence. It also requires that probable cause be shown before a warrant permitting the search and seizure can be issued. The warrant itself restricts the search to a specific place and the seizure to particular objects or persons. When the police gain evidence by violating Fourth Amendment rights, that evidence cannot be used in court. This is known as the *exclusionary rule*.

Fifth Amendment.   We have already mentioned one of the essential clauses of this amendment: the right of an accused person to not give evidence against him- or herself. In this instance too, if a person accused of a crime inadvertently makes a self-incriminating statement to the police without advice of counsel, that statement cannot be used as evidence against the person in court. Again, the exclusionary rule comes into play. The most famous example of the exclusionary rule in a criminal case is *Miranda v. Arizona* (1966) in which Ernesto Miranda's confession to a crime was set aside and his conviction overturned.

This clause has been widely used not only by criminals, but also by high-ranking government officials and political dissidents under investigation by Congress. When one says he or she is "taking the Fifth," this clause is meant.

There are also several other important clauses in the amendment. Major crimes can be tried only after an investigation and indictment by a grand jury. An accused person is protected from being tried a second time for the same crime; this is protection against double jeopardy. A person cannot be deprived of life, liberty, or property without due process of the law. This clause links up with the due process clause of the Fourteenth Amendment, which virtually repeats it verbatim and applies it to the states. Finally, private property cannot be taken by the government without adequate payment.

Sixth Amendment.   This amendment assures the accused of a fair trial by an impartial jury. It also guarantees that the person knows what the accusation is and can confront his or her accusers. The accused can also use government power to get supporting witnesses, and has the right to an attorney.

Eighth Amendment.   "Cruel and unusual punishment" as well as excessive fines and bail are prohibited by this amendment.

These four amendments lay out the procedures that must be followed in criminal cases. The Supreme Court is often called upon to review and interpret these procedural protections. As new cases appear before it, the Court refines and sometimes changes its interpretation of the constitutional protections of those accused of crime. Through the due process clause of the Fourteenth Amendment, each of the procedural rights has been applied to the states by recent Court decisions.

THE REMAINING AMENDMENTS

The country has been much involved with the amendments we have just discussed and has only intermittently paid attention to the other parts of the Bill of Rights.

For example, the Second Amendment reserves to the people the right to bear arms, which the Framers thought of as providing for state militias that could serve in place of a national army; a national military force seemed threatening because it could support an oppressive federal government. Gun-owners' associations, citing the Second Amendment, are vehemently opposed and have so far effectively lobbied against controls.

The next amendment that may be involved in controversy is the tenth. This amendment reserves to the states the powers that are not prohibited to them or claimed for the federal government by the original Constitution. Advocates of states' rights point to this amendment when they argue against the nationalization of the Bill of Rights. Minority groups, women's organizations, and other vulnerable individuals and groups, on the other hand, have found relief in the nationalization of the Bill of Rights.

Other amendments are not now controversial. The Third Amendment protects homeowners from being forced by the government to house troops. This had been a major complaint against the British before the Revolution. The Seventh Amendment provides for jury trial in civil cases and requires review of law rather than facts on appeal. Juries decide the facts in a trial, but the judge decides the law. If a judge makes an error, the case can be appealed to a higher court.

The Seventh Amendment as well as those protecting the accused afford procedural safeguards for the First Amendment. They also, as we have seen, enlarge the rights implicit in the First Amendment, the rest of the Constitution, and the concept of fundamental rights. The currently enlarged scope of the Bill of Rights, however, is due mainly to the Fourteenth Amendment.

THE FOURTEENTH AMENDMENT AND THE BILL OF RIGHTS

After the Civil War, the United States ratified three amendments affecting the former slaves. The Thirteenth Amendment outlawed slavery, the Fourteenth made the former slaves citizens, and the Fifteenth gave them the right to vote. Of the three amendments, the one that has had the greatest impact beyond its original purpose is the Fourteenth. In large measure this is because the Fourteenth Amendment is the broadest of the three in its sweep.

The essential achievement of the Fourteenth Amendment was to apply the restraints on government to the states. Traditionally, we believe the Founding Fathers intended the Constitution to restrict the federal government and leave the states free to act as they wished. But it is not absolutely certain that this was indeed their intention, or that the intention was unanimous. In his letter of October 24, 1787, James Madison described to Thomas Jefferson some of what took place at the Constitutional Convention and his own feelings about the issues discussed. Here we will quote only that which is relevant to state sovereignty.

The second object, the due partition of power, between the General & local Governments, was perhaps of all, the most nice and difficult. A few contended for an entire abolition of the States; some for indefinite power of Legislation in the Congress, with a negative [veto power] on the laws of the States: some for a limited power of legislation, with such a negative. . . . The question with regard to the Negative underwent repeated discussions, and was finally rejected by a bare majority. . . . I will take this occasion of explaining myself on the subject. Such a check on the states appears to me necessary . . . to prevent instability and injustice in the legislation of the States.[7]

Madison, as well as a number of other Framers of the Constitution, felt that the people needed protection from the states as much as from the federal government. But it was not until the rebellion of the states in 1860 to 1865 that Congress was persuaded to assert its authority over state governments. Abolitionist leaders wanted to be certain that the prevailing antiblack sentiment in both the North and South did not frustrate their efforts to enfranchise the newly liberated slaves.

Prior to the Civil War, the chief constitutional mechanism used to regulate the states was the commerce clause. By broadly interpreting the national power to regulate commerce, the Supreme Court enlarged the authority of the federal government over the states. After the war, the Court was able to use the Fourteenth Amendment as well. Section 1 of the Fourteenth Amendment has the breadth and depth of the Bill of Rights, which in some ways it seems to purposely echo. Here is what Section 1 says:

All persons born or naturalized in the United States and subject to the jurisdiction thereof, are citizens of the United States and of the State wherein they reside. No State shall make or enforce any law which shall abridge the privileges or immunities of citizens of the United States; nor shall any State deprive any person of life, liberty, or property, without due process of law; nor deny to any person within its jurisdiction the equal protection of the laws.

The congressional sponsors of the Fourteenth Amendment expected that the Bill of Rights, which limited only the national government, would apply to the states under the privileges and immunities clause. But an 1873 decision by the Supreme Court held that this clause did not include the Bill of Rights. In contrast, the due process clause might include a portion of those rights because it so closely resembles the due process clause of the Fifth Amendment. Subsequently, the Court ruled that the Fifth Amendment's due process restrictions were the only part of the Bill of Rights that could apply to the states.

THE DUE PROCESS CLAUSE

From the 1880s until the mid-1930s, the Court applied the due process clauses of the Fifth and Fourteenth amendments to economic matters. For the most part, the high court used these clauses to strike down government efforts to regulate the excesses of big business. For example, Congress had passed a law in 1898

[7]From *The Papers of James Madison*, vol. 10, *27 May 1787–3 March 1788*, ed. Robert A. Rutland et al. (Chicago: University of Chicago Press, 1977), p. 209.

that made it a crime to fire a worker because of membership in a union. The Court struck down the law because it was ''an arbitrary interference with the liberty of contract.'' Again using the liberty-of-contract argument, the high court ruled in 1905 against a New York law limiting the workday to ten hours. In 1894, Congress passed a modest income tax. In 1895, the Court declared the tax unconstitutional and warned that it was an ''assault on capital [that would] be but the stepping stone to others. . . .''

It was not until 1925 that the Supreme Court declared the First Amendment guarantees of free speech and press could be included within the due process clause of the Fourteenth Amendment and applied to the states. But at that time the Court had not applied its finding. Six years later, in 1931, the high court struck down a state's law censoring the press. Prior restraint of the press, the Court held, was permissible only for the most compelling reasons, such as a threat to national security during wartime. This was the first time the Bill of Rights was ''incorporated'' into the due process clause.

THE INCORPORATION DOCTRINE

To *incorporate* means to bring a thing from outside into the ''body'' of some other thing so that they become one. Metaphorically, that is what happened with the Bill of Rights and the Fourteenth Amendment. Because it was thought of as part of the due process clause of the Fourteenth Amendment, the Bill of Rights could be applied to the states. But progress was slow. As we just saw, the freedom of the press was first used to restrain a state in 1931, six years after the incorporation doctrine was first enunciated. It took another six years for several other parts of the Bill of Rights to be applied to the states. In 1937, Supreme Court Justice Benjamin Cardozo provided a short list of the rights that restricted abuses of power by the states.

Freedom of expression

Just compensation for private property taken for public use

Right to counsel for defense in criminal cases

Justice Cardozo also thought the Fourteenth Amendment's due process required a fair trial, but not necessarily the provisions called for in the Bill of Rights.

State laws restricting freedom of religion were struck down by the Supreme Court starting in the late 1930s, after Justice Cardozo made his list. In the late 1940s, the Sixth Amendment's public trial provisions were incorporated into the Fourteenth's due process clause. The Supreme Court under Chief Justice Earl Warren nationalized most of the remainder of the Bill of Rights during the 1960s. Only a few of the provisions of the Bill of Rights have not been incorporated so far.

The incorporation doctrine has come under fire since its inception and has remained controversial to this day. Perhaps most of the criticism centers on questions of federalism. Has the Supreme Court, through the incorporation doctrine, infringed on the right of the states to govern themselves? The question has arisen chiefly because of the incorporation of the Bill of Rights' safeguards for the accused. Questions have also been raised by the Supreme Court's decisions on abortion rights.

The Supreme Court's decision on abortion in *Roe v. Wade* in 1973 has probably caused more heat than any other of its decisions since its school desegregation cases of the 1950s. The Court held that Jane Roe's fundamental right to liberty and privacy were violated by Texas's antiabortion laws. The due process clause of the Fourteenth Amendment, the justices argued, incorporated rights implicit in the first ten amendments. Antiabortion forces asserted that the Court usurped the rights of states to make law and tried to get Congress to overturn the Supreme Court's decision by constitutional amendment. So far they have been unsuccessful. But they did get Congress to pass a law preventing the use of federal funds for abortions.

THE EQUAL PROTECTION CLAUSE

For almost a century after the states adopted the Fourteenth Amendment, its equal protection clause was ignored. Segregation was made possible by the Court's "separate but equal" doctrine that was first put forward in the 1896 case known as *Plessy v. Ferguson*. In 1890, Louisiana passed a law that required "equal but separate accommodations" for white and black railroad passengers. The law was challenged and the Court found in favor of the state. After this ruling, state laws mandating segregation were virtually unassailable.

Desgregation.   The tide began to turn during the liberal years of the late 1930s and 1940s. In a series of decisions based on the Interstate Commerce Act and the equal protection clause, the Court struck at segregation in trains and education. By 1954, the campaign to reverse *Plessy* was in high gear. At that time the Supreme Court, now known as the Warren Court, was presented with *Brown v. Board of Education*. The Court's unanimous decision was that segregated public education on any level and of whatever quality was in violation of the Fourteenth Amendment's guarantee of "the equal protection of the law."

This ruling brought about a social as well as constitutional revolution. State laws enforcing segregation were struck down throughout the South. The federal government sent troops into the South to enforce the courts' antisegregation rulings over the resistance of the state officials. Several civil rights acts were passed by Congress, voting rights laws were strictly enforced, segregation was prohibited on all forms of interstate transportation. Subsequently, the courts called for busing to overcome segregation in schools that resulted from the separate neighborhoods in which the races lived. This ruling, as well as later ones, affected the North for the first time and caused violent opposition by parent groups in such cities as Boston and New York. Federally assisted low- and middle-income housing was desegregated, and efforts to keep blacks out of white neighborhoods were outlawed. In 1965, President Johnson issued an executive order requiring that all federally funded projects have affirmative action programs.

Affirmative Action.   Affirmative action programs are intended to correct the injustices caused by past discrimination. They demand that schools and employers

Breaking barriers: Another decision from the justices sympathetic to feminists.

receiving federal money establish policies and programs to achieve racial and gender balance. Under the Civil Rights Act of 1964 and the affirmative action regulations that followed, sex discrimination was prohibited for the first time. Since their adoption, women have been able to take on jobs that were once denied them, teach subjects in which they were once thought incompetent, and rise to the highest levels in business, government, and scholarship.

But like the issue of desegregation, affirmative action has met with considerable opposition. Some have argued that giving preferential treatment to previously disadvantaged groups is reverse discrimination. Others object to the use of *quotas* (set numbers of people) to assure the presence of racial minorities and women. Still others argue that advancing people on the basis of sex or race means giving up merit as the prime criterion of success. The Supreme Court's own decisions on affirmative action have reflected the conflict within society. The problem arises in situations where there is a scarcity of desirable positions. Offering a scarce position to one person often means denying it to another. When this is done by the government or at government instigation, the equal protection clause is being violated. Or so some Supreme Court justices have argued.

In Conclusion

Throughout history the idea of liberty or freedom has been in conflict with the demands of authority. Because of this long history, the Founding Fathers were very concerned to protect the liberty of the individual from abuses by governmental authority. To secure what they thought of as the most threatened freedoms, the founders refused to ratify the newly created Constitution until they received the promise that a Bill of Rights would be included.

Initially, the Bill of Rights was thought of as restricting only the federal government. With the ratification of the Fourteenth Amendment, portions of the Bill of Rights were slowly applied to the states. At first used in the economic area to protect big business, the due process clause was in the twentieth century extended to include most of the protections of the Bill of Rights. As a result, freedom of expression and religion along with important civil rights are protected from violation by state governments. Under the Fourteenth Amendment's equal protection clause, women and racial minorities also have gained increased rights. Today, more people enjoy more civil liberties and rights than at any time in the past. However, with a Supreme Court dominated by political and social conservatives, these rights may soon be restricted.

Suggested Readings

Henry J. Abraham. *Freedom and the Court,* 4th ed. New York: Oxford University Press, 1982.

Jason Epstein. *The Great Conspiracy Trial.* New York: Random house, 1970.

Fred W. Friendly. *Minnesota Rag.* New York: Random House, 1981.

Anthony Lewis. *Gideon's Trumpet.* New York: Random House, 1964.

J. Harvie Wilkinson III. *From Brown to Bakke.* New York: Oxford University Press, 1979.

FEDERALISM

*It is not by the concentration of powers, but by their
distribution, that good government is effected.*

Thomas Jefferson

In recent years, there has been a persistent call to reestablish the principles of
federalism in the United States. The central argument is that the national
government is too large and too intrusive in state affairs. The counter argument
is that the states are too indifferent to the needs of vulnerable classes of people
and too ready to trample on their rights. Throughout our history, federalism has
been a source of contention and irritation.

As we understand the term today, *federalism* is a system of government in
which authority is divided between national and local governments, such as prov-
inces, cantons, or states. The local constituent governments usually possess a
significant amount of independent authority. Theoretically, they also have an equal
amount of power within their own domains and give up an equal amount to the
central government. As we have seen from our own history, the amount of power
actually yielded to the national government depends on the political and economic
circumstances at a given time.

BACKGROUND

In one sense, *federalism* refers to a confederation or league of independent states. Such leagues go back to ancient Greece. One of the most famous is the Delian League, named for the island of Delos, which housed the league's treasury. Originally an alliance of equally independent Greek city-states, the individual members eventually fell under the complete dominance of Athens, the most powerful member. When a member state rebelled and tried to withdraw, Athens crushed the rebellion and enforced adherence. The Delian League lasted about seventy-five years until it was destroyed by another alliance of Greek city-states under the leadership of Sparta.

Federations or leagues of independent states had been a regular part of European history since the ancient Greeks. Gradually they evolved over time into the types of national systems we understand as federalism. One of the oldest examples of a federated state is Switzerland or, as it is often called, the Swiss Confederation. Originally formed in the Middle Ages as a military alliance of three city-states or cantons in the Alps, the Swiss Confederation grew in size and power until the mid-sixteenth century. At about the middle of the nineteenth century, several of the cantons moved toward increased centralization. At the same time most of the cantons shifted from an oligarchy of wealthy burghers to wider representation. Today, Switzerland is a federal republic.

The United States also started as a defensive alliance of independent states. As we saw in Chapter 2, we were a confederation of thirteen states between 1776 and 1788, when the Constitution was ratified by the required nine states. The federal system of shared powers was created by compromises struck between those who wanted a strong national government and those who wished merely for a more effective confederation. The dispute came down to whether the national or the state governments were to be supreme. As Madison explained to Jefferson, the delegates to the Constitutional Convention had a difficult time apportioning power between the federal government and the states. Although there were many differing views, the extremes were between those who advocated doing away with the states entirely and those who wished to restrict the national government without any restraint on the states. According to Madison, the latter group won and created "a feudal system of republics."[1] In part, the history of the United States can be seen as a gradual shift from "feudal system" to a national one.

From the very beginning of our nation's history, advocates of states' rights called for a return to "federalism" and charged the national government with usurpation of power. When Congress passed the Alien and Sedition Act of 1798, Jefferson drafted what has come to be called the *Kentucky Resolutions*. He there presented the basic argument of those who call for a return to federalism.

> *Resolved,* That the several States composing the United States of America, are not united on the principle of unlimited submission to their General Government; but

---

[1] Madison's letter of 24 October 1787 to Jefferson in *The Papers of James Madison,* vol. 10, *27 May 1787–3 March 1788,* ed. Robert A. Rutland et al. (Chicago: University of Chicago Press, 1977), p. 210.

"It is unthinkable that the citizens of Rhode Island should ever surrender their sovereignty to some central authority located way off in Philadelphia."

... they ... delegated to that government certain definite powers, reserving, each State to itself, the residuary mass of right to their own self-government; and that whensoever the General Government assumes undelegated powers, its acts are unauthoritative, void, and of no force. . . .[2]

Madison had written a similar resolution for Virginia, which, together with Jefferson's Kentucky Resolutions, asserted the right of the states to decide for themselves what was constitutional. He and Jefferson wrote their resolutions because they were ideologically opposed to denying freedom of conscience.

Calls for federalism, like the insistence on strict construction of the Constitution, have always had as their underlying purpose some interest other than adherence to the Framers' intentions. At times that interest is one of principle, as with Jefferson and Madison. At other times it may be private gain or the desire for power. A prime example of the uses to which "federalism" may be put can be found during the administration of Andrew Jackson. As the election of 1828 approached, Jackson's congressional supporters introduced an extremely high tariff bill, expecting it to be defeated. They counted on both the South and North voting against it and the middle states favoring it. The plan was that despite the defeat of the bill, the middle states would be grateful and vote for Jackson. He was already sure of the South, so that with middle-state support he could wrap up the election. To everyone's surprise, the tariff passed.

---

[2]Thomas Jefferson, *Writings,* p. 449.

South Carolina objected strenuously to the tariff because it cut its export trade in cotton and increased the cost of imported consumer goods. Previously extremely nationalistic, South Carolina asserted the federalism principle of states' rights and passed the Ordinance of Nullification of 1832 and threatened secession. Jackson, who had been an advocate of states' rights and had won the South because of that, issued a Proclamation to the People of South Carolina. He asserted that every state was subordinate to the national government and that no state had the right to secede. Jackson also backed up his claim by threatening to use force and sent additional troops to Fort Sumter in South Carolina. Both sides backed off and the scene was replayed about thirty years later.

It was Jackson who reversed the nationalist trend of the Supreme Court by appointing the states' rights man Roger B. Taney as chief justice. For about a century, the Supreme Court followed a rigid system of separate jurisdictions based on the principle of states' rights and called *dual federalism*. Efforts by Congress to regulate the abuses of private industry were struck down time and again on the grounds that the federal government did not have the constitutional authority to regulate actions that took place within a state. The federal government could intervene only in situations that occurred between states, as in interstate commerce. This view of the limited power of the national government ended when Franklin D. Roosevelt threatened to "pack" the Supreme Court in 1937. Since then, the relationship between national and state governments has changed. Today, the different levels of government operate on the basis of *shared authority* in certain areas. This means that some powers are possessed solely by the states, some only by the central government, and some by the two levels of government equally.

Since the states are so important to the concept of federalism, let us look a little more closely at them.

STATE GOVERNMENTS

The United States, as the name implies, is a union of political entities that claim complete sovereignty within their borders. At the time the union was formed, the states gave up to the central government a certain amount of sovereignty. For the most part, they also adjusted their individual governmental structures to fit the constitutional principle of the separation of powers. At the time of the Convention of 1787, Pennsylvania, for example, had a *unicameral* (one-chambered) legislature, an executive council with a president appointed jointly by the council and legislature, and no independent judiciary. Although Virginia had a bicameral legislature, as did most other states, the state's chief executive was chosen by and subordinate to the legislature. The constitution closest to what was adopted at Philadelphia in 1787 was that of Massachusetts, written by John Adams. Today, all states have tripartite governments in which authority is dispersed among the executive, legislative, and judicial branches of government.

THE STRUCTURE OF STATE GOVERNMENTS

Constitutions.   Like the national government, ultimate authority in the states derives from their constitutions. Although far more detailed than the federal charter, state constitutions share certain features with the national one. They all have bills of rights, separation of powers among the three branches, checks and balances, and provisions for being amended.

Constitutional amendment procedures in the states differ in several significant ways from those of the federal government. State amendments are voted upon by eligible citizens directly rather than indirectly, as with national amendments. State amendments can be proposed in one of several ways. The most common is through the use of the *referendum,* a statewide vote by the citizenry on a measure or act presented to it by the legislature. Another is the *initiative,* in which a private citizen can have a proposal placed directly on the ballot in a statewide election after collecting a specific number of signatures on a petition.

Executives.   Governors are the chief executives of all states since the national Constitution was adopted. They have many of the same functions and powers as the president of the United States. Most of them can veto legislation they disapprove of. In a certain way they have even more power than the president. Many of those who have the veto power can reject a specific item without turning down an entire bill. This is called the *line-item veto,* and presidents have been trying unsuccessfully to get that authority for years. In many states, a governor's veto can be overturned only by a three-fourths majority of both houses of the legislature; the president can be reversed by a smaller number, two-thirds of the Congress. In the event a statewide elected official, such as a U.S. senator or state treasurer, dies or is otherwise incapacitated, most governors have the power to appoint a replacement to serve until the next election.

All governors have control over the administrative apparatus of their states, although ultimate authority rests with the legislatures, as it does in the national government. The administrative structures of the states vary enormously; however, there is uniformity in some offices. For example, all states have chief financial officers, although the title may vary considerably. But in some states the head of the school system is an individual, in others it is a commission composed of several members, as is the Board of Regents in New York. The state agencies perform functions that are similar to and often closely connected with the national bureaucracy. State agencies regulate health, education, banking, law enforcement, gas, electric, and phone utilities as well as other public services.

Legislatures.   Most state legislatures consist of two houses; the only exception is Nebraska, which has one. Past this level of uniformity, they vary considerably. State legislatures differ a good deal in the number of representatives their voters have. For example, New Hampshire has 363 representatives in its legislature for a population of 774,000 people, while California, with a population of 20 million, has only 120 members in its legislature. In most states, members of the upper house of the legislature are elected for four-year terms, while those in the lower house are elected for two years. There are about twelve states, however, in which the members of the upper chamber serve only two years, and four states in which lower house representatives serve four-year terms.

Although state legislatures resemble Congress in most respects, they do differ in some signal ways. Not all state legislatures meet every year; some hold sessions every other year. In some states, the length of time a legislative session can last is set by the constitution. However, all state legislatures function more or less as does Congress. They all have standing committees that deal with special legislative matters. They also all hold hearings, some of which may be open to the general public, before writing up bills or passing legislation. Bills are passed in most states by majorities of those present at the time of voting. Some states require a majority of the full membership for passage. All bills require approval of both houses of the legislature before going to the governor for signature.

State Judiciaries.   The justice systems of the states differ from one another enormously, probably more than any other part of state government. For a discussion of the essentials of state judicial systems, see Chapter 11, pages 260–261. In summary, state courts share with the federal courts jurisdiction over certain kinds of cases. These are suits over $10,000 that involve citizens from different states and crimes that violate both state and federal laws. Otherwise, state courts deal solely with the civil and criminal violations of their local laws. Specific laws differ markedly from state to state, as, for example, with respect to divorce, consumer protection, or penalties for theft.

The greatest difference between the federal and state judicial systems is the way judges are selected. Federal judges are appointed for life by the president with the approval of the Senate. Most state judges are elected, usually for terms of four to fifteen years. Several states have a judicial committee or council, often composed of senior judges, that recommends someone whom they consider well qualified to the governor for appointment. In some states, the governor makes the appointment with the approval of a mixed judicial-political commission. And in a few states, governors nominate judges for approval by the upper house of the legislature, much as is done in the federal government.

Local Governments.   To govern their inhabitants, states have created several levels of local government. The top level below the state is usually the county, although in two states the word *county* designates a geographical area rather than level of government. Everywhere else counties are governmental structures that are responsible for particular territorial areas. The counties' political organization varies widely; many counties, for example, do not abide by the separation-of-powers doctrine that characterizes our national and state governments. Both executive and legislative functions are performed by the lawmaking bodies of these counties. In other counties, also organized on the principle of legislative supremacy, lawmakers hire or appoint a county manager as their chief executive. Still other counties follow the separation-of-powers principle and elect independent executive and legislative officials.

Below the level of counties, states have evolved municipal forms of government. These are cities, boroughs, towns, villages, and hamlets, with cities having the most people and hamlets the least. Most of these government units are *incorporated* by the state, that is, they are granted a state charter. Some small units, such as villages and hamlets, are *unincorporated,* which means that the inhabitants have not requested a charter from the state.

Forms of government vary a great deal, although most cities have a mayor or city manager, city council or board of aldermen or commissioners, and an independent judiciary that carries to the local level the separation-of-powers doctrine of the national system. Towns often have boards of supervisors usually composed of the supervisors from the villages that make up the town. These boards customarily function as both legislative and executive branches of local government. Very often major local issues, such as school budgets and taxes, are decided at town meetings, even when there are town boards. The boards usually make local laws within the restraints set by county and state governments.

THE FUNCTION OF STATE GOVERNMENTS

The national government has a few constitutionally mandated functions, mainly to conduct international relations, provide the national defense, and guarantee the general welfare. State governments, by contrast, have a multitude of responsibilities. The states are responsible for public education from kindergarten through graduate school; public health services in hospitals, clinics, and the like; social services for the needy; business regulation; law enforcement; transportation; highway maintenance; and other similar statewide functions. In addition, each state has its own laws governing marriage and divorce, traffic, voting, drinking age, and so forth.

Beyond direct responsibilities, states allocate funds to assist local governments in the performance of certain public services. Among these are the furnishing of public health care, low-income housing, mass transportation in urban areas, public education, and the like. Although local governments raise some of the money for these services on their own, and some of them receive funds from the federal government, the bulk of the money comes from the state. For example, in the late 1980s state governments spent on average about $65 billion per year on elementary and secondary education. That is more than twice as much as local governments and six times as much as the federal government. Although states set guidelines for local education, local governments largely determine the quality of their school systems. That quality varies according to the local community's wealth and willingness to pay property taxes. Starting in the early 1990s, some states, following the example of New Jersey, have tried to offset the obvious educational inequality resulting from differences in wealth. They have reallocated special state funds to poorer communities in an effort to upgrade the educational quality in these areas and have increased the taxes on members of the wealthier communities to collect the funds needed for that reallocation.

Except for the costs of maintaining interstate highways, the federal government pays little toward the other services provided by state and local governments. States, rather than the national government, determine the quality of these services by their expenditures. The allocation of money reflects a state's priorities. For example, Massachusetts ranks fifth among the fifty states in the aid it grants hospitals and twenty-third in the funds it spends on highway maintenance.

State regulation of the local economy also reflects its policies. In order to do business within a state, private firms must register with the state government and be licensed as a corporation, partnership, or sole proprietorship. To encourage business, some states grant tax concessions or provide other benefits. To protect their residents from abuse by business firms, some states set minimum standards affecting working and environmental conditions. Some state regulations are mandated by the federal government, as for example in prohibitions against racial discrimination or polluting the physical environment. To a large extent, it is federal regulations such as these that have raised a hue and cry against "big government" and for a return to "federalism," meaning states' rights.

THE ESSENTIALS OF FEDERALISM

Despite the hue and cry, states are not merely passive instruments of the national government. The reality is much closer to a cog-and-wheel relationship, without it being entirely clear which is the cog and which the wheel. Fairly recently, it was the national government that turned the country around in certain areas. During the 1930s, the national government turned many states toward providing economic benefits and security for the needy; in the 1950s and 1960s, the turn was toward increased civil rights. But starting in the late 1970s and continuing into the 1980s, it had been the states that turned the wheel with the tax revolt that began in California and was carried by former President Reagan to the national level.

Although state autonomy has been curtailed for the past fifty years, it has been far from eliminated. Power, since our nation's founding, has shifted back and forth between the national government and the states. The character of federalism has always been determined by the balance of political forces at any given point in time. In all instances it is a matter of which aspect of federalism would best serve the interests of the dominant group of the moment. Yet even during the period when the power of the national government was ascendant (from about 1937 to 1967), the states retained control in many areas and continued their individual differences.

STATE EXPERIMENTATION WITH PUBLIC POLICY

The large degree of state independence makes possible state experimentation in public policies. As the late nineteenth-century Englishman James Bryce observed about the virtues of federalism: "A comparatively small commonwealth like an American state easily makes and unmakes its laws; mistakes are not serious, for they are soon corrected; other states profit by the experience . . . of the state that has tried it."[3] This may be too rosy a view—it ignores the power of vested interests, which play as big a role in state policy-making as in national politics— but it does contain a shiny nugget of truth.

Individual states have at different times been the seedbed of major national policies. We have already seen some of this earlier in the chapter. Massachusetts' experimental tripartite government, only a little more than seven years old at the time of the Constitutional Convention, was the model for the federal government hammered out in 1787. Virginia's Statute of Religious Freedom of 1786 (written

---

[3]James Bryce, *The American Commonwealth,* ed. Louis Hacker (New York: G. P. Putnam, 1959), p. 85.

"They have very strict anti-pollution laws in this state."

by Jefferson and maneuvered through the state legislature by Madison) became the basis of the First Amendment to the national Constitution. To come closer to our own time: Franklin Roosevelt's New Deal was based in part on relief laws he had passed while governor of New York during the very first years of the Great Depression. They were successful in New York, so he tried them with some expansion for the nation as a whole.

States have also experimented, for good or ill, in such areas as divorce, urban development, automobile insurance, energy conservation, environmental protection, and regulation of nuclear power plants. The states, however, do not have unlimited power to experiment. They are constrained by the federal Constitution. States cannot enact legislation that conflicts with federal laws. Nor can they intrude on the federal domain; for example, they cannot regulate interstate commerce or make separate treaties with foreign nations, although states, and sometimes major cities, have arranged special business deals with foreign governments. Some states have also worked out special arrangements among themselves, as New York and New Jersey have done with the Port Authority.

DIVISION OF POWERS

Some of the Framers of the Constitution were very suspicious of the national government they had just created and wanted a number of checks on its power.

A number of others were fearful of the bigotry and "injustice" of the states and wanted a check on their powers. As Madison so cogently explained to Jefferson: "In the extended Republic of the United States, the General Government would hold a pretty even balance between the parties of particular States, and be at the same time sufficiently restrained by its dependence on the community...."[4] Thus the Framers conceived a structure in which the excesses of the states are controlled by the central government and the possible excesses of the national government are restrained by the states.

Over the 200 years of our national existence, the federal and state governments have evolved a tradition of separate domains of power and of overlapping authority (see Figure 4.1). In certain areas the two levels of government have similar responsibilities. Their duplicated authority is called *concurrent powers*. The concurrent powers affect the same activities directly. For example, both state and federal governments tax the same individuals, and both make laws that regulate the same business firms, such as commercial banks. Certain kinds of crimes, such as kidnapping, involve local, state, and federal police. As we saw a bit earlier, court cases involving citizens of two different states and more than $10,000 may be tried by either a federal or state judge.

The doctrine of concurrent powers has come to serve as a major theoretical basis for overturning the belief in dual federalism, the concept that the separation

---

[4]Madison's letter of 24 October 1787, in his *Papers,* p. 214.

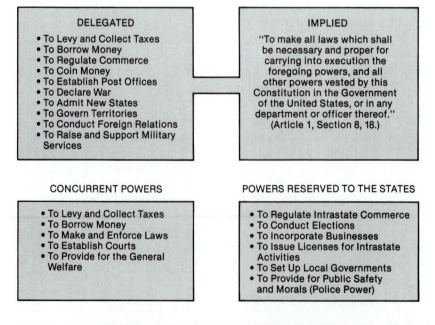

POWERS DELEGATED TO THE NATIONAL GOVERNMENT

DELEGATED
- To Levy and Collect Taxes
- To Borrow Money
- To Regulate Commerce
- To Coin Money
- To Establish Post Offices
- To Declare War
- To Admit New States
- To Govern Territories
- To Conduct Foreign Relations
- To Raise and Support Military Services

IMPLIED
"To make all laws which shall be necessary and proper for carrying into execution the foregoing powers, and all other powers vested by this Constitution in the Government of the United States, or in any department or officer thereof." (Article 1, Section 8, 18.)

CONCURRENT POWERS
- To Levy and Collect Taxes
- To Borrow Money
- To Make and Enforce Laws
- To Establish Courts
- To Provide for the General Welfare

POWERS RESERVED TO THE STATES
- To Regulate Intrastate Commerce
- To Conduct Elections
- To Incorporate Businesses
- To Issue Licenses for Intrastate Activities
- To Set Up Local Governments
- To Provide for Public Safety and Morals (Police Power)

FIGURE 4.1   THE AMERICAN FEDERAL SYSTEM: DIVISION OF POWERS BETWEEN THE NATIONAL GOVERNMENT AND THE STATE GOVERNMENTS

between the jurisdictions of national and state governments is absolute. As Archibald Cox so succinctly expressed it: "The division of a federal system does not preclude concurrent jurisdiction.... Today one marvels at ... the [once] prevailing theory of dual federalism."[5] The federal government may now legislate in areas that were once reserved to the states. Federal regulation of business practices within the states was at one time prohibited by the Supreme Court, for example. Since the court's 1937 decision in the *National Labor Relations Board v. Jones & Laughlin* case, which upheld the authority of the NLRB (a federal agency) to regulate worker-management relations within Pennsylvania, the federal government has been empowered to intervene in state matters.

With the shift from dual federalism to the concept of concurrent jurisdictions, the enormous expansion of federal power became possible. That enormous power, however, operates through the states. Even when the national government provides funds, as in its grant-in-aid programs, to states for highway construction or Medicaid, for example, state and local officials actually make the decisions on how the money will be spent. That is why there had been so much resistance from state and local officeholders to Reagan's attempt to cut back on national funding to the states. To many state officials his "new federalism" meant a cutback in funding and a corresponding loss of power. They preferred the "old federalism" to the new.

Despite the national government's regulations, the states have considerable independence. Thus, from a practical point of view, the original balance of powers between national and state governments remains as the Framers conceived it. Archibald Cox observed:

> Hamilton's nationalistic theory of the spending power finally prevailed. It has also become plain that attaching regulatory conditions to an offer of federal grants [to the states] in such areas as housing, highway construction, education, medical care, and local law enforcement raises no constitutional difficulty.... Given this principle ... the vast congressional expansion of federal activity seems quite consistent with a proper understanding of the original intent.[6]

FEDERAL GRANTS TO STATE AND LOCAL GOVERNMENTS

We tend to think nowadays that federal grants to the states are a modern invention of the Roosevelt administration. As it happens, the "federal government" of the Confederation promulgated a Land Ordinance in 1785 that granted 640 acre lots for the maintenance of public schools in newly created towns in the Northwest territories. And in 1787, as the Constitution was being debated, the Confederation Congress virtually gave away these territories to land speculators so as to encourage settlement. After the creation of the present United States, land grants, especially for educational and developmental purposes, became relatively common in the early years of the Republic. Among the most famous were land grants

---

[5]Archibald Cox, *The Court and the Constitution* (Boston: Houghton Mifflin, 1987), pp. 140, 141.
[6]Ibid., pp. 170, 172.

made during the Civil War. One grant was to the railroad companies in 1862 that gave them a checkerboard of land sections adjacent to the tracks they built. Another was the grant, also in 1862, of 30,000 acres to each Union state for the establishment of what have come to be called land-grant colleges.

Grants-in-Aid Programs.   Money grants to states also have a long, pre-Roosevelt history. But it was not until the Roosevelt era that federal grants dealt in significant sums of money. During the 1930s, the sixteen New Deal grant-in-aid programs cost over $2 billion. One of the most important developments in federal funding was the Federal Housing Act of 1937, which provided monetary aid to municipal public housing programs. Local officials had considerable discretion under the housing law, which became a model for direct assistance to the cities.

After the depression ended and we entered World War II, the Roosevelt programs were cut back. After the war, the grant-in-aid programs came back. They expanded from about $1 billion in the early 1940s to $8 billion in the early 1960s. From 1964 to 1968, during the administration of Lyndon B. Johnson, federal funding programs grew exponentially. Johnson's Great Society programs went from $8 billion in 1963, when he took over the government from John F. Kennedy, to $19 billion in 1968, when he left office. Beginning in 1964, Congress passed, under Johnson's leadership, bills authorizing funds for mass transit, the war on poverty, medical care for the elderly and the poor, aid for elementary and secondary education, rent subsidies for the poor, assistance for low-income housing, training programs for the unemployed, and endowments for the arts and humanities. The Great Society programs carried to its pinnacle the New Deal promise of caring for "the forgotten man at the bottom of the economic pyramid."[7] And like the New Deal, the Great Society resulted in a vast expansion of national power.

Even after Johnson left office and was replaced by the far more conservative Richard Nixon, grant-in-aid programs continued to expand despite the yearning to get "the government off the people's back." In response to this widely felt desire, Nixon instituted a "New Federalism." The promise was to return power to the states. In 1972, at Nixon's urging, Congress passed the State and Local Fiscal Assistance Act, which provided revenue sharing. Unlike the grants-in-aid, which have a multitude of federal requirements attached, revenue sharing has no strings attached. Governors and mayors loved revenue sharing, but Congress and the federal bureaucracy did not. Thus, money was slow in coming and low in quantity.

Critics of revenue sharing charged that it discriminated against the poor, ethnic minorities, the inner cities, the aged, and other beneficiaries of the grant-in-aid programs. State and local officials, however, supported Nixon's program. Revenue sharing did not require that the states or municipalities put up matching funds, as the grant-in-aid programs did. Because of the requirements attached to grants-in-aid, these programs are often called *categorical grants.* When Ronald

---

[7]Franklin D. Roosevelt in a radio speech on April 7, 1932, quoted in Samuel Eliot Morison, *The Oxford History of the American People* (New York: Oxford University Press, 1965), p. 948.

Reagan assumed the presidency, all federal funding for social programs was severely cut, ostensibly to reduce the deficit. The deficit has not been reduced (indeed, it has grown phenomenally), and over 400 categorical grants have, despite Reagan's best efforts, remained in place. Indeed, funding for categorical grants is now more than five times as much as expenditures for revenue sharing.

The Politics of Federal Funding. Political as well as economic realities have determined the distribution of federal grants. State and local governments have established powerful lobbies to work for what they consider their fair share of federal funds. But, as we saw in connection with Nixon's revenue-sharing program, there are also other interest groups contending for those funds. The very lack of restrictions on revenue sharing disturbs such groups as organized labor and advocates for the poor and underprivileged. In their view, state governments often do not use the funds in ways to benefit their constituents or as Congress intended. As one political scientist observed: "If your overall purpose is to reduce benefits to the needy without appearing to do so, then the answer is to shift responsibility to state and local governments."[8]

From the opposite end of the political spectrum, objections to categorical grants come from conservative groups such as the National Conservative Caucus, the National Tax Limitation Committee, and the American Enterprise Institute. Conservatives argue that categorical grants have distorted the American system by producing an overly powerful national government that has reduced state initiative and independence. These advocates gain their main support from suburban middle-class taxpayers who are dismayed by increasing taxes for programs that seem to favor inner-city residents, many of whom the conservatives feel are "welfare cheats."

EVOLVING CHARACTER OF FEDERALISM

Political, social, and economic forces continue to act on our concepts of federalism. During the Roosevelt era, the nation was hit with a devastating economic crisis, with which state and local governments did not have the wherewithal to deal. Only the national government could mobilize the resources to cope with the desperate circumstances of millions of people from all walks of life. Although Roosevelt intended his programs only as emergency solutions, some of them became fixtures in the political landscape. Johnson enlarged the scope of federal involvement in state activity, and the Supreme Court since the Roosevelt presidency has expanded national power even further. In each of these expansions, deprived and underprivileged people have benefited from increased national authority. By contrast, most of these people had no voice when the states were relatively supreme during the approximately 144 years between the administrations of George Washington and Franklin Roosevelt.

After World War II, the nation as a whole became relatively affluent. With the passing of the years, the generation that matured during the Great Depression

---

[8]Quoted in Ed Magnuson, "New Federalism or Feudalism?" *Time,* 8 Feb. 1982: 19.

passed away and a later generation came to power. Strong attachment to community values and the belief that those who are well off are responsible for those who are not was weakened. At the same time, costs for the supportive programs started during the Roosevelt-Johnson years were increasing and straining taxpayers' patience. The tax revolt of 1978 to 1980 brought the Reagan administration to power. Since Reagan took office, federal assistance has been sharply reduced. In 1987, state and local governments received five times as much revenue from their own citizens as they did from the federal government. In many states and cities, this has resulted in a curtailment of services. It has also resulted in more independence for the states. Some states, such as Massachusetts, have been innovative and undertaken experimental programs in health benefits for everyone. Others, especially in the economically hard-hit Midwest, have pulled back, as in their education programs. At this point, one can only say that the "New Federalism" has produced mixed results.

In Conclusion

The outcome of a peculiar historical and political circumstance at the founding of the nation, federalism in the United States has continued to be subject to history and politics. The term refers to the relationship between the state and national governments. In a sense, that relationship has been in constant flux, sometimes within the same period and sometimes within the same person. Thomas Jefferson is the perfect example of someone who believed firmly in state supremacy, but while president often acted to enhance the power of the national government.

For most of American history, however, the central government was weak, and political dynamism and power were located in the states. The reverse of this situation occurred in the mid-1930s when the economy collapsed in the Great Depression and state and local governments were unable to meet the needs of their people. To deal with this crisis, the central government under the leadership of Franklin Roosevelt moved swiftly and aggressively. As a consequence, national relief, regulatory, and funding programs overshadowed and replaced inadequate state and local efforts. To carry out those programs, the national government had to expand its power and Alexander Hamilton's concept of national supremacy became reality.

In large measure, national supremacy derived from the regulatory and funding programs of the federal government. From 1937 to 1987, the power of the central government over the states came from the money it gave away and the strings it attached to that cash. Categorical grants are among the federal establishment's chief instruments for fashioning national domestic policy. The Supreme Court's power of judicial review is another. Both Congress and the Court have brought about a greater degree of social equity and justice than there had been in the nation's past.

The federal programs had been possible while the nation's wealth was growing. Starting in the mid-1970s, America's productive capability slowed down and our wealth diminished as our commitments either grew or at best remained the same.

President Carter tried retrenchment in military power, which proved politically disastrous. When President Reagan took office he cut back from the other side of the budget—he reduced as much as he could federal funding of social welfare programs. In so doing, he returned a considerable amount of responsiblity and independence to the states. All indications are that President George Bush will continue Reagan's policies. It remains to be seen how well the states have picked up the ball and how far they have carried it.

Suggested Readings

Robert Jay Dilger. *The Sunbelt/Snowbelt Controversy: The War Over Federal Funds*. New York: New York University Press, 1982.

Morton Grodzins. *The American System*. Chicago: Rand McNally, 1966.

George E. Hale and Marian Leif Palley. *The Politics of Federal Grants*. Washington, D.C.: Congressional Quarterly, 1981.

William H. Riker. *Federalism: Origin, Operation, Significance*. Boston: Little, Brown, 1964.

James L. Sundquist. *Making Federalism Work*. Washington, D.C.: The Brookings Institution, 1969.

chapter

5

POLITICAL PARTIES

Party platforms are contracts with the people.

Harry S Truman

Political parties are organizations whose purpose is winning elections and gaining government power. By competing with one another, they offer choices to voters. Usually, parties appeal for votes on ideological and practical grounds. The Democratic party in the United States, for example, traditionally appeals to a coalition of working-class, minority, and professional groups. It argues for social justice and sponsors programs to help the poor and otherwise disadvantaged. The Republican party, by contrast, has traditionally appealed to small and big business interests. It is seen as concerned with fiscal programs that promote economic strength and corporate growth.

BACKGROUND

The Founding Fathers viewed political parties with great suspicion. They thought parties—''factions,'' they called them—were opposed to the public interest and were divisive. Nevertheless, parties or factions formed as the nation was formed at the Constitutional Convention in Philadelphia. Of the fifty-five delegates to the

Convention, only thirty-nine signed their names to the Constitution. These people came to be known as Federalists. The remaining sixteen are known as Anti-Federalists and were supporters of the previous Confederation with its admitted faults. Both "factions" competed for votes during the ratification process, and each won some and lost some.

Once the country was established, the governing elite split along ideological and practical lines. The Federalists favored a strong centralized government that would intervene in the economy to encourage industrial growth. Their opponents, the Democratic-Republicans, preferred a minimal, decentralized government and an agrarian economy. As happens in the United States, these were two contending visions of what was best for the country as a whole. As also happens here, each side saw the other as out to destroy the country. Very quickly, these two parties came to stand for different regions and classes that were opposed to each other.

With the election of John Adams as the second president, the parties became formal organizations that offered candidates for political office. Following Thomas Jefferson's election as third president in 1801, the Democratic-Republicans became the dominant party until the election of John Quincy Adams a quarter century later. Andrew Jackson, who followed Quincy Adams as president, transformed the Democratic-Republicans into the Democratic party we know today.

Jackson, who owned many slaves and was an extremely wealthy land specu-lator, turned the Democrats into the party of "the common man." The Democrats then went on to hold office with but a few interruptions until the election of Abraham Lincoln in 1860. After Lincoln, the Democrats did not occupy the White House for an extended period until Franklin D. Roosevelt won it in 1932. The old Federalist party, meanwhile, had gone through several transformations until it turned into the Republican party we know today.

THE CONSTITUTION AND POLITICAL PARTIES

The Constitution does not make any provision for political parties. The founders were themselves so divided by "faction" and at the same time so distrustful of it that they did not wish to become directly enmeshed in the issue. However, in designing the Bill of Rights they tried to make certain that political parties could operate freely. Generally, the First Amendment assures parties the freedom to organize and publicize their views. The Supreme Court usually looks askance at governmental efforts to regulate political activity. Parties are free to organize as they wish, providing they do not violate explicit constitutional restraints such as those prohibiting racial discrimination.

FEDERALISM AND PARTY ORGANIZATIONS

Unlike European parties, American "national" parties are in actuality small local parties that come together every four years to elect a president. It is only within the last several years that the two major paties have had permanent national staffs and a semblance of national organizations. Neither national party tells the local organizations what to believe or whom to nominate for office on any level. In that European sense they are not national parties.

American parties developed in response to our historical predisposition to decentralized government. For almost 200 years, the central or federal government was "weak" while the state and local governments were relatively strong. Most patronage jobs were and still are given out by local and state officials. There are over 700,000 elected officials, only a very small number of whom serve on a national level. Most serve in one or another of the fifty states and innumerable local governments.

State and local parties are separately organized to fill the many elected and appointed government positions on their levels. These different organizations have their own leaders, programs, and constituencies. For the most part, they do not depend on the national party for money or organizational support. Indeed, the dependency is generally the other way. The national party, as a rule, looks to the local organizations for money and campaign workers. Until very recently, national parties existed only during presidential elections. Power within a party had been for the most part centered in county or state organizations. To some extent this is now changing. Since national organizations have started to maintain continuity between elections, they have increased their influence on the local parties slightly. National organizations will occasionally provide advice on campaign strategies for senatorial and congressional races. They may also offer training sessions for new candidates, but local organizations are still largely independent.

SEPARATION OF POWERS AND PARTIES

Not only is official power in the United States divided between the national and local governments, it is also divided on every level of government. This tends to make for corresponding splits within party structures. Each of these centers of power has its own constituency, as we discussed in Chapter 2. The function of the parties is to mobilize these constituencies at election times. That mobilization ultimately takes place within the smallest political unit, the precinct. At other times, and on another level, it takes place in Congress. One of the party functions is to get members of Congress to vote the party line.

The president develops a program, usually consistent with the platform on which he ran for office, which he then submits to Congress. The members of the president's party are expected to support that program. However, as we saw previously, the members of Congress and the president are beholden to entirely different constituencies. This usually means that some congressional members of the president's party will refuse to follow his leadership, as happened with President Reagan's nomination of Judge Robert H. Bork to a seat on the Supreme Court.

Congress is usually divided between two parties: that party which controls most of the seats and is known as the majority party, and the minority party, which has fewer seats. Division continues, for Congress consists of two houses, and in each house two parties sit. Although senators and representatives are either Democrats or Republicans, they do not always vote with the party leaders. Some-

at the Constitutional Convention in Philadelphia. Of the fifty-five delegates to the times individuals cross party lines and vote with the other side. Further divisions continue. Within each of the parties there are conservative and liberal wings, and for some legislators this can be more significant than party affiliation. Party identification within Congress is a sometimes thing—generally less a matter of conviction than of convenience.

THE PRESIDENT AND THE PARTY

Presidents are usually the chiefs of their parties when they are in the White House. Once out, they are treated as ''elder statesmen,'' even if they are young, and are shunted to the sidelines, as the Republicans did to Teddy Roosevelt. In his case, this was a mistake. The Bull Moose bellowed, the Republicans lost, and a Democrat occupied the White House for two terms. Presidents, even out of office, generally have a loyal following in their party and often in the electorate.

In addition to enormous prestige, presidents also have patronage that they can dispense to loyal cohorts and wealthy contributors to the party. Some of the patronage appointments are federal judgeships, cabinet-rank jobs, ambassadorships, and policy-level positions within the bureaucracy. Presidents can use patronage to appoint individuals to whom members of Congress are indebted and thereby gain congressional support for their programs. They can also influence Congress through their ability to veto legislation particularly beneficial to specific senators and representatives. Finally, if the president is an effective speaker, he can go over the heads of the Congress and appeal to his national constituency, as Ronald Reagan has done several times. These various instruments of persuasion give presidents enormous leverage over other centers of power within the government and their party.

ESSENTIALS OF POLITICAL PARTIES

Although the founders were fearful of the "baneful effects of the spirit of party," as George Washington put it, they also created a system that required parties. Our system of government is based on conflict. Conflict within government was intended to protect us from the tyranny of government. But conflict means taking opposing sides, and once those sides are organized, there are parties. At the very beginning of our nation's history, as it happened, two main concepts of government were in contention.

THE TWO-PARTY SYSTEM

At the time the United States was formed, Great Britain had had a two-party system for over a hundred years. The Royalists and Parliamentarians of the seventeenth century evolved into the Tories and Whigs of the eighteenth. As in other things, America followed Britain. Divergent political interests submerged their differences and formed two competing parties here.

Although nationally we have had a two-party system throughout our history, on local and state levels we have had many one-party and multiparty arrangements. For about eighty years following the Civil War, the South was a one-party region; it was solidly Democratic. To complement the South, large areas of the North, such as the rural Midwest, had during the same period a one-party system of its own—a Republican one. In some areas, such as New York state, there have been as many as five or six parties on the ballot at one time.

As is true elsewhere, too, the leadership in one-party states and cities could ignore large segments of the electorate. Party discipline in such circumstances was tightly maintained, and effective control was exercised over political and governmental apparatuses. In effect, political life was controlled by a minority. The multiparty system ends in the same place from the opposite side of the playing field. The electorate may be so splintered among different groups that a minority party can determine victory in an election by telling its supporters to vote for a major party's ticket. Whether either system is suited to democracy as we understand it is open to question.

When the two-party system works properly, it can offer a meaningful choice to voters. By assimilating a fairly broad spectrum of beliefs, each of the parties tends to stay clear of extremes. Yet each also provides its extreme wing with an opportunity to vent its anger and frustration. As the extremists of right and left increase their chances of success, they come closer to the center, as happened with Ronald Reagan in the Republican party and Jesse Jackson in the Democratic party. When that occurs, the center is broadened and the extremes seek new leaders.

On the whole, both the Democratic and Republican parties try to gather under their "umbrellas" the widely divergent interests of American society. They each welcome support wherever they can find it. Where they possibly can, they try to make inroads into their rival's base, as occurred when Ronald Reagan captured large segments of the traditionally Democratic blue-collar vote. That's effective politicking.

THE FUNCTION OF POLITICAL PARTIES

Effective politicking can be said to be the main function of political parties. Their purpose is to win elections. In this way, they can attract voters and politicians to their banners. If all goes well, they may even be able to put their policies into effect. But mainly, parties serve to link the voting public to the government and to help bring about changes when they are desired by enough people. They achieve these ends in a number of ways.

Selecting Candidates. The major parties have several candidate selection processes. In the old days, party bosses got together in "smoke-filled rooms" and

DRAWING BY STEVENSON; © 1983 THE NEW YORKER MAGAZINE, INC.

"I just want somebody clearly established as a front-runner, and, frankly, I don't give a damn who it is."

picked candidates from among their favorites. That process was not as bad as its critics, past and present, charged. It gave us some of our greatest presidents. In the election of 1800, Alexander Hamilton convinced his supporters in the House of Representatives to vote for Thomas Jefferson rather than Aaron Burr. Hamilton, who worked best behind the scenes, was perhaps America's first political boss. After national conventions became the norm, bosses, who ran those conventions, picked such presidential candidates as Abraham Lincoln, Theodore Roosevelt, Woodrow Wilson, and Franklin Roosevelt.

Since the 1970s, candidates have been chosen in ever-more exhausting primaries. A primary is an election within a party in which as a rule only registered party members can vote. In primaries for president, party members vote for delegates to national conventions. At those conventions, party bosses have lost influence and single-issue social movements with special agendas have gained power. One result is that there is sometimes a great divergence of interest between the party activists and the party's rank-and-file supporters. For the Republicans this happened in 1964 with the nomination of Barry Goldwater, who was too rigidly conservative for the majority of his party. It happened again in 1972, this time with the Democrats who chose George McGovern. He was too far to the left of the mainstream and, like Goldwater, alienated many rank-and-file members of his own party. This kind of situation may no longer be possible because in recent years traditional power brokers may have regained some of their previous influence within their respective parties.

Supporting Candidates.   Whether candidates were chosen in smoke-filled rooms or in state primaries, the parties have always made efforts with more or less enthusiasm, more or less success, to put their candidates across. The parties send out their workers to canvass door to door, set up phone banks to call possible voters, and arrange for car lifts to get elderly voters to polling places in the hope that all those contacted and assisted will pull the lever or mark the ballot for the party's candidate. Parties also assist in fund-raising campaigns, running polls, and contributing to advertising.

Although party organizations still perform these tasks to some degree, they play a much reduced role in today's elections. Since the late 1960s and early 1970s, when the tightly controlled party organizations we call "machines" lost power, individual candidates have built their own organizations and to a great extent run their own campaigns. But the traditional party machinery is still functioning, although on a diminished scale, and provides a kind of political infrastructure for candidates. National conventions, for example, which are still run by the party, can bring new bright lights onto the horizon. It was his speech nominating Goldwater at the 1964 Republican convention that brought Ronald Reagan national prominence. Twenty years later, New York Governor Mario Cuomo also gained nationwide attention from a speech delivered at the 1984 Democratic convention. The party may also arrange for endorsements of new candidates by popular elected officials, such as the president. Often these endorsements work, but sometimes they do not, as happened when President Reagan campaigned for several members of Congress in 1986.

PARTY ORGANIZATION

Party organizations differ at the national, state, and local levels of government. Generalizations about party structures are difficult to make because the parties have been and are still in flux. For example, from the late 1960s to the late 1970s, newly politicized groups such as racial minorities, women, and youth had a voice in determining Democratic party policies. This new influence was reflected in rules for choosing candidates, holding primary elections, seating delegates at state and national conventions, writing the party platform, and selecting the presidential nominee. More traditional party interest groups such as union leaders, as well as elected political officials such as congressmen, senators, and governors, were less influential than they had been in party decision making. Since the mid-1980s, this has changed. Under the chairmanship of Paul G. Kirk, the more traditional power brokers have been brought back into the decision-making process of the Democratic party to help balance grass-roots forces that nevertheless remain important.

Even though American political parties are in a continuing process of change and generalizations about them are risky, we will nevertheless hazard a few. The two major parties are based on local politics, usually organized on a precinct or ward level. These party groups join together to form the county organization, and the counties join to form state organizations. At the top are the national organizations.

National Organizations.   Traditionally, there was one national organ for each of the parties. These were—and still are—the national committees. The Republican and Democratic National Committees (RNC and DNC, respectively) are composed of representatives from the state parties. These committees make the rules that govern their parties, especially in connection with their quadrennial nominating conventions. The presidential nominees choose the chairmen of the national committees. The chairmen run the party apparatuses, which are oriented principally toward raising money and providing technical assistance to state and local party organizations. Unlike what occurred in the past, these activities are nowadays carried on between presidential elections as well as in election years. At this point, national organizations under the headings of the RNC and DNC seem to be developing permanent bureaucratic structures.

In recent years, the Republican and Democratic parties in the two houses of Congress have developed nationwide committees of their own. These organizations have as their principal function raising funds, although they also try to provide services in the local campaigns of their members. Senators and representatives also receive some financial backing from their national committees, the RNC or DNC.

Party contributions to campaigns of individual candidates, however, are limited by federal election laws. Thus, although the national committees are important sources of financial support to candidates, they are not critical. The technical services they provide, such as mailing lists of contributors or training sessions for candidates, may be as valuable as the money. Most of the money raised by candidates is from the efforts of their own election committees combined with matching funds from the federal government. Political action committees (PACs) are also major contributors. This situation makes it difficult to impose a party line on members of Congress and can explain in part why presidents may sometimes have difficulty with members of their own party.

State and Local Parties.   Members of Congress are often more concerned with what the people in their state and local constituencies want than with the desires of their national leaders. It is on these levels that elections are won and lost. Moreover, the precinct, county, and state organizations have a continuity that the national parties have not yet achieved. State and local parties, largely candidate-based and organized, are also wholly independent of the national organizations.

There is little nationwide uniformity among the parties. Most are organized according to party charters and state laws. In some states, for example, delegates to national conventions are chosen in direct primaries. Other states hold "caucuses" at which registered party members vote for delegates to their state conventions. The state conventions choose delegates to their party's national convention. A few states choose delegates to the national convention at state committee meetings. These states have neither caucuses nor primaries, and the ordinary registered party member has little say in the choice of delegates. Once common, this method is now very rare.

Although they follow very different rules, most state parties tend to have somewhat similar formal structures. Typically, the party starts on the bottom, or "grass-roots," level. The grass root is the ordinary registered Democrat or Republican, who is a member of the party's precinct or ward organization. Precincts elect members of the county committee. The county committee chooses a chairman, who in the old days was "the boss of the political machine" in a city or state. County committees elect the members of state committees. In some state organizations, the precincts have their own committees as well and it is these committees, rather than ordinary party members, that elect members to the county level. Obviously, committee members constitute an elite cadre within their parties.

NATIONAL NOMINATING CONVENTIONS

The glue that holds these distinct and often divergent organizations together is each party's national convention, held every four years to nominate candidates for president and vice president. Since their invention in 1832, national conventions have served as major political arenas in which powerful antagonists battled one another in an effort to determine the direction of the country.

Traditionally, these struggles took place behind the scenes in the Republican party and on the convention floor in the Democratic party. As with almost all other generalizations about parties, this too is in the process of change. In the 1976 Republican nominating convention, Ronald Reagan presented a strong challenge on the floor to a sitting Republican president, Gerald R. Ford. During the 1988 primary season, six Republican hopefuls went at each other hammer and tongs in public. The noisy Republican campaigns were more acrimonious than the primary contest among the Democrats, but the Democrats, too, went their own ways in developing candidate parties that competed intensely for the prize of the presidential nomination.

The national committees organize the conventions. This means that they not only prepare for the circuslike hoopla we see on television, they also arrange for the selection of candidates and make the rules governing the convention. The rules indicate who will be accepted as a delegate and how many delegates a state may have. The number of voters a state has and the strength of the party in the state determines the number of delegates it is allowed at the convention. This tends to weight voting in favor of state delegations that have strong party showings in previous elections.

Each party's delegate-selection rules are intended to make sure the party nominates a candidate who stands a good chance of winning. This purpose may be in conflict with the ideal of equal participation in the democratic process. In the direct primaries, grass-roots party members may vote for delegates pledged to a candidate who has little broad appeal. Critics say this undermines party responsibility and effectiveness. They also complain that party loyalty among voters is already in decline and that direct primaries are causing further deterioration. Some

"Every four years at just about this time, he ups and hits the old campaign trail."

critics even attribute the increasingly low voter turnout in national elections to the increased participation of grass-roots voting in the primaries.

It seems there is an ever-growing separation between people who join political parties and the general voting population. For most of this century, our presidents and legislators have been elected by less than 40 percent of those eligible to vote. This means that a minority of our citizens decide who will run the country and what the nation's policies will be. For example, President Reagan's "landslide election" in 1984, when he received about 59 percent of the popular vote, meant that actually only a little more than 35 percent of eligible voters chose him. This was so because only about 60 percent of those entitled to vote took part in the election. In 1988, George Bush was elected president by even fewer voters. Only 27 percent of the electorate voted for him. This was so because a mere 50 percent of those eligible to vote did so, and, of the 50 percent, 54 percent voted for Bush.

VOTERS AND ELECTIONS

In our political system, the majority of citizens should play a critical role in choosing the direction the government takes. As fearful of the majority as the founders were, they nevertheless expected most citizens to take part in the electoral process. They thought they were creating a popular, democratic government. And indeed, majority rule is considered the defining characteristic of democracy. It is therefore ironic that the world's "oldest continuous democracy" should have one of the lowest voter turnout records of any major nation.

FACTORS CONNECTED WITH VOTING PATTERNS

Many complex matters influence voter participation. Among these are education, income level, occupation, race or ethnicity, and family background. All these factors are linked and may affect one another. Middle-class people, for example, usually have more education than poor or working-class individuals. Persons with a college education are more likely to vote than those with only a high school diploma or less. Studies have found that larger percentages of the middle class than of the lower classes vote in elections. Individuals with a family history of voting, studies also show, have a greater tendency than others to participate on all levels of the political process.

Occupation.   As important as education, family, and social status are, other parts of life influence voting patterns as well. A person's occupation often correlates with whether one votes or how one votes. For example, professionals are more likely to vote than unskilled laborers, and a stockbroker is more likely than not to vote Republican while a unionized factory worker is more likely to vote Democratic. But even here it is difficult to be sure. In 1980, 1984, and 1988, large numbers of workers ignored their unions and voted for the Republican candidates for president, Ronald Reagan and George Bush. Occupation, of course, is closely related to income level, education, and social class (see Table 5.1).

Religion.   Another factor that links up closely with voting behavior is religious identification. As with all other supposed influences, religion has an uncertain predictive value. For example, the majority of Catholics have historically voted for the Democratic party. But in four recent elections—1972, 1980, 1984, and 1988—more than 50 percent voted for Republican presidents (see Table 5.2). Nor are there easy explanations for the votes of a religious denomination. For instance, George McGovern favored the Arab cause over Israel's; nevertheless, he received 57.1 percent of the Jewish vote in 1972. Despite the apparent uncertainties, there does seem to be a correlation between religious identification and overall party preferences. The majority of white fundamentalist Christians have voted overwhelmingly for Republican candidates for president in 1980, 1984, and 1988, for example.

Race.   Unlike the situation with measures of religion, the link between race and party preference is very strong. Large percentages of black voters consistently favor the Democratic party in presidential elections, as shown in Table 5.3. Since Franklin D. Roosevelt's New Deal, blacks have voted for the Democratic party because they believe it rather than the Republican party will carry out programs to improve their condition. Blacks share the Democrats' belief that government

Table 5.1   Voting by Occupation, Income, and Education

	VOTE, 1980			VOTE, 1984		VOTE, 1988	
	Reagan	**Carter**	**Anderson**	**Reagan**	**Mondale**	**Bush**	**Dukakis**
National Totals	51%	41%	7%	59%	40%	54%	46%
Occupation							
Prof'l or Mgr	57	32	9	62	37	59	40
White-collar	50	41	8	59	40	57	42
Blue-collar	47	46	5	54	45	49	50
Student	—	—	—	52	47	44	54
Teacher	46	42	10	51	48	47	51
Unemployed	39	51	8	32	67	37	62
Housewife	—	—	—	61	38	58	41
Farm worker	36	59	4	—	—	55	44
Retiree	—	—	—	60	40	50	49
Income Level							
Under $12,500	42	51	6	45	54	37	62
12,500–24,999	44	46	7	57	42	49	50
25,000–34,999	52	39	7	59	40	56	44
35,000–49,999	59	32	8	66	33	56	42
50,000 & over	63	26	9	69	30	62	37
Educational Level							
No high school	46	51	2	49	50	43	56
High school grad	51	43	4	60	39	50	49
Some college	55	35	8	61	37	57	42
College grad	52	35	11	58	41	62	37
Post graduate	—	—	—	—	—	50	48

SOURCE: Adapted from *The New York Times,* 10 Nov. 1988: B6. Copyright © 1988 by The New York Times Company. Reprinted by permission.

intervention is necessary to assure equal opportunity and advancement for racial minorities. As Figure 5.1 clearly indicates, whites and blacks have radically different perceptions of the extent of discrimination. As the principal victims of discrimination, blacks understandably welcome the Democrat's persistent efforts to eliminate it. Whites, on the other hand, have a much more mixed view of the situation and of Democratic programs such as affirmative action, integration, busing for desegregated schools, and the like. Hence, the shifting allegiance of the white voter.

As Table 5.3 indicates, a varying majority of whites have voted consistently for Republican presidential candidates since 1952, except for one instance in 1964. The reason may perhaps be found in the identification of the Democratic party

Table 5.2   Religious Factors in Voting

Election Year	Religion	Voted Democratic	Voted Republican	Voted Other
		(Stevenson)	(Eisenhower)	
	Protestant	37%	63%	
1952	Catholic	56	44	
	Jewish	77	23	
		(Stevenson)	(Eisenhower)	
	Protestant	37%	63%	
1956	Catholic	51	49	
	Jewish	75	25	
		(Kennedy)	(Nixon)	
	Protestant	38%	62%	
1960	Catholic	78	22	
	Jewish	81	19	
		(Johnson)	(Goldwater)	
	Protestant	60%	36.7%	
1964	Catholic	79.8	17.1	
	Jewish	91.3	4.6	
		(Humphrey)	(Nixon)	(G. Wallace)
	Protestant	32.6%	50.1%	13.5%
1968	Catholic	50.3	36.2	8.4
	Jewish	81.3	11.6	(Not available)
		(McGovern)	(Nixon)	
	Protestant	27.7%	66.9%	
1972	Catholic	41.1	51.8	
	Jewish	57.1	42.8	
		(Carter)	(Ford)	
	Protestant	46%	54%	
1976	Catholic	55	45	
	Jewish	68	32	
		(Carter)	(Reagan)	(Anderson)
	Protestant	31%	64%	5%
1980	Catholic	41	53	6
	Jewish	46	40	14
	White fundamentalist Christian	33	63	3
		(Mondale)	(Reagan)	
	Protestant	27%	72%	
1984	Catholic	45	54	
	Jewish	67	31	
	White born-again Christian	21	78	
		(Dukakis)	(Bush)	
	Protestant	33%	66%	
1988	Catholic	47	52	
	Jewish	64	35	
	White evangelical Christian	18	81	

SOURCES: Ivan Hinderaker, ed., *American Government Annual 1961–1962* (New York: Holt, Rinehart and Winston, 1961), p. 74; releases of the American Institute of Public Opinion (Gallup Poll); and the Roper Survey. Data for 1976 and 1980 are from the CBS Almanac and from *The New York Times,* 10 Nov. 1988: B6; for 1984, from *The New York Times,* 8 Nov. 1984: A19. Copyright © 1984 by The New York Times/CBS News Poll. Reprinted by permission; for 1988, from *The New York Times,* 10 Nov. 1988: B6. Copyright © 1988 by The New York Times Company. Reprinted by permission.

Table 5.3   Racial Voting Patterns

Election Year	Race	Voted Democratic	Voted Republican	Voted Other
1948	White	53%	47%	—[a]
	Black	81	19	—
1952	White	43	57	
	Black	79	21	
1956	White	41	59	
	Black	61	39	
1960	White	49	51	
	Black	68	32	
1964	White	59	41	
	Black	94	6	
1968	White	38	47	15%[b]
	Black	85	12	3
1972	White	32	68	
	Black	87	13	
1976	White	49	51	
	Black	83	17	
1980	White	36	56	7
	Black	86	10	2
1984	White	35	64	1
	Black	89	9	2
1988	White	40	59	
	Black	86	12	

SOURCES: Ivan Hinderaker, ed., *American Government Annual 1961–1962* (New York: Holt, Rinehart and Winston, 1961), p. 74; CBS Almanac; releases of the American Institute of Public Opinion (Gallup Poll); *The New York Times*, 8 Nov. 1984; A19. Copyright © 1984 by The New York Times/CBS News Poll. Reprinted by permission; and *The New York Times*, 10 Nov. 1988: B6. Copyright © 1988 by The New York Times Company. Reprinted by permission.

[a]Percentages for the candidates for the States' Rights and Progressive parties were not tabulated.

[b]Percentages are for the American Independent party.

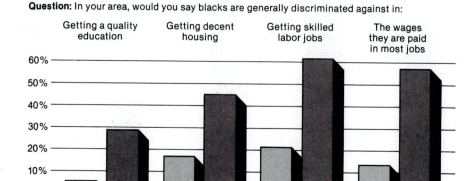

Question: In your area, would you say blacks are generally discriminated against in:

Note: The sample size is 1,872 with a black oversample of 446. "Don't know no opinion" calculated out for comparison purposes. The highest "don't know no opinion" response = 13%.

FIGURE 5.1   BLACK VERSUS WHITE OPINION ON DISCRIMINATION

SOURCE: Survey by ABC News, *The Washington Post*, February 26–March 6, 1981. Reprinted from *Public Opinion*, April/May 1981, p. 35. Reprinted with permission of The American Enterprise Institute for Public Policy Research.

with the interests of black people. In 1948, President Harry Truman, the Democratic candidate for reelection, split the party by advocating a strong civil rights platform and, by executive order, integrating the armed forces. Blacks were seen as the chief beneficiaries of Truman's action. Although Truman was able to hold a majority of white voters in '48, the party lost them in the 1952 election when the very popular General Dwight Eisenhower ran for president on the Republican ticket. Except for a short trip back in 1964, most whites have voted against the Democrats in national elections since.

Gender and Age.   There are no clearly discernible connections between gender or age and voting patterns. Each of these categories is so large and encompassing that it is virtually impossible to isolate the factor of age or sex in relation to voting behavior. There are, for example, poor women, rich women, white women, black women, Jewish, Catholic, and Protestant women. Each of these factors can influence behavior in a voting booth. In any case, the voting pattern of women is not statistically different from that of men, as can be seen in Table 5.4. By the way, the term *gender,* which originally designated masculine and feminine endings of words in certain inflected languages, now refers to sexual differentiation and

Table 5.4   Vote by Gender in Presidential Elections Since 1952

	1952		1956		1960		1964	
	Stevenson	Ike	Stevenson	Ike	JFK	Nixon	LBJ	Goldwater
National	44.6%	55.4%	42.2%	57.8%	50.1%	49.9%	61.3%	38.7%
Male	47	53	45	55	52	48	60	40
Female	42	58	39	61	49	51	62	38

VOTE BY GENDER IN PRESIDENTIAL ELECTIONS SINCE 1952 (CON'D)

	1968			1972		1976			1980			1984		1988	
	HHH	Nixon	Wallace	McGovern	Nixon	Carter	Ford	McCarthy	Carter	Reagan	Anderson	Mondale	Reagan	Dukakis	Bush
	43.0%	43.4%	13.6%	38%	62%	50%	48%	1%	41%	51%	7%	40%	59%	46%	54%
	41	43	16	37	63	53	45	1	38	53	7	37	62	41	57
	45	43	12	38	62	48	51	[a]	44	49	6	44	56	49	50

[a]Less than 1 percent.

Note: 1976 and 1980 results do not include vote for minor party candidates.

SOURCE: The Gallup Opinion Index, December 1980, Report No. 183; *The New York Times*, 8 Nov. 1984; A19; *The New York Times*, 10 Nov. 1988: B6. Copyright © 1988 by the New York Times Company. Reprinted by permission.

is used in political science, sociology, and other related fields when discussing factors influencing behavior.

The elderly also encompass the same subgroups as the general population. As a result, there are no statistically significant differences between the votes of the elderly and other people. Because of improved health and medical conditions, longevity has increased and there are therefore many more elderly voters than in the past. So far they have not voted noticeably as a bloc. This may change if they feel threatened as a group. For example, if one or the other party comes out strongly against Social Security, the likelihood is that the elderly will vote en masse against that party and its candidates.

WINNING ELECTIONS

The reason to learn the characteristics of voters and to form parties is to win elections and run the government. To achieve this goal, politicians have used a variety of techniques, probably from the beginning of time. Julius Caesar regularly won election as Roman consul by bribing large numbers of poor citizens with free food and lavish entertainments as well as by lending money at low interest to the aristocracy. Almost 2,000 years later, some of the same tactics were used by "Boss" Tweed of Tammany Hall in New York. In the mid-nineteenth century, Boss Tweed was regularly reelected to the state Senate by holding giant rallies and buying booze and food for the poor and the needy among the voters. Not only were the poor always with us, but in pre-New Deal days they outnumbered all other classes. With changes in the distribution of wealth and advances in communication technology, electoral tactics have changed somewhat since the days of Julius Caesar and Boss Tweed.

Reaching voters and persuading them that one is the best candidate for an office has always been a main purpose in electoral politics. From the ancient Greeks to the present day, this has required skill in public speaking and a platform from which to speak. In the old days, one gave speeches in the marketplace, the agora of ancient Athens or the forum at Rome. In late nineteenth- and early twentieth-century America, people running for national office spoke from the rear platforms of trains. Their trains stopped at the smallest towns, which came to be known as whistle stops. President Harry Truman was the last national figure to run a whistle-stop campaign, although later candidates for president would speak sporadically from the back of a train. For the most part, though, the television screen has replaced the rear train platform.

The Impact of TV.   Whistle-stop campaigns were conducted so that a candidate could be seen by the largest number of voters possible. On an exhausting whistle-stop tour lasting weeks, a candidate might be seen by several hundred thousand voters over all, while on television, by contrast, he or she could be seen by several million voters at one time. Obviously, TV has some important pluses for politicians.

But TV has certain minuses as well. For one, the focus in television is much more on image than on substance. How one looks may be as important as what one says. Feeling comfortable in front of the camera becomes extremely significant. Many analysts believe that John Kennedy defeated Richard Nixon in 1960 because he projected a much more attractive image than did Nixon during their one TV debate. In similar fashion, many attribute Jimmy Carter's loss in 1980 to his stiff, awkward image on screen in contrast with Ronald Reagan's easy, comfortable manner in front of the camera.

In addition to focusing on style rather than substance, televison forces on candidates a kind of simplicity. Aside from the fact that candidates most often present themselves in thirty-second spots and thus do not have enough time for a full discussion, the medium itself works against the presentation of complex ideas. As a rule, complicated ideas do not lend themselves to oral presentations, and television is an oral medium as well as a visual one.

Despite all the negatives connected with TV, it is still the medium of preference because it reaches so many more people than any other means of communication.

Other Media, Other Methods.   Television is the most modern way to reach people, but is not the only way. In many instances, the cost-benefit ratio of TV is such that there is little reason to use it. More traditional ways of reaching voters

then come into play. Newspapers and radio are the primary alternatives. Ads in newspapers can be more thoughtful than ones in the electronic media. There is a problem with the print media, though. Fewer and fewer people are willing to read. Radio does not pose the risks inherent in the visual medium of television, but like the print media, it too reaches a much smaller audience than TV and has its own hazards. The principal one is that it requires control of one's voice to project an attractive persona.

Handbills, posters, buttons, and other even more ancient devices are still in use as ways to reach voters and garner support in an election. All of these methods—television, radio, newspapers, handouts, posters, and so forth—appeal to voters essentially as isolated individuals, whether in the privacy of their living rooms or alone on the streets. Only speaking on the proverbial "stump" before a crowd of listeners establishes the sense of community necessary for sentiments of party loyalty. Yet for so many candidates, there are so many drawbacks to this method of reaching people that it is practiced less and less often.

Party Identification and Voter Loyalty.   In the past, voters generally identified with one party and voted a straight party line. Since the late 1960s, however, there has been a decline in party loyalty, if we take voting the party line as

Table 5.5   Trends in Party-Line and Split-Ticket Voting, 1952–1984

	1952	1956	1960	1964	1968	1972	1976	1980	1984
				PARTY-LINE VOTING[a]					
House	80	82	80	79	74	75	72	69	70
Senate	79	80	79	79	73	69	69	71	72
President	77	76	79	79	69	67	74	68	80
				SPLIT-TICKET VOTING[b]					
President-House	12	16	14	15	26	30	25	34	25
Senate-House	9	10	9	18	22	23	23	31	20
Local	27	30	27	41	48	56	NA	59	52

[a]A party-line vote is defined as a Democrat or Independent Democrat voting for a Democratic candidate for the offices listed and a Republican or Independent Republican voting for a Republican candidate.

[b]A split-ticket vote is defined as casting a ballot for candidates from different parties for the offices listed.

SOURCE: SRC/CPS National Election Studies. Reprinted by permission from Martin P. Wattenberg, *The Decline of American Political Parties, 1952–1984* (Cambridge, Mass. Harvard University Press, 1986), p. 151.

indicating loyalty. As can be seen in Table 5.5, except for 1984, there has been a steady increase in split-ticket voting since 1952. This increase corresponds to an increase in the number of people who list themselves as independents and are not affiliated with any party (see Figure 5.2). Moreover, party adherents are with increasing frequency joining independents in splitting tickets. This makes for a great deal of uncertainty when running a campaign.

The loss of party loyalty by voters is bound to affect all elected officials. Members of Congress have less motivation to abide by party discipline if significant portions of their constituencies consider themselves independents. This situation tends to make other factors, such as personality or ideology, become highly significant. As Table 5.6 suggests, party loyalty is still an important determinant of voter behavior when it is reinforced by these other factors. But knowing how to appeal to voters has become a very uncertain skill, as President Reagan discovered in the 1986 election. Although he had campaigned strenuously for a number of conservative senators, they were subsequently defeated and he lost control of the one house of Congress that had been dominated by his party.

THE 1988 PRESIDENTIAL ELECTION

Whether or not "the Reagan Revolution" reflected a long-term shift in the voting habits of Americans remained in doubt in 1988, although Republican candidate George Bush won an overwhelming victory over Democrat Michael Dukakis, the governor of Massachusetts. Bush captured 17 percent of the Democratic vote, somewhat less than Ronald Reagan's score in 1980 and 1984. Eighty percent of the voters who identified themselves as conservatives, however, remained in the Republican party, approximately the same number who had supported Reagan.

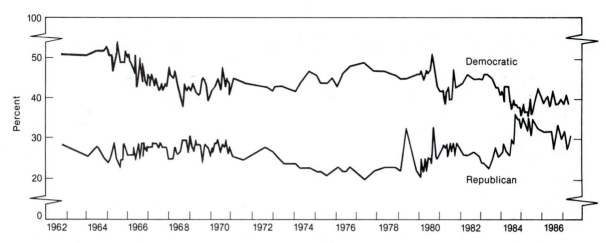

In politics, as of today, do you consider yourself a Republican,
a Democrat, or an Independent?

FIGURE 5.2   PARTY IDENTIFICATION 1963–1987

SOURCE: Surveys by the Gallup Organization in *Public Opinion*, September/October 1987, pp. 32–33.
Reprinted with permission of The American Enterprise Institute for Public Policy Research.

"My God! I went to sleep a Democrat and I've awakened a Republican."

Table 5.6   Voting by Party and Ideology, 1980–1988

	Vote in 1980			Vote in 1984		Vote in 1988	
	Reagan	**Carter**	**Anderson**	**Reagan**	**Mondale**	**Bush**	**Dukakis**
Party							
Republicans	86	8	4	93	6	91	8
Democrats	26	67	6	24	75	17	82
Independents	55	30	12	63	35	55	43
Ideology							
Liberals	25	60	11	28	70	18	81
Moderates	48	42	8	53	47	49	50
Conservatives	72	23	4	82	17	80	19

SOURCE: *The New York Times*, 10 Nov. 1988: B6. Copyright © 1988 by The New York Times Company. Reprinted by permission.

TYPES OF ELECTIONS

President Reagan's inability to persuade voters to elect the conservative senators he endorsed indicates some volatility in the electorate. To complete his program for the nation, Reagan had to maintain his support in the Senate and increase it in the House of Representatives. His failure to do so makes us realize that there are various types of elections.

The most common type is the "maintaining election," which results in the continuation of the party in power. These elections, of course, are always won by the party in power. Although Americans tend to vote for legislative incumbents (candidates running for reelection), which should favor maintaining elections, as we saw with President Reagan's failed effort, this is sometimes difficult to achieve. Nevertheless, maintaining elections occur with greater frequency in legislative elections than any other type.

When large numbers of voters change their party affiliations, we have what is known as a critical or realigning election. This occurred in 1932 when Franklin D. Roosevelt defeated Herbert Hoover. The Republican dominance of national politics for the previous seventy-two years came to an end. Republican analysts believe or hope that a new realignment has occurred with the 1980 and 1984 elections of Ronald Reagan and that the Democratic dominance of the preceding fifty years has finally ended. Whether this has indeed occurred is still unclear. Because of the large and increasing number of independent voters, neither party may again achieve a complete hold on the electorate. Moreover, the many different party levels and elections confuse the measurement of election outcomes in terms of party power and voter alignment. A party victory at the presidential level, for example, is unlikely to be reflected in Congress.

In addition to maintaining and realigning elections, there are two other types. Deviating elections occur when the results of national voting shift temporarily from expectations based on party alignments, as happened when Dwight D. Eisenhower was elected president despite a Democratic majority among voters. Reinstating elections restore the balance after the deviation has passed, as when the Republicans returned to the White House after an absence of eight years during Woodrow Wilson's presidency.

In Conclusion

Political parties are mechanisms for gaining power. Despite their distaste for "factions," the founders themselves developed the first parties. Because the Constitution is based on a conflict model, it virtually calls for the organization of political activities into party structures. In response to the dispersal of power required by the Constitution, America's national parties are actually decentralized, independent organizations. These organizations join together every four years in one of two parties to try to elect a president and vice president.

Although ours is basically a two-party system, the two major parties try to pull together a wide range of interests. This enables large numbers of disparate groups to participate in the political process. However, less than 60 percent of the voting-age population takes part in national elections.

While political parties require a certain degree of loyalty to be effective, increasing numbers of voters are independent of party entanglements. Perhaps because of this factor and modern election techniques, many voters seem to make choices based on personality or ideology. It is difficult to predict the long term effects of changing patterns in voting.

Suggested Readings

Doris A. Graber. *Mass Media and American Politics*. Washington, D.C.: Congressional Quarterly Press, 1980.

Gary C. Jacobson. *American Parties in Decline*. Boston: Little, Brown, 1980.

E. O. Key, Jr. *The Responsible Electorate*. Cambridge: Harvard University Press, 1966.

Everett C. Ladd, Jr. *Where Have All the Voters Gone?* New York: Norton, 1978.

Edwin O'Connor. *The Last Hurrah*. Boston: Little, Brown, 1956.

chapter

6

INTEREST GROUPS

The private interest of every individual may be a sentinel over the public rights.

James Madison

nterest groups and political parties are similar in some ways and different in others. Both seek power, not for its own sake, but rather to achieve specific goals. Both represent interests they consider vital. And both are focused on government, whether federal, state, or local. Their differences, however, are as significant as their similarities. While parties seek to gain political office as a means of reaching their objectives, interest groups seek only to influence those who occupy the office. Also, political parties must balance a broad range of interests if they are to survive. Interest groups, on the other hand, are usually concerned with only one interest or a very narrow range of interests.

Interests are concerns, needs, benefits, or rights that groups or individuals have or would like to have. Some areas that people have interests in, for example, are business, work, environment, health, education, religion, race, nation, state, city, town, and so forth. Because interests are shared by greater or lesser numbers of people, groups are organized and mobilized around them. Interest groups can be defined as associations of persons who share common concerns, needs, benefits, or rights and have as their purpose the satisfaction of claims to these. Usually, the claims are made on the government, and are met as a result of pressure. Even when claims are made by one interest group on another, those claims are generally made through pressure on the government.

Clearly, interests can be—and often are—in competition. We are familiar with a fair number of these conflicting interests. The interests of management and labor are, as we know, often opposed to one another. To choose another common example, the interests of industry and other users of the environment are also often in conflict. The government tries to balance these competing, essentially private interests while weighing something called the "public interest." We may define *public interest* as that which benefits or meets the needs of the nation as a whole. Thus, private interests may not only be opposed to one another, but some of them may clash with the public interest as well. One example of this collision is represented by the survival need of the nation for a military force and the opposing right of young people not to risk their lives and futures. This particular conflict of interests is morally complex.

BACKGROUND

Interest groups of all kinds have existed since before the founding of the country. The peculiar structure of our governmental system is the result of conflicts of interests. At the Philadelphia Convention in 1787, the large and small states had opposing interests, for example. They arrived at what we call the Great Compromise in which all states, large and small, had equal representation in the Senate, while states with large populations had a greater voice in the House of Representatives. There were other conflicting interests as well, such as between the East Coast and the western frontier or between the developing industries of the North and agriculture in the South. These competing interests are still with us, although they may have changed somewhat through our history. Today, we have an enormously complex array of economic, social, ideological, and political interests, all of which interact with the government.

From the very beginning, the federal government sponsored certain private interests at the expense of others. Starting in Washington's administration, Congress acted to support the growth of business, especially manufacturing. At Hamilton's urging, Congress assumed the debts of the Revolutionary War and founded the Bank of the United States, both of which helped business interests, especially investment capital. Hamilton argued that this action would improve our credit standing and thus help the economy become strong.

Hamilton also wanted to subsidize manufacturing directly and encourage it by having Congress impose protective tariffs on foreign imports. Both actions would help the economy, he argued, and thereby strengthen our independence. He was defeated by agrarian interests, which had money tied up in land and felt threatened by the tariff. These interests, under the leadership of Jefferson, also argued for minimum government intervention in the market, preferring what we today call a "free economy."

The quarrel over protective tariffs, favored by the industrial North and opposed by the agricultural South, was especially intense in the years leading up to the

Civil War. In any case, government intervention in the economy was established by 1798. With the financial aid of a government military contract gained him by Hamilton, Eli Whitney was able to develop mass production techniques. Hamiltonian principles of government assistance to private interests have since been a hallmark of the American system.

Throughout the nineteenth century, federal, state, and local governments aided business interests with tax policies, land grants, direct subsidies, and bank practices. In conflicts with labor, the governments sided with business, using troops to crush strikes and the courts to jail union leaders. These practices continued into the twentieth century. It was not until the mid-1930s that labor was able to gain government support for its interests. In the 1980s that support ceased, and the federal government reversed directions by supporting business interests.

AVENUES OF INFLUENCE

Interest groups are primarily concerned with affecting public policy to their own advantage. They can use a number of avenues to reach their objectives. Some are connected with the structure of our government and some are related to the nature of the democratic process.

VIA THE CONSTITUTION

Federalism and the separation of powers have enhanced the influence of interest groups instead of diminishing it, as the founders had hoped. The division of power between the national and local governments on the one hand and among the three branches of government on the other has increased the number of pressure points available to interest groups. These groups can often increase their influence by winning support on one level of government and then using that support to overcome resistance on other levels. For example, an interest group can bring pressure to bear on several legislators to get Congress to pass laws favoring its position. Since our system has been designed so as to require cooperation between the executive and legislative branches, a president has to be dead set against a law before he will refuse to approve it and thus risk antagonizing Congress. In many instances, presidents and even legislators have approved bills they did not entirely like.

Contact between the executive and legislative branches is most often made by administrative departments and agencies. The heads of these organizations frequently appear before Congress either to seek support (e.g., funding) or to explain some departmental activity. The activities of most government departments affect the interests of some group or other. As a consequence of this relationship, bureaucratic chieftains are often susceptible to influence from various private interests. As bureaucracies also have their own interests to advance and protect, their chiefs often need the support of interest groups when negotiating the tricky currents of interest politics.

Sometimes pressure is brought to bear first on state governments and then on the federal government. For example, a tax revolt that began in California and spread to the Midwest reached Washington with such great public hostility to taxes that Reagan was able to gain support from several congressional Democrats for cutting federal taxes. What started as a local rebellion had gained national force.

VIA POLITICAL PARTIES

Sometimes the most effective means of influencing public policy is through one or another of the political parties. By gaining influence within party circles, a particular interest or set of interests can win powerful advocates in the halls of government. The classic examples are, of course, the influence of economic interests in the two major parties. Since the Franklin D. Roosevelt era, labor unions have been closely identified with the Democratic party, whereas big business has been similarly linked to the Republican party since at least the days of presidents Calvin Coolidge and Herbert Hoover.

Interest groups can bring a fair amount of pressure to bear on political parties in several ways. Wealthy interest groups use money as leverage. Through their political action committees, they contribute to the party's coffers and to the election campaigns of individual candidates. In many instances, the same interest group will contribute at the same time to opposing candidates and parties. The group's purpose is to win influence and gain a bargaining chip. It does not matter who the victor is, as long as the interest group gets what it wants. Either way, it intends to win.

Another way to pressure a political party is by convincing party leaders that the group can call on a large number of campaign workers and voters. Labor unions have long used this tactic with the Democrats. The Moral Majority also proclaimed that it can mobilize vast numbers of supporters. This tactic was very effective in the 1980 presidential campaign, when Reagan, convinced he would receive the votes of the majority of fundamentalist Christians, served as the spokesman for their social agenda.[1] In 1987, the failure of fundamentalist Christians to advance the candidacy of former television preacher Pat Robertson for the presidential nomination of the Republican party exposed deep divisions within the movement. However, as the 1988 election returns showed, more fundamentalists voted for the Republican candidate than in any of the previous elections for which there are data.

Still a third way to pressure a political party is to split off a portion of the regular members and form a splinter or "third" party that can, by running its own slate of candidates, draw support from the regular party. The very threat of a third-party slate is often enough to bring about a desired result. Third parties have been a regular feature of the political landscape in the United States. But not since the Republican party was formed by assimilating a number of smaller parties have third parties played any significant role except as a means of pressuring the two main parties. The classic example of the threat posed by a third

---

[1]Fundamentalist Christians believe in the literal truth of the Bible. Most strongly oppose abortion and favor prayer in the schools.

party is Teddy Roosevelt's defection from the Republicans in 1912. He opposed the Republican administration's foreign policy, which he termed "dollar diplomacy," and its antitrust policy, which he considered far too kind toward large monopolies. At the national convention, he tried to get his program adopted and win the nomination. He failed and bolted the party. Roosevelt and his Republican followers formed the Progressive party, which ran him for president. Enough Republicans voted for Roosevelt to enable a Democrat, Woodrow Wilson, to win the election.

STRATEGIES FOR INFLUENCING POLICY

Forming a third party is, as we have just seen, a way to exert pressure. There are also other ways to affect policy-making. In almost all instances interest groups try to use the avenues we just discussed to reach the centers of power. The many decision makers on all levels of government afford interest groups ample opportunity to gain their objectives.

LOBBYING

The application of pressure on government by interest groups is called *lobbying*. The term comes from the old practice of people gathering in the lobbies of legislatures to speak to lawmakers to try to get some benefit from them. Today,

"Thanks, sport—and here's a little something for you.".

lobbyists seek out not only lawmakers but all other government decision makers, and not only in lobbies but also in hallways, offices, restaurants, parties, and elsewhere as well. Nor is the gentle art of lobbying as crude as is implied by the word *pressure*.

Lobbyists are highly skilled professionals, often lawyers and even more frequently former government officials. They are employed both for what they know and for who they know. Often they can get a hearing from someone in a position of power when others cannot. Part of the reason for this accessibility is that they provide a high level of ready expertise. Lobbyists seek to make themselves invaluable adjuncts of the legislative and executive processes. They often appear before Congress to give expert testimony; they often assist administrators and others of the executive bureaucracies to draft regulations, reports, and proposed legislation. In addition to these activities, many lobbyists help with speech writing and fund-raising for reelection campaigns. They also provide valuable contacts to members of Congress and the bureaucracy by inviting them to parties, dinners, and various entertainments.

But all lobbyists are not so benign. Some are thoroughly corrupt, and their actions may seriously affect policy. No recent period has had as much scandal associated with it as the Reagan-Bush decade. In a good many instances, individuals close to the two presidents have been implicated in the unethical use of personal influence. Perhaps one of the most prominent has involved a former aide to President Bush. The former aide used his influence to help a client convicted of fraud buy failed savings and loan banks from the government with borrowed money and receive from the government a promised subsidy of almost $2 billion. In this instance, President Bush's policy of bailing out the savings and loan industry was perverted by his own former aide, whose remarkable success called into question the entire bail-out program.

Former members of Congress are especially effective lobbyists because they have an insider's knowledge of the legislature and continue to have floor privileges (i.e., they are permitted on the floor of the House or Senate to talk to whomever they wish). Lobbyists are also drawn from former congressional staff members. These individuals have considerable knowledge of congressional procedures and a good number of influential contacts. Just as ex-congresspersons and staff people have a lobbying advantage on Capitol Hill, so do former bureaucrats in the executive areas. They know the ins-and-outs of the administrative world as well as many of the people who inhabit that world. An example of bureaucratic lobbying know-how may be seen in what has come to be known as the HUD scandal. Many Reagan appointees earned millions of dollars as lobbyists for little more than calling old friends at the Department of Housing and Urban Development (HUD) and obtaining lucrative contracts for clients.

Often, these various types of lobbyists form an effective network. Getting Congress to act on a lobbyist's interest is just the first step. How an agency implements a congressional act determines its real content and impact. Similarly, getting an agency to issue regulations on a matter of interest to a lobbyist is but the first step. The next step is enforcing the regulations, either in the courts or in administrative hearings. For each of these steps, special skills are required. To gain their goals, major interests employ staffs of lobbyists who can provide the

range of skills needed. They also interact among themselves and with the congressional and administrative people they wish to influence.

The link among congressional committees, executive departments and agencies, and lobbyists is often called an "iron triangle." In many areas of public policy, especially those involving government regulations and subsidies, iron triangles may determine the course of government. Regulatory agencies have often become "the captives" of the industries they presumably regulate. Both the White House and congressional leaders have tried to break the triangles, but with limited success and after much resistance. The problem posed by highly paid lobbyists is an old one, as is the effort to control it.

Even before the Civil War, rich corporations bought off more than a few state and sometimes federal legislators, making them virtual puppets and gaining privileges the businesses might not have otherwise gotten. The most famous, perhaps, were the land grants made by state and federal governments to the railroads. In 1850, the first land grant bill passed Congress, and by 1860, about 28 million acres of public land was slated for the railroads. Toward the end of the century, this and similar situations raised a hue and cry against big business and their lobbyists.

Efforts to regulate lobbying began at the state level in the nineteenth century. The national government, however, did not begin serious regulation until well into the twentieth century, passing the Federal Regulation of Lobbying Act in 1946. From that time onward, lobbyists have had to register with the government and report their financial and other activities. However, in their reports lobbyists reveal very little about their activities or the legislation they are trying to influence. Their statements are usually put in the broadest and most general terms possible.

Although the courts have accepted some restrictions on their activities, lobbyists are protected for the most part by the First Amendment guarantees of free speech, press, and the right to petition government for a redress of grievances.

POLITICAL ACTION COMMITTEES

In addition to employing a lobbying corps, interest groups also use political action committees (PACs) to bolster their influence in government circles. In 1925, Congress prohibited both corporations and unions from making direct contributions to political figures or parties. To get around this prohibition, first the unions and then, in the 1970s after new campaign practice laws went into effect, the corporations formed political action committees to fund the candidates they favored. Political action committees soon developed the tactic of supporting both candidates in a race, although they discriminate a bit by usually contributing larger sums to incumbents. PACs have come to be used by an enormous number and variety of interest groups. Today there are over 4,000 PACs.

Political action committees are fund-raising and distributing organizations that serve private interest groups. Their main purpose is to help finance the election campaigns of candidates for office. They are allowed to give each candidate $10,000 in direct contributions, $5,000 for the primary and $5,000 for the general election, and an unlimited amount in "indirect expenses." Table 6.1 illustrates the enormous amounts that PACs contribute to congressional campaigns. By the mid-to-late 1980s congressional candidates relied more than ever on PACs to finance their campaigns (see Figure 6.1). All told, PAC contributions to the 1986

Table 6.1   Major PAC Contributions to Congressional Elections, 1985–1986

Total Contributions by Broad Categories	
Corporations	$49,400,000
Trade Associations and Others[a]	34,400,000
Unions	31,000,000
Contributions by Individual Organization	
National Association of Realtors	2,782,338
American Medical Association	2,107,492
National Education Association	2,055,133
United Auto Workers	1,621,055
National Association of Retired Federal Employees	1,491,895
National Association of Letter Carriers	1,490,875
International Brotherhood of Teamsters	1,457,196
National Association of Home Builders	1,424,240
Association of Trial Lawyers	1,404,000

[a]"Others" covers "membership groups and health associations."
SOURCE: *Congressional Quarterly Weekly Report*, vol. 45, no. 21, 23 May 1987, p. 1062. Reprinted by permission of Congressional Quarterly, Inc.

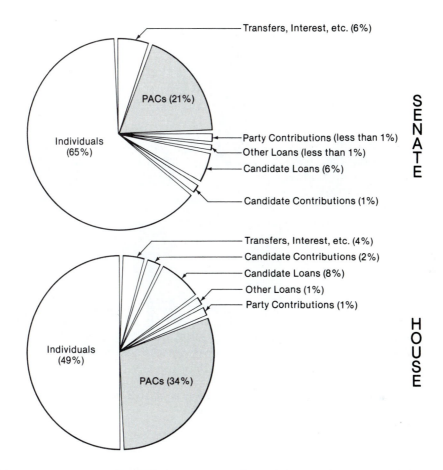

FIGURE 6.1   SOURCES OF INCOME FOR CONGRESSIONAL CAMPAIGNS IN THE TWO-YEAR PERIOD OF JANUARY 1, 1985, THROUGH DECEMBER 31, 1986

SOURCE: *Congressional Quarterly Weekly Report,* vol. 45, no. 20 (May 16, 1987), p. 991. Reprinted by permission of Congressional Quarterly, Inc.

congressional races came to over $132 million. Whereas congressional candidates rely on PAC funds, presidential races are publicly funded. Presidential candidates do receive some PAC money as they compete for their party's nomination, and in the general election they may benefit from indirect PAC expenditures in their behalf; but, generally, PAC money has little impact on the presidency.

PACs try to exert influence through other means as well as by giving money. Many, especially ideological PACs, cultivate grass-roots support both as a source of funds for themselves and as a body of voters they can call on. They then target individuals they oppose and make a concerted effort to defeat them. For example, Democratic Senator Frank Church of Idaho, as one of a group of liberal senators, had been targeted by the National Conservative Political Action Committee (NCPAC, or "nicpac") in the 1980 election and lost his seat largely as a result of its efforts.

"According to our estimates, a campaign budget around six point two million is needed to successfully sing your praises."

PACs also spend a good deal of money on advertising in newspapers, radio, and television for the candidates of their choice. A good amount of money is also spent by the PACs on direct mail campaigns. These are "indirect expenditures" and, although reported to the Federal Election Commission, are not restricted by government regulations.

PUBLIC OPINION: THE MEDIA AND DIRECT MAIL

To win office, elected officials have to appeal to collections of individuals called "the public." In primaries, candidates try to convince one kind of public; in general elections, another. As a rule, politicians prefer appealing to as broad a public as possible, and they are very uncomfortable antagonizing any part of it. They therefore pay close attention to the strongly held views of all segments of the populace, and are very sensitive to anyone who can manipulate public opinion.

That is precisely what some interest groups do—they manipulate or try to manipulate public opinion. Certain interest groups have always tried to influence the attitudes and beliefs of the public. In ancient Athens, the great orator Demosthenes urged the crowds in the *agora* to resist the attempt of Philip of Macedon to conquer Greece. Several hundred years later, the gladiator Spartacus urged his fellow slaves into a great rebellion against the wealthy classes of Rome. To skip over almost eighteen hundred years, Patrick Henry in the Virginia House of Burgesses argued for freedom from Britain. Closer to our own day, speakers of all persuasions have harangued crowds from "soap boxes" for all causes. All of these, from Demosthenes to the soap-box radicals of yesterday, have tried to mold public opinion.

Television.   Today, the agora is the tube. The most powerful medium of persuasion is television. Almost 90 million households own television sets. Major events, such as presidential debates, often reach over 100 million viewers, and perhaps as much as 45 percent of the public gets most of its information from television. Yet it is still questionable as to how much TV influences the attitudes or behavior of its viewers. For example, in 1982 President Reagan asked his TV viewers to write or call their congresspeople and express support for his military budget. The members of Congress were inundated with phone calls and postcards backing the president. Four years later, he made a similar appeal on television and there was hardly any response at all. Studies have also shown that those who depend mainly on TV for their information tend to participate less in the political process. Nevertheless, Reagan's enormous personal popularity despite strong disagreements with many of his policies can be attributed only to the attractive image he projects on the television screen.

Newspapers and Magazines.   Although these media reach smaller audiences, they may have greater impact, at least as measured by political participation. The print media allow somewhat more room and time than either radio or television for detailed treatment of issues and therefore may be a bit more persuasive than the electronic media. Moreover, cost is also an important consideration. A thirty-second spot on television is much costlier than a full-page ad in most newspapers or journals of opinion. For these reasons, the print media is generally used more often than the electronic media. Nevertheless, as a campaign reaches its climax or peak, interest groups will often invest in television and radio spots as well.

Direct Mail.   When measurable impact and cost-benefit ratios are important, interest groups turn to direct-mail techniques. With the arrival of computers, mailings can be churned out en masse and targeted at very clearly defined groups. Indeed, mailings can be made to appear highly individualized and personal by inserting the addressee's name within the text of a letter. Often they further the illusion of personal interest by soliciting responses to a questionnaire that is at the same time a request for money. As was shown by fund-raiser Richard Viguerie's ability to get huge sums of money from vast numbers of $20 donors to arch-conservative causes, direct mail is perhaps one of the most effective fund-raising methods available to interest groups. It is also a very effective means of mobilizing an already committed group and getting them to take action, such as writing letters, traveling to Washington to appear in mass demonstrations, or going out on a cold and nasty day to vote.

© 1986 BOB ROGERS AND *THE PITTSBURGH PRESS.*

ESSENTIALS OF INTEREST GROUPS

An enormous number and variety of interest groups continually try to influence government. However, for purposes of discussion and analysis, they are usually grouped together into several broad categories: business, labor, professional, agricultural, ideological, and what might be called "public interest" groups. It is important to recognize that the members of these categories do not hold identical views. Indeed, they often hold opposing views on exactly the same subjects and are classed together for this very reason. Instead of resembling monoliths, our groupings are more like jigsaw puzzles that fit together in such a way that they reflect most attitudes and opinions on issues that matter to people.

BUSINESS INTERESTS

We often think of "corporate America" as if this were a single entity striving for a uniform goal. But this mistaken notion is contrary to what is actually the case. There is a tremendous variety of business interests, and these are represented by a huge array of trade associations and other organizations. Sometimes they have similar interests and goals, sometimes they have opposite ones. For example, many manufacturers have sought high protective tariffs during the eighties to discourage imports. By contrast, merchants have fought protectionism because it tends to raise domestic prices and, for those in the export business, risks foreign retaliation.

RICH, NEW HAVEN REGISTER, 1990.

Even within the manufacturing group, there is little unity. In the late 1950s and 1960s, for example, the American textile industry was hard hit with foreign imports and therefore asked for raised tariffs to protect their market here. The automobile industry, which at the time was exporting many vehicles to Europe and Asia, strenuously opposed such protective tariffs. They were afraid their overseas markets would be closed to them in retaliation. In the late 1970s and early 1980s, American autos did not hold up well against competition from Japan and Germany. Chrysler almost went under while Ford and General Motors lobbied for protective tariffs. At that time the electronics industry carried on a brisk export trade and therefore strongly opposed protectionism. On the issue of trade restrictions, clearly the business community splits along lines of self-interest, and that self-interest is in constant flux.

Even in areas where businesses have common interests, such as low taxes, there are occasional divisions within the community. For example, in the fall of 1987 the stock market plunged over 500 points in what some described as the Second Great American Crash. Many within the financial community attributed the enormous drop in the market value of stocks to the huge government deficit the Reagan administration had accumulated. They called on the government to reduce the deficit by cutting services and increasing taxes. Other sections of the business community vehemently opposed any tax increase. On the whole, American business is united in its opposition to taxes as it is to any other cost that takes away from profits.

Environmental controls are another cost to which business is generally opposed. To accommodate this opposition, the Reagan administration virtually dismantled the Environmental Protection Agency (EPA). Strong opposition by environmental groups in combination with charges of corrupt practices by EPA heads forced the administration to make an abrupt about-face. Regulatory policy is generally under considerable pressure from business interests, which usually strive for minimum government interference in their pursuit of profit.

Government departments, however, are under constant pressure to award contracts to various business firms. Perhaps the largest contracts go to the defense industry. Giant manufacturers of military hardware, such as McDonnell Douglas or Rockwell International, usually get jobs worth billions of dollars from the Department of Defense (DOD). The Pentagon also awards millions of dollars for research and development to corporate giants such as AT&T, IBM, or TRW in addition to billion-dollar production contracts. The goal of all these organizations and others like them is to continue to receive DOD largess. The Reagan administration has been especially generous in awarding defense contracts and particularly lenient in monitoring them. These contracts have served as huge subsidies to America's industrial giants, which of course is a form of government interference in the working of the "free market."

To achieve their goals, businesses are represented in their dealings with government in various ways. The corporate giants, such as General Electric or Union Carbide, often employ their own lobbyists in addition to joining many other businesses large and small in trade associations such as the Chamber of Commerce or the National Association of Manufacturers. Some other major business representatives are the National Association of Realtors, American Bankers Association, National Association of Home Builders, and Automobile and Truck Dealers Association.

LABOR INTERESTS

The other side of the economic equation is labor, the workers who actually produce the goods that make the profits for business. Just as all business firms, large and small, are interested in maximizing profits, so all workers are interested in earning more than a subsistence wage, having job security, and working under "decent" or reasonable conditions. And just as businesses are not monolithic, so labor is not also. Indeed, there is a major division within labor itself. There is on the one side organized labor—the unions—and on the other, unorganized labor—nonunion workers. When we think of the interests of labor, we think of those interests that have been expressed by unions. Nonunion workers, who are in the majority, are assumed to share these interests, but there is no certainty that they are indeed conscious of a common interest. The membership of unions, which never represented the majority of workers, has steadily declined from a high of about 36 percent of the work force in 1945. Yet unions have had and still have an enormous impact on the American economy.

Part of the explanation for the impact of unions can be sought in their political activity and, by comparison to European unions, their avoidance of radical ideologies. Radicalism tends to rigidity, and its absence allows for flexibility. Most American unions have been closely identified with the Democratic party since the 1930s, but some have contributed to the Republican party. Further, some of their leaders, such as the late Jackie Presser of the Teamsters, have had close relations with leading conservative Republicans, all of whom are strongly anti-union. Nevertheless, Presser and other "Republican" union leaders are tough negotiators when it comes to bargaining for benefits to their members.

Over the years, unions have fought on picket lines and in the halls of Congress for the right to collective bargaining. They have won some and lost more. Their classic defeat was the passage in 1947 of the Taft-Hartley Act, which outlawed labor's strongest weapon, the closed shop (a business in which all employees must be members of a union). A recent major loss for unionism was the destruction of the air controller's union by President Reagan in 1981 and the forced "give-backs" in many union contracts negotiated since. The most recent loss for labor is President Bush's 1989 veto of an increase in the minimum wage, for which the unions had campaigned hard. Congress sustained his veto.

Traditionally, unions have lobbied vigorously for minimum-wage and maximum-hour laws, Social Security and unemployment benefits, and government regulation of health and safety in the workplace. Among the most active lobbyists for labor interests are the American Federation of Labor-Congress of Industrial Organizations (AFL-CIO), United Automobile Workers (UAW), International Brotherhood of Teamsters, the International Ladies Garment Workers Union (ILGWU), and United Steelworkers of America. There are, of course, many other unions that also try to exert influence on legislation.

AGRICULTURAL INTERESTS

In the early years of the country's history, the major opponents of business interests were farmers and planters. Some historians have analyzed the Civil War as a conflict between the economic interests of these two groups, especially Southern planters and Northern industrialists. After the Civil War and with the advent of modern machinery, agriculture began to change. Small family farms began to go down under debt and agribusinesses began to replace them. With the arrival of business people came business savvy and professional lobbyists to represent agricultural interests.

Those interests vary according to what is grown and the kind of farming that is done. For example, wheat growers do not share many of the problems of cattle ranchers, and both are distant from the concerns of dairy farmers. However, many tend to come together on some basic interests. A few of these issues are price supports, soil conservation, control of industrial pollution believed to cause acid rain, and maintenance of low tariffs to assure foreign trade. The ongoing effort to unionize migrant workers and other farm laborers has been a constant problem for agribusinesses in the past fifteen to twenty years. So too has the government's persistent attempt to control the entry of illegal aliens who come north mainly from Mexico to work on farms in southern California and the Southwest.

If we discount Jefferson and the agrarians from the South, farm pressure groups started with the National Grange in 1867. Two other major farm organizations are the National Farmers Union and the American Farm Bureau Federation. Curiously, the Federation opposes farm subsidies while producer groups endorse government supports. Some of the more specialized associations are the National

Milk Producers Federation, the National Livestock Feeders Association, the American Meat Institute, and the National Wool Growers Association.

PROFESSIONAL INTERESTS

Doctors, lawyers, educators, engineers, scientists, accountants, and other professionals have also created organizations to represent their interests before government. At this moment, their interests are more diverse than those of any of the other groups we looked at. Unlike the other categories, the different professions hold no recognized interests in common. And some of the professions, such as the doctors and lawyers, are often in conflict, as these two are about medical malpractice court cases.

Despite the fragmentation of the professions, individual organizations have a good deal of influence in their specialties. The American Medical Association, for example, has so far successfully blocked a national health program, which it labels "socialized medicine." It has strongly influenced the training requirements of doctors and other health care professionals and has largely determined which categories of health services will be licensed by the states. Other highly influential organizations are the American Bar Association, which has a large voice in the selection of federal judges, and the National Education Association, which virtually forced President Jimmy Carter to create a new Department of Education and prevented President Ronald Reagan from dismantling it. The education establishment has enough clout with the general public to have affected George Bush's rhetoric during the 1988 presidential campaign. When running for office, candidate Bush promised he would be "the education president."

IDEOLOGICAL INTERESTS

So far we have discussed explicitly economic interests. As we have seen, there is a fair amount of conflict within a category and between classes of interests. This conflict is even more intense in the ideological realm, as we might expect. But there is a good deal of cooperation as well. For example, the two premier ideological organizations, the National Association for the Advancement of Colored People (NAACP) and the American Civil Liberties Union (ACLU), often cooperate with one another. The ACLU has also cooperated with a number of other groups, such as the National Abortion Rights Action League (NARAL), in appearances before the courts.

The members of ideological interest groups share a political philosophy, even though they may come from widely divergent economic, social, racial, and religious backgrounds. The glue is their shared belief. Sometimes the belief is so strong that it will outweigh an obvious self-interest. For example, the ACLU, which is devoted to civil rights and civil liberties for everyone, has defended members of the American Nazi Party and of the Ku Klux Klan, each of which would have happily destroyed the ACLU if it had the power.

To varying degrees, other ideological groups are also attached to their beliefs. One can list on the liberal side several outstanding groups from among a large number. People for the American Way is devoted basically to resisting the effort

THE COMMERCIAL APPEAL, 1977. REPRODUCED BY PERMISSION.

Congress is often pictured as the captive of outside interests.

of certain religious groups to break down Jefferson's "wall of separation between church and state." The National Organization of Women (NOW) is dedicated to women's issues, particularly to assuring women equality in the workplace and the political arena. The NAACP is dedicated to civil rights for blacks and has been a powerful force in winning over the courts and legislatures to its cause. Americans for Democratic Action (ADA) is devoted to a broad range of human rights and civil liberties. And, of course, the ACLU, which is perhaps the nation's principal defender of the Constitutional guarantees of civil liberties.

Opposed to these liberal advocates are a number of conservative interest groups. Among these are Americans for Constitutional Action, which opposes welfare programs and the expansion of the Bill of Rights; the National Taxpayers Union, which favors elimination of the deficit and a balanced budget amendment; and the American Conservative Union, which supports a broad range of programs such as cutting taxes, building military strength, opposing international communism, as well as rolling back welfare, balancing the budget, and generally curtailing the expansion of individual rights.

PUBLIC INTERESTS

While somewhat similar to ideological interests in the strong passions they arouse, public interests are nevertheless very different. Although politically active and sophisticated, groups claiming to represent public interests do not hold to a particular political belief system. Both conservatives and liberals, for example, are members of the Sierra Club or Common Cause. They differ from all the other interests we have discussed in that there is little or no conflict among the various interests or the groups representing them.

At this time, there appear to be mainly three kinds of public interests: consumer, environmental, and good government concerns. The leading advocate of good government is Common Cause. Ralph Nader's Public Citizen is possibly the best-known consumer advocate, and the Sierra Club is perhaps the most famous representative of certain environmental interests. Environmental concerns are more broadly spoken for by the League of Conservation Voters, and consumer interests are further represented by the Consumer Federation of America.

Public interest groups seek to achieve goals that in essential ways would benefit the entire population. For example, we are all consumers, even if some of us manufacture goods and others raise crops. That means we all benefit from the activities of consumer advocates, even if we are not members of any of their groups. In that latter instance, we gain the benefits of consumer protection without paying the price of membership. This is precisely the justification for public interest advocacy—the whole society is presumed to benefit from the efforts of public interest groups.

Of course, there are nonpublic interest groups that feel that society as a whole loses from activities of public interest lobbies. For example, in the Northwest woodlands, both labor and management in the lumber industry are very opposed to the efforts of several environmentalist groups to save the trees. The environmentalists want to preserve some of the few remaining large tracts of forests in the United States. The lumber companies argue that preventing them from cutting the forests would drive them into bankruptcy, the reverberations of which would result in a regionwide depression and, through its effect on housing costs, possibly a nationwide recession.

MEMBERSHIP OF INTEREST GROUPS

As with almost all voluntary organizations, interest groups have basically two kinds of members—those who are active and those who are passive. Passive members pay dues, contribute money to special fund-raising drives, occasionally write letters or sign petitions, and sometimes appear at gatherings or demonstrations. In most organizations, these people make up the majority of the membership. As a rule, they, like most people, have a fairly large number of interests and often join several groups representing the variety of their concerns. They also may join an interest group for a variety of reasons aside from the group's focus. Many join to gain insurance benefits, job possibilities, travel or vacation discounts, and the like. The groups, of course, appeal to these extraneous interests as a means of increasing their membership. In a democratic system numbers count, and a large enrollment in an interest group gives that group influence in the corridors of power.

In contrast, the activists are relatively few in number and more deeply committed to the interest represented by their group. It is the activists who try to rouse the large numbers of passive members to action. The activists generally perform the low-level chores needed by all interest groups, such as stuffing envelopes or making phone solicitations, and can be counted on to write their legislator or other elected official. Unlike passive members, activists can be trusted to vote an interest group's party line. It is usually from the ranks of the activists that leadership slots are filled in organizations.

In Conclusion

Interest groups have always been a vital part of the political process. Although the founders had mixed feelings about them, they counted on a multitude of competing private interests to protect the country from tyranny. And indeed a large number of economic, ideological, consumer, and environmental interests vie, with varying degrees of success, for influence over public policy and government actions. So far, they have helped maintain the system created by the founders.

Suggested Readings

Jeffrey M. Berry. *The Interest Group Society*. Boston: Little, Brown, 1984.

Theodore Lowi. *The End of Liberalism*. New York: Norton, 1969.

Andrew McFarland, *Public Interest Lobbys*. Washington, D.C.: American Enterprise Institute, 1976.

Larry J. Sabato. *PAC Power*. New York: Norton, 1985.

David B. Truman. *The Governmental Process,* 2nd ed. New York: Knopf, 1971.

chapter

7

PUBLIC OPINION
and the MEDIA

*For however strong a ruler may be, he will always have
need of the good will of the inhabitants if he wishes to
remain in power*

Machiavelli

hat the citizens of a country think or believe is of central importance
to all forms of government. Knowledge of those opinions or views
helps determine public policy. If a government enunciates a policy
that is counter to the views of a significant number of its citizens, the government
will have difficulty carrying out the policy. Prohibition is a prime example from
within the American experience. Collectivization can serve as an example from
the totalitarian regime of Stalin's Russia. In both instances strenuous and costly
efforts at enforcement were undertaken. In the Soviet case, the effort to collec-
tivize the farms resulted in violent resistance, severe famine, the relocation of
huge populations, and the death of millions of people. In the United States,
Prohibition led to increased corruption, the rise of organized crime, and the willing,
if not joyful, flouting of the law by millions of otherwise law-abiding citizens.

The trick then is in finding out what the citizenry believes. Today, the usual
way of doing so is by commissioning public opinion polls. But there are problems.
First, that wonderful creature, "the public," needs to be defined. Then, it needs

to be questioned in such a way as to gain a reasonably accurate understanding of its "opinion." These problems are more easily solved on paper than in action.

But politicians do not just want to learn the opinions of the public. They often also want to influence those opinions. In the contemporary world, this is tried largely through the media. The media—instruments of communication—provide most people with most of the information they have about subjects with which they have little or no personal acquaintance. It is one thing, though, to provide people with information which they may ponder; it is quite another to shape people's opinions about that information.

The endeavor to shape the opinions of the public soon involves a thinking person in the issues associated with propaganda or the arts of persuasion. Essentially, these issues concern problems of truth, credibility, the uses of art, and freedom of expression. And, as in almost all political matters, informing the public and shaping its view of the world raise questions about ends and means. Each of these matters is complicated and difficult.

Beyond these more or less philosophical issues are very practical ones. The media, especially the mass media, in modern America are privately owned. They are business enterprises that are geared essentially to making a profit for their owners. But our constitutional guarantee of a free press is based on the supposition that the press or media perform a vital public service in a democratic society. The question arises as to how well that public service requirement is satisfied by profit-seeking businesses. Here too, both question and answer are complex and fraught with difficulties.

Finally, there is another practical question: How effective are the mass media— that portion of the media that appeals to a vast, general audience? How effective are they in changing our perceptions of political realities, for example? of getting us to recognize our own best interests? or in getting us to act against our own best interests? In this case, the answer may be easy, but finding it is very hard.

Clearly then, public opinion and the media are closely related. And that relationship is a complex one. Moreover, it connects one way or another with our politics. But, because of its complexity, we sometimes have difficulty grasping the nature of that relationship.

One way to begin to understand the relationship among public opinion, the media, and politics is to look at these connections within a historical context.

BACKGROUND

From its beginning, one of the purposes of government has been to influence the beliefs of its citizens.[1] Very early on in the American political scene, major figures

---

[1]For an instance of the antiquity of government efforts to control public opinion, we can turn to the ancient Roman historian Livy. In his *History of Rome,* he tells a charming tale about Numa, the first king of the city after Romulus, its founder. As Livy put it, Numa wanted to give warlike Rome "a second beginning, this time on the solid basis of law...." To reach his goal, Numa felt he had to exploit his subjects' fear of the gods. He "pretended, therefore, that he was in the habit of meeting the goddess Egiria by night" and receiving from her the laws he made. The "rough, ignorant" Romans, to use Livy's terms, were so taken by Numa's invention that they renounced war and turned to law and peace during his 43-year reign.

President Bush's popularity was at an all-time high during the Persian Gulf War.

used the available instruments of communication in an effort to sway public opinion. So, political leaders hired or sponsored those skilled in the art of communication. This was first done when Thomas Jefferson persuaded the poet Philip Freneau in 1791 to edit the antifederalist newspaper, *The National Gazette*. After some time, Alexander Hamilton followed suit by hiring William Coleman, an experienced polemicist, as editor of his newly founded *New York Evening Post*. These journals were dedicated to promoting particular political views. They were unashamedly partisan and biased.

Nor were these papers alone in being biased. The early press and public speakers generally were extremely partisan. Henry Adams describes those members of the press whom he calls "scurrilous libellers":

> Perhaps none of these habitual libellers deserved censure so much as Fisher Ames. ... He saw no harm in showing "the knaves," Jefferson and Gallatin, "the cold-thinking villains who lead, 'whose black blood runs temperately bad,' " the motives of "their own base hearts. ...."[2]

The early partisan press wrote for an upper- and middle-class audience. Increased literacy down the social scale, improved printing methods, and cheaper paper enabled the press to publish for the lower classes. In 1833, the mass media was born with the first appearance of the penny press in New York City. The *New*

[2]Henry Adams, *History of the United States of America during the Administrations of Thomas Jefferson* (New York: Library of America, 1986), p. 83.

York Sun was sold on street corners to all and sundry for one penny. It was not long before the *Sun* was faced with competition, and other newspapers costing a penny began appearing in New York and other cities. Alexis de Tocqueville, a politically astute observer from France, provides a description of the newspapers of this period:

> In America three quarters of the bulky newspaper put before you will be full of advertisements and the rest will usually contain political news or just anecdotes. . . . [T]he hallmark of the . . . journalist is a direct and coarse attack, without any subtleties, on the passions of his readers; he disregards principles to seize on people. . . .[3]

The press continued its intemperate style to the Civil War. This conflict was a watershed of American history in more ways than one. From our point of view, it changed the look, feel, and character of the press. News stories drove advertising from the front page and polemical harangues back into the midsection of the paper. For the most part, news reporting was fairly straightforward and, because of the invention of the telegraph, more immediate than in previous wars. There were more reporters in the field than in earlier years. Line-cut illustrations from the front were used more widely than previously. Readers had much more the sense of being directly involved in the war than in earlier accounts. One consequence was that papers grew in size and circulation.

But also a new style and standard of writing began to appear in newspapers and magazines. News stories were no longer polemical. For the most part, they were eye-witness accounts and were written as if reporters were neutral observers. This new manner was called "objectivity," which, it was believed, would yield the "unvarnished truth." *Objectivity* may be defined as the suppression of individual interpretation or personal opinion and the practice of a wholly descriptive style of representation. Whether objectivity is possible is a difficult philosophical question that we need not deal with here. It is enough to recognize that objectivity in journalism is a matter of style that lays claim to the expression of truth.

But the unvarnished truth is, to put it crudely, rather boring. Truth without varnish didn't sell many newspapers, and selling papers became the name of the game toward the end of the nineteenth century. After the Civil War, some newspapers began selling over 100,000 copies daily. The larger the circulation, the larger the number of readers who might buy goods, the higher the cost of advertising, the higher the profits the paper earned. So, newspapers started to compete for readers, which meant that papers had to be entertaining as well as informative, perhaps even entertaining while being informative. Comics, sports, gossip began to appear in the daily papers. And some varnish on the truth also began to appear.

Those newspapers that treated information as a species of entertainment practiced what is often called "yellow journalism." The term *yellow journalism* derives

---

[3]Alexis de Tocqueville, *Democracy in America,* tr. George Lawrence, ed. J. P. Mayer (New York: Doubleday, 1969), pp. 183–184, 185.

from the title of one of the earliest comic strips, "The Yellow Kid." The phrase also continues nicely the metaphor of varnished and unvarnished truths: Varnish tends to yellow with age, and truths that have been "varnished," usually with exaggeration if not outright lies, have generally been exposed over time.

In any case, the basic idea behind yellow journalism, aside from making money, was to conceive the news as a type of high drama or melodrama. War, scandal, corruption, evil had been the stuff of drama for the ancient Greeks and were the same for the newspaper tycoons at the end of the nineteenth century and beginning of the twentieth. The journals that published this kind of news were often referred to with contempt as "scandal sheets." And the reporters who dramatically exposed scandal, corruption, and evil in high places were called angrily, first by Teddy Roosevelt and later by others, "muckrakers." We still have scandal sheets, and occasionally a muckraker will arise among today's erstwhile journalists. And we still have newspapers that carry to our own time the late nineteenth-century pretense of objectivity that was most fully articulated by the *New York Times*.

But the truth, if there is such a thing, was under assault not only from within the media itself but from without as well. At the beginning of the twentieth century, giant corporations, since they were often the targets of the muckrakers, began using "publicity experts" to counter the bad press they were receiving. Government officials also did not take long to recognize the advantages of controlling the flow and character of information to the media and thereby influencing public attitudes.

The manipulation and dissemination of information for the purpose of affecting public opinion is precisely the definition of *propaganda*. Government use of propaganda first reached its apogee during World War I, when the United States undertook a massive campaign to sway opinion in favor of the war. Government propaganda was crude back then; it has been refined since, but its effectiveness is still in question. So many countervailing pressures influence public attitudes that neither the government's nor any one else's effort to affect those attitudes can be assured success. But, what are those attitudes? How can we find out?

ESSENTIALS OF PUBLIC OPINION

Even before trying to discover the public's attitudes, we have to have some idea of what the public is. What in the world is that mysterious creature called the public? Well, first off, it's an abstraction. Or, to put it somewhat differently: the *public* is actually a set of characteristics possessed by a group of people. For example, homeowners living in the suburbs of major cities are one public; persons renting apartments in inner cities are another.

Clearly, there are several different publics, and they are defined by ignoring individual differences among people and concentrating only on those features that are shared. When American pollsters try to learn the views of the "general public," they choose individuals from all the categories that make up the nation's entire population. The categories the pollsters are mainly concerned with are age, sex, occupation, income, education, region, race, political ideology, and religion.

MEASURING PUBLIC OPINION

But pollsters cannot ask the opinion of every man and woman in the United States. So, the poll takers randomly select a sample of the general population. This means that theoretically every person within the categories that make up a relevant population has the same chance to be polled. Ideally, randomness protects the sample against bias and allows for the statistical probability of accurate results. The larger the sample, the greater the chance for reliable readings. Since a polling organization rarely can survey a truly large segment of the population, sampling errors are possible that may skew the results. Research organizations try to limit the degree of sampling error to statistically insignificant amounts, usually 3 to 5 points.

Sample size is not the only source of possible error; how a survey is conducted is another source. Today, the most common method of conducting a survey is by telephone. Unfortunately, respondents are often not willing to answer questions for more than about 10 or 15 minutes, and their responses cannot be verified by visual observation. As the *New York Times* put it: "In addition to sampling error, the practical difficulties of conducting any survey of public opinion may introduce other sources of error into the poll."[4] Some of these practical difficulties arise when recording answers during interviews or entering data into the computer, to choose but two common sources of errors.

The question asked is itself a possible source of inaccurate data. It can influence responses and is sometimes contrived to do precisely that. The following question is obviously calculated to elicit a desired response: "Do you believe that it is fair for Congress to give themselves a 39% pay raise for an annual salary of $120,000.00 and then reduce benefits for senior citizens to reduce the deficit?"[5] In this instance, the poll taker is not really interested in finding out what the respondent thinks. But in other circumstances, pollsters want accurate results and fail to get them because of poorly phrased questions. For example, the frequently asked "Do you think the president is doing a good job?" is so broad that it is virtually meaningless. A well-constructed question will sharpen the focus of the question and keep it neutral. Our question rephrased might be "Do you approve of the president's tax policies?" or ". . . of the president's economic policies?"

Finally, the respondents themselves may be a source of error. Most people are decent folk and want to "give a new fella a chance," so the approval rating of a president in the first few months of his term is often 65 to 70 percent when he may have barely squeaked to electoral victory with 50 percent. The classic instance of this is the approval rating of John F. Kennedy six months after taking office. He won the election with only 49.7 percent of the vote, but 71 percent approved of him six months after he entered the White House.[6] Sometimes people questioned in polls do not want to admit their ignorance of a subject and thus will

---

[4]From an explanation of how a presidential ratings poll was conducted in *The New York Times*, 14 Oct. 1990: 25.

[5]From a questionnaire sent to retirees by Retired Americans Legislative Lobby, Inc.

[6]The sixth-month figure for JFK's approval rating comes from a comparative study of presidential ratings by Gallup Polls appearing in *The American Enterprise*, Sept./Oct. 1990: 99.

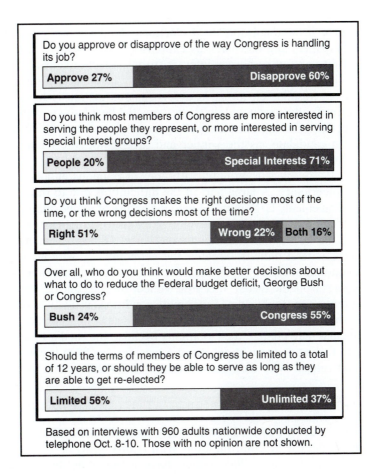

FIGURE 7.1   ASSESSING CONGRESS: MIXED REVIEWS

SOURCE: *The New York Times,* October 12, 1990: A21. © 1990 by The New York Times Company. Reprinted by permission.

express an opinion on a topic when they actually have none. And the very processes of polling—the way questions are asked, the structure of interviews—may affect responses.

Given all the uncertainty connected with polling, it should not come as a surprise when the surveyed public seems to contradict itself. The poll in Figure 7.1 may serve as an example of the difficulty in gaining a coherent view of public opinion. The survey was conducted in the midst of the budget debacle of 1990. At that time, the Bush administration and congressional leadership (both Republican and Democratic) had worked out a "budget deal" that was thoroughly rejected by the rank-and-file members of Congress.

The opinion of the public is not only sought and expressed in scientifically conducted surveys, it is also elicited in *vox populi* interviews by the press and of course in national and local elections. Media interviews, although paraded in newspapers and television as expressing the sentiment of the people, have little validity except as human interest stories. Elections, of course, are the polls that count in the final analysis. Although as a rule election results are fairly close to survey results, elections in a few famous instances have given the lie to the scientifically conducted polls. Perhaps the best known of these is the presidential election of 1948, when the polls generally predicted Thomas Dewey, the Republican candidate, as the winner and the Democratic incumbent, Harry Truman, actually won.

Clearly, measuring public attitudes or opinions entails a considerable amount of uncertainty. A large part of the difficulty is due to the nature of polling itself. But an equally large part is due to the nature of public opinion itself. As a scholarly work noted: "Americans develop opinions toward an astonishing variety of issues that lie far outside their own experience. [T]hey ... manage to decide whether huge federal deficits threaten the economy ... without undertaking their own economic analysis. ..."[7] The information about the threat posed by federal deficits comes from the media. It is little wonder then, as one observer noted, that "Public attention to troublesome but remote conditions is likely to be ephemeral, changing forms as the news high-lights different issues or unrecognized facets of old ones."[8] People may change their opinions because the media focuses on certain issues, but feeling concern about those issues derives from previously existing attitudes and values. Where do those attitudes and values come from?

THE FORMATION OF PUBLIC ATTITUDES AND VALUES

Our values are formed continuously throughout our lives and just as continuously are modified by confrontations with reality. But, first we need to examine what we mean by *value*. Philosophers have argued about the concept since the ancient Greeks. We will cut through the myriad complexities surrounding the concept and offer a simple definition. *Value* refers to a fundamental principle by which we judge actions, events, or other principles. For example, many people believe they value human life above all else. In these instances, they may argue against abortion or capital punishment. But, if the nation is attacked, then they may be willing to go to war, and that of course involves taking human life. In this case, the continued existence of the nation is valued above life. Here, there is a shift in values. In effect, these people have said, "human life is a supreme value, except when the life of the nation or community is threatened." In philosophy, values form the bases for ethical judgments—in politics, they underlie our ideological commitments and political attitudes.

Generally, values shift very gradually. As we have just seen, attitudes and opinions, however, may change quickly according to changing circumstances. We

---

[7]Shanto Iyengar and Donald R. Kinder, *News That Matters* (Chicago: University of Chicago Press, 1987), p. 2.

[8]Murray Edelman, *Constructing the Political Spectacle* (Chicago: University of Chicago Press, 1988), p. 32.

may change our attitude toward government intervention in the economy, for example, because of price gouging by the oil industry. Or, perhaps because of heavy media coverage, we may come to feel that a formerly trusted political leader can no longer be believed, as in the case of Marion Barry, the mayor of Washington, D.C., even though the evidence against him was very weak.

We acquire our opinions, attitudes, and values through a process of socialization, from families, schools, friends, professional associates, the media, and life experiences in general. *Attitudes* are inclinations or tendencies toward or away from some fact or belief. They are generally fairly vague until expressed, at which time they are identical with *opinions*. When those opinions are held by large numbers of people or society as a whole, they become *public opinions*. As we noted at the beginning of this chapter, public opinion is central to the political process. To be effective, political decisions must take into account the views of the public.

Most of us first gain our political values and attitudes from our families. Although those attitudes and values may never have been clearly or formally stated in the family they nevertheless seem in most cases to have a lasting and quite pervasive influence on our later views. Often, people raised in families that do not believe in the electoral process and therefore do not vote are themselves nonvoters later in life. So too, people raised by Republican or Democratic parents often remain with the same political affiliations as those of the parents. Very often these party affiliations correlate with the religious and ethnoracial identities of the voters and their families. Of course other sources of influence may modify (or reinforce) the attitudes and opinions inherited from the family.

Beyond the family, school and later professional associations will influence our political attitudes and opinions. Both education and occupation generally sharpen awareness of political and social issues. Since economic matters, such as taxes or recessions, usually affect our income-gaining abilities, we quickly learn what political positions are in our own best interests. Moreover, as individuals move up the educational and income ladders, they have a greater stake in our society and thus have a livelier interest in political affairs with correspondingly stronger views on public issues than those on the lower rungs of the ladder. This may in part account for the large number of union members who voted for Reagan and against their own best interests. But the opinions of all of us—Democrats and Republicans, rich and poor—are shaped largely by the information we receive. And most of our information comes from the media, especially the mass media.

THE ESSENTIALS OF THE MEDIA

No period before our own has been as inundated with information. More of it flows over and around us than we can reasonably assimilate. One consequence of this information overload is a tendency to simplify and compartmentalize the information we do receive. The media contribute mightily to this process. They fix the content of our concerns and our conversations in politics, art, and social life. Fashion reports in the media tell us what the smart set wears and how to look chic. Film reviewers tell us what to see at the movies and what to think of that which we do see. And news stories, especially when covered intensely, tell us what is important and how to think of that which is important.[9]

We can see this last in the impact the media has had on the public's view of the American-Iraqi confrontation in the Persian Gulf. When Iraq invaded its much smaller neighbor Kuwait at the beginning of August 1990, few Americans were involved or interested. The media barely paid attention. There had been prior to the invasion an occasional muddled story about some "sabre rattling" by Saddam Hussein, the leader of Iraq.

When President Bush decided to respond some short while after the invasion by sending American troops to the region, the media perked up its ears, and the public began getting a steady stream of information on what came to be known as the Gulf crisis. It looked like there might be a war, and the media as a whole loves conflict—high drama. So Ted Koppel of ABC and Dan Rather of CBS raced to the Middle East and soon were broadcasting from Baghdad, Iraq. Between August 1st and 15th, the television networks devoted 80 percent of their newscasts to the Gulf crisis, which was twice as much as the coverage of the first 15 days of the Panama invasion or the early days of the national election.[10] As a former producer for CBS commented on the coverage, it is "a wonderful opportunity for the networks to get out there, to sell themselves, to have great footage and great backdrops for their anchor."[11]

But the media did not just sell themselves, they also "sold" George Bush. During those initial days all the networks and major newspapers were full of stories about how effectively Bush had organized "worldwide" condemnation of Iraq, had gotten Arab countries to join us against Iraq, and had persuaded the nations of the world to cooperate with our blockade of Iraq. The American military buildup in the Gulf was also portrayed as fast and efficient, and this too was by implication credited to Bush. Thus, it shouldn't surprise anyone that all this early adulation enhanced Bush's standing in the polls. Shortly before the Iraq confrontation, Bush's ratings had dropped to a low of 60 percent in the Gallup Polls. A week or so after he committed U.S. troops to the defense of Saudi Arabia, Bush's Gallup Poll ratings shot up to 74 percent.[12] The former CBS producer "believes," according to the *Washington Post* story, "that all the action created a sense of urgency about the crisis, which in turn helped President Bush sell his policy and improve his popular standing."[13]

However, a couple of months later, after a bruising battle with Congress over the budget for the fiscal year 1991, Bush's popularity plummeted to the lowest point of his presidency. The budget battle had received intense, highly dramatic,

---

[9]This is known as agenda setting and has been described by Maxwell McCombs and Donald Shaw, "The Agenda-Setting Function of Mass Media," in *Public Opinion Quarterly* 36 (Summer 1972): 176–187, and studied under controlled conditions by Iyengar and Kinder, *News That Matters*.

[10]*The Media Monitor* as reported in the *New York Post*, 18 Sept. 1990: 53.

[11]Quoted in E. J. Dionne, Jr., "Mainstream Reporting and Middle East Extremities," *The Washington Post*, 1 Sept. 1990: C6.

[12]Quoted in *The American Enterprise*, Sept./Oct. 1990: 99.

[13]Dionne, "Mainstream Reporting," C6.

and extremely widespread media attention, especially during the month of October. Toward the end of that month, Bush's Gallup Poll approval rating had dropped a precipitous 26 points to 48 percent.[14]

By mid-November, when the budget brouhaha was over, the media returned to the crisis in the Persian Gulf. Having just completed a highly dramatic miniseries on the budget, the media sought the same success for their drama in the Gulf. They shifted attention from Bush's successes in confronting Iraqi aggression to conflict within the populace over his policy in the Gulf. As *Newsweek* put it: "Bush found himself at the epicenter of what may yet be the most wrenching foreign-policy debate since Vietnam."[15] So the media pounded away at the President's presumed failure to convincingly explain his reasons for threatening war against Iraq. Support for confronting Iraq dropped from a mid-August high of 77 percent to a low of 47 percent just a few days before the United States launched its attack.[16] After the initial attack, accompanied by dramatic television footage of American "successes," popular support for military action shot back up 32 points to 79 percent.[17]

The media are such powerful instruments of persuasion that they are kept under tight control in totalitarian states and are carefully manipulated in democratic ones. For example, a primary objective of the Soviet Union in reasserting its power in Lithuania was control of the media. One of the first moves the Soviet Union made was to gain control of the printing presses and broadcast studios. As the *New York Times* expressed it: "Moscow authorities have made broadcasting [and the press] a major battlefield in cracking down on Lithuanian sovereignty."[18] In democracies, every effort is made to gain maximum coverage for a politically significant story or, at other times, to keep that same story from reaching the press. Presidents, executive departments, members of Congress, interest groups, large corporations, and unions all have high-paid public relations people to handle the press.

What accounts for this power of the press that makes everyone so interested in manipulating it? In large part, the power derives from the credibility most of us grant the mass media, especially television. Despite insistent denials, people tend to believe in the truth-telling function of the media. Why?

TRUTH AND OBJECTIVITY

We tend to believe that if someone is reporting the facts as they are, without prejudice or interpretation, then he or she is "objective" and hence telling the

---

[14]Gallup Polls, Oct. 25–26, in *Newsweek*, 5 Nov. 1990: 21.

[15]Tom Morganthau et al., "Should We Fight?" *Newsweek*, 26 Nov. 1990: 26.

[16]The mid-August figure comes from a *New York Times*/CBS News poll reported by Michael Oreskes, "Bush Regains Record Rating in Crisis," *The New York Times*, 22 Aug. 1990: A13, and the mid-January figure is from a poll reported by Michael R. Kagay, "Approval of Bush Soars," *The New York Times*, 19 Jan. 1991: L9.

[17]Kagay, "Approval of Bush Soars": L9.

[18]Francis X. Clines, "Lithuanians, Improvising, Resume TV Broadcasts," *The New York Times*, 19 Jan. 1991: 3.

"truth." And, indeed, this has been a long-time claim of journalists. The claim was probably most clearly articulated by Adolph Ochs, an early owner of the *New York Times*. He said in 1896, "It will be my earnest aim that *The New York Times* . . . give the news impartially, without fear or favor, regardless of any party, sect or interest involved. . . ."[19] Since then, many journalists, not only for the *Times* but for other media organs as well, have laid claim to this standard of objectivity. The problem: How valid is that claim?

For the past 20 or so years, the very possibility of being objective has been called into question. As one scholar noted: "Millions of significant events take place daily, forcing journalists to make choices about . . . specific stories to be published. . . . [These] highly skilled professionals . . . put together an interesting collage of events selected for . . . attractiveness to media audiences. . . ."[20] Clearly, choosing events to report on because of their "attractiveness to audiences" is not the same as giving the "news impartially, without fear or favor." To favor news stories because they arouse and hold the interest of readers and viewers is to practice a form of bias. That is hardly objectivity.

Beyond the problem of choice is the issue of accuracy. It is very often extremely difficult to get down exactly what has happened or been said.[21] Events sometimes happen so quickly and are seen only from one vantage point so that distortion and error are hard to avoid. Sometimes what we hear is so garbled or mumbled that here too it is difficult to be accurate. Accuracy is so difficult a problem that many newspapers have special columns set aside for the public correction of errors that they have previously published. In many journals, these corrections occur in the section devoted to letters to the editor.

Related to the problem of accuracy in conveying an event or statement is the purposeful distortion introduced by a reporter or editor. Such distortion may result from sheer bias or ideological commitment. This sort of reporting usually occurs in a political context. Distortions of this kind are not, however, just errors; they are out-and-out falsehoods, often trading on our belief in the objectivity and truthfulness of the press.

Among the things we are most prone to believe are the photographs of people and events we see on televison and in newspapers. "Photos don't lie," we say. We think the camera shoots only that which is in front of its lens. This fact alone probably accounts for the reason people first gave tabloids—which pioneered photojournalism—and now give TV such great credibility.

But photos can indeed, and sometimes do, lie. They can be manipulated—*doctored* is the term—to show virtually anything that is desired. The photo on page 136 shows Robert Bowen creating a photo of an event that never took place. The photo was produced by computer for *Newsweek*. In the article accompanying

---

[19]Reprinted in Ronald Berkman and Laura W. Kitch, *Politics in the Media Age* (New York: McGraw-Hill, 1986), p. 25.
[20]Doris A. Graber, *Mass Media and American Politics* (Washington, D.C.: CQ Press, 1989), pp. 76–77.
[21]This can sometimes result in some comic contrasts. The February 26, 1990, issue of *The New Republic* reprinted the following headlines: "Barbara Bush backs women's combat role" from the *Miami Herald* of January 17, 1990; and "Barb no Amazon fan. Women not up to combat roles, she feels" from the *New York Daily News* of the same day.

this doctored photo, *Newsweek* tells of some earlier, politically significant instances of doctoring:

> In the 1950s, allies of Sen. Joseph McCarthy doctored a photo to make it seem as if a senator was talking to a communist. In the 1980s, an official White House photo of President Ronald Reagan in the hospital had the intravenous tube cropped out so that the public would not see how sick he was.[22]

One cannot but think of a slight adaptation of a line from George Orwell's *1984*, written in 1948:

> This process of continuous alteration was applied not only to photographs, but also to newspapers, books, periodicals, pamphlets, posters, leaflets, films, sound tracks, cartoons—to every kind of literature or documentation which might conceivably hold any political or ideological significance.[23]

The falsification of facts for political purposes has a very ancient history. And, although the media may not change fact or photo, they often unquestioningly publish those they receive from others. But the media cannot always afford the luxury of absolute devotion to truth and the practice of a rigorous policy of verification. They often have neither time nor people to check the facts given them. Nor dare the media consistently offend powerful politicians. To quote a great French political philosopher: "The avocation of the politician does not always tolerate the utterance of truth."[24]

Well then, if the media do not purposely lie but cannot always be relied on for the truth, how do they perform their function, and what is that function?

THE OPERATION OF THE MEDIA

Almost all the media in the United States have one overriding function or purpose—to make money for their owners. Some small segments of the media serve other purposes, as for example PBS in television and radio, interest group publications, and newsletters or journals of opinion representing specific ideological positions. But the mass media—those which have the greatest impact on the largest number of people—are entirely devoted to earning a profit, as are most other businesses within our system. This central purpose determines the way in which the mass media approach all situations.

The mass media make their money primarily from advertising. They charge advertisers huge sums for space in the *print media*—newspapers and magazines—and for time in the *electronic media*—radio and television. But, before paying these huge sums, advertisers want to know that they will reach enough people to

---

[22]Jonathan Alter, "When Photographs Lie," *Newsweek*, 30 July 1990: 44.
[23]From George Orwell, *Nineteen Eighty-Four: Text, Sources, Criticism*, 2d ed., ed. Irving Howe (New York: Harcourt Brace Jovanovich, 1982), p. 28.
[24]Raymond Aron, *History, Truth, Liberty: Selected Writings*, ed. F. Draus (Chicago: University of Chicago Press, 1985), p. 352.

Robert Bowen puts together a picture on a computer showing a number of different people who would not otherwise appear together.

make the costs worthwhile. Hence, circulation figures for print and listener-viewer ratings for electronic media are extremely important.[25]

To get and hold large numbers of readers, listeners, and viewers, the media offer their audiences a wide mix of subject areas: hard news, such as stories about government, economics, crime, war; soft news or human interest, such as stories about the marital and financial travails of Donald Trump, the New York entrepreneur; sports, fashion, reviews of events in the entertainment industries (film, theatre, music, art, literature, dance, night spots); and political commentary.

These subjects compete with one another for space and time, the two essential components of the media. To keep audience interest high, all the media, whether print or electronic, try for the most dramatic stories and presentations; those that will grab the attention of their audience and at least hold it for a while. In the political arena, this focus on the dramatic tends to get reduced to a set of clichés. As noted by Paletz and Entman: "The locations may change, but the political explanations recur eternally: bureaucratic inefficiency, congressional corruption, the cynical desire by politicians for more power, prestige, votes."[26] What is wrong

---

[25]This is not to suggest that owners and advertisers influence the content of news stories directly. But business's emphasis on the "bottom line" does affect the style of news presentations. And style may affect the way we understand the news.

[26]David L. Paletz and Robert M. Entman, *Media Power Politics* (New York: Free Press, 1981), p. 23

Differences among the media are often more a matter of style than of substance. The **New York Times** *and the* **New York Post** *headline the same event on the same day.*

with the media's approach is that their explanations are extreme oversimplifications of frequently complex situations. At the very moment of speaking the truth, the media often produce falsehoods.

In part, the uniformity of explanation comes about because there is in fact very little competition between media organizations. The *New York Times* and the *New York Post,* for example, have carved out separate niches for themselves in the marketplace of goods and ideas. Each paper has its own distinctive, highly individual verbal style in reporting events while providing essentially the same interpretation for very different readers.

There is a little more competition among the major networks, NBC, CBS, and ABC. But here, competition works to reduce individuality and to enforce a high degree of conformity. As Ben Bagdikian, a veteran media watcher, commented: "There are 1,000 television stations in the country and three national networks, but a person unacquainted with the personalities involved would have trouble distinguishing anything individual about any one station, either in its entertainment, which is literally interchangeable, or in its news. The three networks, it has been observed, are one network in triplicate."[27] To a large extent we can check out Bagdikian's observation ourselves. The evening news programs on the three networks are each a half hour. All three are anchored by men of approximately the same age, general appearance, and personality. An occasional viewer might have the impression that Dan Rather, Tom Brokaw, and Peter Jennings pass among themselves the same trench coat when on foreign assignment. Depending on the breaking stories, each of the networks allot about the same amount of time to national and international news, and recently special features. Local news, weather, national sports, and a smattering of national and international news are usually handled by local affiliates.

SOURCES OF NEWS STORIES

News stories do not just happen. Someone tells the media that some event has or is about to take place. That someone is either outside the media or is inside one of the media organizations. The one inside the media is usually a journalist, generally on a news beat. Another person within the media that might generate stories is an editor. Both of these individuals can determine what will appear in their medium of communication and become part of public discourse.

Gatekeepers: Journalists and Editors.   The reporters and editors who decide on the stories to write up and either print or air are called *gatekeepers*. There are several levels of these people: reporters on the scene who might phone in a story; the rewrite person in the office; a copy editor who checks a story for house style and content; a senior editor who decides if, when, where, and how a story will be played in print or on television. The senior editor may have that as his/her title or may be the managing editor, bureau chief, or executive editor. In television, that senior editor may be the news program's anchor (the newscaster who introduces stories by other reporters, reads some himself or herself, and provides commentary and continuity) or television news executive. These people are called gatekeepers because they control a metaphoric gate through which the news flows to the public. The number of gatekeepers involved in a story varies greatly.

---

[27]Ben H. Bagdikian, *The Media Monopoly,* 3d ed. (Boston: Beacon Press, 1990), p. 132.

Pack Journalism.   Certain beats are regularly covered by large numbers of reporters. Washington news conferences, such as White House press briefings, are prime instances of massive media coverage. Wars, major disasters, elections also draw packs of journalists. The pack usually consists of reporters who know each other well, are accustomed to working together, often rely on each other for additional information or insights, and invariably influence each other's perception of an event. As Berkman and Kitch point out: "The pack regards the same issues, events, and activities as worthy of coverage."[28] This situation lends a striking uniformity to reportage,[29] and that uniformity will generally reinforce the illusion of objectivity and truth in any story "composed" by the pack and written individually by pack members. When all reports agree, we usually consider them highly believable, even if in fact they are totally erroneous.

External Sources.   Although the media generate many stories on their own, they get most news reports from press agents working for government officials or departments. We have already seen this when considering pack journalism. The pack usually gets its information from a government spokesperson (read "press agent")—in case of war, someone from the Department of Defense; if at a summit, either from the White House or the State Department; and so on. Several scholars have shown that 50 to 60 percent of front page news stories in the print media originate with government sources.[30] The study by Iyengar and Kinder showed that lead stories strike readers and viewers as more important than those further back in a newscast or newspaper.[31]

As a rule, journalists depend heavily on their sources for their stories and background information. Indeed news people have a strong symbiotic relationship with their sources. Thus, journalists are not very quick to challenge the information given them by a source, although they will rush to an opposing source for a contrary view on controversial issues. In this way journalists maintain the illusion of objectivity. They also, albeit incidental to their main purpose, perform a public service by providing information to their readers and viewers.

In Conclusion

To govern, officials need to gain the consent of most of those whom they govern. In a democracy, to gain office and hold it, politicians need to gain the approval, that is, the consent, of the majority of those whom they hope to govern. To

---

[28]*Politics in the Media Age*, p. 83.

[29]Uniformity was very much present in the 1990 midterm elections. ABC, CBS, NBC, and CNN used the same voter survey to project election results across the country. So much for the vaunted competition among the media.

[30]Paletz and Entman, *Media Power Politics*, pp. 19–20, and Graber, *Mass Media and American Politics*, p. 79.

[31]*News That Matters*, pp. 42–46.

achieve their ends, politicians and government officials need to learn and manipulate the opinion of the public whose consent they must win. Public opinion is learned from polls or surveys conducted by research organizations. The opinion of the public is manipulated through the mass media.

The power of the media to shape the public's opinion derives from the credibility granted them by most people. The credibility of the media stems largely from a popular belief that news stories are written without bias. In fact, however, there is little basis for this belief. The media are commercial enterprises and therefore write, produce, and publish news stories contrived to gain and hold the largest possible number of readers and viewers. Large numbers lead to large advertising revenues, which end in large profits. The profit motive drives the mass media. But, incidental to gaining a profit, the media also perform a valued service by providing their readers and viewers with information on public issues.

C ★ A ★ S ★ E   S ★ T ★ U ★ D ★ Y

CENSORSHIP AND WAR IN THE PERSIAN GULF

In the first few months of 1991 the issue of censorship and a free press arose once again in the United States. At that time, the United States led United Nations armed forces in a war against Iraq. It also led the press by the nose. As one journalist reported:

> In the days leading up to the ground war, reporters were so frustrated by their lack of access to the battlefield that they jumped at the chance to cover rehearsals for a massive amphibious landing on the Kuwaiti coast. As the exercises carried on, press coverage mounted and anticipation grew. Only one problem: the landing never came. The amphibious assault was a diversionary tactic intended to fool the Iraqis. And the press coverage, as General Norman Schwarzkopf pointedly observed, was a big help."

And Richard Zoglin, the teller of this tale, also pointedly observed that "[t]hroughout the war, the Pentagon did a masterly job of controlling the flow of information."[1] The military's strategists not only trounced the armies of Iraq, they also outmaneuvered the press corp of America.

It may be a source of pride and delight that "know-it-all" journalists were outsmarted by "heroic" generals, but that sort of thing raises serious questions

---

[1] Richard Zoglin, "It Was a Public Relations Rout Too," *Time,* March 11, 1991: 56.

for a democratic society. No national event has greater import than war for any country. In all societies, the sovereign must be fully informed of all circumstances during a war. In democratic societies, the sovereign is the people. Justice Hugo Black of the Supreme Court offered, in the Pentagon Papers case, an excellent explanation of why freedom of the press is critical to democracy even in wartime:

> The press was protected [by the First Amendment] so that it could bear the secrets of government and inform the people. . . . And paramount among the responsibilities of a press is the duty to prevent any part of government from deceiving the people and sending them off to distant lands to die of foreign fevers and foreign shot and shell.''[2]

But, informing the people may increase the dangers suffered by the people. Justice Oliver Wendell Holmes, the great advocate of liberal principles, put the case for wartime censorship: ''When a nation is at war many things that might be said in time of peace are such a hindrance to its effort [to gain victory] that their utterance will not be endured so long as men fight. . . .''[3] It was in this opinion that Holmes articulated the ''clear and present danger'' doctrine used by the American government to censor the press.

For most of American history, the United States government exercised control over the flow of information to the American people, especially during periods of perceived crisis. This began during the Sedition Act of 1798 when the administration of John Adams arrested Antifederalist editors on the grounds that they gave aid and comfort to ''radical'' supporters of the French Revolution. During the Civil War, the Lincoln administration ''took to suspending newspapers that had broken [its] censorship rules, arresting editors . . . and banning correspondence from the front. . . .''[4] This dreary picture continues with depressing variations throughout the rest of American history until the Vietnam War.

VIETNAM: THE MILITARY VERSUS THE PRESS

In the beginning, the usual censorship restrictions were enforced in Vietnam. But this time there was a difference. Because American operations in Vietnam were at first covert, the small group of war correspondents there confronted the stark contrast between the official line that Americans were only ''advisers'' and the reality that many were directly involved in early fighting, particularly as pilots. Journalists reported the early participation of Americans in the war and brought down on themselves the wrath of Vietnamese and American government authorities.

As the war progressed and American involvement increased, newspaper and television correspondents began to report the truth as they saw it, which was

---

[2]*New York Times Co. v. United States,* 403 U.S. 713 (1971).
[3]*Schenck v. United States,* 249 U.S. 47 (1919).
[4]Phillip Knightley, *The First Casualty* (New York: Harcourt Brace Jovanovich, 1975), p. 27

often directly at odds with Pentagon reports. Even before American involvement in the war got underway in earnest, President John F. Kennedy's press secretary Pierre Salinger described news reports from Vietnam as "emotional and inaccurate."[5] Undeterred, war correspondents continued to report the often brutal and unfavorable realities of the Vietnam war vividly and sometimes emotionally. Vietnam was also different from earlier wars in another signal way. It was the first "TV war." For the first time, the horrors of war were presented in "living color" in the parlors and bedrooms of America. TV cameras went everywhere and showed everything, it seemed. The ugliness of war was etched into the American mind by electronic blips on a TV screen.

In the end the White House and the Pentagon felt that the unbridled press that operated even in the face of strict censorship had undermined public confidence in the war and even caused the defeat of American forces. They promised themselves that the strictest press censorship and controls would be imposed in future wars.[6]

THE PERSIAN GULF WAR: THE MILITARY VERSUS THE PRESS

Government censorship of the press during the Persian Gulf War took the form of channeling war correspondents into a "pool" that the Pentagon would strictly control. No longer could correspondents on the front roam from Pentagon-assigned locations. Both electronic and print media journalists objected to the arrangement and some, such as CBS's Bob Simon and his televison crew, "did a unilateral," the term the press used for ignoring pool arrangements, only to find themselves captured by the Iraqis. Correspondents were subject to being treated as prisoners of war by the American military if they disobeyed the rules.

IN DEFENSE OF CENSORSHIP

No one argues about the need for military censorship during wartime, but the nature and degree of restraint on the media is the subject of heated debate. The government, of course, wants unlimited censorship, while the media, understandably, wants fewer restrictions.

The Reagan and Bush administrations imposed a tight military censorship during the Grenada invasion and the Persian Gulf War, respectively. They saw no

---

[5]Ibid., p. 380.
[6]See Malcolm W. Browne, "The Military vs. The Press," *The New York Times Magazine*, March 3, 1991, pp. 27–30, 44–45, for a vivid contrast between the role of the press in Vietnam and in the Persian Gulf War.

need to justify what for them was an obvious requirement for military secrecy. Ironically it was Jody Powell, former President Jimmy Carter's press secretary, who, during the Grenada crisis, forcefully argued for government management of the news.

After commenting on his role in hiding information from the press that in view of the White House would have endangered the American hostages held in Iran during the Carter administration, Powell went on to defend the Pentagon's tight restraints over the press before and during the invasion of Grenada. The press "charged that the [Reagan] administration had repeatedly lied to them on matters that were in no way vital to national security or the protection of lives."[7] While in Powell's opinion some of the White House restrictions on the press during the Grenada operation were unnecessary and unsupportable, "if the government has in this and other instances been guilty of excess in the exercise of what I believe to be its legitimate right to mislead and even deceive on matters of vital import, the fourth estate [the press] has also been guilty of excess in its cavalier insistence on the right to do as it pleases with little regard for good judgment, good taste, or the consequences of its actions—and the American people know it."[8]

The public, whose right to know the press constantly defends, strongly supported restrictions on war correspondents during the Grenada invasion and the Gulf War. Wyoming Senator Alan Simpson represented the views of many Americans when he even went so far as to attack CNN's Peter Arnett for remaining in Baghdad and continuing to report under Iraqi censorship. Simpson charged that Saddam Hussein was using Arnett for his own purposes, to undermine American public opinion in support of the war by allowing Arnett to report only the death and destruction of civilians while censoring any references to military targets.

For his part Arnett was reminded of Vietnam, when he came under attack and was put on a White House enemy's list because of his vivid reporting. During the early stages of the war in the Persian Gulf, his reports challenged White House and Pentagon optimism. Arnett did the best that he could to call his shots as he saw them despite strict Iraqi censorship. For example, Arnett succeeded in pointing up the fact that the hastily manufactured signs surrounding a bomb factory, which the Iraqi's claimed produced baby milk and not chemical weapons, were printed in English and thus were obviously intended as propaganda. Defending his role, Arnett said, "you just report what is going on around you. I said on the air that when you unload enormous amounts of weaponry on a place like this [Baghdad], you are going to hurt civilians. Pretending it's not happening is silly. It's better . . . to learn this stuff up front so that we don't have surprises and start being ashamed later for what we didn't know or didn't want to know at the time."[9]

[7]Jody Powell, *The Other Side of the Story* (New York: William Morrow, 1984), pp. 223–240.
[8]Ibid.
[9]William Prochnau, "If There's A War, He's There," *The New York Times Magazine,* March 3, 1991, p. 34.

THE PENTAGON AND ITS RULES

Predictably, the Pentagon defends its rules limiting media access on the grounds that secrecy is necessary to protect military operations and the lives of troops. Testifying before the Senate Governmental Affairs Committee which held hearings on press censorship during the Persian Gulf War, Pentagon spokesperson Pete Williams defended the pool arrangement that restrained the press. But he also admitted that "he knew of a number of cases in which military officials needlessly delayed for more than a day the transmission of news dispatches that had already been cleared by officers in the field. He also acknowledged that some reporters had been denied interviews because their coverage was regarded as unfavorable by military officials." Williams continued, "we tried to weigh in on those cases. I can't say that military commanders aren't human, but it's certainly not policy, and it's certainly something we discourage."[10]

No one denies the need for military security, and for press censorship during wartime. Clearly information that jeopardizes specific military operations cannot be reported to the American public lest it aid the enemy. However, a far more difficult question arises concerning the public's right to know in a democracy about the causes, consequences, and potential outcomes of war. Government and military deception may be appropriate to avoid jeopardizing specific military operations, but it is unsupportable in a democracy if it is intended to distort the truth so as to gain public support. The government practices military censorship not only to protect the troops and military security, but also to maintain public support. During the Persian Gulf War, White House Press Secretary Marlin Fitzwater acknowledged, "we have a tightrope to walk—between unrealistic public expectations of victory in a matter of days and an anxious skepticism about whether the U.S. is going to win at all." A senior White House official said, "in this video-game war, we have been so successful so far that people may really be shocked if Saddam gets off an Exocet [missile] and sinks one of our ships or pulls some other big surprise."[11]

MEDIA REACTION TO MILITARY CENSORSHIP

Every quarter of the media strongly criticized the Pentagon's pool arrangements during the Persian Gulf War. "One casualty of the Gulf War appears to be the independent itinerant war correspondent," wrote Peter Schmeisser for the *New Republic*. He continued, "The press pool system used in the Gulf encouraged the most docile sort of pack journalism. Only one hundred and sixty reporters were allowed near the front lines, and these had to travel in groups of a half dozen or more, with military public affairs officers close behind. The most gripping reports

---

[10]Richard L. Berke, "Pentagon Defends Coverage Rules, While Admitting to Some Delays," *The New York Times,* February 21, 1991, p. A14.
[11]*Time,* February 4, 1991, p. 18.

came from correspondents who violated ground rules and hitched up with Egyptian or Saudi units, despite the fact that this was overwhelmingly an American operation—and an American victory. As one seasoned journalist put it, throughout the war American correspondents were 'like senior citizens on a package tour.' ''[12]

A seasoned war correspondent agreed, ''we have found ways to see the war. Those of us who made it to the skirmish at Khafji, where a small Iraqi mechanized force briefly occupied Saudi territory, did so as part of a Saudi pool, not an American pool.'' Regardless of tight military censorship, he continued, ''I think [covering the war] is worth the effort. News correspondents have their share of problems reporting this war—problems that seem to evoke little sympathy from some of our countrymen. But aside from the introduction of some spectacular new technology and communication systems, the Gulf War has much in common with earlier conflicts. Americans still need to know what is happening, and it is still the task of the press to maintain the flow of information.''[13]

Speaking for all reporters, Joseph L. Galloway of *U.S. News and World Report* complained about the sacrifice of truth to expediency. ''One of the earliest casualties in America's desert war,'' he wrote, ''was the truth, wounded by an information directorate bent on controlling the words and images that flow from the battlefields. Political managers who seem determined to apply the same spin control to war news that they routinely use on campaign news have, with the acquiescence of a military haunted by Vietnam, clogged a vital artery leading to America's brain.''[14]

In Vietnam, continued Galloway, ''the ground rules totalled only three: Don't compromise operational security. Don't reveal troop movements until they are completed. Don't report actual battle casualties while the battle is continuing. Reporters made their own calls and wrote their own stories.''[15]

Galloway concludes, ''Some two hundred and twenty-eight American or American-employed correspondents have died since 1941 covering America's wars. More than sixty correspondents died covering America's Indochina wars. Asked why he permitted the press to accompany his battalion, and later his brigade into the terrible [Vietnam] battles of 1965 and 1966, then-colonel Hal Moore replied: ''We are an army of free men, defending a nation of free men and women who have a right to know what we are doing in their names.' ''[16]

Undoubtedly the Pentagon-media battle over freedom of information will continue during times of war. The press will never be happy to submit to military censorship; war correspondents will have little choice but to acquiesce during war time to what the military considers best. The public overwhelmingly supports military censorship, and the courts have recognized that prior censorship is con-

---

[12]Peter Schmeisser, ''Shooting Pool,'' *New Republic,* March 18, 1991, p. 21.
[13]Malcolm W. Browne, ''The Military vs. The Press,'' *The New York Times Magazine,* March 3, 1991, p. 45.
[14]Joseph L. Galloway, ''Who's Afraid of the Truth?'', *U.S. News and World Report,* February 4, 1991, p. 49.
[15]Ibid.
[16]Ibid.

ZIPPY "Everybody Outta the Pool" by Bill Griffith

stitutional during wartime. While the public's right to know may have to be deferred over the short term, the media's critical role in reporting the truth over the long term sustains a viable democratic process.

Suggested Readings

Ben Bagdikian, *The Media Monopoly*. Boston: Beacon Press, 1983.

Doris A. Graber, *Mass Media and American Politics*. Washington, D.C.: Congressional Quarterly, 1980.

David Halberstam, *The Powers That Be*. New York: Knopf, 1979.

Richard Joslyn, *Mass Media and Elections*. Reading, Mass.: Addison-Wesley, 1984.

V. O. Key, *Public Opinion and American Democracy*. New York: Knopf, 1961.

Thomas G. Leonard, *The Power of the Press: The Birth of American Political Reporting*. New York: Oxford University Press, 1986.

Walter Lippmann, *Public Opinion*. New York: Free Press, 1965.

James Reston, *Artillery of the Press*. New York: Harper & Row, 1967.

CONGRESS

There is nothing more wonderful or more impressive than a great orator discussing great affairs in a democratic assembly.

Alexis de Tocqueville

The keystone of our democratic structure is Congress. It stands at the center of government and through it flows the authority of the people as a whole. Today, the American Congress is an assembly or gathering of individuals elected directly by the people to represent their collective interests. Jointly with the president, who is elected indirectly, it makes the nation's laws.

Although Congress is the primary legislative body, the president shares this function by proposing legislation in some instances and vetoing laws in others. When a president is especially powerful, as was Franklin D. Roosevelt or Lyndon B. Johnson, he is as much the lawmaker as Congress. To a lesser degree, the courts also share in the legislative function. By interpreting the laws and applying them to particular cases, judges are necessarily "making law" almost as much as is Congress. But Congress is the formal lawmaker in our system.

BACKGROUND

Representative assemblies are very ancient, especially in the Anglo-Saxon tradition. The ancient Germanic tribes that occupied Old England were ruled by a king and council or assembly of notables called the *witenagemot*. The Norman conquerors did away with the Anglo-Saxon council, but found after several hundred years that to tax the people they had to convene an assembly called *parliament*. Slowly the English Parliament claimed the right to petition the king for redress of grievances. Over time, this right to petition the monarchy was extended to the right to present bills or laws for his or her approval. In the seventeenth century, Parliament asserted legislative supremacy, which it has had since.

At the time the Framers of the Constitution met in Philadelphia, Parliament had consisted of two chambers for several hundred years. It had an upper House of Lords and a lower House of Commons. Most of the legislatures in the thirteen American colonies were patterned on Britain's Parliament. It does not require much imagination to see the source of America's bicameral legislature. But it does require an imaginative leap to sympathize with the Framers who were nervously giving birth to a "democratic" regime.

Although the Framers wanted to create a popular government, they were very suspicious of the people. Even James Madison, that strongest advocate of popular government, worried about the fickle emotions of the people. As he expressed it in *The Federalist,* No. 63:

> ... there are particular moments in public affairs when the people, stimulated by some irregular passion, or some illicit advantage, or misled by the artful misrepresentations of interested men, may call for measures which they themselves will afterwards be the most ready to lament and condemn. In these critical moments, how salutary will be the interference of some temperate and respectable body of citizens.... Popular liberty might then have escaped the indelible reproach of decreeing to the same citizens the hemlock on one day and statues on the next.

Madison used this argument to explain why the Senate was necessary as a balance against the "irregular passions" of the House of Representatives, the "popular" branch of government. Others looked upon the Senate as the "aristocratical" branch of government and the House of Representatives as the "democratical" one. Originally, members of the Senate were chosen by state legislatures rather than by the people directly. This indirect mode of election was decided upon because since "... the State legislatures who appoint the senators will in general be composed of the most enlightened and respectable citizens, there is reason to presume that their attention and their votes will be directed to those men who have become the most distinguished by their abilities and virtues," as John Jay expressed it in *The Federalist,* No. 64. In other words, the Senate would be composed of the "best men" in the nation. By contrast, the House of Representatives has been chosen directly by the people from the beginning. Since 1913, the Senate has also been chosen in direct popular elections, which makes Congress the only branch of government that is fully democratic in the sense in which the founders used the word.

CONSTITUTIONAL STRUCTURE OF CONGRESS

Article 1 of the Constitution describes in ten sections the nature, power, requirements, and membership of the Congress. The features of Congress enumerated in the original Constitution have, to some degree, been modified by later amendments. Moreover, Congress's power and authority have remained unsettled since its inception.

THE NATURE AND POWER OF CONGRESS

The first section of Article 1 states that Congress consists of two chambers and is the only lawmaking body in the federal government (see Box 8.1). This seems simple and straightforward enough with respect to the bicameral structure of Congress but is far less simple with regard to its lawmaking function.

Throughout the nineteenth and well into the twentieth century, controversy raged over the extent of congressional power, especially with regard to the exercise of federal authority over the states. In large measure the controversy ended in 1937, when the Supreme Court used the commerce clause of Section 8 to assert that Congress can do virtually anything it wished that was "essential and appropriate to protect . . . commerce from burdens and obstructions"[1] in what is known as the *Jones & Laughlin* decision. After this decision, political factors rather than judicial interpretation determined congressional power. The Bill of Rights has regularly provided the only limitations on congressional authority. Even in this area the Supreme Court has granted wide latitude to Congress, especially in connection with national security laws.

REQUIREMENTS OF MEMBERSHIP IN CONGRESS

Practical politics as well as political theory dictated the bicameral structure of Congress. The Great Compromise at the Philadelphia Convention divided Congress between the Senate, representing state interests, and the House of Representatives, representing the people. While each state has two senators, it has a congressional delegation based on population. The Constitution requires that a census be taken every ten years to indicate population shifts among states. This information is then used to apportion state delegations, which are figured on a percentage of the total number of representatives in the House. However small the population, the Constitution guarantees each state at least one representative.

In addition to determining the number of representatives and senators, the Constitution establishes their qualifications. All members must be citizens and residents of the states they represent. In the case of the House of Representatives, however, members do not have to live in the districts they represent. House members must be at least twenty-five years old and citizens for at least six years prior to election. Senators, on the other hand, must be no less than thirty years

---

[1]Chief Justice Charles Evans Hughes writing for the majority of the Supreme Court in *National Labor Relations Board v. Jones & Laughlin Steel Corp.*, 301 U.S. 37 (1937).

BOX 8.1 Powers Granted Congress by the Constitution

IN ARTICLE I

From Section 1:

Congress has the sole power to make laws.

From Section 2:

The House of Representatives has the sole power of impeachment.

From Section 3:

The Senate has the sole power to try impeachments.

From Section 7:

All taxes or other revenue bills start in the House.
Both chambers of Congress can jointly override the president's veto by a two-thirds majority.

From Section 8, Congress has the power to:

pass taxes; provide for national defense and the general welfare.
borrow money.
regulate commerce between the states and with foreign nations.
set naturalization requirements and make bankruptcy laws.
coin money, punish counterfeiting, and establish the post office.
provide copyright and patent protection.
establish federal courts below the Supreme Court.
define and punish piracy and offenses against international law.
declare war.
raise, support, and regulate an army and navy.
call up state militias, suppress rebellions, and repel invasions.
govern the District of Columbia and the national capital.
make all laws which are "necessary and proper" to function.

IN ARTICLE II

From Section 2:

The Senate shall give the president advice and consent on treaties and appointments of ambassadors, consuls, justices of the Supreme Court, and lower-level judges of the federal courts.
Congress can by law delegate authority to make lower-level appointments to the president, to the courts, and to department heads.

IN ARTICLE IV

From Section 3:

Congress can admit new states into the union and can regulate or dispose of all federal territories and properties.

IN ARTICLE V

Two-thirds of both houses of Congress can propose amendments to the Constitution.

of age and citizens for a minimum of nine years. Each chamber is the sole judge of the qualifications of its members.

DISTRIBUTION OF POWER WITHIN CONGRESS

The Constitution says very little about the parceling out of power within each congressional chamber. It does, however, provide for the Speaker of the House of Representatives to be chosen by a majority of that body. As a result of this constitutional provision, the Speaker is one of the most powerful elected officials in the federal government. The Speaker decides who will speak from the floor and who will not; he, or she perhaps sometime in the future, also chooses the committees that consider new laws (which can thus receive a friendly hearing or a hostile one); and he assigns members to special committees. Informally, the Speaker has a major voice in the selection of committee chairmen and in the choice of the bills that come to the floor for a vote.

Although he has no vote except in a tie, the vice president of the United States is designated by the Constitution as President of the Senate. In the absence of the vice president, the Constitution provides that the Senate choose a president *pro tempore* (Latin meaning "for the time being," and often shortened to *pro tem*). By custom the president pro tem is elected by the majority party from among its senior members. He (or possibly she) then usually appoints an acting president pro tem on a rotating basis to chair the Senate.

THE POLITICAL ENVIRONMENT OF CONGRESS

As the founders intended, Congress reflects the political interests of the broader society. In addition to making for a good deal of conflict, this also makes for a high degree of inefficiency. TV newsman David Brinkley has observed that it takes hours to make instant coffee on Capitol Hill. However, that very inefficiency may be the greatest safeguard against tyranny that we have. Fascism has been characterized by its extreme efficiency and its ability to make the trains run on time. Our democratic system has stumbled along for over 200 years enlarging the scope and range of human rights and freedoms. Inefficiency has its virtues.

The broader society brings to bear a wide variety of pressures on Congress through a number of agencies, chief among which is the presidency.

PRESIDENTIAL DEMANDS

Both the Constitution and politics make the president a major force in the legislative process. His veto can be overridden only by a two-thirds vote of both the House and Senate, which is extremely difficult to muster. This fact by itself gives the president a great deal of power in the lawmaking process. Moreover, his proposals are at the top of the legislative agenda and, with the support of his party leadership in Congress, are generally pushed toward adoption. In the twentieth century, several presidents have been very effective in getting their legislative programs through Congress. Because they have dominated their legislative opponents, these chief executives are thought to have created what is called the imperial presidency. But even with nonimperial presidents, Congress must consider their wishes when putting together a bill.

INFORMAL DEMANDS

While presidents have formal input in the legislative process, other forces affect legislation informally. Although political parties are weak and decentralized, the majority of party members in Congress still vote the party line most of the time. Interest groups also put pressure on Congress, usually working closely with the committees that deal with their concerns. This generally gives the interests considerable influence on congressional actions. While we expect the demands made by their electoral constituencies to have the most influence on members of Congress, this is often not the case.

No two of the 435 House electoral districts are alike, which of course tends to diffuse electoral pressures in most instances. Even within each district there are usually different economic, political, social, and demographic forces at play. If they wish to be returned to office, representatives must take these forces into account. This is not always an easy task. There are often as many different and conflicting interests within a district as outside it. Moreover, there is quite a bit of apathy within the voting populations of most districts. The voter turnout in most congressional elections is considerably less than 50 percent of eligible voters, and in many districts voters do not even know the name of their representative. All of these factors give members of Congress a good deal of latitude in their legislative behavior. Therefore, senators and representatives are not simply rubber stamps for their constituents. As a rule, constituent demands are so diffuse and unclear that Congress has a good deal of legislative independence.

No discussion of the political environment of Congress would be complete without a discussion of the influence of Congress on itself. Congress as an institution shapes the behavior of its members perhaps more than any other single factor. Every organization develops norms that affect its members, and Congress is no exception. Members spend as much time within Capitol Hill as outside it. This is their world, and if they are to be effective within it they must respect and follow established ways of doing things.

FUNCTIONS OF CONGRESS

Congress has two primary functions, to represent the will of the voters and to make the laws of the nation. As it happens, these are interlocking responsibilities. Ideally, either the laws reflect the desires and interests of the people or the lawmakers face rejection in the next election. In point of fact, as we have noted several times, the people are rarely if ever united in their "desires and interests." For this reason, the laws of the nation more often than not reflect the interests of highly articulate and politically active minorities.

Whatever interests a law may reflect, it is always applicable to an entire class of actions and individuals. For example, the Civil Rights Act of 1964 prohibits discrimination on the basis of race, religion, or national origin by places of public accommodation. That means that restaurants and hotels, for example, cannot refuse service to an African-American, a Moslem, or a Korean. In other words, laws are rules of conduct that have the force of commands and apply to everyone engaged in that conduct.

Congress enacts several types of laws in response to different political needs. It passes a wide variety of legislation for taxes, such as income and excise taxes. It also appropriates funds for government agencies and departments, such as the State Department. Congress also grants subsidies for various parts of the American economy such as agriculture, and enacts regulations such as those covering safety and health in industry. It also establishes government departments and agencies such as the Environmental Protection Agency. Each of these legislative actions, as well as a number of others, is directed at meeting the requirements of government and the larger society. Congress's ability to make laws that apply to the nation as a whole constitutes its ability to set national policies.

The need for continuity in policy-making as well as conflicting political pressures have led Congress over the years to delegate substantial lawmaking authority to the bureaucracy. Many legislators think of executive agencies as creatures of Congress. Since laws are necessarily generalized, the agencies are expected to fill in the details as they implement congressional policies. Of course, there are times when executive departments and agencies attempt to frustrate the intent of Congress instead of carrying out its policy.

To assure that executive agencies act according to their legislative mandates, congressional committees periodically conduct oversight hearings. Since the Leg-

"These S&L lobbyists do such a great job of welcoming us back to Washington!"

© 1990 BRUCE BEATTIE, DAYTONA BEACH NEWS JOURNAL.

islative Reorganization Act of 1946, Congress has assumed oversight responsibilities because the executive has its own priorities and they do not always accord with those of the legislature. Agencies and departments, such as the Central Intelligence Agency, must report on a more or less regular basis to the legislative committees and subcommittees that have jurisdiction over them. Often there is cooperation and accommodation between agency and committee, but sometimes there is considerable friction.

Often, as a means of assisting them in fashioning laws, congressional committees hold hearings or conduct investigations. In recent years several such investigations have been conducted regarding possible violations of law by Reagan administration officials. One of the most prolonged and frustrating has been the congressional hearings into charges of unethical and illegal behavior in the Department of Housing and Urban Development (HUD). Jack Kemp, Bush's Secretary of the Department of Housing and Urban Development, estimated that more than $2 billion had been lost due to fraud and mismanagement at HUD during the Reagan years. A program designed to provide housing for the poor was apparently used to pay off wealthy contributors to the Republican party. Although many fingers pointed at Reagan's Secretary of HUD, Samuel Pierce, Congress has not succeeded as of this writing in getting him to answer the charges that have been made against him.

To get witnesses to testify, Congress may grant them limited immunity. In all investigations, congressional committees must follow due process requirements, especially if testimony might be self-incriminating. Thus, a witness may be accompanied by a lawyer, may invoke the Fifth Amendment's protection against self-incrimination, and, if granted immunity, may not have testimony used as evidence against him- or herself in a later trial.

As part of their function as representatives of the people, all members of Congress try to resolve citizen complaints or difficulties with government. Each congressional office, in Washington as well as at the district and state levels, has staff people to deal with constituents' problems. In a sense, members of Congress function as ombudsmen for the nation. They intervene on behalf of citizens in their relations with a frequently insensitive government bureaucracy.

ESSENTIALS OF CONGRESS

Every organization both shapes and is shaped by the goals of its members. Congress is no different. Congressional scholar Richard Fenno has discussed three basic goals of all members of Congress.[2] These are:

- reelection
- power and influence within Congress itself
- good public policy

---

[2]Richard F. Fenno, Jr., *Congressmen in Committees* (Boston: Little, Brown, 1973).

In one way or another, these objectives influence all or most actions by individual senators and representatives.

One of their primary goals is assignment to a committee that will enhance a congressperson's chances of reelection. For example, representatives from farming districts will try to get seats on agricultural committees and subcommittees so that they can protect their constituents' economic interests. Others from urban areas seek assignments to committees on banking, housing, welfare, and the like for the same reasons.

One of the prime reasons for getting on a committee that is important to constituents is to enable members to claim credit for the benefits that may flow to the district from government action. Given the high level of political indifference and lack of ideological unity in most districts, congressmen and women often take middle-of-the-road positions rather than extreme ones. In that way, they hope to offend the least number of voters and hold their seats in the next election. Of course, all this effort would be for nought if the member's constituents were not aware of all the good they are getting from the congressperson's presence in the legislature. The principal means for accomplishing this is the periodic newsletter sent by almost all members of Congress to their constituents (see Box 8.2).

The ability to accomplish something is power, and politics is a power game. Like all politicians, congressmen and women strive for power within their arena, which is Capitol Hill. Power provides its own satisfactions, but it also strengthens the chances for reelection and thus increased influence and power. In other words, power tends to be circular, building on itself. The most powerful members of the

BOX 8.2 Informing One's Constituents

letter to new york ————————————————

Daniel Patrick
Moynihan

United States Senator from New York

Pindars Corners
November 25, 1987

Dear New Yorker,

Last Friday afternoon, November 20, in time for the evening news and ahead of a midnight deadline, the White House announced agreement on a two-year deficit-reduction plan; $30 billion to be cut from this year's deficit; $46 billion from next year's (technically fiscal years). The agreement was the result of a month of tortured negotiations that began after the stock market fell 508 points on Black Monday.

Nobody cheered. Democratic Senators gathered in the Lyndon B. Johnson room to go over the spare details. Some are hokey. $4.5 billion to be gained by improved "IRS compliance," which is to say tougher tax collection. Some are real. Defense spending down $13 billion; non-defense $6 billion.

But again, nobody cheered. In his Saturday radio talk President Reagan, who announced the agreement in the company of Congressional leaders, said it was "probably not the very best deal that could have been struck." Speaker Wright allowed as how there had been a shortage of heroes.

This is not going to be an account of this particular deficit package. Rather, I wonder if you would join me on an afternoon walk around this general subject. Like the fields here in the hollow, the budget landscape is especially clear just now. But winter is coming. We will be forced to remember what we can now actually see.

If not the best companion for this ramble, I am not the worst. I am chairman of the Subcommittee on Social Security of the Finance Committee, and of the Subcommittee on Water Resources, Transportation, and Infrastructure of the Committee on Environment and Public Works. One-third of the budget of the government of the United States goes through these two committees. It is my job down there to know where the money comes from and where it goes and why.

I hope we can get a fix on this subject. If we don't, we are going to be distracted for the rest of the century as one "crisis" follows another.

TWO PROPOSITIONS ARE KEY:
    FIRST, SOCIAL SECURITY IS FINE. IT IS NOT BROKE
      AND IT DOES NOT NEED FIXING.
      IT ASKS ONLY TO BE LEFT ALONE!

Bob Dole of Kansas, Republican Leader of the Senate, has a standard stump speech as he campaigns for his party's nomination for President. It is about Making A Difference. It starts with an account of how in twelve days in January 1983, a small group of us reached agreement on changes in the Social Security system that left it solid, solvent, secure for a half a century to come. Journalists who have been with him on the campaign trail report that he always begins at the beginning, recounting how I came over to him on the Senate floor on the morning of January 3 and said let's do it.

Social Security is vitally important to large numbers of elderly New Yorkers, many of whom vote regularly. Senator Moynihan is pointing out how instrumental he was in saving the system.

Senate and House are those with the greatest longevity. It is usually they who acquire the emblems of power—chairmanships of prestigious committees, leadership positions in their respective chambers, or seats on the most important policy-making committees—and use them to strengthen their chances for reelection even more.

Power is desired not only for its own sake or for its own perpetuation, it is also desired for what it can achieve. "Satisfy the pork-barrel needs of your constituents and you will be returned to office" might be one congressional maxim. But "Get returned to office enough times and you stand a good chance of moving policy in the direction you want" may certainly be another. Another way of saying the same thing might be "Power derived from satisfied constituents can eventually be used to do what the power holder thinks is good for the nation."

Most people first enter politics from idealistic motives. In the scramble for power, some may lose their first bloom of innocence (they may discover that pacts with the devil must be made daily if they are to be effective representatives), but may retain some desire to do what they believe is best for the nation within the realm of the possible. Once secure in their position, tough-minded senators and representatives can turn their attention to affecting public policy. At this point, they may give up powerful positions on high-status committees to take positions on policy-making ones. For example, Senator Edward Kennedy of Massachusetts gave up his claim to the chairmanship of the prominent Judiciary Committee to chair the Human Resources Committee where he can influence policy affecting the poor, elderly, sick, and others in need of government assistance. From this position, for example, he can try to promote a program of national health insurance for all Americans, a major interest of his. Members of Congress can, of course, pursue policy objectives from any level, not just the senior ones.

From what has just been said, you can clearly see that the work of Congress is done in committees.

COMMITTEE ORGANIZATION

All legislative bodies create committees to do their basic work. Even the Continental Congress created a committee of five to write the Declaration of Independence. Jefferson, Adams, Franklin, and the others were appointed by the entire Congress. The process is much different today. As Figures 8.1A and 8.1B indicate, members request assignment and are appointed to one or more of the full committees by the selection committees of their respective parties.

Full Committees.   Today, Congress has about thirty-seven permanent committees (see Figure 8.2), which are called *standing committees* because they "stand" or continue from one session of Congress to the next. The House Ways and Means Committee, for example, has "stood" since 1795 and the Senate Finance Committee since 1816. *Joint committees,* consisting of both senators and representatives, are usually created for special purposes, as with the joint committee investigating the Iran-contra affair. Some joint committees are temporary, as was the case in the Iran-contra matter, and others are virtually permanent, as is the Joint Economic Committee, which was created in 1946. A *conference committee*

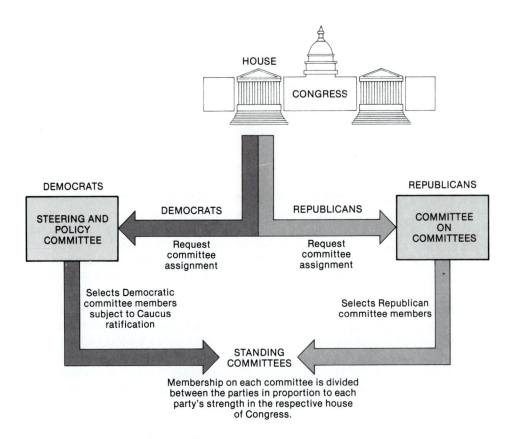

FIGURE 8.1A   COMMITTEE SELECTION: HOUSE OF REPRESENTATIVES

is a temporary joint committee to resolve differences between the Senate and House on a piece of legislation.

Subcommittees.   Because of their heavy legislative schedules, the committees have created subcommittees that number in the hundreds. House subcommittees and their chairs have greater independence than their counterparts in the Senate. The full membership of parent committees, however, has the authority to abolish or change the subcommittees. In the Senate, this authority, albeit informal, is possessed solely by the chairs of standing committees.

Select and Special Committees.   These committees are established to deal with particular tasks. In some instances, their creation is temporary, in others seemingly permanent. For example, the House has a Permanent Select Committee on Intelligence. The House Select Committee on Aging and the Senate Select Committee on Ethics are also long-lasting committees.

   The Speaker appoints the members of the select committees of the House. In the Senate the same task is performed by the majority leader after consulting informally with appropriate colleagues. As with other congressional committees,

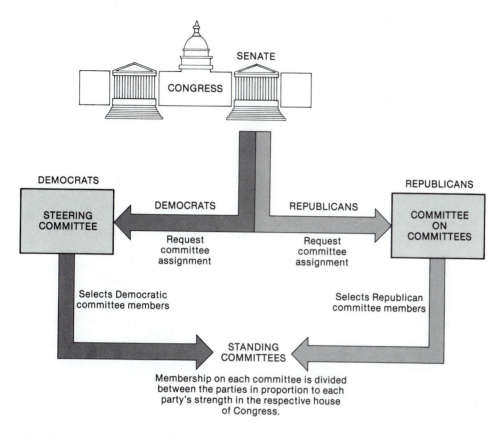

FIGURE 8.1B   COMMITTEE SELECTION: SENATE

membership on a select committee can enhance one's position of power. Former Senator Howard Baker, for example, was so effective on the Senate Select Committee on Presidential Campaign Activities that he first became Republican minority leader, then majority leader, and later an oft-mentioned presidential possibility.

Committee Functions.   Committees perform some vitally important legislative functions. Both houses of Congress have appropriations committees that, following broad outlines drawn by the budget committees of both chambers, actually write funding bills for government operations and programs. The House Ways and Means Committee originates tax legislation that pays for the appropriations that Congress had approved. Funding for congressional operations—cost of offices, staffs, travel, maintenance, and so on—is authorized by the House and Senate administration committees. Other than these committees devoted to what may be thought of as housekeeping functions, congressional committees perform policy, investigative, oversight, and legislative functions in their special domains, such as agriculture or armed services. For a list of the different committees, see Figure 8.2.

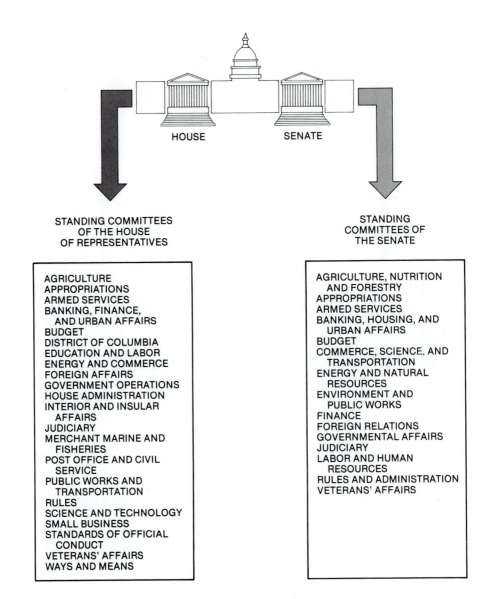

FIGURE 8.2   STANDING COMMITTEES OF CONGRESS

CONGRESSIONAL PARTIES

Although it has become traditional to bewail the decline of parties, party organization still performs vital functions in Congress, as can be seen in Figures 8.3A and 8.3B representing the current legislative term. True, committees, staff members, state delegations, interest groups, and constituents may influence a congressperson's behavior more than party affiliation, but his or her effectiveness is most likely to be affected by party connections.

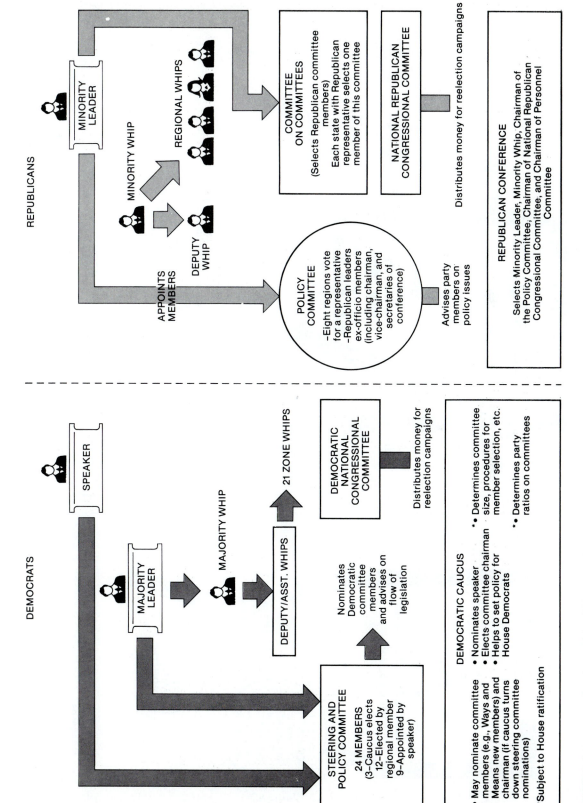

REPUBLICANS

MINORITY LEADER

MINORITY WHIP

REGIONAL WHIPS

DEPUTY WHIP

APPOINTS MEMBERS

COMMITTEE ON COMMITTEES
(Selects Republican committee members)
Each state with Republican representative selects one member of this committee

NATIONAL REPUBLICAN CONGRESSIONAL COMMITTEE

Distributes money for reelection campaigns

POLICY COMMITTEE
-Eight regions vote for a representative
-Republican leaders ex-officio members (including chairman, vice-chairman, and secretaries of conference)

Advises party members on policy issues

REPUBLICAN CONFERENCE
Selects Minority Leader, Minority Whip, Chairman of the Policy Committee, Chairman of National Republican Congressional Committee, and Chairman of Personnel Committee

DEMOCRATS

SPEAKER

MAJORITY LEADER

MAJORITY WHIP

DEPUTY/ASST. WHIPS

21 ZONE WHIPS

DEMOCRATIC NATIONAL CONGRESSIONAL COMMITTEE

Distributes money for reelection campaigns

Nominates Democratic committee members and advises on flow of legislation

STEERING AND POLICY COMMITTEE
24 MEMBERS
(3–Caucus elects
12–Elected by regional member
9–Appointed by speaker)

• May nominate committee members (e.g., Ways and Means new members) and chairman (if caucus turns down steering committee nominations)
*Subject to House ratification

DEMOCRATIC CAUCUS
• Nominates speaker
• Elects committee chairman
• Helps to set policy for House Democrats

• Determines committee size, procedures for member selection, etc.
• Determines party ratios on committees

FIGURE 8.3A HOUSE OF REPRESENTATIVES

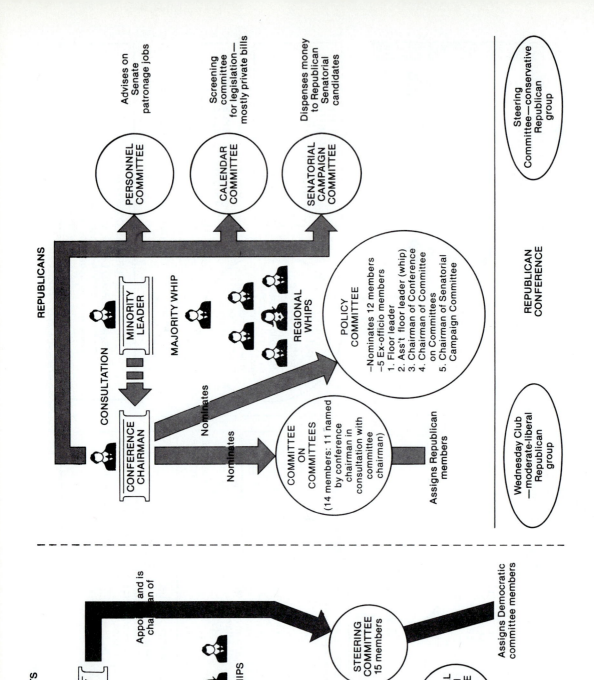

DEMOCRATS

MAJORITY LEADER

Appoi... and is
cha... an of

Appoi... and is
cha... an of

WHIP

REGIONAL WHIPS

STEERING
COMMITTEE
15 members

Assigns Democratic
committee members

-POLICY*
COMMITTEE
(7 members)
-LEGISLATIVE
REVIEW
COMMITTEE
(4 members
also whips)

COMBINED

SENATORIAL
CAMPAIGN
COMMITTEE

*Reviews legislative
proposals and agenda
for the party.

REPUBLICANS

Advises on
Senate
patronage jobs

PERSONNEL
COMMITTEE

Screening
committee
for legislation—
mostly private bills

CALENDAR
COMMITTEE

Dispenses money
to Republican Senatorial
candidates

SENATORIAL
CAMPAIGN
COMMITTEE

MINORITY
LEADER

MAJORITY WHIP

REGIONAL
WHIPS

CONSULTATION

CONFERENCE
CHAIRMAN

Nominates

Nominates

POLICY
COMMITTEE
–Nominates 12 members
–5 Ex-officio members
1. Floor leader
2. Ass't floor leader (whip)
3. Chairman of Conference
4. Chairman of Committee
   on Committees
5. Chairman of Senatorial
   Campaign Committee

COMMITTEE
ON
COMMITTEES
(14 members: 11 named
by conference
chairman in
consultation with
committee
chairman)

Assigns Republican
members

Steering
Committee—conservative
Republican group

REPUBLICAN
CONFERENCE

Wednesday Club
—moderate-liberal
Republican group

FIGURE 6.3B THE SENATE

Leadership.   Majority and minority leaders are elected by their respective party organizations. In the House the Speaker is elected by the majority party and is the party chieftain in that chamber. His constitutional and party roles reinforce one another and give him a firm base from which to exercise a great deal of power. Below the Speaker is the majority leader, who together with several levels of "whips" (an appropriate metaphor) rounds up votes for the party line, especially on heated partisan issues. The minority party in the House has a parallel structure starting with the minority leader. For a graphic depiction of party hierarchies in the House, see Figure 8.3A.

The Senate has a somewhat similar party structure, except that the constitutionally designated presiding officer is politically unimportant. In this chamber the top people are the majority and minority leaders. Jointly, they schedule the bills that come to the floor and the debates that take place. Highly skilled majority leaders with dominating personalities, such as Lyndon B. Johnson, can have enormous influence on the Senate. Otherwise, Senate leaders are much less powerful than their House counterparts. See Figure 8.3B for a graphic picture of the Senate structure.

Party Committees.   An important part of the hierarchical structure of the congressional parties is the cluster of committees that perform the screening, selecting, and funding operations necessary to effective management of party goals. At the top of the ladder are the steering committees that select or assign party members to the committees in the respective chambers. The House Democrats call theirs the Steering and Policy Committee, while the Republicans call theirs the Committee on Committees. The Senate Republicans have kept the same title for their steering committee, while the Democrats call theirs simply the Steering Committee.

Below the steering committees are the policy committees for each party, although the House Democrats have joined their steering and policy functions in one committee. Policy committees try to develop coherent stands on public issues that party members could subscribe to and thus vote as a cohesive group. So far they have had only moderate success. Below these are the campaign committees created to help finance the reelection efforts of party members. These committees are independent of the party's national committees and have a marked influence on the funding decisions of associated PACs.

The Party Line Vote.   One of the prime purposes of the complex apparatus we just examined is to assure adherence to the party line. The party line may be defined as the policy stance that the party has taken on a public issue. Although party discipline may be weak, Table 8.1 indicates that the vast majority of party members hew to the line when their leaders take a clear stand.

When party members do not vote a straight line, we must look to other factors influencing behavior. There are a number of formal and informal groups within Congress that may affect a member's actions. As members go about their business, they may be swayed by members of their staffs, their state delegations, colleagues, and ideological groups. Congresspersons are heavily dependent on staffers for information and assistance, and thus are very vulnerable to staff influence. In the

Table 8.1   Party Unity History

Composite party unity scores for Democrats and Republicans in recent years. The composite is the total number of votes cast by Democrats and Republicans in support of their party divided by the total number of votes cast by members of that party. It shows the percentage of Democrats and Republicans voting with their party on the average party unity vote.

Year	Democrats	Republicans
1989	81%	73%
1988	79	73
1987	81	74
1986	78	71
1985	79	75
1984	74	72
1983	76	74
1982	72	71
1981	69	76
1980	68	70
1979	69	72
1978	64	67
1977	67	70
1976	65	66
1975	69	70
1974	63	62
1973	68	68
1972	57	64
1971	62	66
1970	57	59
1969	62	62
1968	57	63
1967	66	71
1966	61	67
1965	69	70
1964	67	69
1963	71	72
1962	69	68
1961	71	72
1960	64	68

SOURCE For 1960–87, *Congressional Quarterly Weekly Report*, 16 January 1988, p. 104; for 1988 and 1989, *Congressional Almanac 1989*, vol. XLV (Washington, D.C.: Congressional Quarterly Inc., 1990), p. 32B.

House, state delegations can have a profound influence on a member's behavior. The mutual interests of state delegates may pull a member away from his or her party's line—split loyalties are common. Colleagues, especially those who serve on the committee concerned with the issue up for a vote, may have a significant effect on a member's decision. Finally, membership in an ideological group or "caucus" may also affect a member's vote.

THE ENACTMENT OF A BILL INTO LAW

Members of Congress introduce thousands of bills in each session of the legislature. Yet the number of bills that become law is very small. Only after going through a complex legislative process can a bill become law (see Figure 8.4). A *bill* is a proposed piece of legislation that does not become law until it has traveled through the maze depicted in Figure 8.4. There are several types of proposed laws that work their way through the complex.

Bills and Resolutions.   The two principal types of congressional proposals are bills and resolutions. A *resolution* is a statement by one or both houses of Congress that has the force of law only when it has gone through a process similar to that of a bill and been signed by the president. There are several kinds of resolutions, just as there are several kinds of bills.

Bills fall principally into two broad categories: public and private bills. *Public bills* are those that affect the community as a whole, such as those dealing with Medicare, welfare, voting, and the like. Within this category, taxing and spending bills are treated separately from ordinary legislation. Tax bills, which are often called *revenue bills,* start in the House Ways and Means Committee, as the Constitution requires. Spending bills also start in the House, but by custom rather than by constitutional requirement. These bills are officially known as *appropriations* and go through the committee of the same name. Bills coming from the Ways and Means and the Appropriations committees are the only ones that may bypass the House Rules Committee and go straight to the floor for a vote.

Private bills are those that affect only the persons named in them. For example, a private bill may suspend immigration rules to permit a person who would otherwise not be allowed entry to come into the country, perhaps to be reunited with family or receive special medical treatment. Private bills are also used sometimes to redress individual grievances without changing existing law.

There are primarily three kinds of resolutions: simple, concurrent, and joint. *Simple resolutions* deal mainly with what might be called the housekeeping chores of the chamber in which they originate, such as changing the rules of debate or rearranging parking privileges. These resolutions affect only the members of the house involved and are not enacted into laws. Neither are the *concurrent resolutions,* which are generally used for such purposes as setting the time for adjournment or expressing the sense of Congress on some domestic or foreign policy issue. *Joint resolutions* are essentially like bills and become laws on the signature of the president. These are usually undertaken to meet some pressing need. The most frequent need in recent years has been for money to keep the government running at the end of the fiscal year, which has been provided by *continuing resolutions,* a species of joint resolution.

Introduction of Bills.   For a bill to be considered, it has first to be proposed, or "introduced," by a legislator or group of legislators. In the House, this can be simply done by placing the bill in a box popularly called a "hopper" or handing it to the Clerk of the House. In the Senate, the sponsor of a bill has to introduce it orally from the floor. From that point on the bill is in the hand of the Speaker of the House or the Majority Leader of the Senate.

This diagram shows the most typical way in which proposed legislation is enacted into law. There are more complicated, as well as simpler, routes, and most bills never become law. The process is illustrated with two hypothetical bills, House bill No. 1 (HR 1) and Senate bill No. 2 (S 2). Bills must be passed by both houses in identical form before they can be sent to the president. The path of HR 1 is traced by a solid line, that of S 2 by a broken line. In practice most bills begin as similar proposals in both houses.

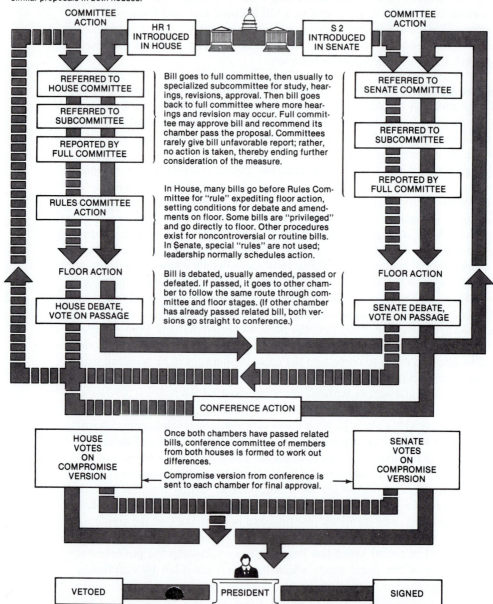

FIGURE 8.4   HOW A BILL BECOMES LAW

SOURCE: *Guide to Congress,* 3rd ed. (Washington, D.C.: Congressional Quarterly, 1982), p. 413. Reprinted with permission of Congressional Quarterly, Inc.

Referral to Committees.   After consulting their parliamentarians and other colleagues, the Speaker and Majority Leader each refer bills to the appropriate committees. For example, a bill dealing with a retirement issue might go to the House Committee on Education and Labor and to the Senate Committee on Labor and Human Resources. In some instances, bills come down the pike that could reasonably go to more than one committee. For example, an authorization for the development of new weapon systems might be referred to the Senate Armed Services Committee, but because it also involves costs, it might be assigned to the Appropriations Committee as well. This sometimes leads to jurisdictional disputes.

The Role of Committees.   When a bill has been referred to a committee, it can move in a number of directions. The committee chairman decides whether to pigeonhole the bill (that is, drop it in the wastebasket), refer it to a subcommittee, or have it studied by the full committee. Whether it is taken on by the full committee or a subcommittee, hearings are then scheduled. At the hearings, members examine expert witnesses, supporters of the bill, and its opponents to learn all views. Most hearings are open to the public, but some, such as those dealing with sensitive intelligence matters, are closed. After the hearings, the committee will modify or amend the bill—"mark it up," as the saying is—and vote on it. Committee members will then write a favorable or unfavorable report. If the committee's sense of the bill is unanimously negative, it may die then and there.

If the report is favorable, the bill is then sent on to the full House or Senate with the committee's recommendations. The committee report is very important because it expresses and explains the legislative intent behind the bill. It serves as a guide to the floor debate and, if made law, to later implementation. Courts also often refer to committee reports as they attempt to determine legislative intent in controversial cases arising from the law.

Most reported bills in the House go to the Rules Committee for hearings and decisions on how the floor debate will be conducted. In the Senate, reported bills go directly to the Majority Leader who, in consultation with the Minority Leader, schedules them for action on the floor.

Legislative Calendars.   When a bill is reported out to the full chamber, it is then put on a *calendar* or schedule for consideration on the floor. The Senate and House have different scheduling systems. The House uses a fairly elaborate system of five calendars, whereas the Senate has two.

IN THE HOUSE

Union Calendar: Money bills, such as taxes and appropriations.

House Calendar: Nonmoney bills, such as voting rights.

Private Calendar: Private bills, such as paying compensation to a particular individual for an injury caused by the government.

Consent Calendar: Noncontroversial bills, which are considered if there are no objections; if there are three objections, then the bill is rescheduled on another calendar.

Discharge Calendar: Discharge petitions requesting that a bill be sent down from a committee and placed on a calendar; requires approval of a majority of the full House.

IN THE SENATE

Executive Calendar: Treaties; presidential nominations, such as to the cabinet or judiciary.

Calendar of Business: All bills reported from committees.

After a bill has been put on the calendar, it goes to the floor.

Floor Action.   By the time a bill reaches the floor of the House or Senate, the real work has been done on it. Congressional leaders rarely bring bills to the floor unless they believe there is adequate support for them. In amost every case, committee approval must precede floor action.

Bills that have no opposition when they come to the floor are dealt with quickly. Others are acted upon by the House sitting as a Committee of the Whole, which needs only 100 members present to conduct business. Business is limited to debating bills. Each speaker is usually allowed only five minutes during the debates. Voting is done by the full House. In contrast to the Committee of the Whole, the full House requires at least 218 members to be present before it can do business, such as debate bills or vote on them. Generally, the House approves the bill favored by the sponsoring committee.

Smooth passage on the floor, however, is not an absolute certainty. Members have, through increasingly sophisticated parliamentary maneuvers on the floor, chipped away at the powers of committees and leaders. Although the rules of debate in the House generally do not permit irrelevant amendments called *riders*

to be attached to bills, members have managed to evade that restriction. If they can get two-thirds of the members present to suspend the rules, they can attach favorite riders. The idea is to attach an amendment that stands little chance of passage to a bill that has strong support and is likely to be signed by the president.

Floor action in the Senate is much simpler than in the House. There are many fewer rules restricting debate and it is much easier to attach riders to popular bills. If a bill is bottled up in committee, senators can attach it to another bill, however unrelated, and get it passed as an amendment. In 1960, while Lyndon B. Johnson was still Majority Leader of the Senate, for example, he pushed through the Civil Rights Act of that year by attaching it as a rider to a minor bill. Although the act had strong opposition in committee, Johnson was able to garner enough support on the floor for passage.

Resolving House-Senate Differences.   Legislation passed by the House and Senate usually have significant differences that must be ironed out before a bill can go to the president for signature. After consulting the chairmen of the sponsoring committees, the Speaker of the House and the majority leader of the Senate appoint members to a conference committee. *Conference committees* are joint committees that meet to adjust House-Senate differences and reach agreement on a version acceptable to both chambers.

Conferences are not always necessary. Many laws are passed when the first chamber in which a bill originates accepts the changes made by the second chamber. Sometimes the leaders of the Senate or House or both oppose the legislation and thus delay the appointment of members for the conference. In other instances, the legislative schedule is so tight that appropriate members are not free to meet in time-consuming conferences. At any rate, if the appointment of a conference committee is delayed beyond the end of a congressional session, the bill is in effect dead. It has to go through the entire process once more—from introduction to joint conference—in the next congressional session, just as if it were a new bill.

On the other hand, if a conference committee is appointed, the process of reconciling the different versions may bring about major changes in the bill. Sometimes the differences are irreconcilable. In that event the bill dies in the conference committee. If the conferees have come to agreement after major changes, the bill may be killed by one or the other of the two houses. However, if the committee report is accepted by the two chambers, the bill then goes to the president for his signature.

Presidential Action.   When the president receives the bill, he has several options available to him. He may sign the bill without hesitation, in which case it immediately becomes law. This frequently happens with bills that were first proposed by the executive branch and are part of the president's program. In those instances, a member of Congress was its legislative sponsor and managed the bill on its intricate journey through the lawmaking process.

But the president may also disapprove of a bill. In that case he may formally veto it, sending it back to Congress with a message explaining his rejection. If Congress accepts the president's reasoning, the bill is then dead. However, if despite the president's objections, Congress still wants to put the bill through as law, it can *override* (set aside or make void) his veto. Overriding a presidential veto requires a two-thirds vote in both houses of Congress, which is very difficult to achieve. Very often a bill has passed Congress with a bare majority of 51 or 52 percent. In that case, it is virtually impossible to muster the necessary 66 to 67 percent support. For this reason, the mere threat of a presidential veto is a formidable weapon and may coerce Congress to accommodate the president when it might not have otherwise wanted to.

When the president vetoes a bill, he has to return it to Congress within ten days so that it has an opportunity to override the veto and make the bill law without his signature. At the end of the second one-year congressional session, when Congress adjourns for its upcoming election, the president has an opportunity to avoid the possibility of having his decision overridden. He can refuse to sign the bill within a ten-day period during which the last session of Congress adjourns. This act of withholding the presidential signature is called a *pocket veto.* Obviously, there is a very limited period during which the president can exercise the pocket veto. Prior to 1972, he was also able to use it at the end of the first session of Congress. In that year Senator Edward Kennedy challenged President Richard Nixon's use of the pocket veto during the summer recess of Congress as unconstitutional. A federal judge agreed that the intersession was not properly speaking an adjournment of Congress, which can occur only at the end of its full term. This decision was upheld on appeal in 1986.

When the president does approve of a piece of legislation, there is customarily an elaborate signing ceremony. As the TV cameras roll, the president, surrounded by the smiling chairmen of the sponsoring committees and the leaders of the House and Senate, signs the document using several pens that he then distributes to a select number of the assembled guests. The bill is now law.

THE PRESIDENT AND CONGRESS: A BALANCE OF POWER

The Constitution intimately involves the president and Congress. Section 7 of Article I and Sections 2, 3, and 4 of Article II make close connections between executive and legislative powers. It is from these connections that the primary system of checks and balances derives. But in point of fact, although the checks have always been there, the balances have not.

Except for a few instances, governmental power has resided in Congress until 1933. During the entire nineteenth century, only three presidents dominated Congress: Thomas Jefferson, Andrew Jackson, and Abraham Lincoln. Each had come into office with both houses of Congress under the control of his own party. However, continuity between the presidential and legislative parties is no guarantee of a dominant presidency. Much depends on the personality of the president. Each of the three was extremely charismatic—in the case of Jefferson and Lincoln, their charisma has lasted to our own day.

But it was not until the second half of the twentieth century that complaints about an "imperial presidency" arose. Many saw the executive branch as acting too independently of Congress in both the domestic and foreign arenas. Many felt that Franklin Roosevelt had made secret deals to carve up Europe after World War II without either consulting or gaining the consent of Congress. Harry Truman committed the United States to the Korean War without seeking either a declaration of war or approval from Congress. The Bay of Pigs invasion of Cuba was secretly planned by the administration of Dwight Eisenhower and carried out by the administration of John F. Kennedy, all without the consent or knowledge of Congress. Richard Nixon ordered the secret bombing of Laos and Cambodia, both neutral countries. Nixon also used the Central Intelligence Agency (CIA) to topple from power Salvador Allende Gossens, the duly elected president of Chile, and install in his place a military dictatorship under General Augusto Pinochet. And Nixon impounded (refused to spend) huge sums of money appropriated by Congress for social programs.

Finally, in 1973, Congress rebelled and started to impose restrictions on the presidency. At that time it overrode Nixon's veto of the War Powers Act. This law requires the president to consult with Congress before sending troops into situations that may lead to armed conflict. If American military forces are engaged in potentially hostile situations, the president must report to Congress within 48 hours. The Act further limits the commitment of American armed forces to sixty days unless preceded by a declaration of war (which can be made only by Con-

FROM *HERBLOCK AT LARGE* (PANTHEON BOOKS, 1987).

gress) or granted an extension by Congress. In response to Nixon's excessive impoundment of appropriated funds, Congress passed the 1974 Budget and Impoundment Control Act, which created the Congressional Budget Office and the Budget committees of the House and Senate and restricted the president's discretion in spending money appropriated by Congress. There is a serious question as to whether either bill could have become law if Nixon's presidency had not been much weakened by the Watergate scandal.[3]

Tension between the presidency and Congress has been largely unremitting since Watergate and has become increasingly severe since the Iran-contra affair during Reagan's second term. But Congress had quietly made efforts to reassert its authority over the executive since 1946 in the Legislative Reorganization Act. The purpose of the Act was to make the operation of Congress more efficient, but it also gave the legislature greater oversight of executive departments and agencies. During the 1960s, for example, the Senate Foreign Relations Committee served as a center of criticism of American policy in Vietnam. The House and Senate Intelligence Committees now require that the CIA notify them of any contemplated covert activities. A number of congressional agencies were created in the 1960s and 1970s to aid in legislative oversight. Also, at about the same time, the General Accounting Office (GAO), created in 1921 as an auditing agency of Congress, became a major investigative arm of the legislature that checks on every aspect of government activity. In 1986, for example, the GAO first indicated the extent of the Savings and Loan (S&L) crisis. At the time, it projected that more than $22 billion would be needed to close down the failed S&Ls and pay insured depositors. The GAO has kept on top of the S&L debacle since, periodically increasing the projected costs of the S&L bailout.[4]

But what might be characterized as an ongoing war between the executive and legislative branches of government did not come to an end with the near impeachment of Nixon. Indeed, the "war" reached new heights during the Reagan administration when members of the president's staff admitted to misleading Congress regularly during the Iran-contra hearings. It gained in intensity when President Reagan nominated federal judge Robert H. Bork, a conservative ideologue, to the Supreme Court and then criticized senators for opposing his nominee on ideological grounds. From all indications, the battle between the two branches will continue indefinitely. It was built into their relationship by the Constitution and has been aggravated by America's international responsibilities as a world power.

---

[3]Watergate is the name of an office building in Washington in which the Democratic National Committee had its headquarters. The DNC headquarters were broken into by men connected to President Nixon's top staff. Nixon covered up their involvement and thus broke the law.

[4]In the early 1980s the Reagan administration and Congress relaxed regulations governing the lending practices of savings and loan banks, also called "thrifts." As a result, many S&Ls made a large number of high-risk loans, particularly in real estate. With a sharp downturn in the economy of the Southwest, most of the loans in that area became uncollectible. The thrifts went into bankruptcy, and, because all deposits up to $100,000 are federally insured, the federal government has to pay the depositors of the failed thrifts.

In Conclusion

Congress was conceived by the Framers of the Constitution as the supreme authority in the nation. In their view, it was the bulwark of democracy. But they were fearful of the people. Thus they set up a system of constraints within the legislature itself as well as outside it. The principal internal constraint was to be provided by the division of Congress into two distinct chambers. Since each chamber makes its laws separately, the chambers need to meet and compromise their differences so as to present one bill for the president's signature.

All legislative bodies find that they need committees to do the preparatory work before they can make laws. This circumstance tends to concentrate a good deal of power in committee chairpeople. Committees not only consider bills within their jurisdiction, they also oversee executive departments and agencies that come under their authority. As an aid in making laws, committees hold hearings at which experts and interested parties testify. They also hold hearings as part of their oversight function, and in the Senate as part of their responsibility to give the president advice and consent on his treaties and nominations.

The president and Congress are intimately involved with one another. They need one another to make the laws of the land. When Congress and the presidency are controlled by different parties, this intimacy often leads to conflict and a vying for dominance. For the most part, Congress had been the dominant branch until the 1930s, when presidents became increasingly powerful. Since the end of the Second World War, presidents have acted with considerable independence of Congress in both domestic and foreign affairs. Often these actions have later met with a great deal of congressional disapproval and sporadic efforts by Congress to reassert its power. America's position as a superpower and its international role have enhanced the potential for conflict between the two branches.

C ★ A ★ S ★ E   S ★ T ★ U ★ D ★ Y

Congressional Policy-Making

President Ronald Reagan met with congressional leaders on the south lawn of the White House on October 22, 1986, to sign what was widely heralded as the most important tax reform of legislation to be passed in recent memory. Before hundreds of spectators, and to their loud applause, the president hailed the end of "the steeply progressive income tax [that] our Founding Fathers . . . never imagined . . . struck at the heart of the economic life of the individual, punishing that special

effort and extra hard work that has always been the driving force of our economy."[1]

Reagan went on to state, "I believe that history will record this moment as something more, as the return to the first principles this country was founded on: faith in the individual, not groups or classes, but faith in the resources and bounty of each and every separate human soul."[2]

The Tax Reform Bill that Congress passed, after interminable struggles pitting the House against the Senate and both at times against the president, was a seemingly impossible piece of legislation. Powerful interest groups covering the economic spectrum opposed tax reform because it eliminated their special benefits under the old tax code. Some groups succeeded in retaining their special "tax expenditure" provisions, which allowed them to take deductions, for example, home mortgage interest, against their federal income tax. But many more groups found, to their dismay, that under the new flat tax they would no longer, for example, be given special treatment for capital gains, or be permitted to deduct consumer loan interest or money set aside for individual retirement accounts (IRAs) if their incomes were over a designated amount.

Because revenue legislation traditionally was riddled with tax expenditure provisions benefiting special interests, the tax code was always difficult to change. How, then, did Congress in 1986 pass a major revision that eliminated a large number of politically sensitive tax breaks?

Enacting Tax Reform

Putting Tax Reform on Congress's Agenda

While former New York Congressman Jack Kemp (R) and New Jersey Senator Bill Bradley (D) had urged the adoption of a flat tax before the advent of the Reagan presidency, they were unable by themselves to put the item on Congress's agenda. But Ronald Reagan found the idea attractive, and made it the keystone of his tax overhaul plan announced on May 28, 1985.

Reagan proposed a three-tiered plan under which incomes would be taxed at 15, 25, and 35 percent depending on the amount earned. Eliminated under the Reagan plan were deductions for state and local taxes, and limits were placed on other deduction categories, such as business entertainment and meal expenses. The Reagan plan retained preferential capital gains treatment and deductions for interest payments on primary residences.

Reagan campaigned vigorously for his tax reform plan around the country, but he stirred little interest. Most of the electorate seemed satisfied with a status quo, and if people were concerned with tax reform at all they saw it primarily as a threat to the preferential treatment their interests received under the prevailing law.

---

[1]*Congressional Quarterly Weekly Report*, 25 October 1986, p. 2668.
[2]Ibid.

When Reagan announced that his tax-overhaul program would be his *major* legislative initiative in 1985, Congress automatically put the plan at the top of its legislative agenda. The president had initiated the proposal; now it was up to congressional leaders, particularly the key chairmen of the House Ways and Means and Senate Finance committees, to put their stamp on the legislation.

Tax Reform Goes to the House of Representatives

Ways and Means Committee Response.   House Ways and Means chairman Dan Rostenkowski, a representative from Chicago who had been trained in the tough ward politics of the Daley machine, announced that he would work with the president to draw up a bill. All tax legislation has to go initially through the House Ways and Means Committee. Its chairman cannot maintain credibility if he lets the president seize the tax initiative from him. A politically astute Rostenkowski knew that maintaining his reputation for political power in the House, a primary goal of senior members, depended on joining the president and taking the lead in the tax reform initiative.

In September 1985, the House Ways and Means Committee staff drew up a tax bill that was very similar to the president's plan. Rostenkowski engaged in skillful behind-the-scenes negotiations to guide the proposal through the intricate committee procedures, which included hearings and markup. Ironically, House Republicans complained that they were left out of the proceedings, and eventually offered a substitute bill that threatened to kill tax reform.

Full House Action.   Because House Republicans were discontented, tax reform became a highly partisan issue in the fall of 1985. President Reagan was disappointed with Rostenkowski's bill because it differed from his in several important respects, although it did continue the flat tax and in a broad sense conformed to the president's program.

After the Democratic version of the tax reform bill was reported out of the Ways and Means Committee, House Republicans, in an unusual move, succeeded in defeating a rule to bring the bill to the floor. The Republican House leadership felt that the White House had abandoned them. President Reagan, however, finally saved the day by intensely lobbying his own party in the House. With a solid Democratic majority behind it, tax reform legislation passed on December 17, 1985.

House Politics.   There was little difference between the Democratic and Republican versions of the tax reform bill in the House. Nevertheless, the politics surrounding its passage was intense and the outcome far from certain. That is because the *substance* of legislation does not necessarily determine how legislators react to it. In the case of tax reform, the relevant political actors were struggling for power. Rostenkowski wanted *his* version of the bill; House Republican leaders wanted *their* version.

In fact, the Republican bill was in ideological terms more akin to Democratic liberal ideology than to conservative Republican views. The Democratic Ways and Means Committee bill, for example, actually cut taxes on individual incomes more deeply than the Republican proposal. Traditionally conservative Republicans have always supported greater tax cuts than liberal Democrats would like to see. Michigan Republican Guy Vander Jagt told his House colleagues in a rousing speech supporting the bill, "If the word 'Republican' wasn't on this alternative [bill], liberal Democrats would be clamoring to get on board."

In the end, House Democrats rallied around their party and Rostenkowski prevailed. The Ways and Means committee chairman had skillfully turned the president's program into a victory for himself. At the same time, the White House could also claim success in its struggle for tax reform.

The Senate Barrier

Congressional politics, of course, is not only that of the House but also of the Senate. Each body is distinctive in many ways. But members share common incentives of internal power, reelection, and good public policy.

When President Reagan sent his tax reform bill to Capitol Hill, Oregon Republican Bob Packwood chaired the powerful Senate Finance Committee. He was the Senate counterpart of Dan Rostenkowski. As the Senate's "feudal baron" in the tax reform arena, Packwood's *personal* approval was critical to the success of the president's and now Rostenkowski's tax reform bill. Personal power often plays an even greater role in the Senate than in the House where broader-gauged party politics is more likely to have an impact on the fate of legislation. Committee chairs are a dominant force in a body whose members consider themselves to be equals, but who recognize that some are more equal than others.

Packwood's Position.   The Senate knew Packwood as a maverick. He could and did play traditional pork-barrel and trade-off politics with the best of his Senate colleagues. He always looked after Oregon timber interests and at first sought to protect tax benefits for them as he embarked upon "tax reform."

But Packwood, like Rostenkowski, knew that his power and influence in the Senate depended on getting out front on the tax reform issue. He realized that Reagan and then Rostenkowski had seized the initiative from him, an initiative that he well might have been given credit for since he had proposed revising the tax code to establish a 25 percent flat-tax rate even before Reagan announced his plan. But he never pursued the idea, and as chairman of the Senate Finance Committee had supported traditional tax-writing politics, which simply amounted to trading and compromising among special interests. "I kind of like the present tax code." Packwood said in 1984.

However, as tax reform gained momentum, *not* in the electorate but because of presidential and House action in 1985, Packwood changed his mind. He began to see clearly, as Congress convened in 1986, that he too had little option if he was to retain his credibility as a leading political figure in the Senate but to support tax reform and even take initiatives of his own.

The Senate and Special Interests

After the president announced his tax reform proposal, and especially after the House adopted the Reagan plan with very few changes, interest groups began in earnest to coalesce on both sides of the issue. Special corporate and business interests, such as the timber and oil industries and the National Association of Realtors, lobbied the Senate Finance Committee to retain the tax benefits they had under the old law. At first Packwood responded, protecting, for example, timber interests that were so important to Oregon. Other Finance Committee members saw to it that interests in their states were also protected.

But when the Finance Committee looked at what it had wrought in April 1986, it found that "tax reform" retained so many special-interest benefits the proposed flat-tax part of the bill would not raise sufficient government revenue.

In an amazing and abrupt turnabout, Finance Committee chairman Packwood decided to scrap the entire bill and, in consultation with his committee chief-of-staff, drop most of the special-interest deductions and adopt a flat-tax schedule.

Behind Packwood's strategy change was a recognition that no tax bill would be acceptable to the president and the House if it was bogged down with special-interest deductions. By rejecting virtually all special-interest claims in establishing a 25 percent tax ceiling, Packwood knew there was a good chance for the bill's passage. The Senate would be in line with the president and the House. And together they were the Senate's most powerful tax constituency, one that over-shadowed the special interests that for the most part had their way on tax legislation in the past.

Conquering Special Interests.   Certainly one of the most unusual aspects of the passage of the tax reform bill was its success against powerful special interests. Congressional committees are usually sensitive to the very interests that are directly affected by the legislation under their jurisdictions. But in the tax reform area, wide-ranging interests come into play that can balance each other. When the president and congressional leaders, not only committee chairmen, take an interest in legislation, special interests can more easily be subdued.

Tax reform also took special interests by surprise. The idea had been floating around Washington for almost a decade before President Reagan announced his plan in 1985. Former Congressman Jack Kemp and Senator Bill Bradley had mentioned the idea on many occasions and have even sought to incorporate it into legislation. But tax reform had no constituency until the Reagan proposal started ever so slowly to forge one.

The initial lack of any pro-tax reform constituency outside of government made many special interests opposing it complacent. Tax reform had always failed in the past, and there was no reason to believe that a new tax initiative would succeed.

Undoubtedly one of the major reasons that special interests failed to defeat tax reform was their inability to develop a concerted strategy. Each interest was out for itself without regard to other tax bill opponents. Proponents of tax reform did not have to employ a divide-and-conquer strategy because their opponents were already divided, each seeking to preserve its special tax benefits.

Pro-Tax Reform Coalition.   At the same time that tax reform opponents could not agree on a course of action, a coalition of interests in favor of the bill began to develop as Reagan and Rostenkowski pushed their proposal to the top of the legislative agenda. While opponents pressured Congress for their individual causes in a scattered manner, such diverse groups as General Motors, the League of Women Voters, and Phyllis Schlafly's Eagle Forum—a right-wing, antifeminist group—joined over 150 other organizations to fight for tax reform. Proponents of the change called themselves the Fifteen/Twenty-seven/Thirty-three Coalition, after the individual and top corporate tax rates proposed in the Senate Finance committee's bill. The coalition included, in addition to General Motors chairman Roger Smith, other large corporations, such as the Aetna Life and Casualty Company, numerous consumer groups, some banks, small businesses, women's organizations, the elderly, African-Americans, and Hispanics.

Divide and Conquer. Some tax bill provisions also helped to divide and conquer the opposition. Provisions were retained, for example, that continued to benefit such powerful groups as the National Association of Realtors—the mortgage interest deduction—which at the same time had the support of a broad cross-section of the public, the millions of home owners throughout the nation. Retaining benefits for only a few powerful special interests helped to diffuse opposition to the tax bill.

Conclusion

In the end, political interests within and without government were able to give tax reform legislation a momentum that could not be stopped. The president and congressional leaders gave the attractive idea of tax reform political reality and impetus. Some powerful interests continued to benefit under the new law, while others lost their tax subsidies. Group politics did not dictate tax reform. Political leadership succeeded because of the coalescence of presidential and congressional incentives to pass the law. Rostenkowski and Packwood boosted their power on Capitol Hill, and their reputations for ''good public policy,'' by adopting and helping to pass the president's plan.

The passage of tax reform legislation revealed Congress in action along with the complexity of the forces that shape legislative behavior. Above all, it suggested the many dimensions of political leadership and the role political incentives—those for power, reelection, and good public policy—play in the system. Congress does not require popular mandates to act. Nor does Congress always rubber-stamp special-interest demands, which often are in conflict. A constituency of sorts did develop outside of government after the president and the House of Representatives had acted. But Reagan met only apathetic public response in his attempt to stir up support for the tax bill in speeches he made throughout the country.

In the end, it was the Washington players who put tax reform on the political agenda and saw it through to passage. Always critical to these players is the maintenance of their reputations for power and good public policy, which add or detract from their credibility with their colleagues in the often insulated Washington and Capitol Hill political environment.

Postscript: Congress Reacts to Bush Initiatives

Death and taxes, so the ancient adage goes, are two of life's certainties. And the inevitability of the latter seems to make tax reform a perennial and thorny issue. President George Bush and Congress fought over tax reform, continuing the acrimonious tax struggle between the two branches that characterized previous administrations. The long, drawn out budget ordeal of 1990 made both President Bush and Congress in the words of one representative, "the laughing stock of the nation."[3]

What the Bush administration labeled "tax reform" was little more than a piecemeal approach that raised excise taxes. It was in essence a flawed continuation of President Ronald Reagan's 1986 effort to reform taxes. But Bush found it far more difficult than Reagan had to persuade Congress to go along with him. Lacking Reagan's charisma and Republican control of the Senate, Bush found that he had little leeway in dealing with the solidly entrenched Democrats on Capitol Hill.

Bush Confronts Congress

In April, 1990, Bush asked congressional leaders to join him in a bipartisan effort to deal with the increasing budget deficit. He invited congressional majority and minority party leaders to a budget summit. Among these leaders were the congressional "prime ministers" who deal with taxes, the chairmen of the tax-writing House Ways and Means and Senate Finance committees. The president hoped he could work through these congressional leaders to gain acceptance of his plan, which consisted mostly of a fragmentary package of excise tax increases and limits on deductions.

Congressional Response

Bush's political logic did not take into account changes in Capitol Hill politics that, in the absence of a charismatic president and an overriding national issue, made Congress difficult if not impossible to lead. Congressional party leaders have no automatic power, and committee chairmen constantly fight among themselves for turf. While the House Ways and Means and Senate Finance Committees control tax policy, a host of other committees claim jurisdiction over government expenditures affecting programs within their jurisdiction. Each committee is a "little legislature" which must, in effect, vote approval of changes over programs they control.

Counting committees and their subcommittees, there are over three hundred little legislatures on Capitol Hill. Bush, however, invited only twenty-one legislators—the party leaders and the two committee chairmen—to his budget summit.

---

[3]*Congressional Quarterly Weekly Report,* October 20, 1990, p. 3471.

Clearly he could not include all of the powerful committee chairmen and members who controlled tax and expenditure policies. Nevertheless, the exclusion of so many congressional chairmen from the budget summit virtually guaranteed congressional defeat of the summiteer's proposals.

Leadership Failure

Effective congressional leadership is difficult under the best of circumstances, even when a popular and forceful president, such as Ronald Reagan, can capitalize on the "honeymoon period" with Congress at the outset of his administration. George Bush, however, not only lacked Reagan's leadership style, but also was past the "honeymoon period" and did not have the former president's flexibility in dealing with budget policies. While Reagan was able to lower taxes, Bush had to find ways of raising them to offset the enormous deficit that resulted from Reagan's tax cuts. Moreover, the difficulties that even Reagan had in cutting expenditures continued unabated and even increased during the Bush administration.

As Bush sought to strike a budget deal he confronted the reality of decentralized congressional power. Congress had returned to its old ways of internal bickering and turf fights among committees as entrepreneurial—that is, self-interested—politics surfaced with a vengeance. Committee chairmen were more concerned to protect themselves and their electoral futures than to follow the president's lead or their own congressional party leaders. Following congressional party leadership does not necessarily serve the interests of individual members in gaining reelection, power, or influence on Capitol Hill. In the end, Bush reluctantly accepted a makeshift package of tax increases and expenditure cuts that reflected parochial congressional interests more than the nation's need to control the budget.

The budget deficit continued to grow under the Bush administration. Bush made "modest" tax proposals in his 1992 budget. But the Democratic Congress partially defeated Bush's recommendations to increase user fees for Medicare, Medicaid, Veterans medical care, and other social programs. The president also wanted to cut $7.1 billion from Medicare's hospital coverage of state and local employees, which had little chance of congressional passage. Bush continued to push for a capital gains tax reduction, but far less vehemently than he had at the outset of his administration. The White House, having been burned in the past, recognized that Chicago Congressman Dan Rostenkowski, Chairman of the House Ways and Means Committee, and Texas Senator Lloyd Bentsen, Chairman of the Senate Finance Committee, would remain in command of tax policies. Their approval was necessary for any presidential program to succeed on Capitol Hill.

Suggested Readings

Richard F. Fenno, Jr. *Homestyle: House Members in Their Districts*. Boston: Little, Brown, 1978.

Morris P. Fiorina. *Congress: Keystone of the Washington Establishment*. New Haven: Yale University Press, 1977.

Gary C. Jacobson. *The Politics of Congressional Elections*, 2nd ed. Boston: Little, Brown, 1987.

Rochelle Jones and Peter Woll. *The Private World of Congress*. New York: Free Press, 1979.

David Mayhew. *Congress: The Electoral Connection*. New Haven: Yale University Press. 1974.

chapter

9

THE PRESIDENCY

A President draws influence from bargaining advantages. The reason for this is simple: most men who share in governing have interests of their own beyond the realm of policy objectives.

Richard E. Neustadt

Those who govern do so not only with the consent of the governed but also with the agreement of others who also have power. This is so not only in a democracy, but also in all other systems of government. The nature of governance distributes power among the members of a ruling group or class. The one who holds the most power—president, prime minister, absolute monarch, dictator—must *persuade* the others in the power "loop" to do his or her bidding. To be persuasive, he or she has to possess a large number of bargaining chips— if possible, the largest number of chips.

As it happens, in the United States the president is handed a number of chips on entering office and, by playing his cards right, he can accumulate more. But, as this metaphor implies, winning at the game is not a sure thing.[1] Much depends

---

[1]For a still excellent discussion of the uncertainties in the use of power by presidents, see Richard E. Neustadt, *Presidential Power: The Politics of Leadership* (New York: John Wiley & Sons, 1960).

on historical circumstance, constitutionally granted powers of office, and personality or political savvy.

Since most of us can do little about history but those of us who vote can do something about who is president, we tend to focus our attention on his personality and political competence. Generally, our approval of a president's performance is based on our belief in his competence and on our acceptance of his objectives. For example, in an ABC News/*Washington Post* poll of early 1990, 62 percent of those polled thought President Bush should get more credit than Democratic leaders for making progress in solving national problems. In the same poll, 64 percent thought Bush was popular because of "the things he has done and the way he has handled himself." Most Americans like a president who displays strong leadership qualities. Following his mobilization of worldwide opposition to Iraq's invasion of Kuwait in August 1990, Bush's rating in the ABC/*Washington Post* poll shot up to 76 percent.

But, the notion that presidents should be strong leaders was not always viewed favorably in the United States. Indeed, the Founding Fathers looked upon a strong president with fear and trembling.

BACKGROUND

During the ratification debate of 1787 and 1788, leading antifederalists complained that the president envisioned by the Constitution would have too much power. Patrick Henry worried that "there is to be a great and mighty President, with very extensive powers—the powers of a king."[2] Henry was not alone in his distress at the power held by the president. Others also saw the president as a king in the making: "Who can deny but the *president general* will be a *king* to all intents and purposes, and one of the most dangerous kind too; a king elected to command a standing army?"[3] Finally, George Mason, one of the leading delegates to the Constitutional Convention, feared that the president would be unaccountable for his actions because he, along with the Senate, "are not the representatives of the people, or amenable to them."[4]

These concerns were so widespread that Alexander Hamilton devoted ten essays to answering them. At the conclusion of *The Federalist,* No. 77, Hamilton attempts to reassure his readers by describing the limits imposed on the presidency.

> Does [the structure of the presidency] also combine the requisites to safety, in the republican sense—a due dependence on the people, a due responsibility? The answer to this question . . . is satisfactorily deducible from these circumstances; the election of the President once in four years by persons immediately chosen by the people for

[2]From Henry's speech to the Virginia Convention of 1788 in *The Antifederalists,* ed. Cecilia M. Kenyon (Boston: Northeastern University Press, 1985), p. 254.
[3]From the letter of "Philadelphiensis" in *The Antifederalists,* p. 72.
[4]Kenyon, *Antifederalists,* p. 192.

"Ladies and gentlemen, the charming President of the United States."

that purpose,[5] and his being at all times liable to impeachment, trial, dismission from office, incapacity to serve in any other, and to the forfeiture of life and estate by subsequent prosecution in the common course of law.

Despite his reassuring words, Hamilton favored a strong president who would occupy the office for life. Most of the others at the Philadelphia Convention, however, were opposed to a strong president and therefore hedged him about with a number of constraints. He must "go to the people" for approval every four years; his major appointments and all treaties have to win the approval of the Senate before going into effect; he has to periodically report to Congress on the state of the nation; his program for the country can only take the form of a set of recommendations that Congress has the power to accept, reject, or change to suit itself; and he can be removed from office by Congress for "Treason, Bribery, or other high Crimes and Misdemeanors."

In the first century of the nation, only six of twenty-two presidents served two terms, and of the six, four were Founding Fathers (see Box 9.1). For the most part, power rested in the legislature during that time, at first in the House of Representatives and later in the Senate. As we mentioned in the preceding chapter, only three presidents dominated Congress and two of them—Jefferson and Lincoln—are figures of mythic proportions in American history.

---

[5]In some states, at the time Hamilton wrote, electors for president were to be chosen by popular vote; but in most states, electors were chosen by state legislatures.

BOX 9.1 TWO-TERM PRESIDENTS[a]

No.	President	First Term	Second Term
1	George Washington	1789–1793	1793–1797
3	Thomas Jefferson	1801–1805	1805–1809
4	James Madison	1809–1813	1813–1817
5	James Monroe	1817–1821	1821–1825
7	Andrew Jackson	1829–1833	1833–1837
18	Ulysses S. Grant	1869–1873	1873–1877
22	Grover Cleveland	1885–1889	
24	Grover Cleveland[b]		1893–1897
26	Theodore Roosevelt	1901–1905[c]	1905–1909
28	Woodrow Wilson	1913–1917	1917–1921
30	Calvin Coolidge	1923–1925[c]	1925–1929
32	Franklin D. Roosevelt[d]	1933–1937	1937–1941
33	Harry S Truman	1945–1949[c]	1949–1953
34	Dwight D. Eisenhower	1953–1957	1957–1961
36	Lyndon B. Johnson	1963–1965[c]	1965–1969
37	Richard M. Nixon	1969–1973	1973–1974[e]
40	Ronald Reagan	1981–1985	1985–1989

[a]Two presidents were elected to two terms but died before the second term was completed. These were: Abraham Lincoln (1861–65) and William McKinley (1897–1901).
[b]Grover Cleveland was elected twice to office for one term each time.
[c]Completes the term of the preceding president, who died in office.
[d]Elected to four terms, only two of which are shown here; the remaining terms were 1941–45 and 1945–48. Roosevelt died April 1945.
[e]The House Judiciary Committee recommended that Nixon be impeached but he resigned before the full House voted on the recommendation.

The second century of the American nation saw a gradual shift of power from the legislature to the presidency. That shift has been sporadically resisted by Congress and is by no means completed yet. But in this century, nine out of nineteen presidents served for two terms, although only five of the nine were elected both times (see Box 9.1). The remaining four—Theodore Roosevelt, Calvin Coolidge, Harry Truman, and Lyndon B. Johnson—completed the term of a president who died in office. Yet three of these—Roosevelt, Truman, and Johnson—were among the most powerful presidents in the twentieth century. The other strong presidents in this century were Woodrow Wilson, Franklin D. Roosevelt,

Richard Nixon, and Ronald Reagan. Clearly not every president has exercised the same amount of power. What, then, makes a president powerful?

SOURCES OF PRESIDENTIAL POWER

Presidential power is many-faceted. Before attempting to understand it, we need to define what is meant by the term *presidential power*. The basic meaning of the word *power* is the ability to do something—lift weights, for example, run a mile in a specified amount of time, or achieve a particular goal. Presidential power is related to our last example. A president is deemed powerful to the extent that he can achieve specific, identifiable goals that he has set. He gains his objectives through a number of means. First among these are the formal powers granted by the Constitution. Constitutional authority is the basis of all other power a president possesses or can exercise.

CONSTITUTIONAL POWERS

The Constitution not only restricts presidents, it also enables them to act. Under the Constitution, presidents are heads of state and chief executives of the federal government. Certain powers flow from these positions, some of which are enumerated in the Constitution and some of which are implicit. But it is important to keep in mind that a president's power is never absolute and in large measure depends on the cooperation of other people.

The presidency is described in Article II of the Constitution.

The President's Executive Authority.   The first sentence of Article II states that the president has the executive power of government. As chief executive, he is required by the Constitution to "take Care that the Laws [passed by Congress] be faithfully executed." In performing this task, he has the assistance of a vast bureaucracy numbering hundreds of departments and agencies that employ about 3.5 million civilian personnel and over 2 million military men and women. To help the president manage this huge apparatus, he has a staff of approximately 2,000 people known as the Executive Office of the President. Many scholars consider the Executive Office an integral part of the presidency.

But the Executive Office does not quite meet the personal and political needs of the president. He therefore has a White House staff that provides him with advice and support on political and administrative matters as well as serving as a buffer against the outside world. Under President Reagan, the White House staff acted in some situations with considerable independence to afford him "plausible deniability," as was revealed at the Iran-contra hearings. This means that if a decision turned out to be politically embarrassing, Reagan was able to say he did not know anything about it, as he did to comic effect at the trial of Oliver North. It also means that individuals who have not been chosen by the people sometimes make basic policy decisions. At that point the president is little more than a figurehead, wonderfully entertaining and much loved but, for all practical purposes, not in control.

Whether the president or his surrogates are in charge, the office of the president—the presidency—has enormous power simply because of the vast organization it commands. That organization affects people in every walk of life on nearly every level of activity. School programs, for example, are often influenced by actions of the Department of Education, as are business decisions by Internal Revenue Service (IRS) rulings. This influence is almost entirely the result of the regulations put forth by executive departments or agencies, and regulations are in effect the same as laws.

One of the chief concerns of the Framers was to make certain that the legislative and executive powers were in different hands. It is, one might say, the fundamental principle of the separation of powers. James Madison made the Framers' point most forcefully in *The Federalist,* No. 47: "The accumulation of all powers, legislative, executive, and judiciary in the same hands, whether of one, a few, or many, and whether hereditary, self-appointed, or elective, may justly be pronounced the very definition of tyranny." Although the executive branch comes perilously close to that "accumulation of all powers," it has so far been constrained by Congress's oversight functions and the Supreme Court's exercise of judicial review.

Fortunately for American democracy, our coequal branches have been sufficiently, if not consistently, jealous of their prerogatives and have generally curbed the excesses of one another. Some of our finest presidents have acted outside the limits set by the Constitution and have thereby expanded the executive powers by established custom if not by constitutional sanction (see Box 9.2). When they have stepped too far out of line, they have been pulled up short by either Congress or the Court. Two examples may suffice.

In 1971, the executive branch tried through the Justice Department to prevent the publication of the Pentagon Papers, a secret Defense Department study of government deception of the American people with regard to Vietnam. The Justice Department claimed in part that the president had the "inherent power"

BOX 9.2 EXPANSION OF PRESIDENTIAL POWER

Presidents have acted without prior approval from Congress and in so doing have thereby expanded the powers of their office. The following is a short list of some of these presidential actions.

In 1794, President George Washington called out the troops to squash a farmers' revolt in Pennsylvania known as the Whiskey Rebellion against a federal excise tax on liquor; established the president's "inherent power" in national security matters.

In 1795, Washington signed an unpopular treaty with Great Britain that had been negotiated by John Jay. The House of Representatives claimed the right to examine documents connected with the treaty negotiation before appropriating funds to implement the treaty's terms. Washington refused. This was the first step toward what has become known as "executive privilege."

Starting in 1801, President Thomas Jefferson carried on an undeclared war against North African pirates for about five years, and in 1803, he approved the purchase of the vast Louisiana territory from France, thus more than doubling the size of the United States; established the president's preeminence in foreign affairs.

In 1807, Jefferson was faced with a subpoena requiring him to turn over a confidential report to the court in the treason trial of Aaron Burr. Jefferson refused, "reserving the . . . right of the president . . . to decide . . . what papers coming to him as president the public interest permits to be communicated."[a] This confirmed the claim of executive privilege.

In 1861, President Abraham Lincoln suspended the "privilege" of habeas corpus (the right of suspension was reserved to Congress in Article I, Section 9, of the Constitution); established the executive's power to override the constitutional guarantees of civil rights in a national emergency.

In 1862, Lincoln issued his Emancipation Proclamation that freed the slaves in the rebellious Southern states; established the president's war powers.

In 1914, President Woodrow Wilson ordered the United States marines to take the Mexican city of Vera Cruz, thus confirming the president's war powers and preeminence in foreign affairs.

[a]Quoted in Archibald Cox, *The Court and the Constitution* (Boston: Houghton Mifflin, 1987), p. 7. Copyright © 1987 by Archibald Cox. Reprinted by permission of Houghton Mifflin Co.

to halt publication of information that "endangered national security." The Supreme Court denied the government's claim and Justice Hugo Black observed rather sharply: "To find that the President has 'inherent power' to halt the publication of news ... would wipe out the First Amendment and destroy the fundamental liberty and security of the very people the government hopes to make 'secure.'"[6]

When a president nominates someone to the Supreme Court, that recommendation is generally ratified by the Senate. Generally, but not always by any means. In 1987, President Reagan nominated federal Judge Robert H. Bork as a justice of the Supreme Court. Judge Bork was widely known within the legal profession as a conservative and as an extremely severe critic of decisions made by the Supreme Court over the previous fifty years. The president's known intention with his nomination of Judge Bork was to change the balance of the high court for years to come and turn it away from its moderate stance toward a far more conservative one. The Senate Judiciary Committee held public hearings in which Judge Bork's opinion of a number of basic rights and his respect for judicial precedent (*stare decisis* in legal jargon) were deeply probed. Many senators were very dissatisfied with Bork's responses, especially with his negative view of the right to privacy. Because of this, a majority of the committee recommended that the full Senate reject Judge Bork's nomination, which it did.

In both of our examples, the president was seen as exceeding his legitimate power. In the case of the Pentagon Papers, Nixon tried to suppress politically damaging information under the guise of protecting national security. With the nomination of Judge Bork, Reagan tried to lock the future into his own ideological bias, and the effort aroused the strong opposition of the Senate.

The President's Role as Commander-in-Chief.   Although the main source of power is the president's executive function, the Constitution provides another major source also—the president's position at the top of the military establishment. But here too the president is hedged about by congressional authority. Only Congress can declare war and appropriate funds for the military. Nevertheless, as commander of all the military forces of the United States, the president controls the major coercive power in the nation, at least theoretically. We have but to remember that as Nixon's impeachment drew closer, his new chief of staff, Alexander Haig, and his Secretary of Defense, James R. Schlesinger, instructed the top military commanders not to accept orders from the president unless it came through them. Thus, even in this area the president's power is limited by external constraints.

As in all other matters, the president's authority as commander-in-chief rests on its acceptance by everyone else involved. When he orders American forces into a hostile situation, the military has to willingly act on his orders. As long as the chain of command is adhered to, the president is in charge and has power. So far there has been no serious challenge to the commander-in-chief's authority, even though, as we have seen in Box 9.2, it has at times been exercised uncon-

---

[6]*New York Times Co.* v. *United States*, 403 U.S. 713 (1971).

stitutionally ever since George Washington marched against the rebellious farmers in Pennsylvania.

Throughout American history, presidents have asserted what has come to be called their war powers. Not only have Washington and Jefferson ordered military actions without seeking prior approval from Congress, others have done so to an even greater extent. Among the major warlike acts of presidents have been:

- In 1846, President James K. Polk ordered General Zachary Taylor into territory claimed by Mexico and only afterward sought approval by Congress. The Mexican-American War followed from this action and prompted Henry David Thoreau to write "Civil Disobedience," his major essay opposing the war and recommending passive resistance.

- In 1861, President Abraham Lincoln ordered a blockade of Southern ports without a declaration of war by Congress. The Supreme Court in what is known as the *Prize Cases* of 1863 confirmed the president's emergency powers in situations that threaten national security. In 1862, Lincoln declared martial law, suspending civil liberties and arresting 13,000 people for the expression of "disloyal sentiments." During the Civil War, the federal government also closed newspapers that were critical of Lincoln's policies. Neither action caused much protest from Congress and the Supreme Court except for a mild rebuke from the high court regarding the use of martial law where no emergency existed.

- In 1903, President Theodore Roosevelt ordered a warship to Panama to support a rebellion against Colombia instigated by the United States so that it could build the Panama Canal. Afterward Roosevelt bragged that he "took" Panama and forced Congress to debate his action rather than the canal. When Woodrow Wilson later tried to indemnify Colombia for its losses, Congress refused.

- In 1912, President William Howard Taft ordered the marines into Nicaragua to protect American interests in what is known as "dollar diplomacy." American troops remained there until 1933.

- From 1914 to 1918, Woodrow Wilson not only sent troops to Vera Cruz before getting congressional approval, he also sent troops to Haiti, Santo Domingo, into Mexico after Pancho Villa, and after World War I into Russia in an effort to overthrow the new communist government.

- In 1940, Franklin D. Roosevelt traded American destroyers for British bases in the Americas; in 1941, prior to American entry into World War II, he ordered U.S. troops to occupy Greenland, Iceland, and Dutch Guiana; throughout this period the U.S. Navy, acting on Roosevelt's orders, secretly escorted allied supply ships across the Atlantic in violation of the Neutrality Acts of 1937 and 1939 passed by Congress.

- In 1950, President Harry S Truman sent U.S. troops under General Douglas MacArthur to South Korea to fight a North Korean invasion. Truman did not seek or receive congressional approval for his "police action" until he fired MacArthur, which led to a Senate investigation that vindicated Truman's policy of "limited war."

- In 1953, President Dwight D. Eisenhower authorized the CIA to secretly take part in restoring the Shah of Iran to the throne by overthrowing the nationalist regime of Premier Muhammad Mussadegh. In 1960, Eisenhower authorized the CIA to train an anti-Castro force of Cubans for an eventual invasion of the island.

- In 1961, President John F. Kennedy approved the Bay of Pigs invasion of Cuba previously planned by the Eisenhower administration. In 1962, Kennedy increased the number of American military "advisers" in South Vietnam from a few hundred to several thousand, and permitted them to serve a combat role; he also authorized CIA operations against North Vietnam. In the same year, he ordered a naval blockade of Cuba when the Soviets tried to deliver missiles, which brought the superpowers close to nuclear war. Kennedy did not seek congressional approval in any of these instances.

- In early 1964, President Lyndon B. Johnson escalated U.S. involvement in Vietnam without seeking a declaration of war or congressional approval until the Tonkin Gulf resolution of late 1964 approved of his policy in the Vietnam War. In 1965, Johnson sent a large marine force into the Dominican Republic to quell a popular uprising against an undemocratic and oppressive government.

- In 1969, President Richard M. Nixon ordered the secret bombing of Cambodia and misled Congress with false reports; in 1970, he ordered an invasion of that country; and in 1973, he authorized the CIA to aid in overthrowing the legitimately elected president of Chile, Salvador Allende, and in replacing him with the military dictatorship of General Augusto Pinochet without informing Congress or seeking its approval. These actions caused Congress to pass the War Powers Act of 1973.

- In 1975, President Gerald Ford ordered air and land attacks against the Cambodian communist regime of Pol Pot, which had seized an unarmed American freighter, the *Mayaguez*. At the same time, he authorized secret aid to the anticommunist side in a civil war in Angola, which was prohibited by Congress in 1976.

- In 1982, President Ronald Reagan sent marines to Beirut, Lebanon, in a misguided effort to stabilize the Lebanese political situation. In 1983, he sent a large military force to invade the Caribbean island of Grenada and overthrow the communist government there. In 1987, he authorized registering several Kuwaiti oil tankers as American ships so that the U.S. Navy could escort them through the militarily dangerous waters of the Persian Gulf during the war between Iran and Iraq. None of these warlike actions had the prior approval of Congress.

- Late in 1989, President George Bush ordered the invasion of Panama to capture the Panamanian strong man, General Manuel Noriega, and bring him to trial in the United States. In 1990 Bush sent a massive military force to the Persian Gulf, ostensibly to protect the territorial integrity of an autocratic kingdom. Both of these warlike acts were done without the prior approval of Congress.

It is clear that presidents have from the beginning done what they thought necessary without first bothering about congressional approval. Often they received that approval in retrospect, as Reagan did almost exactly one year after he sent American forces to Beirut and a little less than a month before a terrorist bombing of the marine compound at the airport there. But in many instances, Congress had been misled, as was the case when Nixon ordered the bombing and later invasion of Cambodia. In an effort to restrain what many considered presidential adventurism, Congress passed the War Powers Act.

None of the presidents since the act was passed have acknowledged its legitimacy, however, contending that it is an unconstitutional invasion of their prerogatives as chief guardians of our national security. For national security reasons among others, Congress has been generally reluctant to curtail the president's freedom of action. For example, despite growing opposition within its ranks, Congress continued to appropriate funds for the Vietnam War. On the other hand, it was severely critical of Nixon's actions when revealed, and many members of Congress had serious doubts about Reagan's belligerent policies in Central America and the Middle East.

The President's Leadership in Foreign Affairs.   In large measure, the use of presidential war powers has been connected with international relations. The majority of warlike actions taken by presidents have been in pursuit of their foreign policies. Both Congress and the Court have long accepted presidential leadership in this area. Yet this dominance is not absolute and does not derive clearly from the Constitution. Indeed, the Constitution divides responsibility for the conduct of foreign affairs between the president and Congress. The dividing line has been, in the words of the constitutional scholar Archibald Cox, "a matter of grave concern" ever since Jefferson sent the marines to the shores of Tripoli in North Africa.

The president's authority in foreign affairs stems from several clauses in Article II, Sections 2 and 3, of the Constitution. Section 2 states that he has the authority to make treaties with the advice and consent of the Senate and the approval of two-thirds of that body, and again with the approval of the Senate he can appoint ambassadors to foreign countries. Section 3 indicates that the president can receive ambassadors from foreign nations without involving the Senate at all. Or he can refuse to receive them, as George Washington did with the ambassador of France, and none could say him nay.

Congress's constitutional prerogatives in foreign affairs derive from Article I, Section 8, and its shared powers with the president in the second section in Article II. As we saw in Box 8.1, Congress can provide for national defense, regulate commerce with foreign nations, set naturalization requirements, define and punish offenses against international law, declare war, and raise an army and navy. Many of the Framers were nervous about granting too much power to the president. James Madison observed:

Mad: agrees w[th] [James] Wilson in his definition of executive powers—executive powers . . . do not include the Rights of war & peace &c. but the powers shd be confined and defined—if large we shall have the Evils of elective Monarchies—probably the best plan will be a single Executive of long duration wth a council, with liberty to depart from their Opinion at his peril—[7]

---

[7]From a speech delivered on June 1, 1787, before the Constitutional Convention at Philadelphia as reprinted in *The Papers of James Madison*, vol. 10, *27 May 1787–3 March 1788*, ed. Robert A. Rutland et al. (Chicago: University of Chicago Press, 1977), p. 22.

The Framers of the Constitution, agreeing for the most part with Wilson and Madison, "confined" the president's warmaking powers. They also used the Senate as a supervisory agent over his peacemaking (read treaty making and foreign relations) power. In the view of most of the Framers, the right to make war and enter into alliances with foreign nations was "monarchical" if exercised by an individual who was not accountable to others with sufficient authority to reject his initiatives. But over time these views were modified through practical necessity.

Although the president still needs to obtain the consent of the Senate in making treaties, he can, when it seems best, conduct foreign policy through executive agreements. An *executive agreement* is an arrangement or agreement made by the president and a foreign nation that is similar to a treaty but does not require Senate ratification. The Supreme Court has granted these agreements the same status as treaties. In politically sensitive circumstances, the president may submit an executive agreement to the Senate for approval. Since only a majority rather than a two-thirds vote is required to approve executive agreements, presidents often prefer these agreements to treaties. The political climate may be such that it would be very difficult to get a treaty through the Senate, as it was for Jimmy Carter when he withdrew from Senate consideration the SALT-II treaty he had signed with Soviet leader Leonid Brezhnev.[8]

In the final analysis, the president can dominate foreign policy only when political considerations permit. Presidents negotiate, manage international crises, use their war powers to achieve foreign policy objectives, enter into binding agreements with foreign governments, and generally conduct international relations, but Congress is forever present as a powerful background influence. A case in point is the congressional response to Bush's Persian Gulf venture. Although members of Congress expressed support for the venture itself, many had serious questions about the immediately preceding events. For about two weeks prior to its invasion of Kuwait, Iraq had massed its troops on the Kuwaiti border, and Iraqi leaders made bellicose noises. The Bush administration seemed indifferent to Iraqi intentions and said as much to Saddam Hussein, Iraq's leader. The administration's much vaunted competence was called into question by Republican as well as Democratic legislators.

Although it does not take a direct part in foreign negotiations, Congress' ultimate approval is almost always necessary, because of the need for either Senate ratification or congressional appropriations. Presidents ignore Congress at their peril. The classic example is that of Woodrow Wilson's stubborn refusal to negotiate with the Senate Foreign Relations Committee in seeking approval for the

---

[8]In 1972, President Nixon signed an executive agreement with the Soviet Union that concluded the first in a series of arms conferences known as the Strategic Arms Limitations Talks (SALT). The talks continued under Nixon, Ford, and Carter. Sufficient agreement had been reached between the Soviet Union and the United States to draw up an arms limitation treaty known as SALT-II, which President Carter signed and at first submitted to the Senate for ratification. Because of the Soviet invasion of Afghanistan in 1979, he withdrew the treaty from a hostile Senate. However, both the United States and the Soviet Union have since abided by most of the treaty provisions.

Treaty of Versailles and our entry into the League of Nations. As a consequence, the treaty was defeated and the United States did not enter the League.

Despite the enormous expansion of executive authority, Congress is still supreme within the confines of the Constitution.

INFORMAL POWERS

The president, however, has sources of power outside the Constitution. Perhaps the most effective source is his popularity with the general public. To a large extent this is because most Americans share the Hamiltonian view of the president as the representative of all the people. In *The Federalist*, No. 68, Hamilton argued most succinctly that the president derives his authority directly from the people as a whole when he wrote: ". . . the executive should be independent for his continuance in office on all but the people themselves." And indeed presidents have relied on popular support in their contests with the other centers of power since "President Jefferson basked in the sunshine of popularity and power," to borrow Henry Adams's words.[9]

In Jefferson's day, nationwide popularity was sought through the newspapers. At a later time, in the days of the railroad train, a national audience was created through cross-country stump speeches. Today, efforts to create national support are made through radio, TV, and videotapes. Of course, past techniques as well as modern ones are now used when presidents reach out to their national constituencies.

The Media.   Presidents reach their publics through the mass media. The media are among our primary sources of current information (there are others, such as special reports, word-of-mouth stories, etc.), which they disseminate very widely. As we saw in Chapter 7, all the media in the United States are commercial enterprises, which means that they are mainly interested in stories that will catch and hold their readers' attention. Although the president is always newsworthy, he may be upstaged by the Super Bowl, or an earthquake, or a particularly horrendous murder. It is therefore important for him to manage as much as possible the flow of information to the press. The modern-day "masters" of the media were Franklin D. Roosevelt, John F. Kennedy, and Ronald Reagan, although Reagan sometimes stumbled through his press conferences.

But for the most part, White House stories are not transmitted to the media by the president directly. Ever since Herbert Hoover, the president has had a large staff headed by a press secretary who controls as much as possible the flow of news from the White House and cabinet departments. The press secretary usually holds daily press briefings, arranges presidential press conferences, and manages "photo opportunities," which are picture-taking events such as a ceremonial signing of a bill or a meeting with a foreign dignitary and at which no

---

[9]Henry Adams, *History of the United States of America* (New York: Library of America, 1986), p. 438.

questions are allowed. Photo opportunities were developed to a high art by the Reagan and Bush administrations.

If the president's press office is successful, it can manipulate the news so that the chief executive gains popular support for his policies. Sometimes popular support can be translated into voter pressure on Congress, which was the main purpose of FDR's radio addresses called "fireside chats." But this is not always effective. In 1938, Roosevelt spoke out against the conservative members of his own party in what was dubbed a "purge" by his opponents. Not only did he lose this battle, but in that year's election conservatives gained seats in the House and

Senate. Nevertheless, by manipulating the media, presidents can more easily rally the nation behind them, as Ronald Reagan did so effectively in his first term. When this happens they stand a better chance of achieving their objectives than when they cannot rally the nation. To a considerable degree, presidential power derives from media interest and personal popularity.

Presidential Personality.   Manipulation of the media is extremely important, but one of its prime purposes is to project an attractive image of the president. The personality of the president has been important since George Washington. Jefferson, who was so fearful that the presidency might turn into monarchy, was reassured by Washington's "perfect integrity" and determination to allow the "republican experiment" a fair trial. We still look for integrity in our presidents and hope that the republican experiment can continue despite their increasing power.

Because of the heavy demands and constant frustrations that presidents are faced with, they must have enormous self-confidence or huge egos. Indeed, it is very difficult to run for office without a sizable ego. John F. Kennedy revealed this in a joke he is supposed to have told about Lyndon B. Johnson, then his vice-president. In the joke both Kennedy and Johnson were senators and the presidential race of 1960 loomed in front of them. Kennedy is speaking.

> I dreamed about 1960 myself the other night, and I told Stuart Symington [another senator and contender for the Democratic nomination] and Lyndon Johnson about it in the cloakroom yesterday. I told them how the Lord came into my bedroom, anointed my head and said, "John Kennedy, I hereby appoint you President of the United States." Symington said, "That's strange, Jack, because I too had a similar dream last night in which the Lord anointed me and declared me President of the United States and Outer Space." Johnson then said, "That's very interesting gentlemen, because I too had a similar dream last night and I don't remember anointing either one of you."[10]

And LBJ certainly seemed to try for omnipotence.

Johnson was able to push through the program Kennedy may have conceived but could not get through Congress. The contrast between these two men may be very illuminating. Kennedy was extremely charming and was very popular, at least with the press, but was on the whole very ineffective in getting his program enacted. Johnson, on the other hand, had a rather unappealing public persona, was generally disliked by the press, and had little national exposure before becoming president. But he was the consummate politician. Not only was he exceptionally skillful in manipulating Congress, but he brought to the presidency a level of energy and determination not seen since Franklin D. Roosevelt. Like FDR, LBJ wrought a revolution of sorts. In his one term in office, Johnson moved through a sometimes recalcitrant Congress Kennedy's tax cut, a controversial bill funding mass transit, the Civil Rights Act of 1964, an act establishing the Office

---

[10]Adapted from James T. Patterson, *America in the Twentieth Century* (New York: Harcourt Brace Jovanovich, 1976), p. 427.

of Economic Opportunity (OEO) and the Equal Employment Opportunity Commission, the Voting Rights Act of 1965, and Medicare, which together with other legislation comprised his Great Society program. Kennedy and Johnson occupied the same office, the media was friendlier to Kennedy than to Johnson, yet Johnson was the more effective president. The main difference between them was their personalities.

Few presidents in American history have been as effective as Lyndon B. Johnson. All of these few had forceful personalities. They were all practical, readily adaptable men—even Jefferson, despite his strong ideological beliefs. They took an office that at first seemed subordinate to Congress and transformed it into one capable of dominating the legislature. One has to look to the personality of the president as well as to the constitutional and historical factors around the office for an explanation of the vast growth of presidential power. When all three factors come together for an individual, then he, and perhaps sometime in the future she, can wield what is perceived by many as the greatest power in the world.

ESSENTIALS OF THE PRESIDENCY

Not only has presidential power grown over the years, but popular expectations have grown correspondingly. Partisans expect the president to lead them to victory in all electoral battles. The Framers of the Constitution thought of the president as above "faction," their word for party. But from the very beginning, when Jefferson formed the Democratic-Republican party, the president has been his party's chief as well as his country's top executive. In recent years, since the era of Franklin D. Roosevelt, Americans have held the president accountable for the economy's performance. He is expected to be, in the words of a leading student of the presidency, the "manager of prosperity." Also since the Roosevelt era, the president is looked upon as the "leader of the free world." But above all, we expect the president to fulfill his constitutional responsibilities as chief executive.

THE ROLE OF CHIEF EXECUTIVE

As we saw earlier, the president is required by the Constitution to make certain that the laws are carried out. That is what the word *executive* means. An *executive* is a person who carries out or "executes" decisions. The term arose in the seventeenth and eighteenth centuries and was used almost immediately with reference to the head of government. When John Locke warned against having the executive and legislative power in one hand, he was thinking of the head of government, whether called, as he said, "Czar or Grand Signior, or how you please."

Certain subsidiary powers flow from the president's role as the nation's chief executive. As head of the vast bureaucracy created to execute legislative policies, the president has appointive, directive, organizational, and discretionary power. Some of these powers are stated explicitly in the Constitution. Others have been delegated by Congress. Under the separation-of-powers doctrine, Congress cannot perform executive functions. In order to realize its objectives, it has created the bureaucracy and empowered the president to run it.

Our earlier discussion of the executive powers of the president depicted a vast multilayered bureaucracy below him. Figure 9.1 will give you some idea of the bureaucracy over which the chief executive presides. As we noted in our earlier discussion, the Executive Office of the President (EOP) was created to help manage this huge bureaucracy. But as Figure 9.2 indicates, the Executive Office is itself a fairly large and complex bureaucracy.

During the 1930s, government experienced phenomenal growth in an effort to cope with the Great Depression. The Roosevelt administration created through

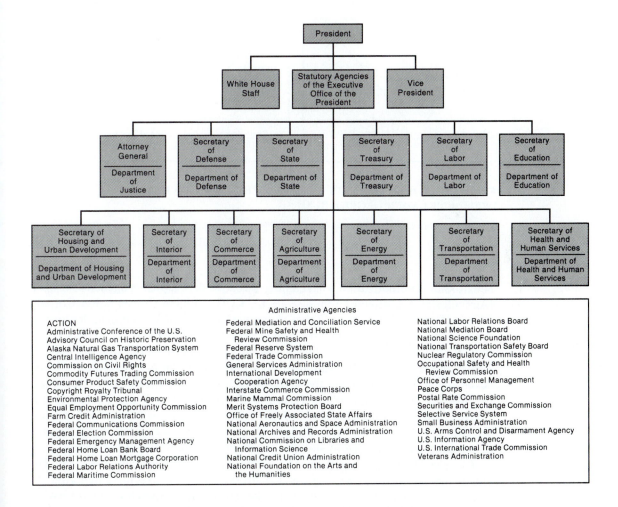

FIGURE 9.1   ORGANIZATION CHART OF THE EXECUTIVE BRANCH

SOURCE: Adapted from *U.S. Government Manual, 1985–86* and *Federal/State Executive Directory*, ed. Nancy Cahill and Pauline G. Green (Washington, D.C.: Carroll Publishing, 1987). Reprinted by permission of Carroll Publishing Company.

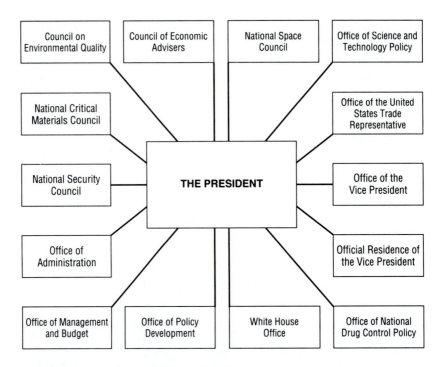

FIGURE 9.2   ORGANIZATION CHART OF THE EXECUTIVE OFFICE OF THE PRESIDENT UNDER GEORGE BUSH

SOURCE: From *U.S. Government Manual 1989/90*, p. 86.

congressional authorization what came to be called the "alphabet agencies": AAA (Agricultural Adjustment Administration), CCC (Civilian Conservation Corps), FERA (Federal Emergency Relief Administration), NRA (National Recovery Administration), TVA (Tennessee Valley Authority), and the WPA (Works Progress Administration), to name just a few. In 1937, a cry for help went up and, in 1939, Congress passed the Administrative Reorganization Act, which gave Roosevelt the authority to create the Executive Office of the President. In doing so, he enlarged his personal White House staff and joined to it the Bureau of the Budget, which was transferred from the Treasury Department and later became the Office of Management and Budget. Over the years since FDR, the EOP and its agencies have changed to suit the president and the needs of the times.

The president does not have sole authority over the executive branch. He shares that authority with Congress. Congress creates the executive departments and agencies under the president and has kept its influence over them by reviewing their activities. The president's authority stems from his appointive power, which must meet with the approval of the Senate for senior administrators, and his ability to fire those administrators at his own discretion, which was granted him in 1789 by Congress. As we saw in Figure 9.1, there are basically three tiers to the executive branch below the president: on the first level there are the White House staff, the statutory agencies of the Executive Office, and the vice president and his staff; on the second level are the cabinet members and their departments; and on the third level are the administrative agencies, some of which are quite independent of the president, such as the Federal Reserve. We will look more closely at the executive bureaucracy in the next chapter.

THE ROLE AS INTERNATIONAL LEADER

The early presidents wished to avoid foreign involvements. In his farewell address on leaving the presidency, Washington suggested: "The great rule of conduct for us in regard to foreign nation is . . . to have with them as little political connection as possible." But of course this was not possible. Still, for most of our history, foreign affairs were a secondary part of our political concerns. Until the late 1930s, American interests focused on domestic issues. Then, with the increasing threat posed by Germany and Japan, Americans began to shift their attention to what was happening overseas. At the end of the Second World War, the United States was the most powerful nation on the globe. Whoever headed our nation had little alternative but to assume leadership in international matters. Most Americans and the rest of the world see the president as heading our nation.

Harry S Truman, who was president at the time, took on the role of world leader, but in a spirit of partisanship that affected our relations around the world. In 1947, he took sides in local conflicts in Greece and Turkey, proclaiming what has become known as the Truman Doctrine and setting the terms of America's postwar foreign policy. In his speech requesting military and financial assistance to these nations, he said:

> One of the primary objectives of the foreign policy of the United States is the creation of conditions in which we and other nations will be able to work out a way of life free from coercion. We shall not realize our objectives, however, unless we are willing to help free peoples to maintain their free institutions and their national integrity against aggressive movements that seek to impose on them totalitarian regimes. . . . I believe that it must be the policy of the United States to support free peoples who are resisting attempted subjugation by armed minorities or by outside pressures. . . . The free peoples of the world look to us for support in maintaining their freedoms.
>
> If we falter in our leadership, we may endanger the peace of the world—and we shall surely endanger the welfare of our own Nation.[11]

The "totalitarian regimes" that Truman had in mind were communist ones. And the "outside pressures" were exerted by the Soviet Union, mainland China, and

---

[11]From a speech before the joint session of Congress on March 12, 1947, reprinted in *American Issues: The Social Record,* vol. 2, eds. Merle Curti et al. (Philadelphia: J.B. Lippincott, 1971), pp. 512–513.

North Korea. Truman's foreign policy fed the rampant paranoia of Soviet Russia's dictator, Joseph Stalin, and together the two leaders brought on what is known as the Cold War. Succeeding leaders of the two regimes have followed the policies set by these two men virtually to this day. Reagan rode to the presidency calling the Soviet Union "the evil empire." He since moderated his rhetoric so that he could sign the Intermediate-Range Nuclear Force (INF) treaty with the Soviets in 1987. Since then, the communist empire has collapsed, and the U.S.S.R. and the U.S. have worked together on a number of ventures.

Truman boasted that *he* made foreign policy. To a great extent he had, and in so doing he largely established the international role and set the agenda of the modern presidency. Presidents throughout our history have taken the initiative in foreign affairs, however. In part this is because foreign nations have always wanted to deal with someone who can make decisions that will hold, and the president is best positioned for that role; in part because the president has the best foreign service apparatus in the nation working for him—the State Department and the intelligence services—and thus can respond more appropriately than Congress, or so it was believed; and in part, perhaps the largest part, because Congress generally, although by no means always, has supported presidential decisions in dealing with foreign nations. But it was not until the modern presidency started by Franklin Roosevelt and Harry Truman that international relations became a central concern.

Truman not only started us down the bumpy road that led from Korea to Vietnam, he also started us down the gilded highway that saved the economies of Western Europe and Japan. George C. Marshall, at the time Truman's secretary of state, proposed a plan for assisting in the recovery of the economies wrecked by World World II. The Marshall Plan was so successful that its principles were copied, somewhat, and extended to Asia, Africa, and Latin America. In Europe, the Soviets rejected the Marshall Plan. In its later incarnations in third world countries, American economic assistance was used as another weapon to combat "communism," which more often than not was local nationalism clothed in socialist rhetoric.

The world has changed considerably in the forty-five or so years since the end of the Second World War. Our international friends are no longer as amenable to our influence as they once were. In many areas, such as economic ones, they have become the most serious rivals we have. Both the Soviet Union and China are no longer seen as a threat to American well-being, thanks to the peacemaking efforts of our two most violently anticommunist presidents, Richard Nixon and Ronald Reagan. In 1988, the United States took the first steps toward entering a new era of international relations that promises to be far more complex and fluid than in the past. And in 1990, we assumed the mantle of Metternich and adopted the role of guardians of legitimacy in the Middle East and perhaps the rest of the third world.[12]

---

[12]Prince Klemenz von Metternich was the chancellor of Austria in the first half of the nineteenth century and the leader of what is known as the "Concert of Europe." He was very concerned to maintain legitimate authority, which he took to be possessed only by royal rulers. The Bush administration had adopted positions in relation to Kuwait that resemble those of Metternich.

THE ROLE AS MANAGER OF THE ECONOMY

On October 19, 1987, the New York Stock Market crashed. The following day the markets in Tokyo and London plummeted, and the one in Hong Kong closed to prevent a crash. Almost immediately, Americans, Europeans, and Asians looked to President Reagan for a solution, although no one had yet come up with a clear description of the problem. Since Franklin D. Roosevelt's mythic "saving" of the American economy during the Great Depression, Americans have held the president responsible for economic performance. Because our economy is intricately entwined in overseas economies and has for many years dominated them, many foreign nations look to us for solutions in economic crises. In large measure that means looking to the president. Both Americans and foreigners expect the president of the United States to manage economic conditions so as to assure everyone a degree of financial security.

As it happens, the decisions of American presidents have had some impact on their own and the world's economy. Although Roosevelt's programs at first pulled the economy a bit out of the depression, it slipped back down again after 1937 and did not recover until our entry into World War II. When Reagan came into office, the budget deficit he inherited from Carter was a little over $70 billion, a figure that was considered outrageously and unacceptably high. Using this figure and everyone's outrage as a wedge, Reagan then cut the Great Society programs benefiting the poor as a means of reducing the deficit. However, he also reduced taxes on the rich and sharply increased military expenditures, so that by 1987 his deficit almost tripled to about $220 billion. On top of this huge growth, the United States imported more than it exported under Reagan, so that the trade deficit skyrocketed from $32 billion in 1982 to $160 billion in 1986. Although conservative economists denied that the Reagan deficits had anything to do with the "Crash of 1987," European and nonconservative economists pointed to the huge "double deficit" of the government and trade as having some causal connection. When the White House indicated it would be willing to raise taxes in an effort to reduce the federal deficit, the stock market stabilized for a while and moved shakily upward. Since then the stock market has remained volatile, and the economy as a whole has been weak.

It is very difficult to determine what impact a president's decisions have on the economy as a whole. It is fairly safe to say that when his budget includes military outlays for advanced weapon systems, arms manufacturers benefit, just as it is fairly safe to say that when a presidential directive cuts food stamps from certain categories of poor people, those people will have difficulty managing their own budgets. But beyond the one-to-one causal relationship, it is almost impossible to connect presidential actions with the general economic conditions prevailing at a given time.

THE ROLE OF PARTY CHIEF

How well the economy does will often determine how successful a president is as head of his party. The reverse is also often true. How successful a president is as leader of his party will often determine how well his economic program does in Congress. If a president fails as party chief, he will often find that many members of his own party in Congress will vote against him. Many congressional members of the Democratic party saw President Jimmy Carter, for example, as a liability, especially after he made a speech bewailing a "crisis of the American spirit." As a consequence, he had a great deal of difficulty getting his program through Congress even though Congress was under the control of his party. Carter could not even rely on friendly support from the leading Democrat in the House, speaker Thomas P. (Tip) O'Neill.

Carter's case was extreme and came about after he was in office a couple of years. Even then, he retained sufficient control of the party apparatus to gain the nomination for a second term despite powerful opposition. As a rule, presidents are seen as the party's leader. Even before winning an election, they gain control of the party machinery as soon as they are nominated for president. As party chiefs they appoint usually close friends and longtime supporters to the chairmanship of the national committee. They also influence the rules governing the selection and seating of delegates to national party nominating conventions. It was this control that helped Carter to withstand the challenge to his second nomination by Senator Edward Kennedy.

Presidents also usually have a large say in shaping the party platform adopted at the convention. But perhaps the major source of presidential power within the party is the control of patronage. As a rule presidents nominate and appoint loyal party supporters to top-level positions in the bureaucracy and to federal judge-

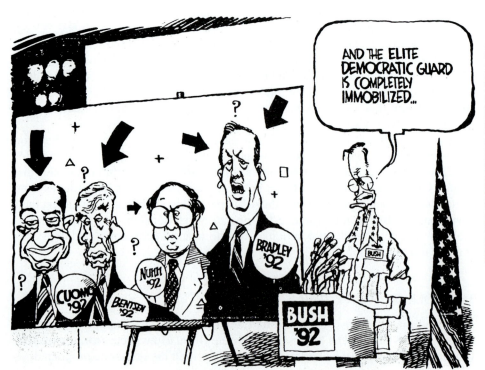

ships. If they are popular and successful, presidents are often called on to endorse and sometimes even campaign for party candidates, especially for those in tight races.

The basic relationship between the president and leading members of his party is one of mutual support. Leading elected or appointed officials support the president's program in return for which he uses some of his patronage on their behalf or lends them his prestige. The idea is that if they scratch each other's back well enough, then he is successful and they are successful. Success is measured by reelection.

But scratching a president's back can be tricky. His interests are usually broader and more national than those of senators or representatives, for example. Their interests are local and may be in conflict with those conceived by the president. In those instances they may well stand in opposition to presidential policies, as happened to Harry Truman when he proposed civil rights legislation and Southern Democrats rebelled against him. Some of these, such as Strom Thurmond, bolted the party and became Republicans. During the 1986 races for Congress, several Republicans in the Northeast asked Reagan not to campaign for them because his policies were unpopular in that region.

But as a rule, presidents and congressional party members try to work together. This means that the president cannot get too far ahead of most of the people in his party. One of the secrets of strong presidents is their ability to accommodate the diverse interests of their parties and at the same time move a little in front of most of their members. Franklin D. Roosevelt was a master at this. Although he was personally opposed to racial discrimination, he refused to propose civil rights legislation because he knew he would lose what was popularly called the Solid South. He needed that support to put the rest of his social program across. If there is too wide a gap between party chief and party, the chief almost always loses. Lyndon Johnson, who was as masterful a politician as Roosevelt, became so obsessed with the Vietnam War that he lost contact with his support groups and found himself faced with a rebellious party in 1968. Perhaps as a result, he gave up the presidency without a fight.

Above all, the president's role as party chief is temporary. It is effective at best only during the period of his tenure as chief executive. Once he leaves office, even if he is popular and much loved, he is generally on the sidelines and given the decorative role of elder statesman. What might be called the ephemeral nature of the presidency acts as another constraint on power and party loyalty.

THE TRANSFER OF POWER: SUCCESSION AND TRANSITION

There comes a time when every president passes from office. This can happen because of an election, because of the completion of the allotted two terms, because of serious disability, because of death in office, or because of forced resignation. The problem then arises of how to transfer power from one person to another. In the Third World, the transfer of power often takes a violent form. In Europe, that had often been the case before the nineteenth century. Fortunately for the United States, the transfer of power here has always been peaceful. Nevertheless, it has been problematic, and the Constitution and its amendments have tried to deal with the issue.

THE PROBLEM OF SUCCESSION

The Constitution provides that the vice president shall take the office of president in the event of impeachment, death, resignation, or "Inability to discharge the Powers and Duties of the said Office." However, it never defined what this "inability" was. Nor did it adequately provide for the possibility that both president and vice president were unable to serve, for whatever reason. After a series of succession acts, each of which was deemed at some point inadequate, Congress passed and the states ratified in 1967 the Twenty-fifth Amendment. It addressed both the question of presidential "inability" and the issue of who comes after the vice president in the line of succession.

After reaffirming that the vice president succeeds to the presidency, the amendment states that if there is a vacancy in the office of vice president, the president shall nominate a vice president who must then be confirmed by a majority of both houses of Congress. Very soon after ratification, the amendment was put to the test. In 1973, Vice President Spiro Agnew virtually admitted to criminal charges and resigned. President Nixon nominated Representative Gerald Ford as his vice president. Ford was confirmed and, in 1974, succeeded to the presidency when Nixon was forced to resign. Ford in turn nominated former Governor Nelson Rockefeller as his vice president, who was of course confirmed.

Presidential disability can be declared in writing either by the president himself or by the vice president and a majority of the cabinet. In this event, the vice president is acting president until the president can return to office. On declaring in writing that he is no longer disabled, the president can resume his office unless challenged by the vice president and a majority of the cabinet. If the challenge does occur, then the dispute is sent to Congress for judgment. Congress then decides by a two-thirds majority whether the president is able to resume his duties or the vice president should continue in office.

ISSUES OF TRANSITION

Presidents do not leave office only because of death or disability. They are succeeded in office more often than not because of elections. When the newly elected president is a member of the same party as the outgoing chief executive, there should be little difficulty, but when they are of opposing parties, some problems in communication may arise. Since Truman inaugurated a system of aiding the incoming president by informing him of crucial matters requiring executive attention, only one president has been succeeded by a president-elect of his own party. Democrat Truman was followed by Republican Eisenhower, followed by Democrats Kennedy-Johnson, followed by Republicans Nixon-Ford, followed by Democrat Carter, who was followed by Republican Reagan. Only Reagan was followed by a Republican, George Bush. As a result, friction between the old and new administrations has sometimes characterized transitions.

Transition teams are usually formed well in advance of entry into office, sometimes well in advance of the election itself. Both Carter and Reagan gathered large cadres of experts to study issues, form task forces, and sift through personnel files much before they knew they would actually need the information. Also, the outgoing administration informs all candidates of critical matters and generally works closely with the incoming president and his transition team to make as smooth a change as possible.

Basically, transition teams help find the personnel for the new administration and help formulate policies that enable the new president to take charge and reach his objectives as soon as he can. As a rule, newly elected presidents have a short time in which to enjoy a highly cooperative Congress before the legislature starts asserting itself and resisting his programs. The faster the president can get going, the more his program will get through Congress.

In Conclusion

Most Americans, and much of the world, see the president as the most powerful part of the United States government. And since the Second World War, he has accumulated increased power, especially in foreign affairs. But constitutionally, Congress is the dominant branch, and it asserts itself every so often. The president's power derives in part from the formal powers granted him by the Constitution and in large part from informal factors, such as his ability to manage the legislature, function as party chief or dispenser of patronage, project a strong personality, and manipulate the media. With increased power have come increased expectations and, because of the growing complexity of the world, less certainty about our future course.

C ★ A ★ S ★ E S ★ T ★ U ★ D ★ Y

Presidential Policy-Making

Americans tend to think of their presidents as personally leading the nation to solutions of economic, political, and social problems. Repeated national crises and the country's role in global affairs have lent force to this view. However, the president's power actually extends only as far as his ability to persuade others that their interests are the same as his.[1] Presidents cannot simply do everything themselves and need to work through others. Moreover, executive action requires the cooperation of other centers of power in order to make or carry out policy.

The following vignette of the start of the Reagan years illustrates the personal and political forces engaged in making policy. These forces were external to President Reagan himself. Nevertheless, they significantly shaped the economic policy that was intended as the showpiece of the Reagan administration. Although our vignette may be an extreme example of the reliance of a president on the skills and intelligence of other people, to some extent all presidents work the same way. President George Washington, for example, depended very heavily on the advice and efforts of his cabinet, especially that of Alexander Hamilton.

Ronald Reagan had a more "laid-back" management style than most other presidents. His relaxed style meant that he was completely detached from the operational details of the White House. In large measure, this resulted in a presidency run more by the members of his staff than by Reagan himself. The character and style of a president has always affected the way in which the White House operates in relation to the rest of the political world. The Reagan presidency was no exception.

The Reagan Revolution

The "Reagan revolution" refers to the president's partially successful attempt to cut federal expenditures and taxes. Tax and expenditure reductions were linked. As the more astute presidential aides hoped, once Congress had reduced taxes, thereby decreasing federal revenues, pressure increased upon reluctant legislators to cut social programs. Reducing the massive federal deficits that had been produced by the administration's tax cuts was the reason given for severe cuts in the budget.

---

[1]The notion that the president is limited by his ability to persuade others to cooperate with him was first developed by Richard E. Neustadt in his classic work *Presidential Power*.

Origin of the Reagan Revolution

At the very heart of the Reagan revolution was the *theory* of supply-side economics, which states that tax cuts to spur demand will produce economic prosperity. Economist Arthur Laffer and *Wall Street Journal* editorial writer Jude Wanniski developed the theory in the academic world. Congressman Jack Kemp (R, N.Y.) took up the cudgels for the theory in Congress, making it the core of his economic program.

Generally in American politics the mix between ideas and politics is nebulous at best. Ideology, which is essentially the linkage of many ideas into broad political or economic philosophies, has been rare because political pluralism and the diversity of ideas that accompany it make ideologies politically unacceptable and ineffective. But politicians, while not seeking ideologies, reach out for ideas such as supply-side economics, which may help them get elected and, once in office, give some coherence to their programs and policies.

Supply-side economics came to the Reagan White House via a circuitous route. David Stockman, a radical college student but a conservative congressman who became Reagan's Budget Director, gave a fascinating account of the Reagan revolution in his best-selling book, *The Triumph of Politics*.[2]

Arthur Laffer, Jude Wanniski, Jack Kemp, and others who advocated the supply-side theory got a sympathetic ear from Ronald Reagan when he was running for president. Stockman, a strong Reagan supporter, agreed with the supply-side approach and helped to coach Ronald Reagan on it and other topics for his debates with Jimmy Carter in 1980. And long before the debates, Stockman recalled, "Governor Reagan's campaign managers had sent him to school for a few days to get brushed up on the national issues. There, Jack Kemp, Art Laffer, and Jude Wanniski thoroughly hosed him down with supply-side doctrine." Reagan "knew instantly that it was true and would never doubt it a moment thereafter."

Designing the President's Program

President-elect Ronald Reagan was closely advised by Ed Meese, a California lawyer who was later to become Attorney General, and Michael Deaver, a close friend. They embarked on a campaign to place conservative Reagan supporters throughout the highest ranks of the bureaucracy.

David Stockman became Reagan's point man in presenting the supply-side program to a resistant Congress, which was reluctant to make the deep cuts in taxes and Great Society programs called for by the economic theory. Interestingly, before the 1980 race, Stockman had little respect for Reagan. He nevertheless joined the Reagan team, feeling that he could use the president to implement the supply-side program he considered essential to the preservation of the American economy.

---

[2]David A. Stockman, *The Triumph of Politics* (New York: Harper & Row, 1986). All subsequent quotes are taken from the Avon paperback edition of this book.

Once in his new position, Stockman "soon discovered that it would be up to him to design the Reagan revolution." Largely on his own initiative, he refined the president's supply-side program. He was the principal Reagan administration spokesperson for the new and radical policy before Congress, shaping at the same time White House strategy to convince Capitol Hill to go along with it.

Launching the Program

President Reagan announced the economic recovery program before a joint session of Congress in February 1981. "The President's speech," observed Stockman, "represented the astonishing triumph of the ideology of a few over the political necessities of the many." Looking back on the event, Stockman concluded after he had left office, "Designing a comprehensive plan to bring about a sweeping change in national economic governance in forty days is a preposterous, wantonly reckless notion. At the time I had thought it was merely an exhausting but exhilarating ordeal. Somewhere deep in my mind, though, lurked a scintilla of doubt."

Dealing with Congress.   Presidents may announce programs, but it is Congress that enacts them. And Congress is a complicated political institution, divided into hundreds of committees, whose chairmen and staffers jealously guard their prerogatives. To enact a law, the administration has to work through committee chairmen and their staffers. Stockman soon found strong resistance on the Hill to a variety of cuts in programs congressional committees had developed and in which they felt a proprietary interest.

Iron Triangles.   Budget cuts were made even more difficult because of the connection among congressional committees, administrative departments or agencies, and pressure groups. These iron triangles believed their interests were threatened by the Reagan cuts. Just as congressional committees do not want their programs sabotaged, executive departments and agencies do not want their budgets reduced, nor do private interests want to lose government benefits.

A fine example of the workings of the iron triangle can be found in Stockman's assault on the transportation budget. Mass-transit funds were among those targeted for sharp reduction in his across-the-board cutting program. "One of my basic fiscal principles," wrote Stockman, "was that the federal government had no business repairing or building local city streets, country roads, bridges or mass transit systems. ... Mass transit operating subsidies were a special abomination, costing the taxpayers over one million dollars per year. ... If there was any single clear-cut case of what the Reagan revolution required, it was dumping the vast local transportation pork barrel."

As economically logical as transportation budget cuts appeared to Stockman, he soon confronted strong and inevitable political opposition. The Secretary of Transportation, Drew Lewis, whom Stockman described as "probably the most astute politician in the cabinet," nevertheless "turned completely white when I first laid out my plans to scrap the local highway and transit subsidies." Lewis insisted on retaining the subsidies and suggested raising gasoline taxes to pay for the programs.

Stockman found that "Lewis's initial reaction to my attack on the transportation pork barrel accurately reflected the consensus of the politicians. The Republicans on Capitol Hill, led by conservatives like Senator Alfonse D'Amato and liberals like Senator Arlen Specter, fought and prevailed on every effort to cut mass-transit. And all of the congressional politicians wanted to keep fixing local potholes, roads, and bridges. We finished up saving hardly a dime of the [proposed] twenty billion dollars."

The Final Outcome

The White House did in the end achieve both budget cuts and large tax reductions. Stockman's brilliant strategy was to link, in the congressional and public minds, all the budget cuts into one large package. Congress had to vote that package up or down as a whole. Individual legislators and committees were not permitted to sabotage the program by protecting their narrow bailiwicks. The White House strategy, enhanced by Reagan's skills as the great Communicator, won the day in the short run.

However, although the tax cuts remained in effect, Congress soon began chipping away at the budget reductions as the iron triangles reasserted themselves. In the end, as Stockman observed, politics triumphed. But that it did so is not bad. Stockman himself admitted that part of the supply-side theory which demanded massive budget cuts "rested on the illusion that the will of the people was at drastic variance with actions of the politicians." In the event, this proved not to be so. The hundreds of federal programs that grant subsidies and benefits to particular interests, and in the case of programs such as Social Security to the general public, reflect congressional responses to felt needs.

"Despite their often fuzzy rhetoric and twisted rationalizations," concluded a chastened Stockman after he left the government, "congressmen and senators ultimately deliver what their constituencies demand." And "those who suggest the existence of an anti-statist electorate are in fact demanding that national policy be harnessed to their own particular doctrine of the public good. The actual electorate, however, is not interested in this doctrine; when it is interested at all, it is interested in getting help from the government to compensate for a perceived disadvantage. Consequently, the spending politics of Washington do reflect the heterogeneous and parochial demands that arise from the diverse, activated fragments of the electorates scattered across the land. What you see done in the halls of the politicians may not be wise, but it is the only real and viable definition of what the electorate wants."

Postscript: Presidential Leadership in the Bush White House

White House insiders have always stressed presidential limits more than powers when writing about their experiences. At the midpoint of his first term President George Bush, though claiming the authority to make war in the Middle East,

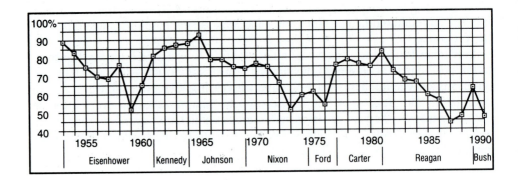

FIGURE 9.3   HOW OFTEN PRESIDENTS WON

SOURCE: *Congressional Quarterly Weekly Report,* December 22, 1990, p. 4185.

faced strong congressional opposition. On the domestic front Bush had a low score with Congress. (See Figure 9.3.) He had particular difficulty with legislators over tax spending policies, which had their roots in prior Reagan administration actions. While Bush's difficulties resulted from the nature of Congress itself (see Case Study, Chapter 8), weak White House leadership was also an important factor. Bush made a capital gains tax cut the mainstay of his program. Not only did he fail to get what he wanted, congressional Democrats succeeded in passing increased taxes on the "rich," a slap in the face of all Republicans!

Bush's Leadership Style

Americans always personalize the presidency, thinking less of the character of the institution than of the man who occupies the oval office; however, both personal and institutional characteristics shape White House leadership. Moreover, presidents cannot dictate to their constituencies, which include Congress, the bureaucracy, political party and interest group leaders, state and local politicians, as well as foreign leaders. The president is not a dictator, but a negotiator who is hobbled by the constitutional system and the political pluralism that is such a dominant feature of American politics.

The Personal Presidency.   Bush took a highly personal approach to the presidency in both domestic and foreign spheres. Knowing that he could not rely upon a disciplined Republican party, which in any case did not have a congressional majority, he touted bipartisanship and tried to forge ad hoc coalitions to get his way on Capitol Hill. He attempted to capitalize on personal contacts with key congressional players, just as in the Persian Gulf War he effectively used his vast network of personal acquaintances among foreign leaders to forge the international coalition opposing Saddam Hussein. Personal leadership, however, works only insofar as presidential and target group interests coincide. On the domestic front Bush found that entrenched parochial interests on Capitol Hill, which most importantly included the incentives of committee chairmen to maintain their power, could not be overcome by White House appeals to bipartisanship and the national interest.

One of Bush's greatest difficulties with Congress was his apparent lack of conviction and lackluster style. Unlike his predecessor, he was not a "Great Communicator." His presidential campaign had been a piecemeal effort that did not stress the need for programmatic changes but rather appealed to popular instincts on such issues as the Pledge of Allegiance to the flag. But, as columnist George Will observed, "even campaigns less negative and vapid than Bush's confer, primarily, an office and initial deference. That is, an election provides less a mandate than an opportunity to fashion a specific mandate while and by governing." But, continued Will, "Bush inherited the presidency from a 'conviction politician' who . . . often aroused public opinion to compel Congress. But Bush seems to regard as *lese-majesty* the idea that he must constantly earn his claim on the public's continuing deference. Such deference depends upon clarity about ideas and principles—'the vision thing.' That is why Bush's inarticulateness, although often comic, is not funny. It is not an esthetic but a philosophic failing. He does not say why he wants to be there, so the public does not know why it should care if he gets his way. Until the public does, he won't. Congress will."[3]

The Bush Staff.   The White House staff has become the most important part of the Executive Office of the President, which also includes the Office of Management and Budget (OMB), the National Security Council, Council of Economic Advisors, Office of Science and Technology, the First Lady's staff, and others that come and go as the president and Congress see the need to make changes in the Executive Office to respond to changing presidential needs.

The effectiveness of the Executive Office depends largely on the *personal* skills of its staff. Those skills derive from the ability of staff members to understand Washington politics, and particularly to know how to operate within the political universe dominated by the legislature. One might easily have expected this sort of ability from Bush's White House Chief of Staff, John Sununu. Sununu had been governor of New Hampshire, and therefore had experience dealing with legislators, albeit on a state level. He may not have had much experience with Washington, but he is a quick study and should have rapidly learned the intricate dance on Capitol Hill. That dance, everyone thought, had surely been thoroughly mastered by Bush's other senior staff member, Richard Darman. Bush's Director of OMB, Darman is the quintessential Washington insider. He had served, with brilliance many said, in the administrations of Presidents Nixon, Ford, and Reagan. Both Sununu and Darman had prime responsibility for cobbling together Bush's budget plan and selling it to Congress. Their failure illustrates the central importance of personal style—what might be called good manners—in dealing with Congress.

Just as Bush's personal style contributed to his difficulties on Capitol Hill, Sununu and Darman's style antagonized the members of Congress. The antago-

[3]*Newsweek*, October 2, 1990, p. 84.

nism had become so severe that even congressional Republicans strayed from the fold. Washington journalist Fred Barnes described the White House staff in action: "Sununu and Darman are on the rampage. Cabinet members and White House aides are afraid of Sununu, leery of Darman. Both are loathed by House Republicans. Before the budget deal Darman had courted dozens of allies in Washington. Many are now enemies. Some Democrats have a good relationship with him, but that's a mixed blessing for a Republican budget chief. Sununu, though short-tempered and combative, was an extraordinarily effective chief of staff. No more. He alienated virtually every member of Congress he came in contact with in the budget talks."[4]

Wall Street Journal Washington reporters Alan Murray and Jackie Calmes summed up the outcome of Bush's battle with Congress over taxes. "The story of the budget accord of 1990 ought to be one of success and triumph," they wrote.[5] However, "the budget travail has proven a political disaster for President Bush. While he has acted with confidence and skill in foreign affairs, he vacillated in dealing with the most critical domestic economic issue of his presidency, sometimes changing positions daily. In fact, it didn't take long before the budget muddle once again had his critics, particularly conservatives in his own party, calling him a 'wimp.'"

The Bush administration, particularly while diverted by the Persian Gulf Crisis, experienced considerable difficulties with Congress on the domestic front. The lack of White House leadership allowed individual and entrepreneurial politics to surface with a vengeance on Capitol Hill. The Bush administration's problems with Congress illustrate once again that presidential leadership depends more upon personal style than upon institutional arrangements.

Suggested Readings

James D. Barber. *The Presidential Character: Predicting Performance in the White House,* 3rd ed. Englewood Cliffs, N.J.: Prentice-Hall, 1985.

Thomas E. Cronin. *The State of the Presidency,* 2nd ed. Boston: Little, Brown, 1980.

Richard Neustadt. *Presidential Power.* New York: Wiley, 1980.

George E. Reedy. *The Twilight of the Presidency.* New York: World Publishing Co., 1970.

Clinton Rossiter. *The American Presidency,* rev. ed. New York: Harcourt Brace, 1960.

---

[4]Fred Barnes, "Beasts of the Beltway," *The New Republic,* December 24, 1990, p. 23.
[5]Alan Murray and Jackie Calmes, "The Great Debate: How the Democrats with Rare Cunning Won the Budget War," *The Wall Street Journal,* November 5, 1990, p. A1.

THE BUREAUCRACY

Government rests on the world of civil servants.

G. W. F. Hegel

F ew things have a worse reputation than bureaucracy. Say the word and everyone immediately thinks of red tape, stupid and rigid rules, waste, and coldly impersonal, lazy clerks. But actually, a bureaucracy is the administrative section of any organization, such as a university, business, fraternal club, or government. Administrators, or bureaucrats if you will, carry out the decisions of policy-makers, keep records of all matters pertaining to those decisions, and make reports to the policy-makers.

Policies are usually stated in broad, general terms. To carry out a policy decision one must first understand it, and that involves interpretation. The interpretive process is essentially subjective, which has two possible consequences. One, of course, is that there is perfect agreement between the policy-maker and the administrator. The other is that both understand the policy differently. This last is a genuine possibility when the general terms of a policy must fit the highly individual circumstances of a particular situation. In this case, the implementation of a policy may work out to be contrary to the intent of the policy-maker, and the bureaucrat is in effect making rather than just executing policy.

Administrators also affect policy in another significant way. By selecting the information they report to policy-makers, bureaucrats may and often do influence later decisions on a given policy. All data are summarized, as for example in statistical tables or graphs, and summaries are based on a selection process. Reports must also be organized and coherent, which affords administrators the opportunity to emphasize those aspects of a policy that they either favor or disapprove. They can thereby encourage decision makers to change a policy or continue it. Here again, bureaucrats may function in policy-making roles rather than just simply as civil servants following orders. The problem always is to make certain that the bureaucrat does not usurp the role of the policy-maker.

BACKGROUND

Although the word *bureaucracy* is a nineteenth-century invention, the function it refers to goes back to the beginning of recorded history. The ancient Mesopotamians living in the delta between the Tigris and Euphrates rivers were ruled by priestly bureaucrats who told them when to plant, when to harvest, how much to keep, how much to store, and how much to deliver to the temple. The earliest writings that we have are records of farming and trading transactions produced by these bureaucrats. Ancient Egypt and Rome also had highly developed bureaucracies. With the collapse of Rome in the fifth century A.D., the Roman state bureaucracy virtually disappeared in Western Europe. For all practical purposes, only the Catholic Church had a working bureaucracy at the time.

In the late Middle Ages, as kings in France and England were establishing dominance over their feudal vassals, the monarchs started to develop their own bureaucracies by borrowing the church's. After the Renaissance, the secular state had a secular bureaucracy. By the eighteenth century, most European states had well-trained and firmly established bureaucracies. From their beginnings, bureaucracies were strongly attached to the head of state, called in the eighteenth century the chief magistrate. Today, we call this person a chief executive. The traditional attachment of bureaucracies to chief executives worried our Founding Fathers.

GROWTH OF THE AMERICAN BUREAUCRACY

To assure themselves that the bureaucracy did not owe its allegiance solely to the chief executive, the Framers of the Constitution split the authority over the bureaucracy between the president and Congress. Nevertheless, some of the founders were still unhappy. For example, George Mason of Virginia, one of the most important figures at the Constitutional Convention, complained bitterly that the president will be "directed by Minions and Favourites ... or the principal Officers of the great Departments; the worst and most dangerous of all Ingredients ... in a free Country."[1] For all that, the Framers did not pay much attention to

---

[1] George Mason, "Objections to the Constitution of Government Formed by the Convention," in *The Origins of the American Consitution: A Documentary History*, ed. Michael Kammen (New York: Viking, 1986), p. 256.

the "executive Departments" other than to have the president and the Senate share responsibility for them.

The Constitution does not directly mention a bureaucracy. It refers only in an offhand way to "the principal Officer in each of the executive Departments." In 1789, Washington asked for and the Senate approved three "principal Officers" with "executive Departments." These were:

- Secretary Thomas Jefferson, Department of State

- Secretary Alexander Hamilton, Department of the Treasury

- Secretary Henry Knox, Department of War

This, in effect, was the first cabinet. The executive departments they headed were tiny. At the urging of James Madison, Congress approved the appointment of four assistants to Thomas Jefferson, who had inherited five from John Jay, the secretary of foreign affairs for the Confederation. The Department of War had even fewer employees and no standing army. Treasury was the largest department with 39 employees, and under Hamilton's energetic leadership it was to grow by the end of 1790 to 70 persons.[2] In 1802, the entire federal government employed a little under 3,000 civilian personnel. By contrast, the federal government today employs over 3 million civilians. In 1789, the president's cabinet consisted of three departments; today, it consists of thirteen.

The growth of the federal bureaucracy was comparatively slow until the Civil War, when there was a huge upsurge in the need for government officials. After the presidency of Andrew Jackson, government jobs were part of the "spoils of war" that went to the victor in a presidential race as a means of rewarding loyal party hacks. This led to a great deal of dissatisfaction with the civil service, and from about 1870 onward there were persistent calls for reform. As a result of the assassination of President James A. Garfield by a disgruntled office seeker, civil service reform was brought about in 1883. Many jobs in the government could now be gotten only through competitive examinations, although most positions were still filled by patronage or, as it is sometimes called, the spoils system.

By the early twentieth century, the government had added several new agencies and was employing over 200,000 persons. But the truly enormous increase in the size of government came with the creation of FDR's "alphabet agencies" mentioned in the last chapter. These agencies were created to deal with both the Great Depression and World War II. By 1945, the United States government employed almost 4 million civilian personnel. Afterward, the government has consistently employed between 2 and 4 million since 1970, despite Ronald Reagan's promises to reduce the size of government. It is interesting to note that when Reagan came into office there were 2.8 million civilian employees in the federal government. When he left office, there were 3.9 million.

---

[2]Sources for Department of State employees are Leonard D. White, *The Federalist* (Westport, CT: Greenwood Press, 1948), p. 136, and *The Papers of Thomas Jefferson*, vol. 16, ed. Julian P. Boyd et al. (Princeton, NJ: Princeton University Press, 1961), pp. 512–513; for Department of War, White, *The Federalist*, p. 147, quotes a visitor to the department who "found two clerks and a servant"; and for the Treasury, *The Federalist*, p. 122.

Although merit is supposed to characterize the civil service, the spoils system still operates on the upper levels of the bureaucracy. As Paul Volcker, the former head of the Federal Reserve, said: "There's a very strong [current] trend toward more political appointments and fewer career appointments." This sort of situation is demoralizing, Volcker believes. He asked challengingly: "Would you want to be bossed round by a deputy assistant secretary who was [really] an advance man?"[3]

THE CONSTITUTIONAL CONTEXT OF THE BUREAUCRACY

The Constitution depicts a simple picture of an executive branch under the president. It says only that he appoints senior officials with the advice and consent of the Senate and may require in writing the opinions of the heads of the executive departments. Beyond these requirements the Constitution does not go. Yet it was enough to set the ground for shared control over the bureaucracy by the executive and legislative branches. But the type of control exercised by each branch is very different.

Separation of Powers and the Bureaucracy.   Congress alone has the authority to create executive departments and agencies, define their scope and powers, and appropriate funding so they can carry out their responsibilities. However, the legislature is prohibited by the separation-of-powers doctrine from the direct exercise of authority over the bureaucracy. The president alone has that authority. Nevertheless, the power Congress does have to set up the agencies and departments is sufficient to enable it to profoundly affect the character of the executive branch.

The separation-of-powers and checks and balances doctrines tend to make for an adversarial relationship between Congress and the presidency. This results in a tug-of-war for control of the bureaucracy. To survive, agencies seek political support wherever they can find it and try to accommodate all power centers. Sometimes this requires great acrobatic skill from agency heads, for they often need to balance conflicting demands without offending anyone in power. As a consequence, many agencies have adopted an independent stance toward the two primary centers of power that concern them—the presidency and Congress. In large measure that effort at independence has almost turned the bureaucracy into a separate branch of government in which it can check and balance the other branches.

Enumerated Powers and the Bureaucracy.   When Congress creates an executive department or agency, it does so by virtue of the authority granted it by the Constitution. Article I, Section 8, enumerates the powers of Congress. The enabling legislation establishing an agency or department always cites the constitutional authority under which it had been created.

---

[3]Martin Tolchin, "The Bureaucracy: Is Quality of Federal Work Force Deteriorating?" *New York Times*, 15 Jan. 1988, Metropolitan section.

"How do you do? I'm an unnamed government offical."

The most widely used of the enumerated powers is the commerce clause. Under its authority, Congress created such regulatory agencies as the Securities and Exchange Commission (SEC), Federal Communication Commission (FCC), National Labor Relations Board (NLRB), Occupational Safety and Health Administration (OSHA), and the Environmental Protection Agency (EPA), among others. Congress has also used other enumerated powers to establish a number of agencies. The Department of Defense was created by Congress's war powers; the Treasury by its power to collect taxes, pay the national debt, enter into debt, and coin money. Still other departments and agencies were set up under the other enumerated powers.

STRUCTURE OF THE AMERICAN BUREAUCRACY

Each of the three branches has its own "little" bureaucracy, and all share responsibility on one level or another for the entire government (see Figure 10.1). However, not all portions of the bureaucracy are equally prominent. The major

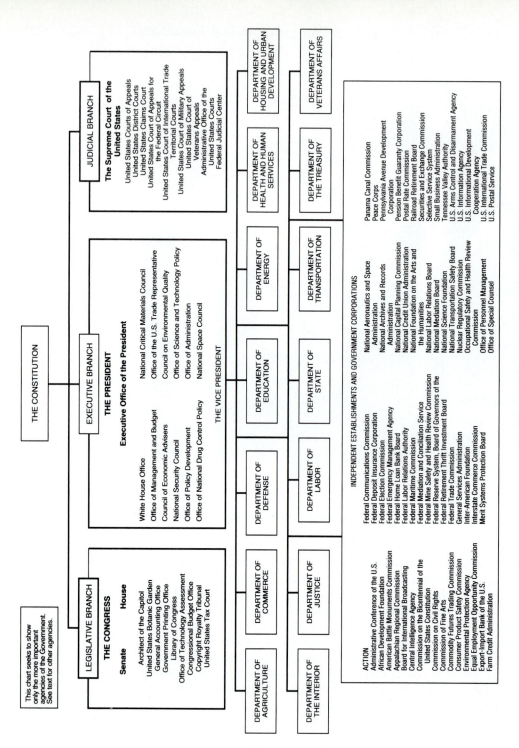

This chart seeks to show only the more important agencies of the Government. See text for other agencies.

THE CONSTITUTION

LEGISLATIVE BRANCH

THE CONGRESS

Senate   House

Architect of the Capitol
United States Botanic Garden
General Accounting Office
Government Printing Office
Library of Congress
Office of Technology Assessment
Congressional Budget Office
Copyright Royalty Tribunal
United States Tax Court

EXECUTIVE BRANCH

THE PRESIDENT

Executive Office of the President

White House Office
Office of Management and Budget
Council of Economic Advisers
National Security Council
Office of Policy Development
Office of National Drug Control Policy

National Critical Materials Council
Office of the U.S. Trade Representative
Council on Environmental Quality
Office of Science and Technology Policy
Office of Administration
National Space Council

THE VICE PRESIDENT

JUDICIAL BRANCH

The Supreme Court of the United States

United States Courts of Appeals
United States District Courts
United States Claims Court
United States Court of Appeals for the Federal Circuit
United States Court of International Trade
Territorial Courts
United States Court of Military Appeals
United States Court of Veterans Appeals
Administrative Office of the United States Courts
Federal Judicial Center

DEPARTMENT OF AGRICULTURE

DEPARTMENT OF THE INTERIOR

DEPARTMENT OF COMMERCE

DEPARTMENT OF JUSTICE

DEPARTMENT OF DEFENSE

DEPARTMENT OF LABOR

DEPARTMENT OF EDUCATION

DEPARTMENT OF STATE

DEPARTMENT OF ENERGY

DEPARTMENT OF TRANSPORTATION

DEPARTMENT OF HEALTH AND HUMAN SERVICES

DEPARTMENT OF THE TREASURY

DEPARTMENT OF HOUSING AND URBAN DEVELOPMENT

DEPARTMENT OF VETERANS AFFAIRS

INDEPENDENT ESTABLISHMENTS AND GOVERNMENT CORPORATIONS

ACTION
Administrative Conference of the U.S.
African Development Foundation
American Battle Monuments Commission
Appalachian Regional Commission
Board for International Broadcasting
Central Intelligence Agency
Commission on the Bicentennial of the United States Constitution
Commission on Civil Rights
Commission of Fine Arts
Commodity Futures Trading Commission
Consumer Product Safety Commission
Environmental Protection Agency
Equal Employment Opportunity Commission
Export-Import Bank of the U.S.
Farm Credit Administration

Federal Communications Commission
Federal Deposit Insurance Corporation
Federal Election Commission
Federal Emergency Management Agency
Federal Home Loan Bank Board
Federal Labor Relations Authority
Federal Maritime Commission
Federal Mediation and Conciliation Service
Federal Mine Safety and Health Review Commission
Federal Reserve System, Board of Governors of the
Federal Retirement Thrift Investment Board
Federal Trade Commission
General Services Administration
Inter-American Foundation
Interstate Commerce Commission
Merit Systems Protection Board

National Aeronautics and Space Administration
National Archives and Records Administration
National Capital Planning Commission
National Credit Union Administration
National Foundation on the Arts and the Humanities
National Labor Relations Board
National Mediation Board
National Science Foundation
National Transportation Safety Board
Nuclear Regulatory Commission
Occupational Safety and Health Review Commission
Office of Personnel Management
Office of Special Counsel

Panama Canal Commission
Peace Corps
Pennsylvania Avenue Development Corporation
Pension Benefit Guaranty Corporation
Postal Rate Commission
Railroad Retirement Board
Securities and Exchange Commission
Selective Service System
Small Business Administration
Tennessee Valley Authority
U.S. Arms Control and Disarmament Agency
U.S. Information Agency
U.S. International Development Cooperation Agency
U.S. International Trade Commission
U.S. Postal Service

FIGURE 10.1   ORGANIZATION CHART OF THE UNITED STATES GOVERNMENT

SOURCE: *U.S. Government Manual, 1989/90.*

government agencies tend to be those that either affect the public directly or otherwise have a significant impact on the political process. For the most part, these may be found chiefly among the organizations of the executive branch and what Figure 10.1 calls "Independent Establishments and Government Corporations." We will discuss only a small portion of the bureaucracy, primarily to give you some sense of its complexity.

THE CABINET

Many of the Framers were concerned that the Constitution had not established a "great council" to advise (and restrain) the president. But as soon as the government was actually formed, President Washington and Congress established a kind of great council, the three departments that eventually became the cabinet. The *cabinet* is the group of secretaries that head the major executive departments of government. Today, there are fourteen of these departments. Each department (except Justice) is headed by a secretary who was appointed by the president with the consent of the Senate. Generally, below the secretary are a deputy or undersecretary and a number of subordinate secretaries holding a variety of titles.

The oldest cabinet departments still receive the most attention from the public and the other units of government. Here is a short description of the three.

Department of State.   Created in 1789, the Department of State at first had responsibility for both domestic and foreign affairs. Jefferson, the first secretary of state, devised the system of weights and measures himself, passed personally on all patent applications, supervised the minting of money, arranged for publication of the laws passed by Congress as well as a number of other domestic matters. In addition, he conducted international relations and served as one of President Washington's principal advisers. In his day, the organization of the department was very simple. Today it is highly complex, as can be seen in Figure 10.2, despite the fact that it now deals only with foreign affairs. Other departments have taken over its domestic functions, as the Department of Commerce has with patents and weights and measures. With the passage of time and America's deeper involvement overseas, the State Department has had to expand and create special subunits or bureaus to deal with areas of international concern.

Department of Treasury.   Also created in 1789, the Department of the Treasury soon took over the responsibility of minting money from State. In addition to its normal responsibilities with fiscal matters—such as collecting taxes and paying the national debt—the Treasury Department ran the U.S. Post Office until 1829. Under Alexander Hamilton, its first head, the Department of the Treasury encouraged the development of business here and abroad, a function that has since been taken on by the Department of Commerce. Over the years, Treasury has narrowed its focus and expanded its functions in the area of financial management (see Figure 10.3). Aside from collecting taxes and proposing fiscal policy, the department is best known for its Secret Service, charged with responsibility for protecting the president, and the Customs Service.

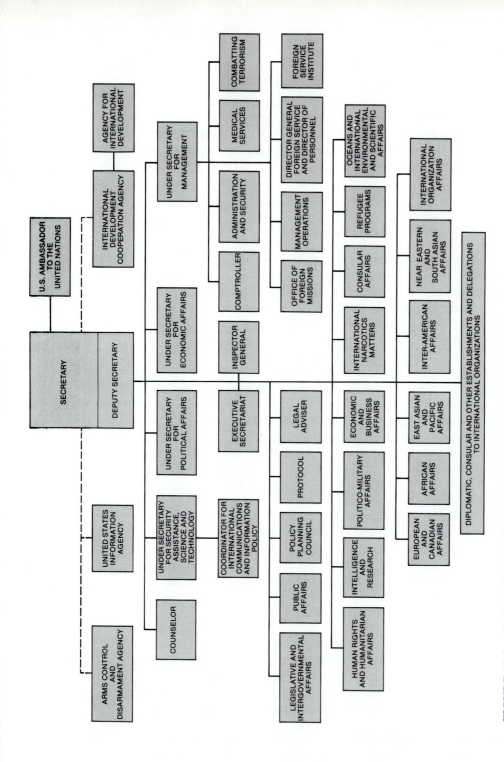

FIGURE 10.2   ORGANIZATION CHART OF THE DEPARTMENT OF STATE

SOURCE: *U.S. Government Manual, 1985/86.*

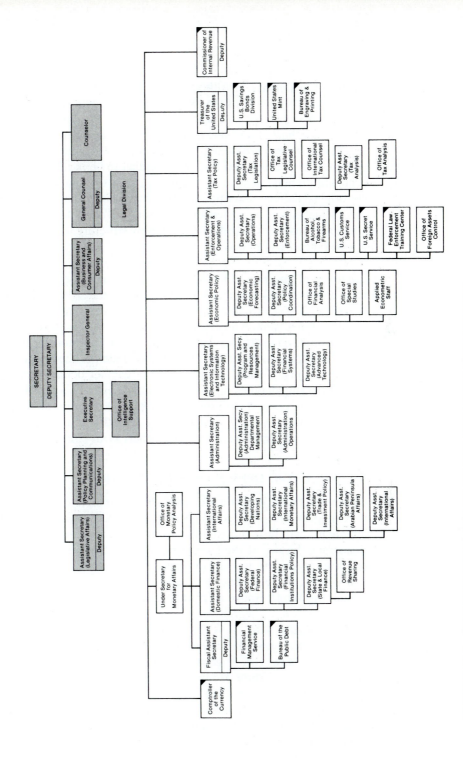

FIGURE 10.3 ORGANIZATION CHART OF THE TREASURY DEPARTMENT

SOURCE: *U.S. Government Manual, 1985/86.*

227

Department of Defense.   Although created in 1947, the Department of Defense, or DOD, has its origins in the War Department, which was established in 1789. Under the first secretary of war, Henry Knox, the department had a tiny work force, smaller than either State or Treasury. Today, DOD is the largest department or agency in the government. Although Knox was a general, control of the War Department was conceived from its founding to be in the hands of civilians since it is constitutionally headed by the president as commander-in-chief. As with the other original cabinet departments, War had a large number of extraneous duties, most of which have since been stripped from it. Today, DOD is focused on military matters and has an extraordinarily complex structure to respond to crises around the world (see Figure 10.4).

Department of Justice.   In 1789, Washington appointed Edmund Randolph, the former governor of Virginia, as his attorney general. Although Randolph was only a part-time adviser to the president, it was sufficient to earn future attorney generals cabinet rank. The Justice Department was created in 1870 because the responsibilities of an attorney general had grown enormously. Figure 10.5 conveys some of the complexity of the present-day duties of the Justice Department.

These are just a small sampling of the cabinet departments. There are nine others of varying degrees of complexity, and several so-called independent agencies that are associated with them. For example, the United States Arms Control and Disarmament Agency works closely with the State Department, although it is listed on the government organization chart as an "independent establishment."

THE EXECUTIVE OFFICE OF THE PRESIDENT

As we noted in the preceding chapter, by the middle of Franklin D. Roosevelt's tenure as president, the federal bureaucracy had grown so complex that he had to create his own little bureaucracy to run the larger one. Since his day, that little bureaucracy, known as the Executive Office of the President, has grown to mammoth proportions. As we saw in Figure 9.2, the structure of the Executive Office has become quite complex. Basically, the office can be divided into two components: the White House staff and what many call the "statutory agencies."

The White House Staff.   At first, the Executive Office was to function as the president's right hand, directly accountable to him and under his immediate control. In time, however, it grew beyond his ability to supervise directly. As a consequence, the White House staff became increasingly important and ever larger, serving as the president's instrument of control over the earlier instrument of control that had far outgrown its original purpose. But, as Box 10.1 clearly indicates, the White House staff itself may have grown in recent years beyond any president's ability to directly manage.

Presidents organize the White House staff according to their individual political styles. Some prefer a direct, hands-on involvement in the affairs handled by the staff. In this case, several top assistants report directly to the president, as they did to Jimmy Carter. Other presidents prefer to have information sifted and predigested for them by a chief of staff, as did Ronald Reagan. Sometimes a presi-

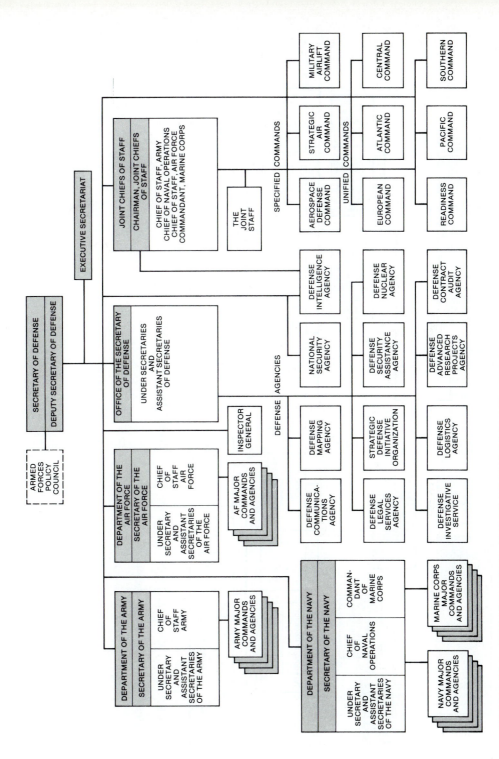

FIGURE 10.4 **ORGANIZATION CHART OF THE DEPARTMENT OF DEFENSE**

SOURCE: *U.S. Government Manual, 1985/86.*

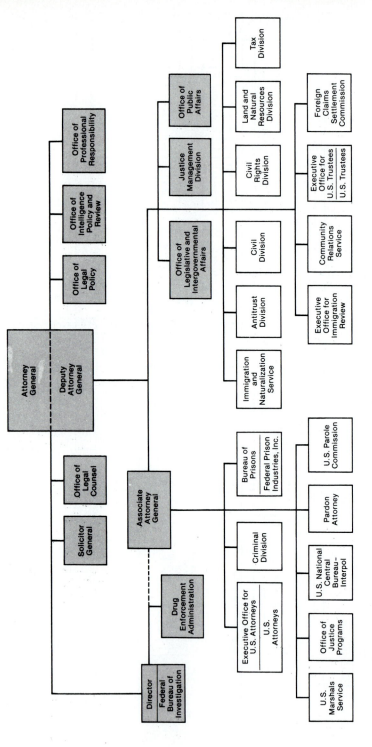

FIGURE 10.5 ORGANIZATION CHART OF THE JUSTICE DEPARTMENT

SOURCE: *U.S. Government Manual, 1985/86.*

dent's top aides try too hard on their boss' behalf, as did John Sununu and Richard Darman, and thereby gain the ire of other centers of power. Sununu, President Bush's chief of staff, and Darman, the head of the Office of Management and Budget, were so high-handed in negotiating the 1991 budget that they offended many members of Congress, including powerful members of their own party. As a result, they were excluded from further budget negotiations by the members of Congress, and the president had to yield even more ground than he had earlier.

Statutory Agencies of the Executive Office. As with the White House staff, the agencies of the Executive Office change according to presidential styles and interests. Nevertheless, certain agencies have remained throughout the many changes. Perhaps the most important one is the Office of Management and Budget (OMB). It is the largest of the Executive Office agencies, employing 550 individuals in 1987, about a third of the Executive Office work force. OMB's prime responsibility

BOX 10.1 White House Staff

The White House Office

Office of the President

  Office of the Chief of Staff

  Office of the Staff Secretary

    Scheduling

    Executive Clerk

    Records Management

    Correspondence

  Office of Communications

    Office of Speechwriting

    Office of Research

    Office of Media Relations

    Office of Public Affairs

    Office of Public Liaison

  Press Secretary

    News Summary

  Office of Management and Administration

  Intergovernmental Affairs

  Office of the Counsel

BOX 10.1 White House Staff

White House Military Office

Office of National Security Affairs

Office of Legislative Affairs

Office of Economic and Domestic Policy

Office of Special Activities and Initiatives

National Service

Advance Office

Office of Issues Analysis

Office of Political Affairs

Office of the Cabinet Secretary

Office of the First Lady

Presidential Personnel

Blair House

Offices of Former Presidents

Office of the Vice President

Chief of Staff

Office of the Deputy Chief of Staff

Office of the Staff Secretary

Legal Counsel

Office of Public Liaison

Office of Administration

National Security Affairs

Press Office

Scheduling

Office of Legislative Affairs

Mrs. Quayle's Office

Advance Office

Office of Vehicle Operations

Vice President's Indiana Office

SOURCE: *1990 Federal Staff Directory/2*, ed. Ann L. Brownson (Mt. Vernon, VA: Staff Directories, Ltd), p. vii. Copyright 1990, Ann L. Brownson.

is to examine and ride herd on the budgets of all departments and agencies. The budgetary process is at the center of government policy-making, for the allocation of funds determines which programs get priority and thus the direction in which the government shall move.

Other important statutory agencies are the National Security Council (NSC) and the Council of Economic Advisers (CEA). The NSC has received a great deal of notoriety due to the Iran-contra hearings. Its head, the assistant to the president for national security affairs (see Box 10.1), is a member of the president's White House staff and at times has had a great deal of influence over foreign policy, as in the case of Henry Kissinger under Richard Nixon and Gerald Ford. The CEA represents the views of professional economists in government and assists the president in preparing his annual federal budget and economic policy. The CEA also reports to Congress, and its three members are appointed with the advice and consent of the Senate.

OTHER AGENCIES OF THE BUREAUCRACY

The cabinet and Executive Office are in a sense "presidential agencies." Their senior personnel are appointed by the president and remain in office at his pleasure. The Senate's consent is almost automatic. The other agencies of the government

DRAWING BY FRASCINO. © 1984 THE NEW YORKER MAGAZINE, INC.

"I warned you about them, Sire. They call themselves the Council of Economic Advisers."

are presumed to be as accountable to the Congress as to the president. In practice, this is the case with only some of the agencies, such as the Small Business Administration or the Veterans Administration. Several agencies, such as the Central Intelligence Agency or the United States Information Agency, consider themselves arms of the executive branch and behave as if their allegiance is primarily to the president. Still other agencies are by statute independent of both branches, such as the Federal Reserve System, whose Board of Governors are appointed for a fixed term. It is supposed to be above "politics" in regulating the supply of money and interest rates. One important agency is entirely responsible to the Congress: the General Accounting Office (GAO), which is a major investigative unit of Congress.

Executive departments are organized hierarchically with a clear chain of command. By contrast, many of the administrative agencies are composed of boards or commissions consisting of five or seven members. All departments and agencies are theoretically accountable to both the president and Congress, but as we have seen, practice varies considerably from theory.

ESSENTIALS OF THE BUREAUCRACY

Congress has created executive departments and administrative agencies to perform a variety of tasks in response to political pressures. Those pressures define the political environment of the bureaucracy and determine the branch to which an agency or department will be most sensitive. Pressures are exerted mainly by interest groups working either within or without the government. The political environment of the bureaucracy may also change because of changing administrations following elections, changing congressional leadership, and changing judicial personnel. Shaped by the vagaries and shifting alliances of the political system, the bureaucracy as a whole has developed over time an instinct for survival that has confounded the efforts at control of presidents and Congress. The contemporary bureaucracy is very far from the simple "executive Department" envisioned by the Framers of the Constitution. It is today a highly complex and varied institution, largely independent of the forces that created it.

THE POWERS OF THE BUREAUCRACY

Congress not only creates and funds the bureaucracy, it also delegates quasi-legislative and judicial powers to the agencies it makes. The enabling statutes that create the agencies are usually stated in very broad terms. This means that the agencies must exercise a great deal of discretion when carrying out their mandate. The agencies then exercise quasi-legislative powers when they make rules governing groups and individuals within their jurisdiction.

Rule-Making.   Under the Administrative Procedure Act (APA) of 1946, agencies must publish their rules in advance of making them official so that those interested have an opportunity to respond, either in person at a hearing or in writing. In some instances, enabling statutes require agencies to hold judicial-style hearings

BASSET FOR *THE ATLANTA JOURNAL.*

(courtlike hearings in which witnesses testify for or against a proposed rule) and that final decisions be based on the hearing record.

The quantity of rules made by agencies is staggering. Agency rules fill thousands of pages in the *Federal Register* and the *Code of Federal Regulations,* official publications of the United States government containing all agency rules. A few examples of rule-making agencies are the Food and Drug Administration (FDA), which sets regulations governing safety, labeling, and other standards in food and drug products; the Environmental Protection Agency (EPA), which sets regulations controlling industrial wastes and pollutants, especially as they affect the air, water, and earth; and the Federal Aviation Agency (FAA), which sets regulations governing safety standards and price ranges for the airline industry.

Many regulatory agencies often make rules on an ad hoc or case-by-case basis rather than through some formal rule-making procedure. There may be several reasons for this. First and foremost, an ad hoc decision will usually have much more limited impact than a broad, general rule. Therefore, the political fallout can be expected to be equally limited. An agency head may believe he or she can survive small explosions, but large ones are much more "iffy." For example, congressional investigations revealed that Reagan appointee Ann Gorsuch Burford, the head of the EPA, and several of her subordinates had permitted several industries to evade EPA regulations covering pollution. Nothing much happened until it was discovered that at Burford's instructions the EPA had installed paper shredders during the investigation, which implied obstruction of justice. Upon that discovery, she was forced to resign.

Rule-Enforcing.   When Congress delegates quasi-legislative powers to agencies, it also grants them quasi-judicial authority. This means that agencies can sit like courts and hold hearings before administrative law judges. In such cases, agencies can bring charges against violators and seek penalties enforceable by the government. Sometimes one interest group may bring charges against another in an administrative law hearing. And sometimes an interest group may challenge an agency ruling in a hearing first and later in the regular courts.

Because agency decisions may be challenged in the courts, hearings are usually adversarial proceedings in which the rules of evidence operate. Accusers and accused face each other, usually have lawyers representing them, call witnesses for their side, and present evidence to support their claims. All agency decisions are subject to judicial review, although the routes of appeal are difficult and most often the courts tend to decide in favor of agencies.

EXECUTIVE RESPONSIBILITIES

Agencies and departments are granted quasi-legislative and quasi-judicial powers so that they may carry out the intent of Congress. This is, after all, the prime reason for the creation of agencies and departments. The bureaucracy performs executive tasks and is often considered identical with the executive branch. It often manages vast government enterprises, as does the Social Security agency, for example, which administers the retirement programs, Medicare and Medicaid, and several public assistance programs such as Supplemental Security Income (SSI) and Aid to Families with Dependent Children (AFDC).

Politics and the Bureaucracy.   In carrying out their responsibilities, agencies and departments are influenced by a number of factors. Sometimes these influences are in conflict. For example, Ronald Reagan came into office promising to do away with the rights of women to choose an abortion. One of the ways in which he tried to do this was by placing restrictions on funding for family planning programs. Funds for these programs are distributed by the Department of Health and Human Services, the head of which is a member of the president's cabinet. Reagan directed the department to prepare rules that prohibit funding to family planning clinics that offer the option of abortion or abortion counseling. Despite the fact that the department is a "presidential agency," it has, to the annoyance of a White House official, "tried to do the least it could in the regulations and still arguably fulfill the President's directive."[4] An official of the department virtually admitted as much.

One can understand the department's resistance. Family planning advocates had filed a lawsuit contending "that the regulations would violate the intent of Congress, deprive millions of poor women of information about abortion and unconstitutionally infringe on the free speech rights of clinic employees who want to offer counseling on abortion."[5] Here, the department is caught in the middle

[4]Robert Pear, "Reagan Will Limit Aid for Abortions," *New York Times*, 21 Jan. 1988: A19.
[5]Ibid.

James Watt on the spot: Opposition to his policies cut across party lines.

between Congress and the president on a highly emotional issue that can galvanize thousands of people on both sides.

Political forces more than formal authority often determine bureaucratic behavior, as in the case with the Department of Health and Human Services. Polls have regularly indicated that a very large majority of Americans support the right to an abortion. Over 4 million people are serviced by family planning clinics, and over 1 million women choose legal abortions each year. That is a very large number of people, and this is bound to have great significance for Congress. Therefore, the department tried to moderate the president's demand, even though its top officials are Reagan appointees who probably share his beliefs and values. Pragmatism—the recognition of practical limitations—many times replaces ideology as the governing principle in bureaucratic behavior.

Strong ideological commitment on the part of a department or agency head can make for problems. For example, Reagan's secretary of the interior, James Watt, shared the president's fervent belief in "privatization," the concept that government functions are best handled by the private sector (business and nongovernmental organizations). Before coming to Washington, Watt had been a vocal advocate of turning federal lands over to the states so that they could be exploited for economic gain by such business interests as mining and lumbering firms. When head of the Department of the Interior, he leased federal lands that had been kept as natural preserves to strip-mining companies, which ripped up the surface of the lands in the search for coal. He also gave off-shore drilling contracts to oil companies, which sometimes resulted in the blowout of an oil well that polluted adjacent breaches.

Watt persisted in these actions despite strong opposition from environmental and conservation groups. Moreover, he was extremely abrasive in his responses to criticism—so much so that Reagan often said that he was constantly waiting for the next time Watt would "shoot himelf in the foot." Opposition to Watt became so loud and clamorous, and from so many different regions, that Congress forced him to resign. Watt's insensitivity to the political realities connected with his position, a common failing of extreme ideologues, caused his departure and eventually the abandonment of his programs.

Although departments operate under the authority of the president, they must beware of arousing strong antagonism within Congress. For this reason, bureaucrats try to establish a relationship of cooperation and mutual trust with Congress, even when they are carrying out unpopular presidential directives, as is often the case with the CIA. Therefore, wise bureaucrats try for an atmosphere of easy communication with members of Congress, especially those on committees that have power relative to their agencies. This is not difficult for those on the top. The nexus of power is relatively small in Washington, and social gatherings tend to include individuals from overlapping power centers.

The Iron Triangle.   Congressional committees or subcommittees and the agencies they oversee are tied to one another by their relationship to the same interest groups. Because they service the same client, so to speak, and agency personnel usually possess expert knowledge needed by committee members for lawmaking, antagonism between Congress and the bureaucracy is rare indeed. When Congress does criticize the bureaucracy it is frequently around election time and it is usually for that great public bogey, red tape. Otherwise, congressional committees, agencies, and their interest groups form a triangular bond that is mutually supportive and, in the view of some critics, as strong as iron.

Agencies often look to the interests they are involved with to lobby on their behalf when appropriations are being decided upon in Congress or to assist them in formulating proposed laws for their congressional committees. Interest groups are also expected to lobby on behalf of the proposed laws. The interest group expects to benefit from its cooperation, as do the members of the congressional committee. When it works, everybody's back is scratched. Sometimes, however, the triangle gets a little rusty and the bolts holding it together pop out. For a variety of reasons, an agency may come into conflict with an interested party, especially if it is a regulatory agency making a politically expedient rule, as in the case of the Department of Health and Human Services in regard to abortion rights. In such an instance, the agency may find itself in a difficult situation with its committee as well as its interest group client. In human relations, triangles, however metallic, are always complicated.

THE PRESIDENCY AND THE BUREAUCRACY

The president's constitutional role as chief executive does not accurately indicate the nature of his relationship to the bureaucracy. It is difficult, and often impossible, for the president to control the countless activities of his vast administrative apparatus. Even with the resources of the Executive Office, the president and his aides cannot keep in daily touch with the wide-ranging activities of the bureaucracy. Moreover, Congress has formally placed important administrative operations outside presidential authority, such as the rule-making and grievance procedures. And, as we have seen, the bureaucracy must to some degree remain independent of presidential control so as to be able to accommodate congressional demands.

Nevertheless, the president has considerable influence on the bureaucracy. First, his influence extends through his power of appointment. Under his direct control are several thousand top-level executive jobs. These are political appointees to which the Senate generally agrees. They are almost always made from among those who are either party stalwarts or strong supporters of the president. In effect, White House appointments spread the president's cohorts throughout the bureaucracy. Thus, in many instances executives holding the same views as the president are in positions of power within the bureaucracy, sometimes for periods extending beyond his own term of office, as in the case of the Federal Reserve. This enables the president's policy positions to be at least represented if not always fully implemented within the bureaucracy. His long-term appointments to some degree can affect future policy decisions, which most presidents strive for, although few with the clear determination of Ronald Reagan.

Another source of presidential influence on the bureaucracy is the Office of Management and Budget. All agency budgets are subject to OMB analyses and

"The Ambassador says he does not care what we have heard—he speaks for both Secretary Weinberger and Secretary Shultz."

recommendations before being submitted to Congress, which gives the office a great deal of input into the agencies' policy decisions. Presidential control is more directly exercised when legislative proposals originating with an agency must be channeled through OMB to prevent conflict with the president's program. In addition, OMB can, and sometimes does, suggest changes in the organization and operations of different departments and agencies of the government. Under Richard Darman, Bush's OMB director, the office has had a profound impact on setting administration policies, as in the effort to cut Medicare benefits during the budget summit of 1990.

Ultimately, however, presidential influence over the bureaucracy depends on his persuasive ability and the cooperation of Congress. In the last analysis, the bureaucracy—even the president's official "family" of cabinet officers and departments—is a creature of Congress.

CONGRESS AND THE BUREAUCRACY

Congress has created the bureaucracy and has retained ultimate power over it. There are chiefly three sources of congressional influence: Congress's enabling statutes that establish agencies, its oversight functions that examine agency performance, and its appropriations authority that funds agencies.

Enabling Statutes.   Congressional legislation establishing agencies usually defines the standards and procedures that administrators are to follow. The courts have required Congress to state its intent clearly so that administrators and, if necessary, judges are able to determine with some assurance the boundaries of agency authority. In stating its intent, Congress sets policy for the agency. But generally, it does so in very broad terms.

Prior to the early 1930s, enabling legislation tended to narrowly define the scope and responsibilities of government agencies. This gave Congress tight control over bureaucratic actions. But to meet the emergency created by the Great Depression, Congress delegated to the executive and the bureaucracy wide discretionary power to make regulations having the force of law. After 1937, the courts upheld Congress's power to broadly delegate legislative authority and "thus opened the door to great masses of regulation by executive and administrative agencies that Congress itself could never prepare and enact."[6] In large measure, this also opened the door to policy-making by the bureaucracy.

Congressional Oversight.   After its creation, a federal agency is subject to supervision by Congress. In most instances, oversight is exercised by a committee or subcommittee responsible for the area in which an agency operates, as for example in agriculture, law enforcement, or education. Committees hold hearings—most of which today are open to the public—at which they consider proposals made by relevant agencies, laws pertaining to areas of interest to particular agencies, reports from the agencies under their jurisdiction, or grievances against

---

[6]Archibald Cox, *The Court and the Consitution* (Boston: Houghton Mifflin, 1987), p. 344.

specific agencies or regulations. At most of the hearings only interested parties appear and present their views, which sometimes may be in conflict, but more often are not.

When Congress investigates an agency, as it has done from time to time, it almost always deals with a controversial issue in which the agency under investigation is on the defensive. Some of the investigations, as of the EPA, are public and widely reported. Others are held in closed session, as several on the CIA, because national security interests are involved. Either way, Congress may subpoena witnesses, hold uncooperative witnesses in contempt, grant immunity to witnesses, and, if it has the proper swearing-in ceremony, charge witnesses with perjury. Members of the agency under investigation may have an attorney present to advice them during the hearing. Because of the adversarial nature of an investigation, it is the most dramatic form of congressional oversight and for this reason will often gain more media attention than other kinds of hearings.

Appropriations. An agency cannot function without funds. This then becomes another means by which Congress can exercise control over agency behavior. If a congressional committee disapproves, for example, of an agency program, it can cut it out of its budget authorization. In order to spend money, an agency must first have the committee under whose jurisdiction it operates enact an authorization bill for the program and its funds. After the funds have been authorized, they must be appropriated, which provides another opportunity for agency review, generally by a committee that is not otherwise involved in agency activity. Here again, the program may be modified, reduced, or cut entirely from an appropriations bill. If passed by the Appropriations Committee, funding must be approved by the House, which affords another chance to members of Congress to change or kill a program. The process is repeated in the Senate. Anywhere along the line, Congress may alter agency decisions and frustrate a president's policy, as happened for several years when the House refused to appropriate military aid for the contra rebels' effort to overthrow the Sandinista regime in Nicaragua.

From a bureaucratic standpoint, Congress is a meddlesome source of potential difficulty. From a citizen's viewpoint, Congress helps keep the bureaucracy accountable. When the bureaucracy is not accountable, it can behave in morally questionable ways, as had the National Security Council during the Iran-contra affair and the CIA from the late 1950s to early 1970s when it arranged either the overthrow or assassination of foreign leaders with whom the American government disagreed ideologically. From a constituent's point of view, Congress may intervene on his or her behalf with an agency involved with the constituent in some way. But as a rule, the relationship between the bureaucracy and Congress is harmonious rather than frictional.

THE CIVIL SERVICE AND THE BUREAUCRACY

In the distant past, the civil service and the bureaucracy were synonyms. A civilian who worked for the government was a part of the civil service, in contrast to a uniformed military person, who was a part of the armed services. With the Civil Service Act of 1883, our conception of the civil service changed. Since then most people think of the civil service as that portion of the bureaucracy in which workers are hired based on the results of competitive examinations and are very difficult to fire. Advancement within the system is based on further examinations. This is known as the *merit system*. For the most part, the merit system is confined to lower-level employees.

The greatest number of federal workers are hired under the merit system. That means these people are largely beyond the reach of the president or Congress. However, most of them are clerks or middle-level managers and therefore have little discretionary power. They can have only a minimum impact on policy. It is the political employees, those outside the merit system and appointed by the president and his staff, who may have the largest impact on the policy-making aspects of government.

MAKING POLICY IN THE BUREAUCRACY

It was generally believed that the head of state, whether king or high priest, made policy and bureaucratic underlings carried it out. The belief was probably never entirely accurate and had only the semblance of truth under strong monarchs, such as Henry VIII of England or Louis XIV of France. The reverse was much more common. Top bureaucrats stood at the very center of the policy-making process.

Under the American system, policy is supposed to be the exclusive province of the president and Congress. To hold that bureaucrats only implement the policy set by others is an extreme oversimplification of what actually occurs. Just as in ancient times, top bureaucrats today are at the very center of the policy-making process. They advise the president and Congress on important and politically sensitive issues, they help congressional committees write bills, they interpret so as to implement broadly worded legislation, and they prepare and publish regulations affecting major economic, social, and other interests. Agency decisions may be subject to review by Congress and the courts (as well as OMB), but this does not deny their impact on policy. Instead, it means that the bureaucracy has been incorporated into our system of checks and balances precisely because of its policy-making role.

Since the mid-1930s, Congress has increasingly given agencies policy-making authority. Agencies are much closer than Congress to the actual circumstances within their jurisdictions and thus are presumably better able than Congress to make the "right" decisions for their constituents. But bureaucratic competence presents certain difficulties for our kind of society.

Bureaucrats—administrators—are appointed officials, not chosen by the people. In a democratic society where government is supposed to reflect the will of the people, that situation raises serious questions. Although it is true that most senior administrators are ultimately accountable to elected officials—either the president or members of Congress—it is also true that these unelected administrators exercise broad discretion in shaping and implementing public policy. Thus at the very core of our democracy is a center of power not directly accountable to the people. What effect does this have on American democracy?

In Conclusion

The vast bureaucracy we have today has its origins in the tiny government of 1789. As the country grew, the bureaucracy grew with it in order to handle the increasing demands placed on government. The largest increases in government came about in response to crises, usually wars. In the 1930s and 1940s, Franklin D. Roosevelt brought about a vast increase in government to cope with two back-to-back crises, the Great Depression and the Second World War. FDR's administration also sought and got major changes in the character of the bureaucracy.

Starting in the mid-1930s, Congress delegated quasi-legislative and quasi-judicial powers to federal agencies. On several occasions, the bureaucracy either abused its authority or neglected its mandate. As a result, agencies found themselves subject to increasing supervision by Congress. Today, federal departments and agencies find that they must balance the demands of Congress, the president, and interest groups if they are to function effectively.

Basically, there are two kinds of agencies. Executive agencies are headed by individuals that the president has the power to remove. These are often called presidential agencies. But where Congress has established independent agencies, it usually limits the president's authority to remove top-level officials even though he has appointed them in the first place. Many of these agencies are headed by people who serve fixed terms and are thus independent of both Congress and the president.

The bureaucracy is intimately involved in setting policy as well as carrying it out. Not only do they help set policy through their influence on the constitutionally designated policy-makers, but agencies also make policy through the regulations they issue. Bureaucratic policy-making raises difficult questions about democracy in the United States.

C ★ A ★ S ★ E   S ★ T ★ U ★ D ★ Y

Bureaucratic Policy-Making

The bureaucracy, "the fourth branch," of government, makes policy in many ways. Congress delegates to executive departments and agencies the authority to make policy, but, at least theoretically, the policy made always must adhere to congressional intent. Congress is the primary lawmaking body, and the bureaucracy is its agent.

In reality, a variety of factors gives administrators wide discretion to make policy. A "policy" decision may consist of general rules that apply to the community as a whole or a class of persons within it. Congress, for example, creates policy under the environmental protection laws when it states certain standards that apply to air and water pollution. But in the regulatory sphere congressional standards are generally vague, requiring further administrative refinement and ultimately enforcement before policy becomes a reality.

While administrators have discretion in both setting and enforcing policy, administrative action can often be questioned. Under the Administrative Procedure Act of 1946, any person aggrieved by an agency decision may oppose it in court. Moreover, specific enabling statutes of most agencies provide that persons adversely affected by agency decisions may oppose them in court.

This case study is an example of the way in which a citizen's group used the courts to win a long political battle over a transportation department decision that authorized the construction of a highway through one of the most important recreational parks in Memphis, Tennessee.

Background

Executive officials always must act under statutory authority. The first step an administrator must take in making a policy decision is to determine what his or her authority is under the law. In the present case, the secretary of transportation derived his authority from the Department of Transportation Act of 1966 and the Federal-Aid-Highway Act of 1968. When he became President Nixon's secretary of transportation in 1968, former Massachusetts Governor John Volpe found that under these acts new standards were imposed upon him that made it more difficult to authorize the release of federal funds to construct highways through public parks.

Prior to Volpe's tenure, both the Bureau of Public Roads in 1956 and the Federal Highway Administration in 1966 had approved the construction of a highway through Overton Park, which "is a 342-acre city park located near the center of Memphis. The park contains a zoo, a nine-hole municipal golf course, an outdoor theater, nature trails, a bridal path, an art academy, picnic areas, and a hundred and seventy acres of forest."[1] The authorized highway was six lanes, and would have severed the zoo from the rest of the park and destroyed twenty-six acres of park land.

Under the 1966 and 1968 amendments, new *policy* and procedural guidelines were established for the secretary of transportation. The amendment laws provided:

> It is hereby declared to be the national policy that special efforts should be made to preserve the natural beauty of the countryside and public park and recreation lands, wildlife and waterfowl refuges, and historic sites ... after [August 23, 1968], the Secretary [of Transportation] shall not approve any program or project which requires the use of any publicly owned land from a public park, recreation area, or wildlife and waterfowl refuge of national, state, or local significance as determined by the federal, state, or local officials having jurisdiction thereof, or any land from an historic site of national, state or local significance as so determined by such officials *unless* (1) there is no feasible and prudent alternative to the use of such land, and (2) such

---

[1] *Citizens to Preserve Overton Park, Inc.* v. *Volpe*, 401 U.S. 402 (1971).

program includes all possible planning to minimize harm to such parks, recreational area, wildlife and waterfowl refuge, or historic site resulting from such use.

Environmental forces had brought about the changes in the law that now made Secretary Volpe's decision far more difficult, or so it appeared.

The Decision-Making Process

Clearly the law obligated Secretary Volpe to take into account the new congressional guidelines that protected environmental interests. But from both a political and a bureaucratic standpoint, the weight of the pressure upon Volpe was to approve the prior action of the Bureau of Public Roads and the Federal Highway Administration. Not only had his own administrator supported the highway, but the Memphis City Council, after a hotly contested debate, had also approved the plan.

Political and economic interests clearly backed the highway, which would channel federal funds into Memphis and increase contractors' revenues and local employment at the same time. The Citizens to Preserve Overton Park, an environmental group, simply were unable to overcome the even broader economic interests supporting the plan.

The general thrust of administrative policy-making has always been for agencies to support what they perceive to be the interests of clientele and constituency. The Bureau of Public Roads and the Federal Highway Administration were created to pave the nation, not to preserve park lands. Administrators heading those agencies have never recognized the importance of environmental interests for they have always drawn their support from the highway lobby, which includes local officials who are only too happy to have federal funds spent in their communities.

Procedural Requirements. While informal political forces usually determine the direction of administrative policy, Congress, through the Administrative Procedure Act of 1946 and agency enabling statutes, requires certain decision-making procedures to be followed. Essentially Congress attempts to ensure administrative fairness, accuracy in the determination of facts upon which decisions are based, and efficiency.

It is almost impossible to reverse the politics that supports administrative decisions. But court challenges can and usually are based on alleged procedural flaws, claims that administrators have not adhered to required procedures. The usual result is, at best, a delay in administrative policy implementation. The courts are reluctant to delve into substantive policy issues, deferring to administrative expertise. If the judges find procedural flaws, cases are remanded back to the agencies for compliance with court directives and statutory procedural requirements.

In the Overton Park case, the Tennessee State Highway Department had requested federal aid to build the throughway. The law required the state highway department to hold "public hearings" and take into account the economic effects of its plan before submitting it to the Federal Highway Administration.

The Challenge

Recognizing that the political forces were against it, the Citizens to Preserve Overton Park decided that the only way they would have a chance to challenge Secretary Volpe's decision was in the courts. The group, which consisted of local and national conservation organizations, contended that the secretary had violated the statutes by authorizing the highway. First, they claimed that the secretary had accepted the Memphis City Council judgment in support of the highway without making formal findings required by the statute. Second, they argued that the administrative decision was not supported by substantial evidence and was unwarranted by the facts, which if true would require the courts, under the Administrative Procedure Act, to overturn the decision. Finally, the challengers argued that the secretary had not in any way explained his decision, and that authorizing the construction of the highway through the park could not be justified under the law because alternative routes were available.

Lower Federal Court Action

The Transportation Department immediately moved for summary judgment against the challengers, which the Federal District Court granted, a decision that the Court of Appeals upheld. The secretary was not required to make formal findings, argued the government attorneys who filed affidavits to lend factual support to the secretary's decision. The lower federal courts, in supporting the Transportation Department's argument, exercised judicial self-restraint. They found, first, that the secretary did not have to make formal findings to support its decision. Second, they refused to order the deposition of the former Federal Highway Administrator because "probing of the mental processes of an administrative decision maker was prohibited."[2] Finally, "believing that the Secretary's authority was wide and the reviewing courts' authority narrow in the approval of highway routes, the lower courts held that the affidavits [filed by the challengers] contained no basis for a determination that the secretary had exceeded his authority."[3]

The Supreme Court's Decision

Associate Justice Thurgood Marshall wrote the Court's opinion in the Overton Park case, holding that under the law the secretary of transportation was obligated to explain his decision more fully than had been done simply by filing affidavits with the lower courts. The secretary's decision, wrote Marshall, was neither rule-making nor adjudication; therefore, the Administrative Procedure Act requirements for formal findings that might have applied under certain circumstances

---

[2]*Citizens to Preserve Overton Park, Inc.* v. *Volpe*, 401 U.S. 402 (1971).
[3]Ibid.

were inapplicable. Such findings are particularly valuable to reviewing courts that must determine whether or not an agency has acted within the boundaries of its statutory authority.

While not requiring formal findings, the Supreme Court did hold that the secretary had to justify his decision either by making informal findings that a court could review or, as a last resort, by requiring administrative officials who were involved in the decision to give testimony before the court.

The Supreme Court concluded:

> [It] is necessary to [remand] this case to the District Court for plenary review of the Secretary's decision. That review is to be based on the full administrative record that was before the Secretary at the time he made his decision. But since the bare record may not disclose the factors that were considered or the Secretary's construction of the evidence it may be necessary for the District Court to require some explanation in order to determine if the Secretary acted within the scope of his authority and if the Secretary's action was justifiable under the applicable [statutory] standard.[4]

The Outcome

Requiring the secretary to justify his decision before the Federal District Court ultimately had profound consequences. After a twenty-five-day trial, which included affidavits from the secretary and testimony from his subordinates, the court concluded that Secretary Volpe had not adequately supported his decision under the law. He had failed, stated the court, adequately to investigate alternative routes and had misinterpreted the law because he did not give due weight to environmental concerns that Congress intended to be taken into account. The district court then returned the case to Secretary Volpe to carry out his responsibilities under the law.

Responding to both the Supreme Court and lower federal court decisions, Secretary Volpe ordered the abandonment of the Overton Park Highway in January 1973. He stated,

> On the basis of the record before me and in light of guidance provided by the Supreme Court, I find that an interstate highway as proposed by the state through Overton Park cannot be approved. . . . I cannot find . . . that there are no prudent and feasible alternatives to the use of parkland nor that the broader environmental protection objectives of the National Environmental Protection Act and the Federal-Aid-Highway Act have been met, nor that the existing proposal would comply with the Federal Highway Act standards on noise."[5]

---

[4] Ibid.

[5] Cited in Walter Gellhorn et al., *Administrative Law: Cases and Comments*, 8th ed. (Mineola, NY: Foundation Press Inc., 1987), pp. 442–443. The state of Tennessee challenged Volpe's decision in federal court, arguing that if he did not approve the Overton Park Highway he should, under the law, designate an alternative route. The District Court ruled in favor of the state, but the sixth circuit Court of Appeals overturned the decision. The Supreme Court refused to grant review.

Suggested Readings

Charles T. Goodsell. *The Case for Bureaucracy,* 2nd ed. Chatham House, 1983.

Randall B. Ripley and Grace Franklin. *Congress, The Bureaucracy and Public Policy,* 4th ed. Chicago: The Dorsey Press, 1987.

David H. Rosenbloom. *Bureaucratic Government USA.* New York: St. Martin's, 1980.

Francis E. Rourke. *Bureaucratic Power in National Policymaking,* 4th ed. Boston: Little, Brown, 1986.

Peter Woll. *American Bureaucracy,* 2nd ed. New York: Norton, 1977.

chapter

11

THE JUDICIARY

*It is emphatically the province and duty of the judicial
department to say what the law is.*

John Marshall

Americans take pride in having a "government of laws," to borrow a phrase from John Adams. Ideally, the power of government cannot be used arbitrarily in the American system. In our conception, might does not make right and power is constrained by law. The problem for Americans from the very beginning has been to determine what is the law. In down-to-earth terms, the issue is one of application. How does the law, which was written in general terms for a large number of situations, apply to this particular case? The person who decides the correct answer to that question is the judge.

But law is not an exact science and judges have often disagreed about the correct application of a law to a specific case. They have even disagreed about the meaning of particular laws. That this should be so is not difficult to understand. Laws are encoded values. We all share many values; that is what makes it possible for us to live together in this huge community called a nation. But we also disagree about some very important ones. For example, the value of human life, how we

...THE CONSERVATIVE EXPRESS...

define those terms ("human" and "life"), and to whom we extend that value are all issues in great dispute today. They are central to our discussion of abortion, capital punishment, or engagement in military ventures overseas. The way in which people answer the questions raised by the values of their society determines how they interpret laws or write them. And values in conflict are rarely simple.

In theory, the legislature and the executive make and enforce the laws, while judges only interpret them. But the very process of interpretation shapes our understanding of that which is interpreted, and our actions are based on our understanding. This is the case in every activity, whether art, science, or logic. It is no different in law. Shaping our understanding of the law is virtually the same as making the law. Throughout our history this notion has been at the center of judicial controversy. Many political figures, from Thomas Jefferson to Ronald Reagan, have wanted to restrict the interpretive scope of judges. Others have wanted to expand it, from Chief Justice John Marshall to Chief Justice Earl Warren.

BACKGROUND

Laws and those who judge behavior on the basis of laws probably go back to the beginnings of society or organized social living. It is difficult to imagine a society without laws, for laws are the codified rules of conduct that the majority have agreed to accept. Laws existed well before the invention of writing, but we know of legal systems only after the appearance of writing. The first written set of laws that we have is that of Hammurabi, a Babylonian king who lived almost 4,000 years ago.

The earliest judges we know of were kings and tribal chieftains. These rulers made the law, executed it, judged violators of it, and inflicted punishment on the violators. With the increasing complexity of society, rulers delegated their law-making authority to agents, who acted on the ruler's behalf. Those who were ruled, the common people, had little or no say in the making or carrying out of the laws under which they lived.

With slight modifications, this set of political relations to law operated in Western civilization until the end of the Middle Ages when, as a consequence of building nation-states, monarchs began to impose a centralized legal system on feudal princes and other local rulers. This had the effect of setting up two systems of law, one local and the other national. With the success of nation-states, national laws eventually dominated.

Political relations to the law, however, remained basically the same. The monarch or his agents made the law, judged according to it, and carried the judgments out. For all practical purposes, this meant that the king was the judge in his own case. In the seventeenth century, this gave rise, especially in England, to a demand for an independent judiciary and the supremacy of the law.

THE FOUNDERS AND THE JUDICIARY

At the Constitutional Convention in Philadelphia, the issue of an independent federal judiciary was of paramount interest. Those present argued intensely over a prolonged period about this matter. Under the Articles of Confederation, there had been no national judicial authority. Thus, many of the Framers of the Constitution disagreed about how to assure the independence of the judiciary. Debates raged over who should appoint judges to the federal court, how long the judges were to be in office, who should determine their compensation, and what their role should be in the national government.

The great concern throughout the debates was to whom the federal judges would be indebted. Many feared that if the chief executive had sole appointive power, the judges would be biased in his favor. On the other hand, an almost equal number felt that the Senate, because there would be so many contending interests, would be irresponsible when making its choice. After a good deal of back-and-forth, the Framers agreed to a compromise proposed by Nathaniel Gorham, a delegate from Massachusetts, and amended by James Madison. The president would appoint, with the advice and consent of the Senate, judges of the Supreme Court. They left to Congress the authority to appoint lower-level federal judges, which was later delegated to the president with the consent of the Senate. Another point of contention was compensation for the judges. As Hamilton noted in *The Federalist*, No. 79, "a power over a man's substance amounts to a power over his will." Still another means of securing judicial independence, all delegates seemed to agree, was to have judges serve for life, or as it was phrased at the time, "for good behavior." A judge could be removed from office only by impeachment.

The independence of judges was not the only judicial issue before the delegates. The Framers were very much concerned also with the authority of the federal judiciary over the states. This too was a contentious issue. Madison, in his *Notes of Debates,* presents a very dramatic picture of the conflict. The conflict centered on the question of whether the national legislature should have the authority to create a federal judiciary below that of the Supreme Court, called by the Framers ''inferior tribunals.''

> M^r [John] Rutlidge [of South Carolina] hav^g obtained a rule for reconsideration of the clause of establishing *inferior* tribunals under the national authority, now moved that that part of the clause in propos. 9. should be expunged: arguing . . . that it was making an unnecessary encroachment on the jurisdiction of the States. . . .
>
> Mr Madison observed that unless inferior tribunals were dispersed throughout the Republic with *final* jurisdiction in *many* cases, appeals [to the Supreme Court] would be multiplied to an oppressive degree. . . . An effective Judiciary establishment commensurate to the legislative authority was essential. A Government without a proper Executive & Judiciary would be the mere trunk of a body, without arms or legs to act or move.
>
> M^r [James] Wilson [of Pennsylvania] opposed the motion [of Rutlidge] on like grounds. . . .
>
> M^r [Roger] Sherman [of Connecticut] was in favor of the motion. . . .
>
> M^r [John] Dickinson [of Delaware] contended strongly that if there was to be a National Legislature, there ought to be a national Judiciary, and that the former ought to have the authority to institute the latter.
>
> On the question for Mr Rutlidge's motion to strike out ''inferior tribunals''
>
> Mass^ts divided. Con^t ay. N.Y. div^d N.J. ay. P^a no. Del. no. M^d no. V^a no. N.C. ay. S.C. ay Geo. ay.
>
> Mr Wilson & Mr Madison then moved, in pursuance of the idea expressed above by Mr Dickinson, to add to Resol: 9. the words following ''that the National Legislature be empowered to institute inferior tribunals.'' They observed that there was a distinction between establishing such tribunals absolutely, and giving a discretion to the Legislature to establish or not establish them. They repeated the necessity of some such provisions.
>
> M^r [Pierce] Butler [of South Carolina]. The people will not bear such innovations. The States will revolt at such encroachments. Supposing such an establishment to be useful, we must not venture on it. . . .
>
> M^r [Rufus] King [of Massachusetts spoke in favor of the Wilson-Madison proposal].
>
> On this question as moved by Mr W. & M^r M.
>
> Mass. ay. C^t no. N.Y. div^d N.J. ay. P^a ay. Del. ay. M^d ay. V^a ay. N.C. ay. S.C. no. Geo. ay.
>
> The Committee then rose & the House adjourned. . . .[1]

Underlying this dispute was the principle of judicial review, a bone of contention since 1787. In one instance, the argument at the Convention was over whether

---

[1] James Madison, *Notes of Debates in the Federal Convention of 1787,* intro. Adrienne Koch (New York: Norton, 1987), pp. 71–73. Madison wrote his *Notes* in the third person, which takes the modern reader a little by surprise.

the Supreme Court should share with the president a veto power over the legislature. Most of the debate was focused on whether it would be proper to involve
the judiciary so directly in the politics of lawmaking. One delegate observed that
if judges were so involved, it would "give a previous tincture to their opinions."[2]
In another argument over judicial review, the issue was whether the Supreme
Court should have jurisdiction over "cases arising under the Constitution."[3]

Although the power of judicial review was not clearly spelled out, it was understood by the Framers as the fundamental purpose of the judiciary. In *The Federalist,* No. 80, Hamilton virtually says so. In his letter of October 24, 1787, to
Jefferson, Madison also recognizes the power of judicial review, although he
complains that it is not strong enough. At this time both Jefferson and Madison
supported the notion of judicial review as a possible control of a tyrannical legislature. In later years, Jefferson was bitter at a Federalist judiciary under the
leadership of John Marshall that at times frustrated his purposes, as in Aaron
Burr's trial for treason. If the concept of judicial review is valid, then the "constitution . . . is a mere thing of wax in the hands of the judiciary, which they may
twist and shape into any form they please."[4] It is important to remember that the
Federalists were vehement opponents of Jeffersonian republicanism and that Jefferson himself was extremely partisan.

The concept of judicial review received its most articulate expression some
twenty years after the Constitution was written. In the case of *Marbury v. Madison,* the Supreme Court declared for the first time that a law of Congress was
unconstitutional. Chief Justice John Marshall, writing for the majority, gave the
basic argument for judicial review. Marshall's reasoning was somewhat like the
following. Essentially, there are two laws that govern the nation: the Constitution
and congressional legislation. The Constitution defines and limits the authority of
the legislature and is therefore superior to any act of Congress. If it were otherwise
Congress would be omnipotent, which would subvert the purpose of the Constitution. Sometimes the laws of Congress are in conflict with the Constitution.
Obviously, in such a case, the Constitution takes precedence. The federal judiciary
is the only branch of government authorized by the Constitution to interpret the
Constitution. Only the Supreme Court can decide if an act of Congress is unconstitutional. This is directly inferable from the clause in Article III, Section 2, that
states: "The judicial Power shall extend to all Cases, in Law and Equity, arising
under this Constitution." But following *Marbury,* most instances of judicial review
by the Supreme Court involved constitutional questions regarding state laws.

THE FEDERAL JUDICIARY AND THE POWER OF THE STATES

The doctrine of separation of powers operates on two levels. On the national
level, the authority of the federal government is divided among three distinct,
competitive, and mutually involved branches. On another level, power is split

---

[2] Madison, *Notes,* p. 462.
[3] Ibid., p. 539.
[4] Thomas Jefferson's letter of September 6, 1819, to Judge Spencer Roane in Jefferson's *Writings,*
ed., Merrill D. Peterson (New York: Library of America, 1984), p. 1426.

between national and state governments. Theoretically, they are coequal and supreme in different spheres. A good many of the *Federalist* papers are devoted to reassuring Publius' readers that the national government will not dominate the state governments. *The Federalist,* No. 46, by Madison is devoted entirely to this issue. There he argues that state governments, holding the affection and interests of their citizens, are in a stronger position than the national government in the event of a contest between them. In short, the states have more power than the central government.

But Madison did not consider this the best state of affairs. He entered the Convention in Philadelphia a committed nationalist. In a letter to Jefferson, while discussing the prospects for a new government Madison clearly stated that what was needed above all was "to arm the federal head with a negative *in all cases whatsoever* on the local Legislatures."[5] After the national government was established and in response to the turn of political events, he changed his position.

Other nationalists did not abandon their preference for a strong central government. Since they controlled the first two administrations, they put in place the mechanism for establishing a powerful national government. The centerpiece of that machine was the Judiciary Act of 1789. The Act created thirteen federal district and three circuit courts under the authority of the Supreme Court, and gave the high court and the newly created federal judiciary the authority to hear appeals from state courts. Moreover, the Act made it clear that the federal courts had maximum authority in constitutional matters.

Under John Marshall, the Supreme Court consistently asserted the supremacy of the constitution and its own superiority over the states as the prime interpreter of that document. This was most fully expressed in a case known as *Martin v. Hunter's Lessee* (1816). The highest court of the state of Virginia had challenged a Supreme Court decision. Virginia, the state court claimed, had equal sovereignty to the United States and thus the Supreme Court had no authority over it. The Supreme Court argued that Virginia surrendered a portion of its sovereignty when it ratified the Constitution and thus was subject to the decisions of the Supreme Court.

In asserting its own supremacy, the Court also expanded the power of the national (federal) government over the states. The classic instance of this expansion of federal power is a case known as *McCulloch v. Maryland* (1819), which arose when the state of Maryland imposed a tax on the local branch of the newly created Bank of the United States. The tax would have driven the bank out of business, and therefore McCulloch, the cashier of the Baltimore branch, refused to pay it. Basing his reasoning on the supremacy clause in the Constitution, Marshall went on to argue that "the Constitution must allow ... the national legislature ... to perform the high duties assigned to it. ... Let the end be legitimate, let it be within the scope of the Constitution, and all means which are ... plainly adapted to that end ... are constitutional." Therefore, the Court found Maryland's tax "unconstitutional and void."[6]

---

[5]Madison's letter of March 19, 1787, in *The Papers of James Madison,* vol. 9, *9 April 1786–24 May 1787,* ed. Robert A. Rutland et al. (Chicago: University of Chicago Press, 1975), p. 318.
[6]See *McCulloch* v. *Maryland,* 4 Wheaton 316 (1819).

FEDERALISM AND THE JUDICIARY

The issue of the equal sovereignty of the state and national governments was finally settled by the Civil War. Although the states were no longer equal to the central government, they still retained a fair amount of sovereignty. As long as they did not conflict with the Constitution or federal laws, state laws were supreme within each state, that is, within its own domain. In many instances, the Supreme Court has recognized the authority of state courts and supported the decisions they arrived at. Between about 1870 and 1935, the Supreme Court consistently decided cases in favor of the states or business interests if these were in conflict. From about 1937 until the early 1970s—during the era of the Roosevelt and Warren courts[7]—the high court revived the national supremacy views of the much-earlier Marshall Court, but struck down state laws only when they were in conflict with national social policy. Since 1976, the Court has alternated unevenly between favoring national and state governments.

Prior to 1945, the great constitutional issues arose in response to economic conflicts. The issue of Supreme Court dominance of the judicial process grew out of a state's attempt to tax a national bank, a state law establishing a steamboat monopoly, and a state's power to set local standards for interstate commerce. Issues related to economic liberty were fought out over whether a state could regulate child labor, set maximum hours of work, or control working conditions in "sweatshops." And issues of federalism arose in connection with efforts on the part of the national government to regulate the formation of trusts, permit the formation of unions, provide aid to an ailing economy, and the like. After the Second World War, great constitutional issues revolved around questions of freedom, equality, privacy, and law and order. Issues related to freedom of the press and of expression arose in a federal-state context, as did conflicts over civil rights, the right of privacy, and rights of individuals charged with a crime.

We can perhaps get a sense of the way the Supreme Court may limit the power of state courts by looking somewhat closely at one case. *Griswold v. Connecticut* (1965) was the first case before the high court in which the right of privacy was articulated. In this case, Estelle T. Griswold, the director of a family planning clinic, and Dr. C. Lee Buxton, a physician at the clinic, were convicted of violating a Connecticut law prohibiting counseling, abetting, or assisting in the use of contraception. They had given medical advice to married couples on the use of contraceptive devices.

Griswold and Buxton claimed the Connecticut law violated the due process clause of the Fourteenth Amendment. In his majority opinion, Associate Justice William Douglas wrote that "... specific guarantees in the Bill of Rights have penumbras [partial shadows, a metaphor for "implications"], formed by ema-

---

[7]The Supreme Court often takes the name of the person who has had most influence on it. During the long—twelve year—tenure of Franklin D. Roosevelt, he appointed nine justices to the Court, all of whom shared his social vision if not his judicial philosophy. Appointed chief justice by President Dwight D. Eisenhower, Earl Warren led the remnants of the Roosevelt Court into making liberal social policy. In the process he changed the prevailing judicial philosophy of the Roosevelt Court, which had been one of restraint, to one of judicial activism.

DRAWING BY JOE MIRACHI; © 1974 THE NEW YORKER MAGAZINE, INC.

"Do you ever have one of those days when everything seems un-Constitutional?"

nations from those guarantees that help give them life and substance. Various guarantees create zones of privacy." Justice Douglas then proceeded to enumerate the amendments that implied the right of privacy. These are the First, Third, Fourth, Fifth, and Ninth amendments. He concluded by observing: "We deal with a right older than the Bill of Rights—older than our political parties, older than our school system." In other words, the right of privacy is a fundamental right, a "natural right" as might have been said in the eighteenth century. The Connecticut law was found unconstitutional because "a government . . . purpose may not be achieved by means which . . . invade the area of protected freedoms."[8]

The post-World War II Supreme Court has taken as its primary function the protection of the rights of individuals against the power of government, whether that government is on a national or state level. That view of the Court's function, however, does not go unquestioned. Many people believe that the state has the right to control individual behavior, especially in the area of private morality. These people have sided with Connecticut against the Supreme Court, for example. They also vehemently oppose a woman's right to choose an abortion, the right of individuals to read whatever they wish, and other private rights.

---

[8]*Griswold* v. *Connecticut*, 381 U.S. 479 (1965).

To favor the rights of individuals against the states is undemocratic, opponents of the Court argue. State laws are enacted by duly elected governments that represent the majority of voters in a state. The Supreme Court is an unelected body of lawyers who are remote from the concerns of the people in a given state. The Court, therefore, should not interfere with what goes on within a state. The Court's opponents usually conclude their argument by asserting that Supreme Court intervention in state affairs is contrary to the "original intent" of the Constitution's Framers. The high court, they charge, is "creating new rights" rather than "finding rights in existing law." Judges must not be creative, for otherwise they intrude on a legislature's right to make laws and set policies.

Those who defend the high court's recent decisions point out that "most private law is common law—that is, law made by judges rather than by legislators or constitution Framers. Judges have been entrusted with making policy from the start."[9] The defense continues by pointing out that the Framers "were, after all, creating neither a pure nor even a representative democracy, but a constitutional democracy."[10] Indeed, as we have seen, the Framers were very suspicious of majority rule and in some instances felt considerable animus toward state governments. As James Madison wrote to Thomas Jefferson describing the Convention debates of 1787:

> A few contended for an entire abolition of the States; some for an indefinite power of Legislation in the Congress, with a negative [veto] on the laws of the States: some for such a power without a negative: some for a limited power of legislation, with such a negative: the majority finally for a limited power without the negative. The question with regard to the Negative underwent repeated discussions, and was finally rejected by a bare majority.[11]

At the time Madison himself felt strongly that a veto power over the states was crucial. He argued: "A constitutional negative on the laws of the States seems ... necessary to secure individuals agst encroachments on their rights.... The injustice of [state laws] has been so frequent and flagrant as to alarm the most stedfast friends of Republicanism."[12]

This brings us to the problem of "original intent." The defenders of the Warren Court's decisions contend that it is impossible to know the "original intent" of the Framers. For one thing, there had been so many different "intents" and so many compromises that few of the delegates were entirely satisfied with the document they produced. Even George Washington had reservations, and a sizable number of delegates refused to sign the Constitution. For another, the language of the Constitution is so broad and generalized that the application of a constitutional principle to a particular case "required the Justices to make conscious choices, influenced by their own vision of the country's needs and po-

---

[9] Judge Richard A. Posner, "What Am I? A Potted Plant?" *The New Republic,* 28 Sept. 1987: 23.

[10] Laurence H. Tribe, "The Final Say," *New York Times Magazine,* 13 Sept. 1987: 70.

[11] Madison's letter of 24 Oct. 1787 in *The Papers of James Madison,* vol. 10, *27 May 1787–3 March 1788,* ed. Robert A. Rutland et al. (Chicago: University of Chicago Press, 1977), p. 209.

[12] Ibid., p. 212.

tential.''[13] The interpretive process itself, as we saw previously, is inherently ''creative.'' Therefore, it is impossible for judges not to ''make law'' and have an impact on public policy.

ESSENTIALS OF THE JUDICIARY

Despite the principle of judicial review, the state and federal courts are parts of largely independent systems. The fifty states are sovereign and can set up whatever judicial systems they wish. As a consequence, there are fifty state laws, sometimes similar, often different. The one unifying feature is that they cannot be in violation of the United States Constitution or federal law. Since each state has limited sovereignty, each can and has set up its own judicial structure. These vary considerably from one another, and from the federal system, although procedures in civil and criminal cases are similar throughout the country. The decisions of a state's highest court is final in all matters of state law. Only when a constitutional issue is at stake can an appeal be made from these courts to the Supreme Court.

FEDERAL AND STATE JURISDICTIONS

Generally, both state and federal court systems are hierarchically organized. The basis for the organization is the authority or jurisdiction of a court to hear and decide certain types of cases. A court's jurisdiction is determined by the legislatures of the federal or state governments within the restraints set by their respective constitutions. Federal courts hear cases that involve constitutional issues, congressional laws, treaties, disputes between states or citizens of different states, controversies in which the United States is a party, and others listed in Article III or limited by Amendment XI of the Constitution. Other types of disputes or cases fall within the jurisdiction of state laws and courts.

Some kinds of cases, however, may be heard by either the federal or state courts. In these instances, the courts have *concurrent jurisdiction*. Basically, two kinds of cases fall within the scope of concurrent jurisdiction: crimes that violate both state and federal law, such as corruption by public officials; and suits involving more than $10,000 between citizens of different states, which may be tried in one or another state court or a federal court at the discretion of the parties to the suit.

In both the state and federal court systems, there are two kinds of jurisdiction. The first is called *original jurisdiction* and refers to the authority to try a case or hear a dispute for the first time. State criminal courts or federal district courts are courts of original jurisdiction. Although the decisions in these courts are generally final, if the handling of the law was flawed or faulty in any way—for example, if a judge revealed bias when instructing a jury—a decision may be appealed to another court. The authority to review an earlier decision of another court is called *appellate jurisdiction*. The Supreme Court is the highest court of

---

[13]Archibald Cox, *The Court and the Constitution* (Boston: Houghton Mifflin, 1987), p. 351.

appeals in the federal system. State courts having final appellate jurisdiction go by varying names: in New York State it is the State Court of Appeals; in New Jersey it is the State Supreme Court, which in New York is the title of a lower state court; and in Texas there are two high courts, the State Supreme Court and the State Court of Criminal Appeals.

TYPES OF CASES

The courts do not get involved in an issue unless an *action,* or court proceeding, is brought by some party claiming injury. Two kinds of actions can be brought. *Civil suits* are actions brought by an individual seeking money compensation for an injury suffered or for recovery of property. A civil suit is most often brought against private persons and organizations, such as corporations, or occasionally government agents. The other kinds of actions are *criminal charges* brought by local, state, or federal attorneys on behalf of the "people." *Crime* is conceived of as an offense against the community, even if a victim is only one person. Here too an injury must be shown to have occurred for a trial to take place. Unlike violations of civil law, which usually result in money damages, breaking criminal law may result in imprisonment or death.

There are two types of crime: *felonies* are major or particularly vicious crimes, such as rape, robbery, kidnapping, or murder, and are punishable by long-term imprisonment or death; *misdemeanors,* by contrast, are minor crimes, such as traffic violations or disorderly conduct, which are punishable by fines or short prison sentences. Federal crimes involve kidnapping when the victim is taken across state lines, counterfeiting, smuggling, bribery or other corruption of federal officials, attacks on federal personnel and property, evasion of taxes, conspiracy to violate federal laws, murder that violates civil rights laws, and the like. Conviction of a federal crime leads to imprisonment.

A case that falls outside the categories we just discussed falls within the province of administrative law. *Administrative laws* pertain to the procedures government agencies must follow in making rules and regulations, which, when published in the *Federal Register,* have the force of law. Hearings must often be conducted according to standard court procedures and usually by an administrative law judge. If a ruling or its application is challenged, this too usually takes place before an administrative law judge. If an aggrieved party is dissatisfied with the outcome, he or she can bring the matter before a federal court of appeals. Agencies must abide by due process requirements in making their rules and must not go beyond the authority outlined in their enabling statutes.

STATUTORY LAW AND COMMON LAW

In addition to the distinction between civil and criminal law, there is a further differentiation within the law. Decisions made by judges in dealing with cases form what is called *common law* or, sometimes, "case law." The American colonists took over the huge body of common law from England and incorporated it into their systems of state and federal laws when the nation was founded. The common law is based largely on precedent and customary practice. *Precedents* are earlier decisions that are used as guides for current decisions. It is important to recognize that the precedents are not themselves law, but rather are indications of what the law is. General principles are inferred from clusters of related decisions or precedents and used to formulate a decision regarding a current case. As an example, here is an excerpt from an opinion written by Justice William Brennan for the majority in applying the Fifth Amendment guarantees against self-incrimination to state cases.

> We hold today that the Fifth Amendment's exception from compulsory self-incrimination is also protected by the Fourteenth Amendment against abridgment by the States. . . . The marked shift to the federal standard began with *Lisenba* v. *California* . . . where the Court spoke of accused's "free choice to admit, to deny, or to refuse to answer." See *Ashcraft* v. *Tennessee* . . . *Malinski* v. *New York* . . . *Spano* v. *New York* . . . *Lynumn* v. *Illinois* . . . *Haynes* v. *Washington*. . . .[14]

As can be seen, precedent and statutory law often interact in the formation of a judicial decision. *Statutory law* is the law enacted by legislatures and represents the "written law" as distinct from the common law, which is thought of as "unwritten." (It should be noted that the vast number of precedents are carefully written down and recorded in huge books. What is "unwritten" is the law the precedents are supposed to reflect.) Legislatures are not bound by the past when they enact statutes as judges are when they decide cases on the basis of common law.

But all law, whether written or "unwritten," deals with the present and, by implication, with the future. As a consequence, the same interpretive processes take place whether a decision is based on statutory or common law. Often an interpretation is governed by the ideological views of the judge or the political climate at the time of the decision. This is particularly so with the great constitutional questions that sometimes face the federal judiciary. Ideology often determines the way a federal judge will respond to the political climate of his or her time. It is for this reason that President Reagan was so determined to place arch-conservatives on the Supreme Court and it is the same reason that made Senate liberals so resistant.

POLITICS AND THE FEDERAL JUDICIARY

Politics are inescapable in any dealings with government. For our purposes here we can define politics as ideology constrained by self-interest. From the beginning, ideology and the federal judiciary were intertwined. However, wise judges trimmed their principles to fit their reality. A perfect example of how this worked is the case in which the Supreme Court first asserted its supremacy as the interpreter of the Constitution.

John Adams, the outgoing president, had pushed through the outgoing Federalist Congress the Judiciary Act of 1801, which created sixteen federal judgeships

---

[14]*Malloy* v. *Hogan*, 378 U.S. 1 (1964).

ostensibly to relieve the Supreme Court. Just days before leaving office Adams appointed the federal judges and a number of minor local judges, one of whom was William Marbury. All of Adams's appointees were Federalists and were chosen with the intention of blocking Jefferson's programs. However, the signed commissions for the judgeships were not delivered to the appointees before Jefferson entered office. Outraged at Adams's maneuver, Jefferson ordered Secretary of State James Madison to hold back some of the commissions for what were called the "midnight judges." One of those midnight judges, actually a justice-of-the-peace, was Marbury, and he brought suit against Madison to get his commission. The case of *Marbury v. Madison* went before Federalist Chief Justice John Marshall, who had also been appointed in 1801 by Adams.

Marshall was deeply suspicious of his cousin Tom Jefferson's republicanism. Jefferson was an advocate of a weak central government, while Marshall, like other Federalists, wanted a strong national government. But by 1803, when *Marbury* came before Marshall, Jefferson had been in office for almost two years and had clearly shown that although he believed in a weak government, he himself was a powerful national leader. Moreover, the likely purpose of Marbury's suit was to embarrass Jefferson since the justice-of-the-peace position was so petty it was not otherwise worth fighting for. But if Jefferson turned the tables on the Federalists, which he was fully capable of doing, and instead embarrassed the Supreme Court by showing it up as weak, this would do irreparable damage to the Court and the constitutional theory of checks and balances.

A direct confrontation with Jefferson on this issue, before the Court had established its authority, could have been disastrous. The chief justice chose the better part of valor and beat a dignified retreat. Marbury had relied on a section of a law passed by Congress to begin his suit on the high court. The Judiciary Act of 1789 gave the Supreme Court the *mandamus* power in original jurisdiction to compel executive and judicial officers to perform their duties under law. But the Constitution can be read as being highly restrictive in granting original jurisdiction to the Court. The Constitution specifically says: "In all Cases affecting Ambassadors, other public Ministers and Consuls, and those in which a State shall be Party, the Supreme Court shall have original Jurisdiction." Nothing is mentioned about the Court's *mandamus* power. But Marbury, in suing a public minister—Madison, who was Secretary of State—requested the Court to issue the *mandamus* writ to Madison to compel him to deliver Marbury's commission.

John Marshall chose to interpret, or "construct," the Constitution strictly, contrary to his usual practice. First, he slapped Jefferson like a good Federalist should by saying that Marbury had a lawful right to his commission; then he rejected Marbury's suit by saying he brought action in the wrong court. The Constitution, according to Marshall, did not permit the high court to have the *mandamus* power in original jurisdiction. The congressional law under which Marbury brought his action, Marshall asserted, was in conflict with the Constitution. He then went on to loosely construct other parts of the Constitution so as to justify his reading of that original document. As former special prosecutor Archibald Cox pointed out, Marshall had been very clever. "By asserting this power of judicial review in a case brought before it, the Supreme Court could maintain the supremacy of the Constitution, build up its own power, and at the same time avoid a disastrous confrontation with President Jefferson by dismissing Marbury's suit as having been brought in the wrong court."[15]

Marshall's reasoning was so clear and compelling that his opinion in *Marbury* has been the basis for the Supreme Court's enormous prestige and overwhelming authority. We must remember that the Court has no means itself of enforcing its decisions and must rely on other power centers, especially the executive, for support. Within the last half century it has enjoyed that support, even when its decisions have been against the president, as it was when Nixon refused to turn over the Watergate tapes to the special prosecutor. But this was not always so. It took many years, and many stumbles, before the Court reached this high plateau.

Not all chief justices of the Supreme Court were as brilliant as John Marshall. The classic instance of a nearly fatal error by the Court is its *Dred Scott* decision. In 1835, John Marshall died after thirty-four years as chief justice and was succeeded by Roger Taney, an Andrew Jackson appointee and a Maryland slaveowner. Dred Scott was the slave of an army surgeon who owned him in a slave state, took him north to a state where slavery was prohibited by congressional law, and then after several years brought him back to the slave state. The surgeon died and Scott sued for his freedom on the grounds that his years of residence in a free state made him a free man. The lowest state court granted Scott his freedom, but the court's decision was reversed on appeal in the higher state courts. The case occurred in the midst of rising passions over the issue of slavery and gained national prominence.

The case was brought to the Supreme Court by Scott's antislavery supporters. Taney wrote the opinion for the majority, which consisted of seven proslavery justices. The majority wanted to settle the highly charged issue of slavery once and for all. Using tortured reasoning based on strict constructionist arguments,

---

[15]Cox, *The Court and the Constitution*, p. 52.

Taney rejected Scott's claim on three grounds. The first is morally offensive to every decent and civilized mind. In Taney's words:

> [Negroes] had for more than a century before [the constitution was adopted] been regarded as beings of an inferior order, and altogether unfit to associate with the white race ... and that the negro might [therefore] justly and lawfully be reduced to slavery. ...

> And, accordingly, a negro of the African race was regarded by them as an article of property, and held, and bought and sold as such, in every one of the thirteen Colonies which united in the Declaration of Independence, and afterwards formed the Constitution of the United States. The slaves were more or less numerous in the different Colonies, as slave labor was found more or less profitable. But no one seems to have doubted the correctness of the prevailing opinion of the time. ...

> No one, we presume, supposes that any change in public opinion or feeling ... should induce the court to give to the words of the Constitution a more liberal construction in their favor than they were intended to bear when the instrument was framed and adopted. ...

> Now ... by [Dred Scott's] own admission he is still a slave; and ... no one supposes that a slave is a citizen ... [therefore, Scott is] incapable of suing in the character of a citizen.[16]

Not only was Taney's reasoning twisted, but the facts central to his argument were wrong, and he should have known better. By the time of his decision, the Journal of the 1787 Convention and the memoirs of the Framers had been made public. He should have known that the delegates were divided on the issue of slavery, and that at the time the Constitution was created, more than half the states did not have slaves. As Madison put it: "It seemed now to be pretty well understood that the real difference of interests lay, not between the large & small but between the N. & South[n] States. The institution of slavery & its consequences formed the line of discrimination. There were 5 States on the South, 8 on the North[n] side of this line."[17] Taney should also have known that the Convention did not write in a constitutional prohibition of slavery only because three states would have refused to sign the document if there were such a prohibition. A large number of delegates agreed with George Mason of Virginia, who looked upon slavery as "this infernal trafic."

In addition to denying Scott his rights because he was black, Taney also denied Congress the authority to make a law freeing slaves or setting aside territory in which blacks could not be enslaved. His third ground for rejecting Dred Scott's suit was that federal courts did not have jurisdiction in the case. Opponents of slavery and many others were outraged at the Court's decision. Its intrusion into a highly charged political and ideological controversy under the guise of rendering a disinterested judicial opinion was completely unnecessary and foolish. Taney could have said simply that federal courts did not have jurisdiction in this case,

---

[16] *Dred Scott* v. *Sandford,* 19 How. 393 (1957).
[17] Madison, *Notes of Debates,* p. 295.

thereby refusing to hear the appeal and allowing the state court's final decision against Scott to stand. All that Taney and the majority succeeded in accomplishing was earning contempt for the high court. Cox said it well: ". . . in a single decision the Court had dissipated its prestige and made itself a political football."[18]

But the Supreme Court's entry into controversial areas does not always have the dire consequences of the Taney decision. Sometimes the Court's prestige is enhanced by a controversial decision. This is what happened with the Warren Court's 1954 decision in *Brown* v. *Board of Education*. The decision, coupled with its 1955 implementation order to desegregate schools with "deliberate speed" caused a violent storm of protest throughout the South. The federal government had to send troops into the South on several occasions between 1957 and 1965 to enforce the Court's ruling. Yet *Brown* became the basis not only of other desegregation cases, but also of the further expansion of civil rights. We may reverse Cox's comment on the *Dred Scott* decision and say "in a single decision the Court increased its prestige and made itself into the ultimate guardian of liberty, equality, and justice in the nation."

Why are the Court's decisions accepted in one instance and not in another? Why have presidents, who control armies, complied with rulings against their actions by a Court that has no physical means of enforcing its decisions? Why has Congress been unwilling to overturn an unpopular Supreme Court ruling, such as the prohibition of school prayer? The traditional answer is that the Supreme Court is regarded by many Americans as possessing a high degree of legitimacy, despite the decline in its popular support.

SOURCES OF JUDICIAL LEGITIMACY

The Court's decisions were not always regarded as having a high degree of legitimacy. Indeed, there were several low points in the Court's standing. The aftermath of the *Dred Scott* decision was the lowest of these. The period between 1935 and 1936, when the Supreme Court struck down FDR's efforts to pull the country out of the Great Depression, was another.[19] Even the Marshall Court hit a low point during the presidency of Andrew Jackson, when the president refused to enforce a Supreme Court decision. Jackson is supposed to have said: "Marshall made his decision. Let him enforce it!"

The Court's highest standing has been during the current period and the recent past, since its involvement in the expansion of civil liberties and rights following its change of heart in 1937. Previously, it had been concerned with the expansion of the national economy and thus favored business interests over the individual and the community. In an important sense one can rightly say that the pre-1937 Court represented the interests of a particular class: the wealthy, and generally those connected with large enterprises, whether in manufacturing, agriculture, or

---

[18]Cox, *The Court and the Constitution*, p. 109.

[19]Starting early in 1935, the Court consistently rejected New Deal legislation, knocking down seven out of nine laws by the end of its 1936 term. The laws were intended to support economic recovery and establish principles of economic and social justice. In his effort to overcome the Court's resistance, FDR had considerable popular and legislative support for his plan to pack the Court.

banking. John Marshall was able to transform that class interest into the national interest. After him, the great visions within the Court came mainly from those writing dissenting opinions until the 1937 turnabout. Oliver Wendell Holmes, who served on the Court from 1902 to 1932, springs first to mind among the great dissenters of the pre-1937 era.

In the major constitutional cases since 1937, the Court has made decisions based chiefly on moral criteria rather than economic ones, even in cases where economic interests were at issue. In so doing, the Court has extended the concept of justice to include the individual's rights of freedom, equality, and privacy against the claims of the state and the majority. Because its decisions have had major consequences for our society as a whole, the Court has been at the center of controversy. Despite the heated arguments that swirl about it, the Court has retained the respect of the elites within the other centers of power. In part it has done so by taking its stand on the moral high ground and turning the Constitution into an instrument of justice as well as an outline of government.

But the "outline of government" character of the Constitution is another source of the Court's legitimacy. The Constitution sets up a tripartite government in which each part is involved in the others and each checks the other. Two of the parts are explicitly political institutions and make their judgments and decisions

DECISIONS, DECISIONS, DECISIONS

DRAWING BY RICHTER; © 1983 THE NEW YORKER MAGAZINE, INC.

in response to public pressures. Their criteria are grounded mainly in expediency rather than principle. The Supreme Court, by contrast, was designed to be "above the fray" and make its decisions based on principle. It checks the other two branches, on those rare occasions when it does check them, according to principles that are presumed to be derived from the Constitution.

By grounding its decisions on what it takes to be constitutional principle, the Court does essentially two things. It lays claim to act in accordance with the most revered document in American history, which strongly implies that its decisions should partake of that reverence. In addition to donning the mantle of tradition, the Court also lays claim to making disinterested judgments. It judges according to the principles that are either implicit or explicit in the Constitution, not, by implication, according to political expediency.

Thus we can say that the sources of the Court's legitimacy are first its constitutional role, second that it makes disinterested judgments drawn from constitutional principles, and third that its decisions enlarge the scope of justice in the nation. When the Court has strayed too far from these sources—or has been perceived as straying too far—it loses some of its legitimacy and comes under attack. To a large extent, the legitimacy found in the Supreme Court carries over to the lower federal courts.

THE STRUCTURE OF THE FEDERAL COURT SYSTEM

The federal judiciary is a complex, highly structured system of courts, as can be seen in Figure 11.1. At the top is the Supreme Court and below it are an array of courts, all of which but one are subordinate to it. Except for the military, the Supreme Court has final jurisdiction. The appeal process can go no further, except when it is carried directly to the president as an appeal for a pardon. Such an appeal was made to President Truman in the espionage case of Julius and Ethel Rosenberg. Many people felt the couple had been convicted unfairly in an atmosphere of anticommunist hysteria. The appeal was rejected and they were executed in 1953.

THE SUPREME COURT

The only court called for in the Constitution, the Supreme Court has had a varying number of members and a variety of functions since it was created. Originally, the Supreme Court consisted of six justices, who also rode the circuit as judges of the Court of Appeals. The high court was reduced to five members at one time and expanded to ten at another. Since 1869, the Supreme Court has consistently had nine members. And since 1891, the justices have not had to serve on courts of appeal, although each justice has some responsibilities with at least one appeals court. The Court has had sixteen chief justices and ninety-five associate justices between its creation in 1789 and 1990. (See Box 11.1.)

Justices are nominated to the Supreme Court by the president, and the Senate either confirms or rejects the nominee. Generally, the president's choice is approved by the Senate, but by no means is this always true. In 1987, President

BOX 11.1 Chief Justices of the U.S. Supreme Court

Chief Justice	Years on Bench	President
John Jay	1789–1795	Washington
John Rutledge	1795[a]	Washington
Oliver Ellsworth	1796–1800	Washington
John Marshall	1801–1835	Adams
Roger B. Taney	1836–1864	Jackson
Salmon P. Chase	1864–1873	Lincoln
Morrison R. Waite	1874–1888	Grant
Melville W. Fuller	1888–1910	Cleveland
Edward D. White	1910–1921	Taft
William H. Taft	1921–1930	Harding
Charles Evans Hughes	1930–1941	Hoover
Harlan F. Stone	1941–1946	Roosevelt
Fred M. Vinson	1946–1953	Truman
Earl Warren	1953–1969	Eisenhower
Warren E. Burger	1969–1986	Nixon
William H. Rehnquist	1986–	Reagan

[a]Rutledge served only a few months and was not confirmed by the Federalist Senate because of his bitter attacks on John Jay's treaty with Great Britain.

Reagan nominated two federal judges, Robert H. Bork and Douglas H. Ginsburg, to the high court. After an extensive hearing that focused on Judge Bork's judicial philosophy, he was rejected by the Senate amid acrimonious debate. Judge Ginsburg withdrew his name when it was discovered that he had smoked marijuana in college; he knew he faced certain rejection. Out of 132 nominees, 27 have been rejected throughout our nation's history.

The Constitution specifies the authority of the Court in Article III, Section 2. The second paragraph of this section also describes in some detail the original jurisdiction and in general terms the appellate jurisdiction of the high court. Most cases that reach the Supreme Court come under its appellate jurisdiction. Today, there are two main ways of gaining a Supreme Court hearing under its appeals authority. Direct appeals from lower courts may be made under certain conditions if the Supreme Court holds that a major constitutional issue is involved. Very few cases arrive at the Court by this route. The majority of cases get to the Court by petitioning for a *writ of certiorari,* an order to a lower court to send the records of a case up to the Supreme Court for review. *Certiorari* can be granted only after agreement by four justices, and that agreement can be obtained only if the justices find that a "substantial federal question" is involved.

When a case does reach the Supreme Court, lawyers for the opposing sides present to the justices their *briefs,* written arguments supported by factual evidence, summaries of lower court decisions in the case, and citations of precedence. The justices read the briefs in their chambers and then hear oral arguments in open court. This enables the justices to question—sometimes quite closely—the attorneys on any aspect of the case. After the oral arguments have been heard, the justices retire to their chambers to consider the issues and to formulate their views.

How the entire Court arrives at its decisions varies to some degree according to the individual styles of the justices. Some, for example, prefer making their decisions in relative solitude after reading and thinking about the case before them and the material researched by their law clerks. Others like to discuss the case with their clerks and brother justices. Then, on the Friday of the week in which oral arguments were presented, the justices meet absolutely alone in the conference room to discuss the cases that had been heard. No one outside the Supreme Court knows exactly what takes place in the conference, but some educated guesses have been made. Here is Archibald Cox's:

> The Chief Justice is said to state each case and present his tentative view of the correct disposition. The Associate Justices follow, in order of seniority. There can scarcely be time in the formal conference for lengthy discussion of even the most important cases, but we know very little of what actually takes place. Typically, a vote is taken at the conference. By tradition, the Justices vote in reverse order of seniority so that the most junior will not feel intimidated. Often, the vote is decisive. Sometimes Justices reserve their votes. Sometimes they change their minds.[20]

Generally, the conference is followed by written opinions that express the views of the justices. A written opinion is customary but not legally required, so that in relatively minor cases opinions are usually short and unsigned. Almost always in major cases, opinions tend to be long, complex, and signed. In the past, there was most often one opinion signed by the majority and one or two dissenting opinions signed by the minority. Today, difficult cases, such as those on affirmative action, generate a number of separate opinions from both the majority and minority.

Still, a fairly standard procedure is followed in choosing the author of the majority opinion. When the chief justice is part of the majority, he will either write the opinion himself or, more often, assign the task to one of the associate justices who shares his opinion. If the chief is in the minority, the assignment is either made or taken on by the senior associate justice in the majority. A draft opinion is then circulated among the justices. The draft often undergoes considerable—sometimes, radical—revision and may on occasion prompt separate opinions from other members of the majority. Sometimes votes are changed during the process of circulating the draft opinions and a new majority may be formed or lost. Eventually, the Court's decision and various opinions are handed down.

The written opinions are not all of one or two kinds, as we may imagine from a group of highly intelligent and strong-minded individuals. Technically, four different types of opinions may be written. On those rare occasions when everyone

---

[20]Cox, *The Court and Constitution*, p. 278.

on the bench votes the same way, a *unanimous opinion* is handed down. When at least five and no more than eight justices vote the same way for the same reasons, they issue a *majority opinion* that they each sign. But when some members of the majority have separate reasons for joining in the decision, they will set forth these reasons in a *concurring opinion*. Those in the minority may write an explanation of their disagreement with the majority in a *dissenting opinion*. If several members hold minority views, they may each dissent for different reasons and therefore write separate opinions. Some of the greatest judicial opinions have come down to us in the form of dissents and have been the basis for later majority opinions, as in the opinions of justices Oliver Wendell Holmes and Louis Brandeis.

CONSTITUTIONAL AND LEGISLATIVE COURTS

The federal courts below the level of the Supreme Court are all creations of Congress. The authority of Congress to create lower federal courts is derived from Article I, Section 8, and Article III, Section 1, of the Constitution. On the basis of this authority, Congress as early as 1789 had created a system of lower federal courts, which at the time consisted of three circuit courts of appeals (a *circuit* is a region or area that can be traveled in a specified time) and thirteen district courts, one for each state. Today, we have eleven circuit courts of appeal (plus one for the District of Columbia) and ninety-four district courts.

Constitutional Courts.   Congress created the courts of appeals, district courts, and three other courts as constitutional courts. *Constitutional courts* are those courts that have been created under Congress's Article III authority. That means that the judges to these courts are lifetime appointees, whose salaries cannot be reduced and who cannot be removed from office except by impeachment. They have the same independence as Supreme Court justices and gain their office through the same process: They are nominated by the president and confirmed (or not) by the Senate.

Legislative Courts.   These were also created by Congress, but under its Article I authority. The courts were established to deal with special situations. In this instance, the judges are subject to congressional authority, unlike the constitutional courts. Congress can remove judges, if it so wishes; it can reduce their salaries and can set fixed or varying terms of office for them. In short, members of the legislative courts do not have the independence of the judges of the constitutional courts.

Congress established four legislative courts. These are courts of the District of Columbia, territorial courts, tax courts, and the Court of Military Appeals. The *Courts of the District of Columbia* are simultaneously legislative and constitutional courts. They have local and federal jurisdiction. *Territorial courts* were established for U.S. territories, such as Puerto Rico and the Virgin Islands. The *Tax Court* has jurisdiction over disputes arising between taxpayers and the Internal Revenue Service. As Figure 11.1 indicates, the decision of this court can be appealed to either the federal District of Columbia Court of Appeals or to the U.S. Court of Appeals. The *Court of Military Appeals* is the court of last resort in courts-martial. It functions like the Supreme Court for the military establishment, except that it follows its own procedures. If constitutional questions are involved, appeal may be made directly to the Supreme Court.

LOWER CONSTITUTIONAL COURTS

Courts of Appeal.   There are twelve courts of appeal consisting of eleven circuit courts and one District of Columbia court. Each court has from four to twenty-six judges, depending on the size of the region and the court's caseload. Each case that appears in court is heard by at least three judges. They may hear appeals only from the district courts in their circuits. In some instances, they may also review decisions from legislative courts. Along with district courts, the appeals courts have the congressional authority to review cases arising from actions of administrative agencies that follow judicial procedures. Congress has also authorized these courts to enforce agency decisions.

District Courts.   These are courts of original jurisdiction. They serve as the federal system's trial courts. Each state has at least one district court, and some

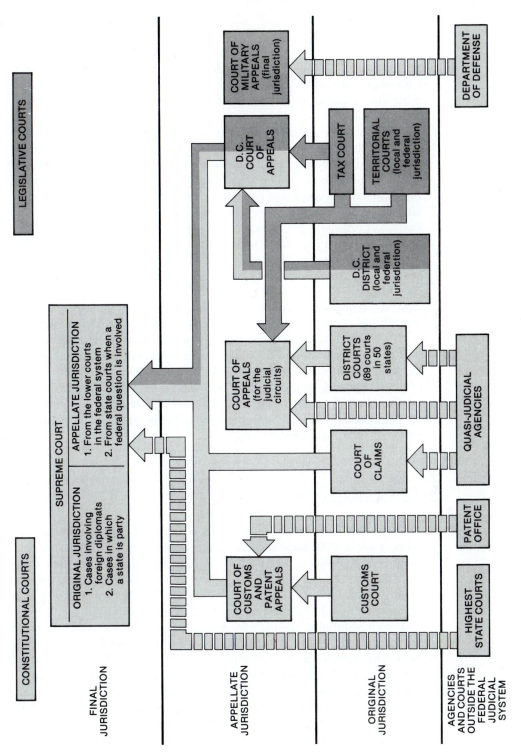

FIGURE 11.1 THE FEDERAL COURT SYSTEM: ROUTES OF APPEAL

273

have as many as four. Congress also set up a district court for the District of Columbia that is both a legislative and constitutional court. Its judges, like the other constitutional judges, are independent and protected from salary reduction or dismissal.

Each court has from one to forty-three judges. In most cases only one judge presides. However, in some cases involving federal questions, Congress requires that at least three judges hear the case. Federal cases involve crimes against the United States, disputes among citizens of different states or between citizens of the United States and a foreign country, and actions arising under the Constitution, federal law, or treaties if the Supreme Court does not have original jurisdiction. District courts, like the appeals courts, have been given the authority to review and enforce the rulings of certain agencies. Although most of the court's decisions are final, they may be reviewed by the Court of Appeals or, in some few cases, sent directly to the Supreme Court.

Special Constitutional Courts.   As Figure 11.1 illustrates, there are a number of constitutional courts set up specifically to deal with special matters. As with all other constitutional courts, the judges assigned to the special courts are protected in their positions and are presumed to be independent. Also, as with the rest of the judicial system, they have original and appellate jurisdictions. Of the courts of original jurisdiction, only the Court of Claims, which handles property claims by American or foreign citizens against the government, may have its decisions appealed directly to the Supreme Court. These courts receive their cases from parts of the bureaucracy.

In Conclusion

The Supreme Court and the lower federal courts play important constitutional roles in our checks-and-balances system of government. To assure that role, the founders attempted to secure for the federal judiciary complete independence from the political branches. Some of the founders were also anxious to establish federal judicial authority over state courts. They desired a strong national government that could exercise a "negative" over state laws.

The constitutional rationale for judicial and national supremacy over the states was presented by John Marshall in a series of landmark decisions from 1819 to 1824. The instrument he used was the power of judicial review. Under Marshall, judicial review served to expand the power of the federal government. Following the Civil War, the Supreme Court used judicial review to restrain government and labor interference with the expansion of big business until the mid-1930s. In response to a serious threat from Franklin Roosevelt, the Court reversed its position and since then has made decisions that have expanded social justice and private rights in the country.

Although the founders wanted to assure an independent judiciary, the judicial system cannot help but be involved with the political process. The decisions that judges make invariably have an impact on the quality of our lives and are necessarily made from a particular ideological position. Since ideological uniformity is virtually impossible in a democracy, the courts run risks every time they hand down rulings on politically controversial issues. The esteem in which the courts were held has fluctuated throughout American history. The Supreme Court's prestige has been high in the 1980s.

The courts in the United States follow a dual track system. Most cases are heard in state courts, which are organized hierarchically along lines somewhat similar to that of the federal judiciary. But there are differences and each state has its own system. At a certain point the tracks cross and a decision made in the highest state court may be reviewed by the Supreme Court. The Court exercises its appellate jurisdiction only when constitutional issues are involved. It also hears on appeal cases that appeared in the lower federal courts. The federal system is also organized along two tracks. The courts have differing jurisdictions and levels of independence according to whether they are constitutional or legislative bodies. For the federal judiciary, except the military court, and for state systems on constitutional questions, the Supreme Court has final jurisdiction. It can function as the court of last resort because most Americans grant the Supreme Court a high degree of legitimacy.

This high regard for the Court's legitimacy derives from the Constitution and the character of the decisions it makes. When those decisions are perceived as unjust, the Court loses legitimacy. But when its decisions are perceived as satisfying the American sense of justice, the Court gains increased legitimacy. Since the Court lacks an enforcement mechanism of its own, acceptance of its decisions depends entirely on the perception of its legitimacy.

C ★ A ★ S ★ E   S ★ T ★ U ★ D ★ Y

Judicial Policy-Making

It is impossible for government elites to escape politics. The justices of the Supreme Court are no exception. Their decisions on constitutional issues invariably involve them in the political world and engage them in policy-making. For example, the Court's "one person, one vote" ruling changed the way electoral districts are drawn, political power is distributed, and representation in state and federal legislatures is allocated. In this instance, the justices intervened directly in a political matter—the nature of our democratic institutions. In other instances, the intervention is indirect.

Basically, the Supreme Court has two ways of dealing with political issues. It can exercise self-restraint or it can actively intervene in matters usually thought of as belonging to the legislative branches of federal and state governments. Either way, the Court is behaving politically. When the Court struck down New Deal legislation prior to 1937, it actively intervened in the political process. When the Court changed its posture in 1937 and afterward exercised self-restraint, it made possible the New Deal programs and was thus as much involved in politics and policy-making as when it was an activist Court.

Starting in 1954, the Supreme Court moved away from the principles of self-restraint enunciated by Associate Justice Felix Frankfurter and back toward an activist stance. Perhaps one of the prime examples of an activist Court and its impact on social policy is the 1973 decision on abortion known as *Roe* v. *Wade*. Prior to that year, a large majority of states had laws that made abortion a crime. Some states permitted abortion, but mostly under extraordinary circumstances only, such as when it was absolutely necessary to save a woman's life. As a consequence, women of limited income who wanted an abortion usually had one illegally under circumstances that were unhealthy and extremely dangerous. Those who were not poor were able to travel to states and countries that allowed abortion. Many women died as a result of illegal abortions, and many more were so severely injured that they were unable to have children in the future. Here was an instance of patent inequality based on wealth.

But the Supreme Court had not previously confronted the issue of a state's right to make antiabortion laws. It had, however, previously faced a case dealing with birth control laws. The direction that the Court was to take in its abortion decision was pointed out in the majority opinion written by Justice William O. Douglas in *Griswold* v. *Connecticut*. That case involved a challenge to an old Connecticut law banning the sale of contraceptives. Douglas's opinion held that the Connecticut law violated a constitutional right to privacy. That right, Douglas contended, was implicit in the First, Fourth, Fifth, and Ninth amendments. As Douglas further argued: "... specific guarantees in the Bill of Rights have penumbras, formed by emanations from those guarantees that help give them life and substance.... [Moreover], we deal with a right to privacy older than the Bill of Rights...."[1] In other words, the right to privacy is prior to the Bill of Rights and is thus more fundamental even than those rights enshrined in the first ten amendments.

To Douglas and a majority of justices, *Roe* v. *Wade* involved the same right of privacy as *Griswold*. In the abortion case, Jane Roe, the pseudonym of a low-income woman from Texas whose pregnancy interfered with her ability to earn enough money "to make ends meet," desired an abortion because of the economic hardship and social stigma resulting from having an illegitimate child. But Texas outlawed abortion. The Court was thus faced with a basic constitutional question. Does the Texas law invade a woman's constitutional right to privacy? It is difficult to imagine any actions more private than decisions about one's own body.

Roe v. Wade: The Decision-Making Process

The Supreme Court took *Roe* v. *Wade* under review in the 1972–73 term primarily to deal with a technical question. It wanted to determine the limits of federal court authority in reviewing state court proceedings. The high court did

---

[1] *Griswold* v. *Connecticut*, 381 U.S. 479 (1965).

not originally intend to face directly the extremely controversial and potentially explosive issue of abortion. But, as in *Griswold,* Justice William O. Douglas became a pivotal figure in the Court's decision-making process. *Washington Post* reporters Bob Woodward and Scott Armstrong, in their chronicle of the Court's deliberations, observed that Douglas "had long wanted the Court to face the abortion issue head on. The laws in effect in most states, prohibiting or severely restricting the availability of abortions, were infringements of a woman's personal liberty. The broad constitutional guarantee of 'liberty,' he felt, included the right of a woman to control her body."[2]

Douglas began to do some head counting. Who were the justices most likely to favor his view? He knew he could count on William J. Brennan, Jr., and Thurgood Marshall, his liberal colleagues. He also felt that Potter Stewart and possibly Harry A. Blackmun would be on his side. Chief Justice Warren E. Burger apparently wanted to stall the decision and deal only with the narrower and safer question of federal judicial review of state action. William H. Rehnquist and Byron R. White could be counted on to dissent. Douglas also felt that Lewis F. Powell, Jr., might very well take a conservative approach and oppose overturning the abortion statutes.

Making the Abortion Decision

As the Supreme Court approaches its final decision, the chief justice traditionally takes a straw vote and assigns the Court's opinion to a justice who is clearly in the majority. Obviously it would make no sense to assign an opinion to a justice opposing the majority decision. Chief Justice Burger, however, faced a difficult task in assigning the Court's opinion for the abortion case. Preliminary discussions did not clearly reveal exactly how the Court would divide on the issue. Douglas counted four unequivocal votes for striking the laws, while Brennan and Marshall counted five, including Justice Blackmun whose vote Douglas considered doubtful. Chief Justice Burger apparently believed that the vote could go either way, and assigned the opinion to Blackmun, who might be able to swing the Court one way or the other. Douglas felt Burger's move was politically motivated to encourage the Court to uphold restrictive abortion laws.

Woodward and Armstrong observed, "Blackmun was both pleased and frightened by the assignment. It was a no-win proposition. No matter what he wrote, the opinion would be controversial. Abortion was too emotional, the split in society too great. Either way, he would be hated and villified."[3]

Blackmun Ponders

The ball was now in Blackmun's hands. Confronting a divided court, Blackmun knew that it was up to him to persuade his fellow-justices to go in one direction

---

[2] Bob Woodward and Scott Armstrong, *The Brethren* (New York: Simon and Schuster, 1979), p. 165.
[3] Ibid., p. 172.

or the other. Blackmun also felt that he was the right choice to write the opinion. Burger, he felt, had difficult alternatives in making his choice. The chief justice did not want to thrust himself into the midst of a political maelstrom, as any decision would certainly produce. Douglas's liberal views would make suspect the pro-choice opinion he would write. One of the most respected members of the Court, Justice William J. Brennan, Jr., also favored a pro-choice position but as a Catholic might find it difficult to write a strong opinion that would strike down state abortion laws. It would be unfair to force him to take the heat from the many Catholic groups that so strongly upheld the abortion statutes. The opinion could have been given to Justice Stewart, but Blackmun felt that although Stewart would "relish the assignment . . . he clearly had trouble going very far."[4]

Blackmun also "was convinced that he alone had the medical background and sufficient patience to sift through the voluminous record for the scientific data on which to base a decision." His view of medical evidence was to become an important part of his opinion, focusing on the issue of viability of the fetus, that is, when the fetus could be considered to be "alive."

Blackmun Decides

Woodward and Armstrong observed, "the abortion assignment really amounted to nothing more than a request that Blackmun take first crack at organizing the issues. It was one of those times when the conference had floundered, when the briefs and oral arguments had been inadequate, when the seemingly decisive issue in the case, jurisdiction, had evaporated. The Court had been left holding the bull by the tail."[5]

Blackmun "was not so naive as to think that the Chief had given him the abortion cases with the intention of having him find a broad constitutional right to abortion."[6] Interestingly, he did not view the case so much as a legal task but "as an opportunity for the Court to ratify the best possible medical opinion."[7] And Blackmun considered himself uniquely qualified among the justices to delve into the medical dimensions of abortion because of his earlier associations with the Mayo Clinic in Minnesota, where he had served for ten years as General Counsel. From that experience as a lay observer and legal adviser, Blackmun felt that he had a direct line into the medical community.

The First Drafts

As Blackmun pondered his course of action, other justices drafted initial opinions. Both Douglas and Brennan proposed invoking the right to privacy to support a right to abortion.

Blackmun retired to the justices' library, wanting to write an opinion that both

---

[4]Ibid., p. 173.
[5]Ibid., p. 174.
[6]Ibid., p. 172.
[7]Ibid., p. 175.

the legal and medical professions would respect. "As general counsel at the Mayo Clinic, Blackmun had advised the staff on the legality of abortions the hospital had performed. Many of them would not have qualified under the Texas and Georgia laws now in question."[8]

Blackmun's opinion was convoluted in many respects, citing in voluminous detail medical evidence concerning what he viewed as the important issue of when a fetus became "viable." In the end, he agreed with Douglas and Brennan that there was a constitutional right to privacy under which women could choose whether or not to have abortions during the first trimester of their pregnancies.

At first, Blackmun's draft opinion did not unequivocally assert a constitutional right to privacy, but merely held the Texas law to be unconstitutional because of vagueness.[9] Blackmun's original draft could have become the Court's opinion, because a liberal majority of justices agreed to join it. Chief Justice Burger, however, was unhappy. He wanted at least to put the decision off, hopefully bringing the Court around to a position of judicial self-restraint that would leave the abortion matter up to the states.

The Outcome

As maneuvering continued among the justices over the abortion decision, it became increasingly clear that the state criminal abortion laws would be overturned. Blackmun finally came to the position that the laws violated a constitutional right to privacy, a right that Douglas had proclaimed in *Griswold* v. *Connecticut*. It took Blackmun many drafts of his opinion, however, and the assistance of his clerks, to sharpen the issue and come out unequivocally for a constitutional right to privacy. At one point Blackmun even withdrew his opinion at the request of Chief Justice Burger, apparently in return for the chief justice's support of Blackmun's position on an entirely unrelated antitrust case.

Burger did succeed in putting the abortion decision off until the 1973 term, but he miscalculated the willingness of a majority of justices to support his view upholding judicial self-restraint and the state criminal abortion laws. Blackmun retreated to the Mayo Clinic in Rochester, Minnesota, during the summer, coming away with even stronger beliefs that the abortion laws should be overturned. In the end, even conservative Justice Louis Powell, much to the surprise of Brennan and Douglas, joined the majority in ruling the abortion laws unconstitutional.

Reaction to the Abortion Decision

Letters mostly critical of the abortion decision poured into the Court and particularly to Justice Blackmun who had authored the majority opinion. "Some letters," wrote Woodward and Armstrong in their account of the case, "compared

---

[8]Ibid., p. 183.
[9]The courts have consistently held that criminal statutes can be voided if they are too vague in asserting exactly what constitutes a crime.

the justices to the butchers of Dachau, child killers, immoral beasts, and Communists. A special ring of hell would be reserved for the justices."[10]

The letters tormented Blackmun. However, after he gave a speech at Emory Law School in Atlanta, Georgia.

> He was chatting with students and faculty when a petite young woman with black curly hair ran up the steps to the stage. She squeezed through the group, threw her arms around Blackmun and burst into tears. "I'll never be able to thank you for what you have done. I'll say no more." The woman turned and ran from the room. Blackmun was shaken but he suspected that the woman was probably someone who had been able to obtain an abortion after the Court's decision. He did not know that, "Mary Roe," the woman who had filed one of the original suits in Texas under a pseudonym, had just embraced him.[11]

Postscript: Webster v. Reproductive Health Services (1989)

Roe v. Wade set the stage for a political battle over abortion rights. The Court's decision in the case mobilized right-to-life forces throughout the nation that pressured politicians at all levels to pass legislation restricting the right to abortion. Many state legislatures responded with restrictive laws that flirted with the boundaries of permissible state action set by the *Roe* decision. At the federal level Congress passed legislation (the "Hyde Amendment") prohibiting the use of federal funds for abortions and Medicaid programs throughout the nation. The Supreme Court upheld this funding restriction in *Harris v. McCrae* (1980).

By the end of the decade of the 1980s the right-to-life movement appeared to be making important strides, especially by influencing President Ronald Reagan to appoint conservative Supreme Court justices, such as Antonin Scalia, who opposed the right to abortion, and others such as Sandra Day O'Connor who favored judicial self-restraint on issues such as abortion. As the Supreme Court continued to rule on abortion statutes the pro-lifers anticipated the overturn of *Roe v. Wade*. The appropriate case appeared to be *Webster v. Reproductive Health Services* (1989) in which the Court reviewed a Missouri law that prohibited the use of public facilities or employees to perform abortions and proscribed the use of public money for abortion counseling. But the Supreme Court delivered a narrow ruling upholding the law and failed to overturn *Roe v. Wade*. Nevertheless Justice Rehnquist's plurality opinion (joined by Justices White and Kennedy), and Justice Scalia's concurring opinion in support of the Court's decision, left no doubt that at least four justices favored overturning *Roe* when an appropriate case arose.

In the meantime, the *Webster* decision suddenly activated the dormant pro-choice forces that had been lulled into complacency by the *Roe* decision. Abortion suddenly became the issue in political races throughout the country, particularly at the state level. Gubernatorial contests in particular focused on the issue, and

---

[10] Ibid., p. 239.
[11] Ibid., p. 240.

governors in several states had to make difficult decisions about whether or not they would veto new laws passed by their state legislatures that severely restricted abortion rights. Whether or not the Supreme Court finally overrules *Roe v. Wade,* pro-choice and right-to-life forces will continue their battle in the political arena of the states.

Suggested Readings

Henry J. Abraham. *The Judicial Process,* 5th ed. New York: Oxford University Press, 1986.

Phillip J. Cooper. *Hard Judicial Choices*. New York: Oxford University Press, 1988.

Joseph C. Goulden. *The Benchwarmers*. New York: Random House, 1974.

Alan F. Westin. *The Anatomy of a Constitutional Law Case*. New York: Macmillan, 1968.

Bob Woodward and Scott Armstrong. *The Brethren*. New York: Simon and Schuster, 1979.

chapter

12

POLICIES and POLITICS

*Though a conclusion has a logical form it in fact
represents a choice of competing considerations of
policy.*

Felix Frankfurter

T he making of policy always presents government leaders with competing
options. The choices they make generally represent their view of what is
in the best interest of the country or of their constituents. We may think
the motives of our leaders are venal and selfish—and for a few, this may be true—
but for most, their motives are mixed. The classic example is Alexander Hamilton.
Born poor, he was sent to New York by friends to study, became a lawyer,
married into a wealthy and politically powerful New York family, and as secretary
of the treasury fashioned government policies that favored the rich. However, he
did not personally benefit from those policies, which were designed to produce a
permanent and strong central government. Hamilton was concerned to seize "the
golden opportunity of rescuing the American empire from disunion, anarchy, and
misery."[1] And the best way to accomplish this, he believed, was to bind the
wealthy to the government by giving them a stake in its preservation and success.

---

[1]Hamilton's letter of July 3, 1787, to George Washington, in *The Origins of the American Constitution*,
ed. Michael Kammen (New York: Penguin Books, 1986), p. 54.

Hamilton saw the interests of a social and economic class with which he identified as crucial to strengthening what he thought of as a weak republican government. About 150 years or so later, Franklin D. Roosevelt, of a wealthy and
powerful New York family, thought the best means for preserving what he saw
as a threatened democratic system[2] was to give the poor and working classes a
stake in its preservation and success. He thus devised policies to carry out his
views. Hamilton's policies, reinforced by Supreme Court decisions, helped change
an agrarian economy into an industrialized one. Roosevelt's policies changed an
unruly capitalist economy into a regulated one. In the process, our view of democracy has changed.

BACKGROUND: THE CHANGING VISION OF DEMOCRACY

Democratic systems never lack topics for policy debates. Because of the dynamic
nature of American democracy and the conflict model of our government structure,
a major topic of debate from the beginning has been the American system itself.
Thomas Jefferson, the leader of the anti-Hamiltonian party, believed that an
agrarian democracy with minimum government would be the surest guarantee of
individual liberty. He looked upon Hamilton as a closet monarchist and opposed
his policies as a threat to the newly won liberties of the American people. Jefferson
won over Madison to his view. For the first half century of American history, the
Jeffersonians and the Hamiltonians struggled for dominance. The Civil War, that
complex American trauma, seemed to have settled the question up to the present
time. Hamiltonian nationalism was triumphant until it was modified by Roose-
veltian nationalism, which emphasized the social responsibility of the federal
government.

Despite the triumph of nationalism, it is still a contentious issue, although
ancient positions are now reversed. Liberals, who share a Jeffersonian belief in
freedom of individual conscience and religious belief, today generally favor a
strong national government to which they look for protection of private rights.
On the other hand, conservatives, who wish to impose a uniform moral standard
on individuals, usually want to weaken the central government and return power
to local communities. Basically, they argue that the majority has the right to
compel a minority to abide by its religious and moral standards. Their opponents
decry the "tyranny of the majority" that Madison worried about.[3]

---

[2]At the end of the 1920s and the beginning of the 1930s, the capitalist economy that characterized
democracies collapsed around the world, including the United States. Here, as in Europe, various
forms of socialism—from communism to fascism—proposed alternatives to uncontrolled capitalism
and to democracy. Both communism and fascism claimed to save the working class and eliminate
poverty by setting up state-run economies in which everyone had a job. Home-grown variations of
these systems were gaining adherents in the United States as a result of the Great Depression.
Roosevelt's programs successfully blunted socialism's appeal.
[3]It must be understood that both the liberal and conservative agendas are much broader than the
relatively narrow perspective described here. But this can serve as an illustration of continuity and
change in a policy arena.

In this instance, democracy is defined differently by the two proponents. Both agree that ours is a "constitutional democracy" in which *the majority of those who vote* determines the political outcome in an electoral contest and thus to some degree the public policy that is followed. Conservatives insist, however, that the essential characteristic of our democracy is that the majority rules. Liberals insist with equal vigor that our democracy is distinguished from other forms of government by our constitutional guarantees of individual liberty that protect us from majority oppression. So far, the contest between these visions of democracy has not been resolved. From about 1932 until 1968 liberalism predominated. Conservatism regained dominance in 1980, when Ronald Reagan was elected as its standard bearer.

In the United States, policy debates take place between the major political parties during presidential elections. At other times, they take place within the parties as factions jockey for power and within the congressional parties as members of Congress maneuver for influence. Policy and power are intertwined. For most of the twentieth century, Republicans have been identified as conservatives, and conservatism has been generally defined in mainly economic terms as favoring business interests. Even Reagan, who came into office on a moralistic platform as much as on an economic one, discovered that it was only on the economic front that he could garner enough Republican congressional support to put across his program. President George Bush has to a large extent continued Reagan's economic policies and paid only lip-service to his predecessor's conservative social program.

The Democratic party has also had several ideological factions warring for control. A recent instance of this occurred when the Democratic leadership in Congress thought it had worked out a "deal" with the Republican congressional leadership and the White House on the budget for the 1991 fiscal year. The deal, which was a budget package of cuts in social benefits and increased excise taxes, hit lower- and middle-income people harder than it hit upper-income individuals. Liberal Democrats cried foul and called the deal "unfair." They therefore rejected the budget package worked out by their leaders and invoked memories of Harry Truman's "Fair Deal." Many Democrats felt thoroughly trounced by the Republicans in 1980, 1984, and 1988. They recalled that in 1948 Truman had beaten what seemed to be an invincible Republican machine by appealing to a basic belief in fairness. Rank-and-file Democrats hoped to repeat Truman's triumph in 1990 and 1992 and were not about to let their leaders stand in the way. But a result of the back-bench revolt may be that the ideological split within the party as a whole has widened.

One of the few major policy differences between the Republicans and Democrats is in the conduct of international relations. Under Reagan and Bush, the congressional Republicans generally supported White House initiatives in foreign affairs, as for example in aiding the Contras under Reagan or invading Panama under Bush. But, just as arch conservatives within the party were unhappy with Reagan's INF (Intermediate-Range Nuclear Force) treaty with the Soviet Union so they were opposed to Bush's military actions in the Persian Gulf. However, they strongly backed Bush's cautious support of Gorbachev's reforms in the Soviet Union, and, although ecstatic at the collapse of communism in Eastern Europe, they generally favored a wait-and-see approach to the events there. On the whole, Republicans have supported strong presidential leadership in foreign affairs since the end of World War II and in consequence have generally favored a strong presidency. With the collapse of communism in Europe, however, this may change. The Republican right wing has been critical of President Bush's overtures to China following the massacre of student protesters in Tiananmen Square as well as of his actions in the Persian Gulf.

By contrast, the Democrats have been much more resistant to the expansion of presidential powers since before the end of the Vietnam War. They look upon that expansion as a form of "imperialism" that threatens to usurp Congress's foreign policy prerogatives. Most Democrats agree that presidents should be bound by the War Powers Act of 1973. Indeed, the Democrats in 1990 were soon critical of the way in which the Bush administration handled the lead-up to the Iraqi invasion of Kuwait. In an effort to reassert congressional authority in foreign relations, Democrats sought reassurances from Bush's secretary of state, James Baker III, that the United States would not launch an attack in the Gulf without prior approval from Congress. Baker made no commitments, and the conflict between the executive and congressional branches over foreign policy continues unabated. According to the Constitution, of course, Congress is the only branch of government that may declare war.

The problem for the Democrats in the 1980s was that they were confronted with the failures of their earlier "welfare state" policies but still drew most of their support from the beneficiaries of those policies. Unfortunately for the Democrats, many of those beneficiaries do not vote. While the economy was growing and the middle classes were relatively affluent, these people, who do vote, were willing to be taxed to support the Democrats' welfare programs. But with the slowdown in heavy industry and the shift from a manufacturing to a service economy (which tends to pay its workers less), middle-class support for the Democratic programs evaporated. The changing domestic situation coupled with a series of Democratic failures in the international arena—Lyndon Johnson's Vietnam War, Jimmy Carter's Iran hostage crisis—turned many voters away from the Democrats. This caused uncertainty among the Democratic leaders, and they were unable to formulate a large vision of American democracy to which all or most party members could subscribe. This may change as Bush also fails to present a broad vision for the country.

Meanwhile, continuing fragmentation in both parties seems to promise a pluralistic (many-sided) politics. Within the Republican party, the ideological contest seems to be between moderate and extreme conservatives. The Democrats also seem to be split between moderate and conservative wings. Among the Democrats, "moderates" are called *liberals*. But in addition to their mainstream constituencies, both parties attract radical, hard-line advocates of their basic cluster of beliefs. Thus, the Republican party attracts hard-line advocates of minimum tax, pro-business, antiwelfare or anti-social service policies. By contrast, the Democratic party attracts extreme antimilitarist, pro-welfare, quasi-isolationist, pro-Third World advocates. The problem of both parties is to retain the loyalty and enthusiasm of their extremists—they are very hard workers—and not lose the broad center where most voters reside.

Political discourse in the late 1980s and early 1990s has focused on a number of policy areas. Uppermost in many people's minds is the economy. The volatile stock market worries many investors and businesspeople. Our huge federal and trade deficits are deeply disturbing. Many people familiar with government finance are seriously concerned by the fluctuating value of the American dollar. This makes it very difficult to attract foreign investments and may force increases in interest rates, which have a negative effect on the economy. The manufacturing sector is weak and sluggish, which bodes ill for the future. Although more people were employed in the late 1980s than in earlier years, many of them were earning less. Thus, a top-level policy concern is our skittish economy as it enters the intensely competitive 1990s.

Another major area that seems to be shaping up as an arena for political conflict is foreign policy. The international policies of the Bush administration have not been sharply focused, and hence Congress may again assert its policy-making prerogatives in the area of international relations. Policy conflicts may also arise over military expenditures since the Soviet Union no longer appears to be a threat. Some Democratic leaders have called for government-provided health care coverage for everyone. They call this "universal health care" and argue that everyone, no matter how poor, should be entitled to decent medical care when needed. Democrats have also called for more federally subsidized housing to help the homeless. The Supreme Court is in transition and may become once again the focus of attention and debate as it has been several times in the recent past. In each of these areas—the economy, foreign affairs, courts, social programs, military costs, executive-legislative relations—there is the potential for making policies that will affect the way democracy develops in the United States.

THE POLITICAL ESSENTIALS OF POLICY-MAKING

Public policies are shaped by a large number of factors. Pressure groups, objective military or economic conditions, political beliefs and commitments all help form the policies that are decided upon. Public policy is a planned course of government action that incorporates within the plan a specific goal or objective. Whatever factors may influence the formulation of policy, the process must be in accordance with constitutional requirements. The Constitution provides the framework within which policy-making can take place.

THE CONSTITUTIONAL FRAMEWORK

Although the Constitution itself does not spell out any specific policies, its preamble does. Since the bicentennial we have all become familiar with its first three words. There is, however, much more to the preamble than just the phrase "we the people." It sets out very clearly the policies of the founders. The preamble says that the Constitution was written to create a stronger national government than had existed under the Articles of Confederation. It also says that government will be just, will ensure peace, will defend the nation against internal or external attacks, will help bring about the well-being of the people, and will assure the permanent existence of freedom. These are closely related policy objectives that the Constitution was designed to make possible.

But the policies outlined in the preamble are very broad generalizations. Taken together, they define what the Framers considered the highest public good of the new republic they were creating. The Framers did not describe in the preamble the way to achieve their policies. That was left to the rest of the Constitution, which sets out the mechanism for realizing their goals. Over the years the Constitution has come to be the guide to legitimacy in the process of making public policy. This is so because the Constitution deals with some of the fundamental issues raised by the policy-making process. The process itself, however, has evolved in ways that the Framers did not anticipate.

Who Should be Legitimately Empowered to Make Policy?   The Constitution does not say directly which branch of government should set the policies for the nation. But through the checks and balances and separation-of-powers system, the policy-making authority is dispersed among the three branches. Policy-making, like power generally in the American system, is constitutionally subjected to a process of critical review. This tends to reinforce a fragmented policy-making process.

Initially, Congress was thought of as the principal policy-making organ of government through the powers given it in Article I, Section 8, of the Constitution. However, Section 7 of Article I requires presidential approval of all congressional acts. The president was also given power to initiate policy in Article II, Section 3, where he is required to report on the state of the union and recommend measures that he deems necessary. Of course, it is up to Congress to act on—or ignore—the president's recommendations. The review system includes the judiciary since it passes on all laws, the embodiment of policies, when cases are brought before it for decision. Although the judiciary seems passive in relation to policy-making, its interpretive role makes it an active participant in the policy-making process, as can be seen in the case study of *Roe* v. *Wade* (pp. 275–281).

Except for a few strong presidents, Congress was the principal policy-maker throughout the nineteenth century. Starting with Theodore Roosevelt, twentieth-century presidents became increasingly the initiators of policies. In part this can be explained by America's greater involvement in overseas ventures following the Spanish-American War of 1898 when we acquired Puerto Rico and the Philippines. At that time, we became more deeply involved in Central America and the Pacific rim countries of eastern Asia than we had been in the past. Since the Great Depression and World War II, presidents have played the part of crisis managers. To fulfill that role, they made policy. Congress played the part of critic and reviewer until the Watergate and Iran-contra scandals, when it reasserted its policy-making power.

The Constitution not only deals with the "who" of the policy-making process, it also deals with the "how."

What Is the Appropriate Mechanism by which to Make Policy?   The Constitution grants both the president and Congress the machinery with which to make policy. We have already glanced at some of this machinery in our discussion of who is constitutionally slated to make policy. But we should look a little more closely at the methods themselves. There are several very important ones.

Economic Policy. The budget is perhaps the first and most important policy-making mechanism. It lays out the government's expected income and outgo for the following year. By allocating money to projects, the budget also sets out policy objectives for the year. Since the mid-1930s the president has proposed a budget that Congress then marks up, and in this way approves or disapproves the president's policy.

In the past, the president's budget was distributed among the separate committees that had jurisdiction over the appropriate spending areas. This meant the budget was broken up among a large number of different committees, and overall control of the process was lost. Since the Budget Act of 1974, this has changed to some degree (see Tables 12.1 and 12.2). Now Congress adopts a consolidated approach to the funding process, and the budget committees of both houses maintain an overview of all revenue and outlay projections. In this way, Congress not only exercises control over the cost of government, it also exercises some control over the policies of government. In recent years, concern over costs has influenced decisions about policy.

TABLE 12.1   CONGRESSIONAL BUDGET TIMETABLE[a]

Deadline	Action to Be Completed
15th day after Congress convenes	President submits his budget, along with current services estimates.[b]
March 15	Committees submit views and estimates to Budget Committees.
April 1	Congressional Budget Office submits report to Budget Committees.[c]
April 15	Budget Committees report first concurrent resolution on the budget to their Houses.
May 15	Committees report bills authorizing new budget authority.
May 15	Congress adopts first concurrent resolution on the budget.
7th day after Labor Day	Congress completes action on bills providing budget authority and spending authority.
September 15	Congress completes actions on second required concurrent resolution on the budget.
September 25	Congress completes action on reconciliation process implementing second concurrent resolution.
October 1	Fiscal year begins.

SOURCE: *Budget Handbook* (Washington, D.C.: Congressional Quarterly, 1980), p. 4. Reprinted with permission of Congressional Quarterly, Inc.

[a]Congress has not always adhered to these deadlines. In recent years, Congress has fallen increasingly behind schedule.

[b]Current service estimates are estimates of the dollar levels that would be required next year to support the same level of services in each program as this year's budget. The Budget Act originally required submission of the current services estimates by November 10 of the previous year. Since the president was still in the midst of developing his budget proposals for the next year, Congress later agreed to permit simultaneous submission of the current services and executive budgets in January.

[c]The Budget Committees and CBO have found April 1 too late in the budget process to be useful; hence CBO submits its report(s) in February, although April 1 remains the date required by law.

For example, in 1990 President Bush hoped to get the budget he wanted by negotiating in secret a package of spending cuts and tax increases with the congressional leaders of both parties. After about five months of pseudo-secret, quasi-public bickering, the negotiators produced a "budget deal" that Bush found acceptable. But Newt Gingrich, an arch conservative and Republican whip in the House, did not like the "deal" and so led a right-wing revolt in Congress against it. Meanwhile, left-wing liberal Democrats also found the "deal" unacceptable, and so they in huge numbers rebelled against their leaders and roundly defeated the budget plan produced by the government elite—the top administration people and bipartisan leadership of Congress.

The conservative Republicans wanted a tax cut for the rich and a spending cut for the poor on the now-discredited theory that wealth would "trickle down." The liberal Democrats wanted to increase taxes on the rich and increase spending for the poor on the traditional liberal theory that wealth "bubbles up from below." Most participants were concerned to reduce an expected budget deficit of $250 billion that did not include the costs of sending troops to the Persian Gulf or the S&L bailout. The question before the administration and Congress was which

TABLE 12.2   DUTIES AND FUNCTIONS OF BUDGET PROCESS PARTICIPANTS

President	Authorizing Committees	Appropriations Committees	Revenue Committees	Budget Committees	Congressional Budget Office
Submits executive budget and current services estimates. Updates budget estimates in April and July. Signs or vetoes revenue, appropriations, and other budget-related legislation. May propose the deferral or rescission of appropriated funds.	Prepare views and estimates on programs within jurisdiction. Report authorizing legislation for the next fiscal year. Include CBO cost estimates in reports accompanying their legislation. *Limitations:* 1. Legislation providing contract or borrowing authority is effective only as provided in appropriations. 2. Entitlements cannot become effective before next fiscal year.	Report regular and supplemental appropriations bills. After adoption of a budget resolution, allocate budget authority and outlays among their subcommittees. Provide five-year projections of outlays in reports accompanying appropriations, and compare budget authority with amounts provided in latest budget resolution. Review rescission and deferrals proposals of the President. *Limitation:* After second resolution is adopted, spending cannot exceed amount set by Congress.	Submit views and estimates on budget matters in their jurisdiction. Can be directed by second resolution to report legislation changing tax laws. *Limitation:* Legislation cannot cause revenues to fall below level set in the second resolution.	Report two or more concurrent resolutions on the budget each year. Allocate new budget authority and outlays among House and Senate committees. Monitor congressional actions affecting the budget. Advice Congress on the status of the budget.	Issues reports on annual budget. Estimates cost of bills reported by House and Senate committees. Issues periodic scorekeeping reports on status of the congressional budget. Assists the budget, revenue, appropriations, and other committees. Issues five-year budget projections.

SOURCE: *Budget Handbook* (Washington, D.C.: Congressional Quarterly, 1980), p. 5. Reprinted with permission of Congressional Quarterly, Inc.

policies would be both most effective in reducing the deficit and best for the country. As history tells us, leaders—whether administrative or congressional— ignore rank-and-file legislators at their peril. Finally, after much haggling, Congress passed a budget that differed from the original "deal" in some significant areas.

Because the president usually proposes the budget, he in large measure sets the main agenda for policy debates. There are, however, other ways beside battling over the budget to set economic policy. Taxation, as we just saw from the 1990 imbroglio, is an integral part of the budget making process although it is a major policy setting device on its own. Establishing tax policies is a complicated process, as can be seen from the Case Study on pages 175–182. Another policy-setting device is the appropriations process for specific projects, such as the "Star Wars" missile system or foreign aid. Although Congress alone has the constitutional authority to allocate funds, the president has considerable input into the decision-making process. For example, because Egypt sent its troops to join our forces against Iraq in the Gulf, President Bush announced that he would "forgive" Egypt's nearly $7 billion debt to us. In approving the foreign aid package, Congress

"And this is for the 1983 military budget."

made provision to forgo the income from Egypt and thereby permitted Bush to set policy in this area.

Foreign Policy: The War Powers of the President and Congress. The power to use military force is another means of setting public policy. As we saw in Chapter 7, presidents since George Washington have exercised their war powers without consistent regard to congressional opinion. Constitutionally, the president's war powers are extremely limited. They are confined entirely to his role as commander-in-chief of the nation's armed forces. But through custom, tradition, congressional acquiescence, and judicial sanction, presidential war powers have expanded enormously in the past 200 years—so much so that presidents have largely ignored the provisions of the War Powers Act since it was passed by Congress in 1973. Congress, on the other hand, has, under the Constitution, unlimited war powers. For the most part, though, it has used its powers to endorse the president's actions, although sometimes in a qualified manner, as when Congress approved President Bush's sending troops to Saudi Arabia but at first refused to sanction the possible use of force against Iraq.

As with budget matters, policy decisions are usually initiated by the president rather than Congress. Here too, then, the president usually sets the terms of debate. Unlike budgetary issues, however, once the president orders the armed forces into a militarily risky situation, Congress has little choice but to back him. Only when there is vocal, popular opposition to warlike actions, as there had been toward the end of the Vietnam War, does Congress sometimes become critical of presidential actions. Even then, when Congress as well as a large segment of the nation was pressing for an end to the war, funding for the military in Vietnam continued. In response to that pressure, however, President Nixon was forced to change his policy in Vietnam and start to seriously negotiate for an end to the war.

Social Policy: Providing for the General Welfare. The well-being of the American people is constitutionally mandated in both Article I, Section 8, and the preamble. In Section 8, this requirement is closely linked with the spending and taxing power given Congress. Prior to the 1930s, the general welfare was presumed to take care of itself despite the innumerable depressions the American economy experienced. Starting in the 1930s, Congress under the leadership of Franklin Roosevelt began to legislate programs that affected the general welfare for the first time. It was during this period that various forms of "relief" were devised for the poor and unemployed. Together with Social Security and unemployment compensation, those relief programs formed the basis of what is called the "welfare state." Some of these programs, such as the retirement pension to which most Americans contribute through their taxes, are considered "rights" or *entitlements* that the government cannot do away with. Other parts of the welfare system, such as food stamps, are subject to the president's discretionary power, and thus can change according to his policy objectives. Even here, though, there are constraints on his power. Reagan wanted to dismantle the food stamp program, for example, but was prevented from doing so by a huge public outcry.

Clearly, the actors in any policy-making situation must take into account the larger political context in which they operate.

NONCONSTITUTIONAL INFLUENCES ON POLICY MAKING

The Constitution provides the formal setting for policy making. However, most of the factors that affect policy decisions come from outside the constitutional framework. Policy is made in response to specific circumstances and within particular ideological constraints. For example, when Roosevelt set up the retirement income part of Social Security, he designed it so that its beneficiaries contributed to the pension and therefore had a permanent and "legitimate" claim on the benefits. This fit the prevailing American belief that one is entitled to what one pays for. One does not have a legitimate claim or right to "charity," which is how most Americans at the time perceived noncontributory assistance.

But ideologies do not arise in a vacuum. They are beliefs that are formulated by groups of people in response to a wide variety of conditions. Most often those who formulate the beliefs are the elite members of the affected groups, whether communistic or democratic, rich or poor, educated or illiterate, black or white, or any other set of contrasts. Nor are these elites always "powerful." But they are, within our context, always articulate.

The chief instrument for expressing beliefs is the media. With the founding of the first political party, the media of the day were enlisted in a battle of rhetoric if not always "ideas." When Jefferson and Madison organized the Democratic-Republican party to promote their program within government, they also persuaded the poet Philip Freneau to publish a newspaper to promote their ideas among the general public. As Jefferson explained to Washington:

> Freneau's proposition to publish a paper, having been about the time that the writings of Publicola [pen name for John Quincy Adams] & the discourses on Davila [by John Adams] had a good deal excited the public attention, I took for granted from Freneau's character, which had been marked as that of a good whig [an anti-royalist in British politics], that he would give free place to pieces written against the aristocratical & monarchical principles these papers had inculcated.[4]

Freneau was sufficiently persuasive to help gain Jeffersonian republicanism a large popular following.

Almost 200 years later, Ronald Reagan proved himself such a master at using the electronic media that he was called "The Great Communicator." But being an effective spokesman is not a guarantee of being able to achieve all one's political goals. Reagan came into office in 1981 determined to reduce the size of government, for example, but found that this was easier said than done. Figure 12.1 illustrates the significant increase in the number of federal employees since Reagan took office. The work force grew by about 180,000 employees despite the significant reductions in the staffs of the departments of Health and Human Services, Education, and Transportation.

Reagan also came into office determined to cut what he had previously attacked as an outrageously high budget with an impossibly high deficit. Yet during his

---

[4]Letter of September 9, 1792, to George Washington in Jefferson's *Writings,* ed. Merrill D. Peterson (New York: Library of America, 1984), p. 998.

Thousands of workers for fiscal years. Figures for 1987 are estimates based on the first eight months.

	1982	1983	1984	1985	1986	1987	Percent change '82–'87
TOTAL	2,871.2	2,878.3	2,911.3	3,001.4	3,046.7	3,050.3	+ 6.2%
Selected Agencies							
Military	1,019.3	1,033.3	1,052.4	1,080.3	1,088.5	1,072.5	+ 5.2%
Transportation	61.5	63.0	62.6	62.4	61.6	61.5	—
Justice	55.4	57.6	60.3	62.9	65.3	66.5	+20.0%
Health and Human Services	149.4	149.5	146.6	141.8	136.9	130.9	−12.4%
Education	5.8	5.6	5.3	5.1	4.7	4.5	−22.4%
State	24.0	24.0	24.4	25.1	25.7	25.3	+ 5.4%

FIGURE 12.1   GROWTH IN THE FEDERAL WORK FORCE DURING REAGAN'S PRESIDENCY

SOURCES: Congressional Budget Office and *The New York Times,* February 16, 1988: D19. Copyright © 1988 by The New York Times Company. Reprinted by permission.

presidency the budget rose from approximately $680 billion at the beginning of 1981 when Carter left office to over $1 trillion in 1987 (see Figure 12.2). The deficit during the same period rose from about $74 billion at the end of 1980 when Carter left office to $148 billion in 1987, with a high of $220 billion in 1986 representing a growth of almost 300 percent in the national debt (see Figure 12.3). In part, the huge budgets and deficits were due to the success of Reagan's policy of cutting

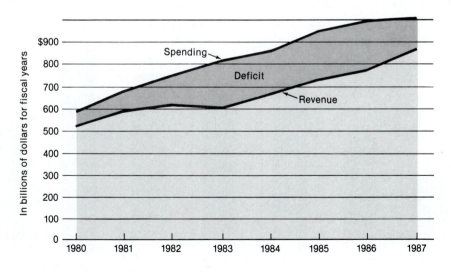

FIGURE 12.2   GROWTH IN THE FEDERAL BUDGET, 1980–1987

SOURCES: Senate Budget Committee and *The New York Times,* February 16, 1988: D19. Copyright © 1988 by The New York Times Company. Reprinted by permission.

taxes and increasing military expenditures. But Reagan's failure to reduce the size and cost of government was also due in part to the circumstances within which he had to operate.

Determined to beef up our military defense posture so as to close what he considered our "window of vulnerability" while at the same time encouraging increased investment by cutting the taxes of the wealthy, Reagan planned to compensate for the increased cost and loss of income by making drastic cuts in federal domestic programs. He soon found, however, that he was blocked in a number of significant areas. Entitlement programs such as Social Security and Medicare are untouchable, for example. So too is interest on the national debt, which has soared under Reagan because of his policy successes and failures. Thus, the cuts he could make affected mainly the antipoverty programs on which the economically vulnerable were dependent. Even so, as devastating as these cuts have been for the poor, they have amounted to only 2 percent of the gross national product (GNP), while the interest on the national debt alone grew during his tenure to about 16 percent of GNP. Also, Reagan found that any attempt to cut or reduce programs that benefited the middle classes, such as guaranteed student loans, caused a political firestorm. As Reagan's OMB director, James C. Miller, noted: "It's very difficult to get Congress to terminate programs for the middle class with its political clout."[5] Thus, the poor, always the weakest and most vulnerable, bore the brunt of Reagan's cuts.

Reagan may not have been as successful as he wanted to be, but he brought his political agenda to the forefront of public debate. Now Democrats as well as Republicans are very conscious of the costs of government programs. Future policy debates—over such issues as national health care, public housing for lower-income people, experimental military projects such as the Strategic Defense In-

Figures in billions of dollars. Each fiscal year's projection was the initial estimate that the President released when proposing a budget for the coming fiscal year.

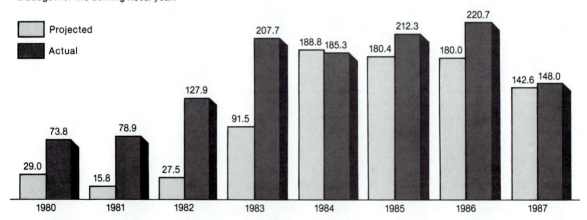

FIGURE 12.3   FEDERAL DEFICIT, 1980–1987

SOURCES: Senate Budget Committee and *The New York Times*, February 16, 1988: D19. Copyright © 1988 by The New York Times Company. Reprinted by permission.

itiative (SDI)—will probably include cost-benefit analyses. Balance-sheet considerations, rather than ethical or sentimental ones as in the civil rights debates of
about thirty years ago or our concern about the homeless today, may play an
important role in supporting policies. But in addition to counting dollars and cents
when evaluating a program, policy makers may also have to take into account
people "with political clout" when deciding on the program. An aroused constituency, as the Reagan people discovered when they tried to cut back on Social
Security, must still be part of any equation when making policy decisions. Not
everything in policy making is quantifiable, as George Bush discovered in the
budget debacle of 1990.

Ideologies and interest groups with "political clout" are not the only factors
in the policy-making equation. The bureaucracy and its constituencies, in and out
of Congress, cannot safely be left out of a policy maker's calculations. Very often
agencies will recommend policies to either Congress or the president. The bureaucracy can also frustrate the policy of the president and Congress by not
enforcing congressional statutes or presidential directives. When Reagan put William Bennett in charge of the Department of Education, he expected Bennett to
do away with the department. Department personnel mobilized so much support
among teachers and their unions, the general population, and members of Congress
that Reagan was effectively blocked, although he did cut heavily into the department's staff before being stopped. In large measure, the same occurred with
the Environmental Protection Agency.

When an agency or politician wishes to mobilize popular support for a policy,
it is most effectively done through the print and electronic media—newspapers,
magazines, radio, film, and television. Achieving policy objectives requires, in
democratic systems, careful handling of the media.

TYPES OF POLICIES

As we have seen, policies are not made in a vacuum. They are intended to fulfill
certain objectives. The political scientist Theodore Lowi had devised a useful
scheme for analyzing policies from the perspective of the purposes they fulfill.
He divided policies into three types: redistributive, distributive, and regulatory.[6]

Redistributive Policies.   A policy that takes a benefit from one segment of society
and gives it to another is *redistributive*. The best known of such policies is the
redistribution of wealth entailed in the progressive taxation and welfare policies
of the past fifty years. As one earns more income one pays, theoretically, a higher
tax, which is then used by the government to help fund one or another of its
programs to assist the poor, sick, elderly, or handicapped. In this instance a
benefit, money, is taken from someone who is considered able to afford the loss

---

[5]Martin Tolchin, "Paradox of Reagan Budgets: Austere Talk vs. Record Debt," *New York Times,* 16
Feb. 1988, Business Section: D19.
[6]Theodore Lowi, "American Business, Public Policy, Case Studies and Political Theory," *World
Politics,* 16 July 1964: 673–715.

and given to someone considered poor, either as cash payments or as food stamps, for example. But this process was reversed during the Reagan-Bush years. As *The New Republic* put it in its customarily blunt fashion: "for the rich, incomes surged upward ... and taxes went down, while for the [working] poor, the tax burdens went up ... and both incomes and government benefits went down."[7] This is not just an observation made by a bunch of liberals. The same point was made at book length by Kevin Phillips, one of the most prominent and original conservative thinkers.[8]

Most often we think of redistributive policies taking place in the economic realm, but they also occur in other areas. Civil rights laws, for example, are redistributive in character. They take from hotels, for instance, the right to discriminate against a person because of race and give to that person the right to be treated as an equal to those of a privileged race. Affirmative action, which requires an employer to ignore race and gender in hiring or promotion, is similarly redistributive.

Redistributive policies are among the most controversial in our society, principally because they have a high potential for conflict built into them. They may also be perceived as self-contradictory. The chief purpose of redistributive policies is to treat everyone as equitably—as fairly—as possible. In our society, so the reasoning goes, we do not share equally in the benefits of society because we do not contribute equally to society. Theoretically, the rewards we receive are based on the contribution we make; or, to put it more crudely, we earn wealth and status according to the value society places on our effort. Nevertheless, the theory says, we should all have our fair share in the rewards of society.

Given a past in which women and members of certain races suffered from discrimination and were deprived of their fair share, they deserve preferred treatment now. In that way, the argument continues, they will have a chance to make contributions equal to their abilities and earn their fair share. Since benefits generally are limited, some individuals will have to give up some benefits to those who have been previously deprived. Often those who are forced to give up some benefit feel this is reverse discrimination and hence unfair. Affirmative action programs often produce this sort of conflict.

Distributive Policies.   Government subsidies to certain groups, such as farmers or disabled veterans, and expenditures for bridge repair or dam construction are examples of *distributive policies*. These policies provide government money for local projects or private interests. In the past, the government subsidized such enterprises as railroads, airlines, ship building, and others. Today, it subsidizes many agricultural products, such as tobacco and wheat, educational projects, medical research, scientific experiments, housing for the poor, and so forth. The justification for government subsidies is that a significant portion of society benefits from the subsidy, not just the ones actually receiving it. Further, the presumption is that we would not receive that benefit if it were not for the government subsidy.

[7]From "Raw Deal," *The New Republic*, 22 Oct. 1990: 8.
[8]*The Politics of Rich and Poor* (New York: Random House, 1990).

For example, we may all benefit from subsidized cancer research that might not exist but for government funding. But some subsidies, such as tobacco, can only be explained by effective interest-group politics. There are pluses and minuses to distributive policies as there are to any other kind.

Regulatory Policies.   Policies designed by administrators to control behavior in certain areas, mainly economic but others such as health as well, are called *regulatory policies*. The principal goal of regulatory action is to resolve group conflict. In response to political demands and practical needs, Congress has created regulatory agencies to act in the public interest by developing and enforcing appropriate policies.

These policies serve several purposes. First, they are designed to prevent abuses of various kinds, such as consumer fraud or unfair labor practices. Second, they are needed as guides for determining the public interest. For example, an agency, such as the Federal Communications Commission, needs criteria to help it decide which competing group will best serve the public interest in markets that are limited, or under what conditions it may enter a market. Some agencies are involved in areas that generate a great deal of public concern, such as the regulation of nuclear power, which raises conflicts between safety and energy needs.

Making policy is a complex process that is characterized more often than not by compromise and accommodation. Many factors intersect to force compromise on policy-makers. President Reagan's last years in office can serve as an illustration. Although the story of the Iran-contra affair broke toward the end of 1986, its full impact was not felt until the joint congressional hearings in 1987. As a result of those hearings, Reagan's standing with the general public was much diminished. His lower stature plus an enormous amount of anxiety created by the Crash of 1987 forced Reagan—one of the most committed ideologues in recent presidential history—to compromise on the last budget proposal of his term and work out an accommodation with a Democratic Congress. He had to, for example, reduce his requests for military expenditures more than a third from his original goal, and increase funds for education a little more than 20 percent over the previous year when he had originally intended to eliminate that department. As David Gergen and Ken Walsh wrote: "The White House failed to capitalize on [Reagan's] 1984 landslide by attacking the budget and trade deficits, leaving the financial markets fragile and Reagan's long-term legacy in doubt."[9] Today, Reagan's legacy is under an even greater cloud than when Gergen and Walsh wrote their assessment. The S&L crisis has been laid at Reagan's door, massive government corruption during his tenure has come to light, and increasing inequities in American society are attributed to his economic policies. As a consequence, the Reagan Revolution has floundered, and the Democrats have tried to mount a counterrevolution. Yet Reagan had achieved in his two terms in office more than any other president since Lyndon Johnson, particularly by reducing inflation, increasing employment, albeit lower-income, and fulfilling much of the conservative economic program of cutting taxes, weakening unions, and strengthening corporate America.

DEMOCRACY IN AMERICA: THE 1990S

Ronald Reagan had hoped to change the direction of American democracy. He had wanted to move the country back to the way it was in the 1890s—before the vast array of rules and regulations, before the huge bureaucracy was fastened onto the country, and before the government turned into a giant give-away store, to borrow conservative rhetoric. But Reagan found that American democracy has a dynamic of its own. It can be pushed in a particular direction only so far, then countervailing forces start pulling in another direction. Alexander Hamilton tried to move the country toward industrial and commercial expansion, which required a strong national government. Thomas Jefferson wanted to keep the country agricultural with a small and weak central government. To some degree he succeeded in slowing down the Hamiltonian movement toward greater centralization of power. But Jefferson doubled the size of the country and as a consequence strengthened the national government when he was president. He also continued many of Hamilton's policies because, as Reagan was to discover almost 200 years

---

[9]David R. Gergen and Kenneth T. Walsh, "Unraveling of a Presidency," *U.S. News & World Report,* 23 May 1988: 23–24.

later, established programs have too many beneficiaries and thus too large a constituency to disregard.

BACKGROUND FOR THE PRESENT AND THE FUTURE

During the nineteenth century, Hamilton's "American empire" had the north American continent to expand across. At the beginning of the twentieth century, the American empire started to expand overseas with the acquisition of Hawaii, the Philippines, and Guam in the Pacific. At the same time, the United States experienced a huge, unprecedented influx of immigrants mainly from southern and eastern Europe. Many of these people accumulated some wealth here and then returned to their native lands. Others brought over relatives and friends from the home country, and formed permanent communities here. In both cases, stronger links than in the past were established between the United States and Europe. Although the United States became more deeply involved in international affairs as a result of its overseas holdings and immigrant population, most Americans did not think of their country as an international power until after World War II. Immediately after the war, the United States had the only solvent economy in the world and was the strongest military power.

Partly to help restore the national well-being of what became the Western powers and partly to support the expansion of American industry overseas, the United States provided economic and military aid to a select group of foreign nations. The basis of selection was whether the country under consideration had a communist government or not. If a communist nation, aid was not given. The world thus split along ideological lines: the communist East and what we insisted on calling the "democratic West," although some of our allies were absolutist monarchies, like Saudi Arabia, and others were military dictatorships, such as the one in Chile.

As our international commitments grew and we took on increasingly the military role of chief protector of the "democratic West," the relationship between the president and Congress changed. Presidents started to act more independently of Congress in the international arena and started using executive agreements with greater frequency than in the past. This relieved them of the need to seek approval from Congress. Presidents also started to use executive orders more frequently than they had previously, which also enabled them to bypass Congress. To avoid probable rejection in Congress, for example, President Harry Truman issued an executive order ending segregation in the armed forces and discrimination against minorities in federal employment. After Truman, presidents were expected to provide "leadership," first in foreign affairs and afterward in domestic matters as well. One might almost say that Lyndon Johnson "ruled" Congress on both the domestic and international fronts with his Great Society programs and the conduct of the Vietnam War.

Under Truman and Johnson, American commitments overseas and at home expanded greatly. Fortunately, during their tenure, the national economy grew— a bit bumpily—to match our commitments until the end of the 1960s. Between 1945 and 1968, the gross national product, a major indicator of economic strength, increased more than 400 percent, from $212 billion to $865 billion. During this period, giant American corporations became giant multinational corporations with branches around the world. At this time we exported far more than we imported, although the gap between exports and imports began to narrow toward the late 1960s. Meanwhile, the nations to which we gave assistance at the end of the war recovered economically and were beginning to compete with us at home and abroad.

THE PRESENT

During the 1970s, the growth of the economy slowed while at the same time inflation increased—wags coined the term *stagflation* to describe the stagnant economy and simultaneous inflationary spiral. Nixon, in the early years of the decade, behaved in an even more "imperial" fashion than any of his predecessors. The Watergate scandal brought Nixon down and Congress rebelled against the "imperial presidency." Partly as a result of Congress' rebellion and partly because of their personalities, presidents Gerald Ford and Jimmy Carter were less "imperial" than any preceding president since Franklin Roosevelt, with the possible exception of Dwight Eisenhower.

By the end of Carter's term, many Americans were again looking for a strong leader, particularly one with a positive message. At the time of his election, Ronald Reagan was wrapped in a mantle of romance. Many voters saw him as the much-needed leader on horseback, a sort of happy hero. They looked to him to lead us back from the brink of defeat and humiliation—the failures of Carter in Iran and of Johnson, Nixon, and Ford in Vietnam. Americans also looked to Reagan to lead us out of what had become by 1980 an economic quagmire from which Carter was apparently unable to extricate us. The country was suffering from runaway inflation, stubbornly rising unemployment, lowered productive capacity, and sky-rocketing interest rates. Some of these trends were reversed under Reagan's presidency, although unemployment and productivity remain murky and other economic problems have arisen.

It seems that in the second half of the twentieth century the traditional concept of American democracy is undergoing significant change. In the early years of the republic, many Americans shared Jefferson's sentiments when he said: "I own I am not a friend to a very energetic government. It is always oppressive."[10] The view of the president that prevailed in the nineteenth century was best expressed by Alexis de Tocqueville: "Beside the legislature, the president is an inferior and dependent power."[11] The ideal of democracy at that time may be described as a weak central government in which the legislature dominates the executive and power is spread over a large area. In essential, especially economic, matters, the government remains uninvolved in the affairs of private individuals.

---

[10]Letter of December 20, 1787, to James Madison in Jefferson's *Writings,* p. 917.
[11]Alexis de Tocqueville, *Democracy in America,* trans. G. Lawrence, ed. J. P. Mayer (New York: Doubleday, 1969), p. 124.

The nineteenth-century ideal held sway through the first third of the twentieth century. It was because the Supreme Court held on to this ideal that Franklin Roosevelt wanted to "pack" it with his supporters and turn the country in a new direction. But the Court yielded. Roosevelt was able to leave the Court unpacked and still alter our conception of democracy. Since Roosevelt's presidency, most Americans expect the federal government to intervene in all sorts of matters. For example, we expect the government to correct injustice, as in racial matters, to solve economic problems, as when Carter bailed out the Chrysler Corporation, and to conduct foreign policy so as to simultaneously protect our interests around the globe and keep us out of conflict. Although when we remember the civics lessons from our school days we recognize that ours is a government of mixed powers, still, we look to the president to handle all these problems. In a way, that is understandable. He is the only national figure we can hold accountable for national problems.

As a result of the demands we place on the executive, we want a strong president. But strong presidents seem to entail certain unacceptable risks. Basically, the problem is that the president may consider himself above the law and thereby assume arbitrary powers. If this goes unchecked, then the democratic system as we know it is endangered. We could end up like imperial Rome, which maintained the form of a republic while in fact having a dictatorship fastened onto it. The Roman Senate theoretically chose the emperor, but in actuality it automatically confirmed—by acclamation—the man presented it by the sitting emperor or the army. So far we have caught up short our presidents when they seemed to exceed our collective sense of their legitimate power. But this has produced considerable tension in our political system. Most of us feel the need for unitary leadership that can act decisively in a crisis, and yet we want to keep the checks and balances of our existing system as the definitive characteristic of our kind of democracy.

THE FUTURE

Gazing into crystal balls is a risky business. Still, faint images may be discerned of the shape of democracy to come. Big government will probably continue and may very well grow even further. Military expenses will also probably continue at about the present level, despite the collapse of the communist threat. Meanwhile, social programs will probably be cut and taxes increased in a vain effort to reduce the shortfall on the $3 trillion national debt. At the same time the weakened American economy may dig itself deeper into a depression. More of the cost for social programs will probably be shifted from the federal government to the states, with fewer and fewer states able or willing to take on the burden. As a result, the average American's quality of life may deteriorate.

On the international scene, the collapse of European communism and the possible disintegration of the Soviet Union may create both new opportunities and hazards. Eastern Europe and the newly separate republics of old Russia may offer enormous markets to the United States. Or, if Eastern Europe joins the European

Community[12] after 1992 and makes its enormous resource potential available to Western Europe, we may be faced with an extremely powerful economic rival just as our own economy becomes weaker. The attempt to integrate the devastated economies of East Europe into the rest of the continent, however, may prove too great a strain for the West and result in a deepening worldwide depression. Due to global interdependence, such a depression might have a disastrous effect on the United States.

Because the world economies are interconnected, threatening the supply of low-cost oil to Europe can affect America's well-being negatively. Hence, we may become considerably more involved in the Middle East, from whence Europe's oil comes. However, if advanced technology can be transferred to the Soviet's vast oil fields, we and the rest of the industrialized West may become far less dependent on Middle East oil. In that case, the United States may withdraw from the area and thus let the intertribal conflicts of the region work themselves out in customary, ancient ways. For moral rather than strategic reasons, we may well continue to support Israel's ability to defend itself, but this support would involve merely the transfer of military hardware, which is economically beneficial to the United States.

As the U.S. economy weakens and more workers are laid off, corporate America will probably intensify its efforts to follow Reagan's lead and break the unions. To the extent that the large corporations are successful, we are likely to experience the same sort of labor strife that plagued America in the nineteenth century and first third of the twentieth. Class and race divisions within our society may become exacerbated, and extremist groups on both the left and right may gain adherents; confrontations between hate groups and their opponents may consequently become more violent. In response, an increasingly nervous federal government may start violating our constitutionally guaranteed liberties in the name of preserving law and order.

As always in American politics, the relationship between Congress and the president remains uncertain. For nearly the first two years of George Bush's presidency he was extremely popular—more so than almost any other president for that period of time. Hence, to a large extent he had his way with Congress. That came to a screeching halt toward the end of 1990 during the budget battle of that year. Not only did his traditional enemies, the Democrats, "whup him," to use the sort of vocabulary the president seemed to favor, but large segments of his own cohort—the Republicans—rebelled against his leadership. As a result of what many felt was Bush's poor handling of the budget situation and increasing criticism of his handling of the Iraq situation, Bush's standing in the polls had plummeted. But, with the start of the Gulf War in mid-January 1991, Bush's

---

[12]The European Community is a group of 12 West European nations which plan to remove all barriers to trade and the movement of people between their nations by 1992 with the ultimate aim of integrating their economies, social programs, and political structures. The 12 nations are: Belgium, Denmark, France, Germany, Great Britain, Greece, Ireland, Italy, Luxembourg, Netherlands, Portugal, and Spain.

popularity skyrocketed once again. By war's end, some six weeks later, his popularity in some polls hovered around 90 percent,[13] higher than any earlier president. This, of course, may herald a return to the strong presidency of the past. Or it may not, since Bush tends to be weak on domestic issues. In that case, he will be back on the roller coaster of popular esteem and thus may be faced with a resistant Congress making ready for the 1992 national election. The French have a phrase for it: "The more things change, the more they remain the same."

In Conclusion

Public policies are generally made to preserve the system that gave rise to them. But of course there are different, often conflicting perceptions of how best to preserve the system and of what is worth preserving. In the United States, these different perceptions usually find expression within one or another of our two parties. Because of the structure of our government, policies can originate within each of the three branches. In the nineteenth century, policies were generally created by Congress. In the twentieth century, especially since midcentury, policies have been made chiefly by the president. Nevertheless, the principal instruments for making policy are legislative, which affords Congress a means of reviewing executive branch decisions.

Policies are not made in a vacuum. External circumstances have a major part in the making of policies. Aside from objective conditions in the national economy or international arena, pressures on the policy-making process are exerted by ideologues, interest groups, bureaucrats, and the media. As a consequence, the process is complex and the policy outcomes are more often than not the result of compromise. The accommodation of opposing views reduces the level of hostility within the system and thus works to preserve the system.

Major policy decisions affect the nature of democracy as we experience it in this country. The decisions Franklin Roosevelt made to preserve the capitalist system altered the character of the democratic enterprise in the United States. Since his day, we have had an activist government with a dominant presidency. However, as a result of several scandals within the executive branch, Congress has periodically reasserted its authority over that branch. But on the whole, the nation looks to the president for leadership and to the federal government for solutions to a wide variety of problems. This represents a major departure from the nineteenth-century view of American democracy.

Democracy in the United States is a dynamic undertaking that still shows a capacity for change after more than 200 years. Yet while changing, in some ways radically, American democracy has managed to retain its original structure and

---

[13]A *New York Times*/CBS poll showed Bush garnering 87 percent while *USA Today* showed Bush with 91 percent. Reported in Maureen Dowd, "War Introduces Nation to a Tougher Bush," *New York Times*, 2 Mar., 1991: 7.

corrective mechanism. It has also retained the opposing ideals of the founders in an ongoing conflict. That very conflict may be the source of our democracy's vitality.

Suggested Readings

Martha Derthick and Paul J. Quirk. *The Politics of Deregulation.* Washington, D.C.: The Brookings Institution, 1985.

Burke Marshall, ed. *A Workable Government?: The Constitution After 200 Years.* New York: Norton, 1987.

Howard E. Shuman. *Politics and the Budget,* 2nd ed. Englewood Cliffs, N.J.: Prentice-Hall, 1988.

David A. Stockman. *The Triumph of Politics.* New York: Harper & Row, 1986, 1987.

Aaron Wildavsky. *Speaking Truth to Power.* Boston: Little, Brown, 1979.

APPENDIX

DECLARATION OF INDEPENDENCE

In Congress, July 4, 1776,

The Unanimous Declaration of the
Thirteen United States of America,—

When in the Course of human events, it becomes necessary for one people to dissolve the political bands which have connected them with another, and to assume among the Powers of the earth, the separate and equal station to which the Laws of Nature and of Nature's God entitle them, a decent respect to the opinions of mankind requires that they should declare the causes which impel them to the separation.

We hold these truths to be self-evident, that all men are created equal, that they are endowed by their Creator with certain unalienable Rights, that among these are Life, Liberty and the pursuit of Happiness. That to secure these rights, Governments are instituted among Men, deriving their just powers from the consent of the governed. That whenever any form of Government becomes destructive of these ends, it is the Right of the People to alter or to abolish it, and to institute new Government, laying its foundation on such principles and organizing its powers in such form, as to them shall seem most likely to effect their Safety and Happiness. Prudence, indeed, will dictate that Government long established should not be changed for light and transient causes; and accordingly all experience hath shown, that mankind are more disposed to suffer, while evils are sufferable, than to right themselves by abolishing the forms to which they are accustomed. But when a long train of abuses and usurpations, pursuing invariably the same Object, evinces a design to reduce them under absolute Despotism, it is their right, it is their duty, to throw off such Government, and to provide new Guards for their future security.—Such has been the patient sufferance of these Colonies; and such is now the necessity which constrains them to alter their former Systems of Government. The history of the present King of Great Britain is a history of repeated injuries and usurpations, all having in direct object the establishment of an absolute Tyranny over these States. To prove this, let Facts be submitted to a candid world.

He has refused his Assent to Laws, the most wholesome and necessary for the public good.

He has forbidden his Governors to pass Laws of immediate and pressing importance, unless suspended in their operation till his Assent should be obtained: and when so suspended, he has utterly neglected to attend to them.

He has refused to pass other Laws for the accommodation of large districts of people, unless those people would relinquish the right of Representation in the Legislature, a right inestimable to them and formidable to tyrants only.

He has called together legislative bodies at places unusual, uncomfortable, and distant from the depository of their Public Records, for the sole purpose of fatiguing them into compliance with his measures.

He has dissolved Representative Houses repeatedly, for opposing with manly firmness his invasions on the rights of the people.

He has refused for a long time, after such dissolutions, to cause others to be elected; whereby the Legislative Powers, incapable of Annihilation, have returned to the People at large for their exercise; the State remaining in the mean time exposed to all the dangers of invasion from without, and convulsions within.

He has endeavoured to prevent the population of these States; for that purpose obstructing the Laws of Naturalization of Foreigners; refusing to pass others to encourage their migration hither, and raising the conditions of new Appropriations of Lands.

He has obstructed the Administration of Justice, by refusing his Assent to Laws for establishing Judiciary Powers.

He has made Judges dependent on his Will alone, for the tenure of their offices, and the amount and payment of their salaries.

He has erected a multitude of New Offices, and sent hither swarms of Officers to harass our People, and eat out their substance.

He has kept among us, in times of peace, Standing Armies without the Consent of our legislature.

He has affected to render the Military independent of and superior to the Civil Power.

He has combined with others to subject us to a jurisdiction foreign to our constitution, and unacknowledged by our laws; giving his Assent to their acts of pretended legislation:

For quartering large bodies of armed troops among us:

For protecting them, by a mock Trial, from Punishment for any Murders which they should commit on the Inhabitants of these States:

For cutting off our Trade with all parts of the world:

For imposing taxes on us without our Consent:

For depriving us in many cases, of the benefits of Trial by Jury:

For transporting us beyond Seas to be tried for pretended offences:

For abolishing the free System of English Laws in a neighbouring Province, establishing therein an Arbitrary government, and enlarging its Boundaries so as to render it at once an example and fit instrument for introducing the same absolute rule into these Colonies:

For taking away our Charters, abolishing our most valuable Laws, and altering fundamentally the Forms of our Governments:

For suspending our own Legislature, and declaring themselves invested with Power to legislate for us in all cases whatsoever.

He has abdicated Government here, by declaring us out of his Protection and waging War against us.

He has plundered our seas, ravaged our Coasts, burnt our towns, and destroyed the lives of our people.

He is at this time transporting large armies of foreign mercenaries to compleat the works of death, desolation and tyranny, already begun with circum-

stances of Cruelty & perfidy scarcely paralleled in the most barbarous ages, and totally unworthy the Head of a civilized nation.

He has constrained our fellow Citizens taken Captive on the high Seas to bear Arms against their Country, to become the executioners of their friends and Brethren, or to fall themselves by their Hands.

He has excited domestic insurrections amongst us, and has endeavoured to bring on the inhabitants of our frontiers, the merciless Indian Savages, whose known rule of warfare, is an undistinguished destruction of all ages, sexes and conditions.

In every stage of these Oppressions We have Petitioned for Redress in the most humble terms: Our repeated Petitions have been answered only by repeated injury. A Prince, whose character is thus marked by every act which may define a Tyrant, is unfit to be the ruler of a free People.

Nor have We been wanting in attention to our British brethren. We have warned them from time to time of attempts by their legislature to extend an unwarrantable jurisdiction over us. We have reminded them of the circumstances of our emigration and settlement here. We have appealed to their native justice and magnanimity, and we have conjured them by the ties of our common kindred to disavow these usurpations, which would inevitably interrupt our connections and correspondence. They too have been deaf to the voice of justice and of consanguinity. We must, therefore, acquiesce in the necessity, which denounces our Separation, and hold the rest of mankind, Enemies in War, in Peace Friends.

We, therefore, the Representatives of the United States of America, in General Congress, Assembled, appealing to the Supreme Judge of the world for the rectitude of our intentions, do, in the Name, and by Authority of the good People of these Colonies, solemnly publish and declare. That these United Colonies are, and of Right ought to be Free and Independent States; that they are Absolved from all Allegiance to the British Crown, and that all political connection between them and the State of Great Britain, is and ought to be totally dissolved; and that as Free and Independent States, they have full Power to levy War, conclude Peace, contract Alliances, establish Commerce, and to do all other Acts and Things which Independent States may of right do. And for the support of this Declaration, with a firm reliance on the Protection of Divine Providence, we mutually pledge to each other our Lives, our Fortunes and our sacred Honor.

JOHN HANCOCK

New Hampshire: Josiah Bartlett
William Whipple
Matthew Thornton

Massachusetts Bay: Samuel Adams
John Adams
Robert Treat Paine
Elbridge Gerry

Rhode Island: Stephen Hopkins
William Ellery

Connecticut: Roger Sherman
Samuel Huntington
William Williams
Oliver Wolcott

New York: William Floyd
Philip Livingston
Francis Lewis
Lewis Morris

Pennsylvania: Robert Morris
Benjamin Rush
Benjamin Franklin
John Morton
George Clymer
James Smith
George Taylor
James Wilson
George Ross

Delaware: Caesar Rodney
George Read
Thomas McKean

Georgia: Button Gwinnett
Lyman Hall
George Walton

Maryland: Samuel Chase
William Paca
Thomas Stone
Charles Caroll of Carrollton

Virginia: George Wythe
Richard Henry Lee
Thomas Jefferson
Benjamin Harrison
Thomas Nelson Jr.
Francis Lightfoot Lee
Carter Braxton

North Carolina: William Hooper
Joseph Hewes
John Penn

South Carolina: Edward Rutledge
Thomas Heyward Jr.
Thomas Lynch Jr.
Arthur Middleton

New Jersey: Richard Stockton
John Witherspoon
Francis Hopkinson
John Hart
Abraham Clark

CONSTITUTION OF THE UNITED STATES

We the People of the United States, in Order to form a more perfect Union, establish Justice, insure domestic Tranquility, provide for the common defence, promote the general Welfare, and secure the Blessings of Liberty to ourselves and our Posterity, do ordain and establish this Constitution for the United States of America.

ARTICLE I

Section 1. All legislative Powers herein granted shall be vested in a Congress of the United States, which shall consist of a Senate and House of Representatives.

Section 2. The House of Representatives shall be composed of Members chosen every second Year by the People of the several States, and the Electors in each State shall have the Qualifications requisite for Electors of the most numerous Branch of the State Legislature.

No Person shall be a Representative who shall not have attained to the age of twenty five Years, and been seven Years a Citizen of the United States, and who shall not, when elected, be an Inhabitant of that State in which he shall be chosen.

Representatives and direct Taxes shall be apportioned among the several States which may be included within this Union, according to their respective Numbers, which shall be determined by adding to the whole Number of free Persons, including those bound to Service for a Term of Years, and excluding Indians not taxed, three fifths of all other Persons. The actual Enumeration shall be made within three Years after the first Meeting of the Congress of the United States, and within every subsequent Term of ten Years, in such Manner as they shall by Law direct. The Number of Representatives shall not exceed one for every thirty Thousand, but each State shall have at Least one Representative; and until such enumeration shall be made, the State of New Hampshire shall be entitled to chuse three, Massachusetts eight, Rhode-Island and Providence Plantations one, Connecticut five, New-York six, New Jersey four, Pennsylvania eight, Delaware one, Maryland six, Virginia ten, North Carolina five, South Carolina five, and Georgia three.

When vacancies happen in the Representation from any State, the Executive Authority thereof shall issue Writs of Election to fill such Vacancies.

The House of Representatives shall chuse their Speaker and other Officers; and shall have the sole Power of Impeachment.

Section 3. The Senate of the United States shall be composed of two Senators from each State, chosen by the Legislature thereof, for six Years; and each Senator shall have one Vote.

Immediately after they shall be assembled in Consequence of the first Election, they shall be divided as equally as may be into three Classes. The Seats of the Senators of the first Class shall be vacated at the Expiration of the second Year, of the second Class at the Expiration of the fourth Year, and of the third Class at the Expiration of the sixth Year, so that one third may be chosen every second Year; and if Vacancies happen by Resignation, or otherwise, during the Recess of the Legislature of any State, the Executive thereof may make temporary Appointments until the next Meeting of the Legislature, which shall then fill such Vacancies.

No Person shall be a Senator who shall not have attained to the Age of thirty Years, and been nine Years a Citizen of the United States, and who shall not, when elected, be an Inhabitant of that State for which he shall be chosen.

The Vice President of the United States shall be

President of the Senate, but shall have no Vote, unless they be equally divided.

The Senate shall chuse their other Officers, and also a President pro tempore, in the Absence of the Vice President, or when he shall exercise the Office of President of the United States.

The Senate shall have the sole Power to try all Impeachments. When sitting for that Purpose, they shall be on Oath or Affirmation. When the President of the United States is tried the Chief Justice shall preside: And no Person shall be convicted without the Concurrence of two thirds of the Members present.

Judgment in Cases of Impeachment shall not extend further than to removal from Office, and disqualification to hold and enjoy any Office of honor, Trust or Profit under the United States: but the Party convicted shall nevertheless be liable and subject to Indictment, Trial, Judgment and Punishment, according to Law.

Section 4.   The Times, Places and Manner of holding Elections for Senators and Representatives, shall be prescribed in each State by the Legislature thereof; but the Congress may at any time by Law make or alter such Regulations, except as to the Places of chusing Senators.

The Congress shall assemble at least once in every Year, and such Meeting shall be on the first Monday in December, unless they shall by Law appoint a different Day.

Section 5.   Each House shall be the Judge of the Elections, Returns and Qualifications of its own Members, and a Majority of each shall constitute a Quorum to do Business; but a smaller Number may adjourn from day to day, and may be authorized to compel the Attendance of absent Members, in such Manner, and under such Penalties as each House may provide.

Each House may determine the Rules of its Proceedings, punish its Members for disorderly Behaviour, and, with the Concurrence of two thirds, expel a Member.

Each House shall keep a Journal of its Proceedings, and from time to time publish the same, excepting such Parts as may in their Judgment require Secrecy; and the Yeas and Nays of the Members of either House on any question shall, at the Desire of one fifth of those Present, be entered on the Journal.

Neither House, during the Session of Congress,

shall, without the Consent of the other, adjourn for more than three days, nor to any other Place than that in which the two Houses shall be sitting.

Section 6.   The Senators and Representatives shall receive a Compensation for their Services, to be ascertained by Law, and paid out of the Treasury of the United States. They shall in all Cases, except Treason, Felony and Breach of the Peace, be privileged from Arrest during their Attendance at the Session of their respective Houses, and in going to and returning from the same; and for any Speech or Debate in either House, they shall not be questioned in any other Place.

No Senator or Representative shall, during the Time for which he was elected, be appointed to any civil Office under the Authority of the United States, which shall have been created, or the Emoluments whereof shall have been increased during such time; and no Person holding any Office under the United States, shall be a Member of either House during his Continuance in Office.

Section 7.   All Bills for raising Revenue shall originate in the House of Representatives; but the Senate may propose or concur with amendments as on other Bills.

Every Bill which shall have passed the House of Representatives and the Senate, shall, before it becomes a Law, be presented to the President of the United States; If he approves he shall sign it, but if not he shall return it, with his Objections to that House in which it shall have originated, who shall enter the Objections at large on their Journal, and proceed to reconsider it. If after such Reconsideration two thirds of that House shall agree to pass the Bill, it shall be sent, together with the Objections, to the other House, by which it shall likewise be reconsidered, and if approved by two thirds of that House, it shall become a Law. But in all such Cases the Votes of both Houses shall be determined by yeas and Nays, and the Names of the Persons voting for and against the Bill shall be entered on the Journal of each House respectively. If any Bill shall not be returned by the President within ten Days (Sunday excepted) after it shall have been presented to him, the Same shall be a Law; in like Manner as if he had signed it, unless the Congress by their Adjournment prevent its Return, in which Case it shall not be a Law.

Every Order, Resolution, or Vote to which the

Concurrence of the Senate and House of Representatives may be necessary (except on a question of Adjournment) shall be presented to the President of the United States; and before the Same shall take Effect, shall be approved by him, or being disapproved by him, shall be repassed by two thirds of the Senate and House of Representatives, according to the Rules and Limitations prescribed in the Case of a Bill.

Section 8. The Congress shall have Power To lay and collect Taxes, Duties, Imposts and Excises, to pay the Debts and provide for the common Defence and general Welfare of the United States; but all Duties, Imposts and Excises shall be uniform throughout the United States.

To borrow Money on the credit of the United States;

To regulate Commerce with foreign Nations, and among the several States, and with the Indian Tribes.

To establish an uniform Rule of Naturalization, and uniform Laws on the subject of Bankruptcies throughout the United States.

To coin Money, regulate the Value thereof, and of Foreign Coin, and fix the Standard of Weights and Measures.

To provide for the Punishment of counterfeiting the Securities and current Coin of the United States;

To establish Post Offices and post Roads;

To promote the Progress of Science and useful Arts, by securing for limited Times to Authors and Inventors the exclusive Rights to their respective Writings and Discoveries;

To constitute Tribunals inferior to the supreme Court;

To define and punish Piracies and Felonies committed on the high Seas, and Offenses against the Law of Nations;

To declare War, grant Letters of Marque and Reprisal, and make Rules concerning Captures on Land and Water;

To raise and support Armies, but no Appropriation of Money to that Use shall be for a longer Term than two Years;

To provide and maintain a Navy;

To make Rules for the Government and Regulation of the land and naval Forces.

To provide for calling forth the Militia to execute the Laws of the Union, suppress Insurrections and repel Invasions;

To provide for organizing, arming, and disciplining, the Militia, and for governing such Part of them

as may be employed in the Service of the United States, reserving to the States respectively, the Appointment of the Officers, and the Authority of training the Militia according to the discipline prescribed by Congress;

To exercise exclusive Legislation in all Cases whatsoever, over such District (not exceeding ten Miles square) as may, by Cession of Particular States, and the Acceptance of Congress, become the Seat of the Government of the United States, and to exercise like Authority over all Places purchased by the Consent of the Legislature of the State in which the Same shall be, for the Erection of Forts, Magazines, Arsenals, dock-Yards, and other needful Buildings;—And

To make all Laws which shall be necessary and proper for carrying into Execution the foregoing Powers, and all other Powers vested by this Constitution in the Government of the United States, or in any Department or Officer thereof.

Section 9. The Migration or Importation of such Persons as any of the States now existing shall think proper to admit, shall not be prohibited by the Congress prior to the Year one thousand eight hundred and eight, but a Tax or duty may be imposed on such Importation, not exceeding ten dollars for each Person.

The Privilege of the Writ of Habeas Corpus shall not be suspended, unless when in Cases of Rebellion or Invasion the public Safety may require it.

No Bill of Attainder or ex post facto Law shall be passed.

No Capitation, or other direct, Tax shall be laid, unless in Proportion to the Census of Enumeration herein before directed to be taken.

No Tax or Duty shall be laid on Articles exported from any State.

No Preference shall be given by any Regulation of Commerce or Revenue to the Ports of one State over those of another; nor shall Vessels bound to, or from, one State, be obliged to enter, clear or pay Duties in another.

No Money shall be drawn from the Treasury, but in Consequence of Appropriations made by Law; and a regular Statement and Account of the Receipts and Expenditures of all public Money shall be published from time to time.

No Title of Nobility shall be granted by the United States: And no Person holding any Office of Profit or Trust under them, shall, without the Consent of the

Congress, accept of any present, Emolument, Office, or Title, of any kind whatever, from any King, Prince, or foreign State.

Section 10. No State shall enter into any Treaty, Alliance, or Confederation; grant Letters of Marque and Reprisal; coin Money; emit Bills of Credit; make any Thing but gold and silver Coin a Tender in Payment of Debts; pass any Bill of Attainder, ex post facto Law, or Law impairing the Obligation of Contracts, or grant any Title of Nobility.

No State shall, without the Consent of the Congress, lay any Imposts or Duties on Imports or Exports, except what may be absolutely necessary for executing its inspection Laws: and the net Produce of all Duties and Imposts, laid by any State on Imports or Exports, shall be for the Use of the Treasury of the United States; and all such Laws shall be subject to the Revision and Controul of the Congress.

No State shall, without the Consent of Congress, lay any Duty of Tonnage, keep Troops, or Ships of War in time of Peace, enter into any Agreement or Compact with another State, or with a foreign Power, or engage in War, unless actually invaded, or in such imminent Danger as will not admit of delay.

ARTICLE II

Section 1. The executive Power shall be vested in a President of the United States of America. He shall hold his Office during the Term of four Years, and together with the Vice President, chosen for the same Term, be elected, as follows:

Each State shall appoint, in such Manner as the Legislature thereof may direct, a Number of Electors, equal to the whole Number of Senators and Representatives to which the State may be entitled in the Congress: but no Senator or Representative, or Person holding an Office of Trust or Profit under the United States, shall be appointed an Elector.

The Electors shall meet in their respective States, and vote by Ballot for two Persons, of whom one at least shall not be an Inhabitant of the same State with themselves. And they shall make a List of all the Persons voted for, and of the Number of Votes for each; which List they shall sign and certify, and transmit sealed to the Seat of the Government of the United States, directed to the President of the Senate. The President of the Senate shall, in the Presence of the Senate and House of Representatives, open all the Certificates, and the Votes shall then be counted. The Person having the greatest Number of Votes shall be the President, if such Number be a Majority of the whole Number of Electors appointed; and if there be more than one who have such Majority, and have an equal Number of Votes, then the House of Representatives shall immediately chuse by Ballot one of them for President; and if no Person have a Majority, then from the five highest on the list the said House shall in like Manner chuse the President. But in chusing the President, the Votes shall be taken by States, the Representation from each State having one Vote; a quorum for this Purpose shall consist of a Member of Members from two thirds of the States, and a Majority of all the States shall be necessary to a Choice. In every Case, after the Choice of the President, the Person having the greatest Number of Votes of the Electors shall be the Vice President. But if there should remain two or more who have equal Votes, the Senate shall chuse from them by Ballot the Vice President.

The Congress may determine the Time of chusing the Electors, and the Day on which they shall give their Votes; which Day shall be the same throughout the United States.

No Person except a natural born Citizen, or a Citizen of the United States, at the time of the Adoption of this Constitution, shall be eligible to the Office of President; neither shall any Person be eligible to that Office who shall not have attained to the Age of thirty five Years, and been fourteen Years a Resident within the United States.

In Case of the Removal of the President from Office, or of his Death, Resignation, or Inability to discharge the Powers and Duties of the said Office, the Same shall devolve on the Vice President, and the Congress may by Law provide for the Case of Removal, Death, Resignation or Inability, both of the President and Vice President, declaring what Officer shall then act as President, and such Officer shall act accordingly, until the Disability be removed, or a President shall be elected.

The President shall, at stated Times, receive for his Services, a Compensation, which shall neither be encreased nor diminished during the Period for which he shall have been elected, and he shall not receive within that Period any other Emolument from the United States, or any of them.

Before he enter on the Execution of his Office, he shall take the following Oath or Affirmation—"I do solemnly swear (or affirm) that I will faithfully execute the Office of President of the United States, and will to the best of my Ability, preserve, protect and defend the Constitution of the United States."

Section 2. The President shall be Commander in Chief of the Army and Navy of the United States, and of the Militia of the several States, when called into the actual Service of the United States; he may require the Opinion, in writing, of the principal Officer in each of the executive Departments, upon any Subject relating to the Duties of their respective Offices, and he shall have Power to grant Reprieves and Pardons for Offenses against the United States, except in Cases of Impeachment.

He shall have Power, by and with the Advice and Consent of the Senate, to make Treaties, provided two thirds of the Senators present concur; and he shall nominate, and by and with the Advice and Consent of the Senate, shall appoint Ambassadors, other public Ministers and Consuls, Judges of the supreme Court, and all other Officers of the United States, whose Appointments are not herein otherwise provided for, and which shall be established by Law; but the Congress may by Law vest the Appointment of such inferior Officers, as they think proper, in the President alone, in the Courts of Law, or in the Heads of Departments.

The President shall have Power to fill up all Vacancies that may happen during the Recess of the Senate, by granting Commissions which shall expire at the End of their next Session.

Section 3. He shall from time to time give to the Congress Information of the State of the Union, and recommend to their Consideration such Measures as he shall judge necessary and expedient; he may, on extraordinary Occasions, convene both Houses, or either of them, and in Case of Disagreement between them, with Respect to the Time of Adjournment, he may adjourn them to such Time as he shall think proper; he shall receive Ambassadors and other public Ministers; he shall take Care that the Laws be faithfully executed, and shall Commission all the Officers of the United States.

Section 4. The President, Vice President and all Civil Officers of the United States, shall be removed from office on Impeachment for, and Conviction of, Trea-

son, Bribery, or other high Crimes and Misdemeanors.

ARTICLE III

Section 1. The judicial Power of the United States, shall be vested in one supreme Court, and in such inferior Courts as the Congress may from time to time ordain and establish. The Judges, both of the supreme and inferior Court, shall hold their Offices during good Behaviour, and shall, at stated Times, receive for their Services, a Compensation, which shall not be diminished during their Continuance in Office.

Section 2. The judicial Power shall extend to all Cases, in Law and Equity, arising under this Constitution, the Laws of the United States, and Treaties made, or which shall be made, under their Authority;—to all Cases affecting Ambassadors, other public Ministers and Consuls;—to all Cases of admiralty and maritime Jurisdiction;—to Controversies between two or more States;—between a State and Citizens of another State;—between Citizens of different States;—between Citizens of the same State claiming Lands under Grants of different States, and between a State, or the Citizens thereof, and foreign States, Citizens or Subjects.

In all Cases affecting Ambassadors, other public Ministers and Consuls, and those in which a State shall be Party, the supreme Court shall have original Jurisdiction. In all the other Cases before mentioned, the supreme Court shall have appellate Jurisdiction, both as to Law and Fact, with such Exceptions, and under such Regulations as the Congress shall make.

The Trial of all Crimes, except in cases of Impeachment, shall be by Jury; and such Trial shall be held in the State where the said Crimes shall have been committed; but when not committed within any State, the Trial shall be at such Place or Places as the Congress may by Law have directed.

Section 3. Treason against the United States, shall consist only in levying War against them, or in adhering to their Enemies, giving them Aid and Comfort. No Person shall be convicted of Treason unless on the Testimony of two Witnesses to the same overt Act, or on Confession in open Court.

The Congress shall have Power to declare the Punishment of Treason, but no Attainder of Treason shall work Corruption of Blood, or Forfeiture except during the Life of the Person attained.

ARTICLE IV

Section 1.   Full Faith and Credit shall be given in each State to the public Acts, Records, and judicial Proceedings of every other State. And the Congress may by general Laws prescribe the Manner in which such Acts, Records and Proceedings shall be proved, and the Effect thereof.

Section 2.   The Citizens of each State shall be entitled to all Privileges and Immunities of Citizens in the several States.

A Person charged in any State with Treason, Felony, or other Crime, who shall fell from Justice, and be found in another State, shall on Demand of the executive Authority of the State from which he fled, be delivered up, to be removed to the State having Jurisdiction of the Crime.

No Person held to Service or Labour in one State, under the Laws thereof, escaping into another, shall, in Consequence of any Law or Regulation therein, be discharged from such Service or Labour, but shall be delivered up on Claim of the Party to whom such Service or Labour may be due.

Section 3.   New States may be admitted by the Congress into this Union; but no new State shall be formed or erected within the Jurisdiction of any other State; nor any State be formed by the Junction of two or more States, or Parts of States, without the Consent of the Legislatures of the States concerned as well as of the Congress.

The Congress shall have Power to dispose of an make all needful Rules and Regulations respecting the Territory or other Property belonging to the United States; and nothing in this Constitution shall be so construed as to Prejudice any Claims of the United States, or of any particular State.

Section 4.   The United States shall guarantee to every State in this Union a Republican Form of Government, and shall protect each of them against Invasion; and on Application of the Legislature, or of the Executive (when the Legislature cannot be convened) against domestic Violence.

ARTICLE V

The Congress, whenever two thirds of both Houses shall deem it necessary, shall propose Amendments to this Constitution, or, on the Application of the Legislatures of two thirds of the several States, shall call a Convention for proposing Amendments, which, in either Case, shall be valid to all Intents and Purposes, as Part of this Constitution, when ratified by the Legislatures of three fourths of the several States, or by Conventions in three fourths thereof, as the one or the other Mode of Ratification may be proposed by the Congress; Provided that no Amendment which may be made prior to the Year One thousand eight hundred and eight shall in any Manner affect the first and fourth Clauses in the Ninth Section of the first Article; and that no State, without its Consent, shall be deprived of its equal Suffrage in the Senate.

ARTICLE VI

All Debts contracted and Engagements entered into, before the Adoption of this Constitution, shall be as valid against the United States under this Constitution, as under the Confederation.

This Constitution, and the Laws of the United States which shall be made in Pursuance thereof; and all Treaties made, or which shall be made, under the Authority of the United States, shall be the supreme Law of the Land; and the Judges in every State shall be bound thereby, any Thing in the Constitution or Laws of any State to the Contrary notwithstanding.

The Senators and Representatives before mentioned, and the Members of the several State Legislatures, and all executive and judicial Officers, both of the United States and of the several States, shall be bound by Oath or Affirmation, to support this Constitution; but no religious Test shall ever be required as a Qualification to any Office or public Trust under the United States.

ARTICLE VII

The Ratification of the Conventions of nine States, shall be sufficient for the Establishment of this Constitution between the States so ratifying the Same. Done in Convention by the Unanimous Consent of the States present the Seventeenth Day of September in the Year of our Lord one thousand seven hundred and Eighty seven and of the Independence of the United States of America the Twelfth In witness thereof We have hereunto subscribed our Names, George Washington, President and deputy from Virginia.

New Hampshire: John Langdon
Nicholas Gilman

Massachusetts: Nathaniel Gorham
Rufus King

Connecticut: William Samuel Johnson
Roger Sherman

New York: Alexander Hamilton

New Jersey: William Livingston
David Brearley
William Paterson
Jonathan Dayton

Pennsylvania: Benjamin Franklin
Thomas Mifflin
Robert Morris
George Clymer
Thomas FitzSimons
Jared Ingersoll
James Wilson
Gouverneur Morris

Delaware: George Read
Gunning Bedford Jr.
John Dickinson
Richard Bassett
Jacob Broom

Maryland: James McHenry
Daniel of St. Thomas Jenifer
Daniel Carroll

Virginia: John Blair
James Madison Jr.

North Carolina: William Blount
Richard Dobbs Spaight
Hugh Williamson

South Carolina: John Rutledge
Charles Cotesworth Pinckney
Charles Pinckney
Pierce Butler

Georgia: William Few
Abraham Baldwin

AMENDMENTS

Amendment I (*First ten amendments ratified Dec. 15, 1791.*)

Congress shall make no law respecting an establishment of religion, or prohibiting the free exercise thereof; or abridging the freedom of speech, or of the press; or the right of the people peaceably to assemble, and to petition the Government for a redress of grievances.

Amendment II

A well regulated Militia, being necessary to the security of a free State, the right of the people to keep and bear Arms, shall not be infringed.

Amendment III

No Soldier shall, in time of peace be quartered in any house, without the consent of the Owner, nor in time of war, but in a manner to be prescribed by law.

Amendment IV

The right of the people to be secure in their persons, houses, papers, and effects, against unreasonable searches and seizures, shall not be violated, and no Warrants shall issue, but upon probable cause, supported by Oath or affirmation, and particularly describing the place to be searched, and the persons or things to be seized.

Amendment V

No person shall be held to answer for a capital, or otherwise infamous crime, unless on a presentment or indictment of a Grand Jury, except in cases arising in the land or naval forces, or in the Militia, when in actual service in time of War or public danger; nor shall any person be subject for the same offence to be twice put in jeopardy of life or limb; nor shall be compelled in any criminal case to be a witness against himself, nor be deprived of life, liberty, or property, without due process of law; nor shall private property be taken for public use, without just compensation.

Amendment VI

In all criminal prosecutions, the accused shall enjoy the right to a speedy and public trial, by an impartial jury of the State and district wherein the crime shall have been committed, which district shall have been previously ascertained by law, and to be informed of the nature and cause of the accusation; to be confronted with the witnesses against him; to have compulsory process for obtaining witnesses in his favor, and to have the Assistance of Counsel for his defence.

Amendment VII

In Suits at common law, where the value in controversy shall exceed twenty dollars, the right of trial by jury shall be preserved, and no fact tried by a jury, shall be otherwise re-examined in any Court of the United States, than according to the rules of the common law.

Amendment VIII

Excessive bail shall not be required, nor excessive fines imposed, nor cruel and unusual punishments inflicted.

Amendment IX

The enumeration in the Constitution, of certain rights, shall not be construed to deny or disparage others retained by the people.

Amendment X

The powers not delegated to the United States by the Constitution, nor prohibited by it to the States, are reserved to the States respectively, or to the people.

Amendment XI   (*Ratified Feb. 7, 1795*)

The Judicial power of the United States shall not be construed to extend to any suit in law or equity, commenced or prosecuted against one of the United States by Citizens of another State, or by Citizens or Subjects of any Foreign State.

Amendment XII   (*Ratified June 15, 1804*)

The Electors shall meet in their respective states and vote by ballot for President and Vice-President, one of whom, at least, shall not be an inhabitant of the same state with themselves; they shall name in their ballots the person voted for as President, and in distinct ballots the person voted for as Vice-President, and they shall make distinct lists of all persons voted for as President, and of all persons voted for as Vice-President, and of the number of votes for each, which lists they shall sign and certify, and transmit sealed to the seat of the government of the United States, directed to the President of the Senate;—the President of the Senate shall, in the presence of the Senate and House of Representatives, open all the certificates and the votes shall then be counted;— The person having the greatest number of votes for President, shall be the President, if such number be a majority of the whole number of Electors appointed; and if no person have such majority, then from the persons having the highest numbers not exceeding three on the list of those voted for as President, the House of Representatives shall choose immediately, by ballot, the President. But in choosing the President, the votes shall be taken by states, the representation from each state having one vote; a quorum for this purpose shall consist of a member or members from two-thirds of the states, and a majority of all the states shall be necessary to a choice. And if the House of Representatives shall not choose a President whenever the right of choice shall devolve upon them, before the fourth day of March next following, then the Vice-President shall act as President, as in the case of the death or other constitutional disability of the President—The person having the greatest number of votes as Vice-President, shall be the Vice-President, if such number be a majority of the whole number of Electors appointed, and if no person have a majority, then from the two highest numbers on the list, the Senate shall choose the Vice-President; a quorum for the purpose shall consist of two-thirds of the whole number of Senators, and a majority of the whole number shall be necessary to a choice. But no person constitutionally ineligible to the office of President shall be eligible to that of Vice-President of the United States.

Amendment XIII   *(Ratified Dec. 6, 1865)*

Section 1. Neither slavery nor involuntary servitude, except as a punishment for crime whereof the party shall have been duly convicted, shall exist within the United States, or any place subject to their jurisdiction.

Section 2. Congress shall have power to enforce this article by appropriate legislation.

Amendment XIV   *(Ratified July 9, 1868)*

Section 1. All persons born or naturalized in the United States and subject to the jurisdiction thereof, are citizens of the United States and of the State wherein they reside. No State shall make or enforce any law which shall abridge the privileges or immunities of citizens of the United States; nor shall any State deprive any person of life, liberty, or property, without due process of law; nor deny to any person within its jurisdiction the equal protection of the laws.

Section 2. Representatives shall be apportioned among the several States according to their respective numbers, counting the whole number of persons in each State, excluding Indians not taxed. But when the right to vote at any election for the choice of electors for President and Vice President of the United States, Representatives in Congress, the Executive and Judicial officers of a State, or the members of the Legislature thereof, is denied to any of the male inhabitants of such State, being twenty-one years of age, and citizens of the United States, or in any way abridged, except for participation in rebellion, or other crime, the basis of representation therein shall be reduced in the proportion which the number of such male citizens shall bear to the whole number of male citizens twenty-one years of age in such State.

Section 3. No person shall be a Senator or Representative in Congress, or elector of President and Vice President, or hold any office, civil or military, under the United States, or under any State, who, having previously taken an oath, as a member of Congress, or as an officer of the United States, or as a member of any State legislature, or as an executive or judicial officer of any State, to support the Constitution of the United States, shall have engaged in insurrection or rebellion against the same, or given aid or comfort to the enemies thereof. But Congress may by a vote of two-thirds of each House, remove such disability.

Section 4. The validity of the public debt of the United States, authorized by law, including debts incurred for payment of pensions and bounties for services in suppressing insurrection or rebellion, shall not be questioned. But neither the United States nor any State shall assume or pay any debt or obligation incurred in aid of insurrection or rebellion against the United States, or any claim for the loss or emancipation of any slave; but all such debts, obligations and claims shall be held illegal and void.

Section 5. The Congress shall have power to enforce, by appropriate legislation, the provisions of this article.

Amendment XV   *(Ratified Feb. 3, 1870)*

Section 1. The right of citizens of the United States to vote shall not be denied or abridged by the United States or by any State on account of race, color, or previous condition of servitude.

Section 2. The Congress shall have power to enforce this article by appropriate legislation.

Amendment XVI   *(Ratified Feb. 3, 1913)*

The Congress shall have power to lay and collect taxes on incomes, from whatever source derived, without apportionment among the several States, and without regard to any census or enumeration.

Amendment XVII   *(Ratified Apr. 8, 1913)*

The Senate of the United States shall be composed of two Senators from each State, elected by the people thereof, for six years; and each Senator shall have one vote. The electors in each State shall have the qualifications requisite for electors of the most numerous branch of the State legislatures.

When vacancies happen in the representation of any State in the Senate, the executive authority of such State shall issue writs of election to fill such vacancies: *Provided,* That the legislature of any State may empower the executive thereof to make temporary appointments until the people fill the vacancies by election as the legislature may direct.

This amendment shall not be so construed as to affect the election or term of any Senator chosen before it becomes valid as part of the Constitution.

Amendment XVIII   *(Ratified Jan. 16, 1919)*

Section 1. After one year from the ratification of this article the manufacture, sale, or transportation of intoxicating liquors within, the importation thereof into, or the exportation thereof from the United States and all territory subject to the jurisdiction thereof for beverage purposes is hereby prohibited.

Section 2. The Congress and the several States shall have concurrent power to enforce this article by appropriate legislation.

Section 3. This article shall be inoperative unless it shall have been ratified as an amendment to the Con-

stitution by the legislatures of the several States, as provided in the Constitution, within seven years from the date of the submission hereof to the States by the Congress.

Amendment XIX   *(Ratified Aug. 18, 1920)*

The right of citizens of the United States to vote shall not be denied or abridged by the United States or by any State on account of sex.

Congress shall have power to enforce this article by appropriate legislation.

Amendment XX   *(Ratified Jan. 23, 1933)*

Section 1. The terms of the President and Vice President shall end at noon on the 20th day of January, and the terms of Senators and Representatives at noon on the 3d day of January, of the years in which such terms would have ended if this article had not been ratified; and the terms of their successors shall then begin.

Section 2. The Congress shall assemble at least once in every year, and such meeting shall begin at noon on the 3d day of January, unless they shall by law appoint a different day.

Section 3. If, at the time fixed for the beginning of the term of the President, the President elect shall have died, the Vice President elect shall become President. If a President shall not have been chosen before the time fixed for the beginning of his term, or if the President elect shall have failed to qualify, then the Vice President elect shall act as President until a President shall have qualified; and the Congress may by law provide for the case wherein neither a President elect nor a Vice President elect shall have qualified, declaring who shall then act as President, or the manner in which one who is to act shall be selected, and such person shall act accordingly until a President or Vice President shall have qualified.

Section 4. The Congress may by law provide for the case of the death of any of the persons from whom the House of Representatives may choose a President whenever the right of choice shall have devolved upon them, and for the case of the death of any of the persons from whom the Senate may choose a Vice President whenever the right of choice shall have devolved upon them.

Section 5.   Sections 1 and 2 shall take effect on the 15th day of October following the ratification of this article.

Section 6.   This article shall be inoperative unless it shall have been ratified as an amendment to the Constitution by the legislatures of three-fourths of the several States within seven years from the date of its submission.

Amendment XXI   (*Ratified Dec. 5, 1933*)

Section 1.   The eighteenth article of amendment to the Constitution of the United States is hereby repealed.

Section 2.   The transportation or importation into any State, Territory or possession of the United States for delivery or use therein of intoxicating liquors, in violation of the laws thereof, is hereby prohibited.

Section 3.   This article shall be inoperative unless it shall have been ratified as an amendment to the Constitution by conventions in the several States, as provided in the Constitution, within seven years from the date of the submission hereof to the States by the Congress.

Amendment XXII   (*Ratified Feb. 27, 1951*)

Section 1.   No person shall be elected to the office of the President more than twice, and no person who has held the office of President, or acted as President, for more than two years of a term to which some other person was elected President shall be elected to the office of the President more than once. But this Article shall not apply to any person holding the office of President when this Article was proposed by the Congress, and shall not prevent any person

who may be holding the office of President, or acting as President, during the term within which this Article becomes operative from holding the office of president or acting as President during the remainder of such term.

Section 2.   This Article shall be inoperative unless it shall have been ratified as an amendment to the Constitution by the legislatures of three-fourths of the several States within seven years from the date of its submission to the States by the Congress.

Amendment XXIII   (*Ratified March 29, 1961*)

Section 1.   The District constituting the seat of Government of the United States shall appoint in such manner as the Congress may direct:

A number of electors of President and Vice President equal to the whole number of Senators and Representatives in Congress to which the District would be entitled if it were a State, but in no event more than the least populous State; they shall be in addition to those appointed by the States, but they shall be considered, for the purposes of the election of President and Vice President, to be electors appointed by a State; and they shall meet in the District and perform such duties as provided by the twelfth article of amendment.

Section 2.   The Congress shall have power to enforce this article by appropriate legislation.

Amendment XXIV   (*Ratified Jan. 23, 1964*)

Section 1.   The right of citizens of the United States to vote in any primary or other election for President or Vice President, for electors for President or Vice President, or for Senator or Representative in Congress, shall not be denied or abridged by the United States or any State by reason of failure to pay any poll tax or other tax.

Section 2.   The Congress shall have power to enforce this article by appropriate legislation.

Amendment XXV   *(Ratified Feb. 10, 1967)*

Section 1.   In case of the removal of the President from office or of his death or resignation, the Vice President shall become President.

Section 2.   Whenever there is a vacancy in the office of the Vice President, the President shall nominate a Vice President who shall take office upon confirmation by a majority vote of both Houses of Congress.

Section 3.   Whenever the President transmits to the President pro tempore of the Senate and the Speaker of the House of Representatives his written declaration that he is unable to discharge the powers and duties of his office, and until he transmits to them a written declaration to the contrary, such powers and duties shall be discharged by the Vice President as Acting President.

Section 4.   Whenever the Vice President and a majority of either the principal officers of the executive departments or of such other body as Congress may by law provide, transmit to the President pro tempore of the Senate and the Speaker of the House of Representatives their written declaration that the President is unable to discharge the powers and duties of his office, the Vice President shall immediately assume the powers and duties of the office as Acting President.

Thereafter, when the President transmits to the President pro tempore of the Senate and the Speaker of the House of Representatives his written declaration that no inability exists, he shall resume the powers and duties of his office unless the Vice President and a majority of either the principal officers of the executive department or of such other body as Congress may by law provide, transmit within four days to the President pro tempore of the Senate and the Speaker of the house of Representatives their written declaration that the President is unable to discharge the powers and duties of his office. Thereupon Congress shall decide the issue, assembling within forty-eight hours for that purpose if not in session. If the Congress, within twenty-one days after receipt of the latter written declaration, or, if Congress is not in session, within twenty-one days after Congress is required to assemble, determines by two-thirds vote of both houses that the President is unable to discharge the powers and duties of his office, the Vice President shall continue to discharge the same as Acting President; otherwise, the President shall resume the powers and duties of his office.

Amendment XXVI   *(Ratified July 1, 1971)*

Section 1.   The right of citizens of the United States, who are eighteen years of age or older, to vote shall not be denied or abridged by the United States or by any State on account of age.

Section 2.   The Congress shall have power to enforce this article by appropriate legislation.

THE ELECTORAL COLLEGE: APPORTIONMENT OF ELECTORAL VOTES

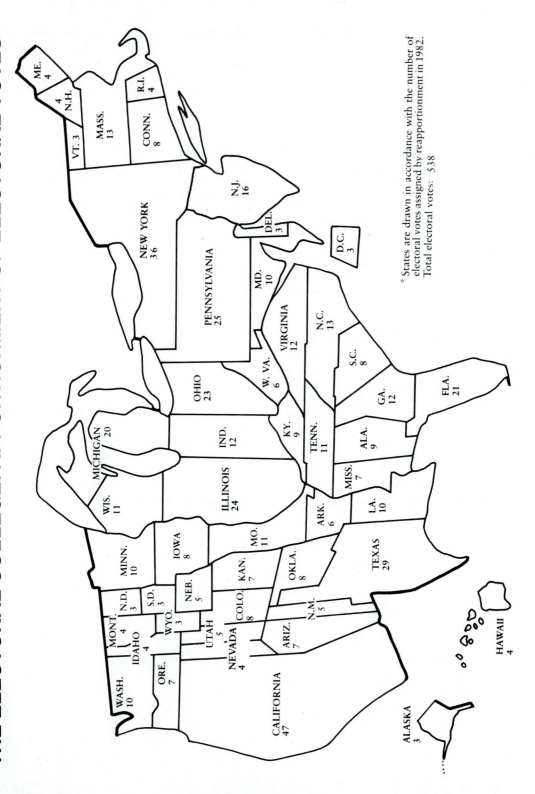

* States are drawn in accordance with the number of electoral votes assigned by reapportionment in 1982.
Total electoral votes: 538

ME. 4

N.H. 4

VT. 3

MASS. 13

R.I. 4

CONN. 8

N.J. 16

NEW YORK 36

DEL. 3

D.C. 3

PENNSYLVANIA 25

MD. 10

VIRGINIA 12

N.C. 13

OHIO 23

W. VA. 6

S.C. 8

MICHIGAN 20

IND. 12

KY. 9

TENN. 11

GA. 12

FLA. 21

ALA. 9

ILLINOIS 24

MISS. 7

WIS. 11

ARK. 6

LA. 10

MINN. 10

IOWA 8

MO. 11

N.D. 3

S.D. 3

NEB. 5

KAN. 7

OKLA. 8

TEXAS 29

MONT. 4

WYO. 3

COLO. 8

N.M. 5

WASH. 10

IDAHO 4

UTAH 5

ARIZ. 7

ORE. 7

NEVADA 4

CALIFORNIA 47

HAWAII 4

ALASKA 3

PRESIDENTIAL ELECTIONS

Year	Number of States	Candidates	Parties	Popular Vote	Percentage of Popular Vote	Electoral Vote	Percentage Voter Participation
1789	11	**GEORGE WASHINGTON**	No party designations			69	
		John Adams				34	
		Other candidates				35	
1792	15	**GEORGE WASHINGTON**	No party designations			132	
		John Adams				77	
		George Clinton				50	
		Other candidates				5	
1796	16	**JOHN ADAMS**	Federalist			71	
		Thomas Jefferson	Democratic-Republican			68	
		Thomas Pinckney	Federalist			59	
		Aaron Burr	Democratic-Republican			30	
		Other candidates				48	
1800	16	**THOMAS JEFFERSON**	Democratic-Republican			73	
		Aaron Burr	Democratic-Republican			73	
		John Adams	Federalist			65	
		Charles C. Pinckney	Federalist			64	
		John Jay	Federalist			1	
1804	17	**THOMAS JEFFERSON**	Democratic-Republican			162	
		Charles C. Pinckney	Federalist			14	
1808	17	**JAMES MADISON**	Democratic-Republican			122	
		Charles C. Pinckney	Federalist			47	
		George Clinton	Democratic-Republican			6	
1812	18	**JAMES MADISON**	Democratic-Republican			128	
		DeWitt Clinton	Federalist			89	
1816	19	**JAMES MONROE**	Democratic-Republican			183	
		Rufus King	Federalist			34	
1820	24	**JAMES MONROE**	Democratic-Republican			231	
		John Quincy Adams	Independent			1	
1824	24	**JOHN QUINCY ADAMS**	Democratic-Republican	108,740	30.5	84	26.9
		Andrew Jackson	Democratic-Republican	153,544	43.1	99	
		Henry Clay	Democratic-Republican	47,136	13.2	37	
		William H. Crawford	Democratic-Republican	46,618	13.1	41	
1828	24	**ANDREW JACKSON**	Democratic	647,286	56.0	178	57.6
		John Quincy Adams	National Republican	508,064	44.0	83	
1832	24	**ANDREW JACKSON**	Democratic	688,242	54.5	219	55.4
		Henry Clay	National Republican	473,462	37.5	49	
		William Wirt	Anti-Masonic ⎫	101,051	8.0	7	
		John Floyd	Democratic ⎭			11	
1836	26	**MARTIN VAN BUREN**	Democratic	765,483	50.9	170	57.8
		William H. Harrison	Whig ⎫			73	
		Hugh L. White	Whig ⎪	739,795	49.1	26	
		Daniel Webster	Whig ⎬			14	
		W. P. Mangum	Whig ⎭			11	

PRESIDENTIAL ELECTIONS

Year	Number of States	Candidates	Parties	Popular Vote	Percentage of Popular Vote	Electoral Vote	Percentage Voter Participation
1840	26	WILLIAM H. HARRISON	Whig	1,274,624	53.1	234	80.2
		Martin Van Buren	Democratic	1,127,781	46.9	60	
1844	26	JAMES K. POLK	Democratic	1,338,464	49.6	170	78.9
		Henry Clay	Whig	1,300,097	48.1	105	
		James G. Birney	Liberty	62,300	2.3		
1848	30	ZACHARY TAYLOR	Whig	1,360,967	47.4	163	72.7
		Lewis Cass	Democratic	1,222,342	42.5	127	
		Martin Van Buren	Free Soil	291,263	10.1		
1852	31	FRANKLIN PIERCE	Democratic	1,601,117	50.9	254	69.6
		Winfield Scott	Whig	1,385,453	44.1	42	
		John P. Hale	Free Soil	155,825	5.0		
1856	31	JAMES BUCHANAN	Democratic	1,832,955	45.3	174	78.9
		John C. Frémont	Republican	1,339,932	33.1	114	
		Millard Fillmore	American	871,731	21.6	8	
1860	33	ABRAHAM LINCOLN	Republican	1,865,593	38.8	180	81.2
		Stephen A. Douglas	Democratic	1,382,713	29.5	12	
		John C. Breckinridge	Democratic	848,356	18.1	72	
		John Bell	Constitutional Union	592,906	12.6	39	
1864	36	ABRAHAM LINCOLN	Republican	2,206,938	55.0	212	73.8
		George B. McClellan	Democratic	1,803,787	45.0	21	
1868	37	ULYSSES S. GRANT	Republican	3,013,421	52.7	214	78.1
		Horatio Seymour	Democratic	2,706,829	47.3	80	
1872	37	ULYSSES S. GRANT	Republican	3,596,745	55.6	286	71.3
		Horace Greeley	Democratic	2,843,446	43.9		
1876	38	RUTHERFORD B. HAYES	Republican	4,036,572	48.0	185	81.8
		Samuel J. Tilden	Democratic	4,284,020	51.0	184	
1880	38	JAMES A. GARFIELD	Republican	4,453,295	48.5	214	79.4
		Winfield S. Hancock	Democratic	4,414,082	48.1	155	
		James B. Weaver	Greenback-Labor	308,578	3.4		
1884	38	GROVER CLEVELAND	Democratic	4,879,507	48.5	219	77.5
		James G. Blaine	Republican	4,850,293	48.2	182	
		Benjamin F. Butler	Greenback-Labor	175,370	1.8		
		John P. St. John	Prohibition	150,369	1.5		
1888	38	BENJAMIN HARRISON	Republican	5,477,129	47.9	233	79.3
		Grover Cleveland	Democratic	5,537,857	48.6	168	
		Clinton B. Fisk	Prohibition	249,506	2.2		
		Anson J. Streeter	Union Labor	146,935	1.3		
1892	44	GROVER CLEVELAND	Democratic	5,555,426	46.1	277	74.7
		Benjamin Harrison	Republican	5,182,690	43.0	145	
		James B. Weaver	People's	1,029,846	8.5	22	
		John Bidwell	Prohibition	264,133	2.2		
1896	45	WILLIAM McKINLEY	Republican	7,102,246	51.1	271	79.3
		William J. Bryant	Democratic	6,492,559	47.7	176	

PRESIDENTIAL ELECTIONS

Year	Number of States	Candidates	Parties	Popular Vote	Percentage of Popular Vote	Electoral Vote	Percentage Voter Participation
1900	45	**WILLIAM McKINLEY**	Republican	7,218,491	51.7	292	73.2
		William J. Bryan	Democratic; Populist	6,356,734	45.5	155	
		John C. Wooley	Prohibition	208,914	1.5		
1904	45	**THEODORE ROOSEVELT**	Republican	7,628,461	57.4	336	65.2
		Alton B. Parker	Democratic	5,084,223	37.6	140	
		Eugene V. Debs	Socialist	402,283	3.0		
		Silas C. Swallow	Prohibition	258,536	1.9		
1908	46	**WILLIAM H. TAFT**	Republican	7,675,320	51.6	321	65.4
		William J. Bryan	Democratic	6,412,294	43.1	162	
		Eugene V. Debs	Socialist	420,793	2.8		
		Eugene W. Chafin	Prohibition	253,840	1.7		
1912	48	**WOODROW WILSON**	Democratic	6,296,547	41.9	435	58.8
		Theodore Roosevelt	Progressive	4,118,571	27.4	88	
		William H. Taft	Republican	3,486,720	23.2	8	
		Eugene V. Debs	Socialist	900,672	6.0		
		Eugene W. Chafin	Prohibition	206,275	1.4		
1916	48	**WOODROW WILSON**	Democratic	9,127,695	49.4	277	61.6
		Charles E. Hughes	Republican	8,533,507	46.2	254	
		A. L. Benson	Socialist	585,113	3.2		
		J. Frank Hanly	Prohibition	220,506	1.2		
1920	48	**WARREN G. HARDING**	Republican	16,143,407	60.4	404	49.2
		James M. Cox	Democratic	9,130,328	34.2	127	
		Eugene V. Debs	Socialist	919,799	3.4		
		P. P. Christensen	Farmer-Labor	265,411	1.0		
1924	48	**CALVIN COOLIDGE**	Republican	15,718,211	54.0	382	48.9
		John W. Davis	Democratic	8,385,283	28.8	136	
		Robert M. La Follette	Progressive	4,831,289	16.6	13	
1928	48	**HERBERT C. HOOVER**	Republican	21,391,993	58.2	444	56.9
		Alfred E. Smith	Democratic	15,016,169	40.9	87	
1932	48	**FRANKLIN D. ROOSEVELT**	Democratic	22,809,638	57.4	472	56.9
		Herbert C. Hoover	Republican	15,758,901	39.7	59	
		Norman Thomas	Socialist	881,951	2.2		
1936	48	**FRANKLIN D. ROOSEVELT**	Democratic	27,752,869	60.8	523	61.0
		Alfred M. Landon	Republican	16,674,665	36.5	8	
		William Lemke	Union	882,479	1.9		
1940	48	**FRANKLIN D. ROOSEVELT**	Democratic	27,307,819	54.8	449	62.5
		Wendell L. Willkie	Republican	22,321,018	44.8	82	
1944	48	**FRANKLIN D. ROOSEVELT**	Democratic	25,606,585	53.5	432	55.9
		Thomas E. Dewey	Republican	22,014,745	46.0	99	
1948	48	**HARRY S TRUMAN**	Democratic	24,179,345	49.6	303	53.0
		Thomas E. Dewey	Republican	21,991,291	45.1	189	
		J. Strom Thurmond	States' Rights	1,176,125	2.4	39	
		Henry A. Wallace	Progressive	1,157,326	2.4		

PRESIDENTIAL ELECTIONS

Year	Number of States	Candidates	Parties	Popular Vote	Percentage of Popular Vote	Electoral Vote	Percentage Voter Participation
1952	48	**DWIGHT EISENHOWER**	Republican	33,936,234	55.1	442	63.3
		Adlai E. Stevenson	Democratic	27,314,992	44.4	89	
1956	48	**DWIGHT D. EISENHOWER**	Republican	35,590,472	57.6	457	60.6
		Adlai E. Stevenson	Democratic	26,022,752	42.1	73	
1960	50	**JOHN F. KENNEDY**	Democratic	34,226,731	49.7	303	64.0
		Richard M. Nixon	Republican	34,108,157	49.5	219	
1964	50	**LYNDON B. JOHNSON**	Democratic	43,129,566	61.1	486	61.7
		Barry M. Goldwater	Republican	27,178,188	38.5	52	
1968	50	**RICHARD M. NIXON**	Republican	31,785,480	43.4	301	60.6
		Hubert H. Humphrey	Democratic	31,275,166	42.7	191	
		George C. Wallace	American Independent	9,906,473	13.5	46	
1972	50	**RICHARD M. NIXON**	Republican	47,169,911	60.7	520	55.5
		George S. McGovern	Democratic	29,170,383	37.5	17	
		John G. Schmitz	American	1,099,482	1.4		
1976	50	**JIMMY CARTER**	Democratic	40,830,763	50.1	297	54.3
		Gerald R. Ford	Republican	39,147,793	48.0	240	
1980	50	**RONALD REAGAN**	Republican	43,901,812	50.7	489	53.0
		Jimmy Carter	Democratic	35,483,820	41.0	49	
		John B. Anderson	Independent	5,719,722	6.6		
		Ed Clark	Libertarian	921,188	1.1		
1984	50	**RONALD REAGAN**	Republican	54,451,521	58.4	525	52.9
		Walter F. Mondale	Democratic	37,565,334	41.6	13	
1988	50	**GEORGE BUSH**	Republican	48,886,097	53.37	426	50.1
		Michael S. Dukakis	Democratic	41,809,074	45.65	111	

Candidates receiving less than 1 percent of the popular vote have been omitted. Thus the percentage of popular vote given for any election year may not total 100 percent.

Before the passage of the Twelfth Amendment in 1804, the Electoral College voted for two presidential candidates; the runner-up became vice-president.

MAJOR THIRD PARTIES IN PRESIDENTIAL ELECTIONS

Year	Party Name	Percentage of Total Votes Cast
1832	Anti-Masonic (William Wirt)	8.0%
1848	Free Soil (Martin Van Buren)	10.1
1856	American Know Nothing (Millard Fillmore)	21.4
1860	Democratic Secessionist (John C. Breckinridge)	18.1
1860	Constitutional Union (John Bell)	12.6
1892	Populist (James B. Weaver)	8.5
1912	"Bull Moose" Progressive (Theodore Roosevelt)	27.4
1912	Socialist (Eugene V. Debs)	6.0
1924	Progressive (Robert M. La Follette)	16.0
1948	States' Rights "Dixiecrats" (Strom Thurmond)	2.4
1968	American Independent (George Wallace)	13.5
1980	National Unity (John Anderson)	7.0

TYPES OF PRIMARIES, BY STATE AND REGION

Northeast
- Connecticut, closed
- Delaware, closed
- Maine, closed
- Maryland, closed
- Massachusetts, closed
- New Hampshire, closed
- New Jersey, closed
- New York, closed
- Pennsylvania, closed
- Rhode Island, open*
- Vermont, open

Midwest
- Iowa, closed
- Kansas, closed
- Nebraska, closed
- Ohio, closed
- South Dakota, closed
- Illinois, open*
- Indiana, open*
- Michigan, open
- Minnesota, open
- North Dakota, open
- Wisconsin, open

Border
- Kentucky, closed
- Oklahoma, closed
- West Virginia, closed
- Missouri, open*

South
- Florida, closed
- North Carolina, closed
- Alabama, open*
- Arkansas, open*
- Georgia, open*
- Mississippi, open*
- South Carolina, open*
- Tennessee, open*
- Texas, open*
- Virginia, open*
- Louisiana, nonpartisan

West
- Arizona, closed
- California, closed
- Colorado, closed
- Nevada, closed
- New Mexico, closed
- Oregon, closed
- Wyoming, closed
- Hawaii, open
- Idaho, open
- Montana, open
- Utah, open
- Alaska, open-blanket
- Washington, open-blanket

*Voter must indicate party affiliation.

SOURCE: Malcolm E. Jewell and David M. Olson, *American State Political Parties and Elections,* rev. ed. (Homewood, Ill.: Dorsey, 1982), p. 110. Copyright © 1982 by Dorsey Press. Reprinted by permission of the publisher, Brooks/Cole Publishing Company, Pacific Grove, Calif. 93950.

SPEAKERS OF THE HOUSE OF REPRESENTATIVES

Name	State	Tenure	Party
Frederick Muhlenberg	Pennsylvania	1789–1791	Federalist
Johnathan Trumbull	Connecticut	1791–1793	Federalist
Frederick Muhlenberg	Pennsylvania	1793–1795	Federalist
Jonathan Dayton	New Jersey	1795–1799	Federalist
Theodore Sedgwick	Massachusetts	1799–1801	Federalist
Nathaniel Macon	North Carolina	1801–1807	Democratic-Republican
Joseph B. Varnum	Massachusetts	1807–1811	Democratic-Republican
Henry Clay	Kentucky	1811–1814	Democratic-Republican
Langdon Cheves	South Carolina	1814–1815	Democratic-Republican
Henry Clay	Kentucky	1815–1820	Democratic-Republican
John W. Taylor	New York	1820–1821	Democratic-Republican
Philip P. Barbour	Virginia	1821–1823	Democratic-Republican
Henry Clay	Kentucky	1823–1825	Democratic-Republican
John W. Taylor	New York	1825–1827	Democratic
Andrew Stevenson	Virginia	1827–1834	Democratic
John Bell	Tennessee	1834–1835	Democratic
James K. Polk	Tennessee	1835–1839	Democratic
Robert M. T. Hunter	Virginia	1839–1841	Democratic
John White	Kentucky	1841–1843	Whig
John W. Jones	Virginia	1843–1845	Democratic
John W. Davis	Indiana	1845–1847	Democratic
Robert C. Winthrop	Massachusetts	1847–1849	Whig
Howell Cobb	Georgia	1849–1851	Democratic
Linn Boyd	Kentucky	1851–1855	Democratic
Nathaniel P. Banks	Massachusetts	1855–1857	American
James L. Orr	South Carolina	1857–1859	Democratic
William Pennington	New Jersey	1859–1861	Republican
Galusha A. Grow	Pennsylvania	1861–1863	Republican
Schuyler Colfax	Indiana	1863–1869	Republican
Theodore M. Pomeroy	New York	1869–1869	Republican
James G. Blaine	Maine	1869–1875	Republican
Michael C. Kerr	Indiana	1875–1876	Democratic
Samuel J. Randall	Pennsylvania	1876–1881	Democratic
Joseph W. Keifer	Ohio	1881–1883	Republican
John G. Carlisle	Kentucky	1883–1889	Democratic
Thomas B. Reed	Maine	1889–1891	Republican
Charles F. Crisp	Georgia	1891–1895	Democratic
Thomas B. Reed	Maine	1895–1899	Republican
David B. Henderson	Iowa	1899–1903	Republican
Joseph G. Cannon	Illinois	1903–1911	Republican
Champ Clark	Missouri	1911–1919	Democratic
Frederick H. Gillett	Massachusetts	1919–1925	Republican
Nicholas Longworth	Ohio	1925–1931	Republican
John N. Garner	Texas	1931–1933	Democratic

SPEAKERS OF THE HOUSE OF REPRESENTATIVES

Name	State	Tenure	Party
Henry T. Rainey	Illinois	1933–1935	Democratic
Joseph W. Byrns	Tennessee	1935–1936	Democratic
William P. Bankhead	Alabama	1936–1940	Democratic
Sam Rayburn	Texas	1940–1947	Democratic
Joseph W. Martin, Jr.	Massachusetts	1947–1949	Republican
Sam Rayburn	Texas	1949–1953	Democratic
Joselph W. Martin, Jr.	Massachusetts	1953–1955	Republican
Sam Rayburn	Texas	1955–1961	Democratic
John W. McCormack	Massachusetts	1962–1971	Democratic
Carl Albert	Oklahoma	1971–1977	Democratic
Thomas P. "Tip" O'Neill	Massachusetts	1977–1987	Democratic
Jim Wright	Texas	1987–1989	Democratic
Thomas S. Foley	Washington	1989–Present	Democratic

U.S. CABINET DEPARTMENTS

Department	Year Created
State	1789
Treasury	1789
Defense	1949 (War, 1789; Navy, 1798)
Justice	1870 (attorney general, 1789)
Interior	1849
Agriculture	1862
Post Office	1872 (became independent, 1970)
Commerce	1913 (Commerce and Labor, 1903)
Labor	1913 (Commerce and Labor, 1903)
Health and Human Services	1979 (Health, Education, and Welfare, 1953)
Housing and Urban Development	1965
Transportation	1966
Energy	1977
Education	1979

GLOSSARY

ABM (antiballistic missile) A missile intended to shoot down missiles fired by a hostile power.

absolutism 1. A form of government that has no constitutional limits on its power. The term is most often used with reference to monarchies in which the ruler can act without restraint. It is sometimes also used with reference to modern totalitarian dictatorships. 2. A belief that certain principles or doctrines are true without exception or qualification and have universal applicability.

ACLU (American Civil Liberties Union) An interest group devoted primarily to the defense of civil rights and liberties guaranteed by the Constitution.

act A bill that has been passed by a legislature and signed by an executive.

activist A person who is strongly committed to a political party or cause and takes vigorous action on its behalf.

administration 1. The president, his cabinet, and other political appointees. 2. The process of managing agencies, bureaus, and other organizations.

administrative agency A government department, bureau, or other organization established by Congress to carry out executive functions.

administrative law judges (ALJs) Independent hearing officers within administrative agencies that conduct initial formal rule-making and adjudicatory proceedings.

Administrative Procedure Act of 1946 (APA) Legislation that imposes judicial-type procedural requirements upon formal administrative rule-making and adjudicatory proceedings.

adversary process The process by which opposing parties contest each other's claims.

advice and consent Approval by the Senate of treaties and presidential appointments.

affirmative action Practices to remedy the effects of past discrimination by granting special benefits to members of the groups which have suffered discrimination. An affirmative action program usually involves an effort to recruit, hire, and promote blacks, women, and other groups that have suffered past discrimination.

AFL-CIO (American Federation of Labor-Congress of Industrial Organizations) An alliance of over 100 labor unions representing worker interests in the United States.

agenda 1. A list of topics for discussion. 2. A political or ideological set of goals or objectives; a political program, such as "empowerment of the poor."

amendment 1. Any change or addition to a formal document, such as a bill under consideration by a legislature. 2. See **constitutional amendment.**

amicus curiae A person or organization that has no standing in a case but is permitted to participate, usually by filing a brief on behalf of one of the parties to the suit. The phrase is Latin meaning "friend of the court."

Anarchism A belief system holding that states produce injustice and should be abolished. Its origins are in the nineteenth century; two of its leading figures were the French thinker Joseph Prudhon and Russian Prince Peter A. Kropotkin, both of whom urged that the state be replaced by communities based on voluntary cooperation.

appellate jurisdiction The power to hear appeals; the judicial authority to review the decisions of a lower court.

appropriations Funds allocated by Congress through appropriation bills for government programs it had previously authorized.

apportionment A computation of the number of legislators that will serve a given number of citizens. The Constitution requires that each state have two senators and a number of representatives based on population. The House of Representatives was fixed at 435 seats by Congress in the Apportionment Act of 1929.

aristocracy   1. Rule by the titled nobility.   2. The titled nobility as a class.   3. In ancient Greece, government by the best.   4. The wealthy upper classes, especially that portion of the upper classes that has inherited its wealth for several generations, such as the Roosevelts, Harrimans, and Vanderbilts.

Articles of Confederation   The agreement between the newly independent thirteen states that united them in opposition to Great Britain. Written in 1776, it was adopted by the Continental Congress in 1777, and was ratified in 1781. From the latter date until 1787 it served as the framework for the United States of America. It was replaced by our present Constitution.

authoritarianism   A system of government in which power is concentrated in one person or a ruling class that demands unquestioned obedience. Military dictatorships generally practice authoritarianism. Compare **totalitarianism.**

authority   Legitimate power. Governments, rulers, representatives, and individuals who have power that is recognized as lawful, just, and moral have authority.

authorization   Legislation approving the expenditure of money for government programs and agencies. See **appropriations.**

autocracy   Government by one individual who possesses absolute power. Some scholars make a distinction between autocracy and absolute monarchy. In this view, an autocrat is limited or restrained only by the quality and level of violence at his command, while even an absolute monarch is constrained by custom, tradition, or concepts of legitimacy.

backlash   A negative response to new social or political developments, such as the reaction of whites to affirmative action and school integration, and of males to women's liberation.

balanced budget   A government budget in which income is equal to expenditures.

balanced ticket   A slate of candidates designed to appeal to a wide variety of political voters. In presidential races a balanced ticket is one in which the presidential and vice-presidential candidates are from different regions of the country and represent different wings of the parties.

balance of payments   The relationship between money moving into a country and moving out of it, set by exports, imports, foreign investments, loans, travel, and so forth. A favorable balance means that more money is coming in than is going out and indicates economic strength. The reverse, an unfavorable balance created when more money is going out than coming in, often reflects some weakness in a nation's economy.

balance of power   A principle of international relations in which rival nations seek to prevent one another from gaining superiority; especially in military force. The latest example of this had been the rivalry between the United States and the Soviet Union. However, the principle extends backward in time to the competition between ancient Egypt and Assyria. See **détente** and **deterrence.**

ballot   A printed list of political candidates.

bicameral   Composed of two chambers, used in reference to legislatures.

bill   Proposed legislation. **Public bills** deal with matters of concern to the public at large; **private bills** concern individual claims against the government, immigration cases, and similar matters.

bill of attainder   A legislative act that condemns and punishes a person without a trial. Congress is prohibited by the Constitution from passing bills of attainder.

Bill of Rights   The first ten amendments to the U.S. Constitution. In summary form these are:

AMENDMENT

   I guarantees freedoms of expression: speech, press, and religion; and protects the rights to assemble and petition the government to redress grievances.

  II guarantees the right to bear arms.

 III prohibits enforced housing of troops in private homes.

 IV prohibits unreasonable searches and seizures of evidence.

  V establishes protection against self-incrimination in criminal cases, guarantees the rights of the accused to due process of law, and prohibits the government from taking private property without ''just compensation.''

VI   guarantees defendants' rights, including jury trial, in criminal cases.

VII guarantees jury trials in certain common-law civil cases.

VIII prohibits excessive bail, fines, and "cruel and unusual punishment."

IX   protects those rights not named in the Constitution or the preceding eight amendments.

X   reserves to the states "or to the people" those powers not given to the federal government by the Constitution.

The Constitution was ratified in 1788 only because of the promise that a bill of rights would be attached. The first ten amendments were ratified in 1791.

bipartisan   Agreement and cooperation between the two major parties on public policy issues, as in bipartisan foreign policy.

block grant   Federal funds given to state and local governments for broad general programs rather than for specific programs. Block grants allow state and local governments a great deal of discretion in the use of the funds. Compare **categorical grant, grant-in-aid.**

boycott   The refusal to do business with a nation, industry, or individual as a means of coercion or an expression of disapproval.

brief   A written argument presented by each side to a law suit.

budget   A financial plan detailing future income and expenses. Usually, the executive branch prepares a budget that it submits to Congress. Congress then deliberates on the various items of the executive budget, makes changes to suit its several constituencies, reconciles differences between the two houses, and sends the revised budget to the president for approval. Federal budgets are the most important statement of government policy available in the United States.

budget deficit   The amount by which expenses exceed income in a budget during an accounting period.

budget surplus   The amount by which income exceeds expenses in a budget during an accounting period.

bureaucracy   1. The administrative departments and agencies of government.   **2.** Any large, hierarchically structured organization stressing formalized procedures, job specialization, and impersonal behavior.   **3.** In popular parlance, any inefficient organization enmeshed in red tape.

cabinet   The heads of the 13 executive departments who are appointed by the president and advise him on public policy.

calendar (legislative)   A listing of bills in the House or the Senate. There are five calendars in the House and two in the Senate.

campaign committee   A fund-raising organization created mainly to win elections. There are presidential, senatorial, and congressional campaign committees as well as committees in the name of individual candidates. See **political action committee.**

capitalism   An economic system characterized by private ownership of businesses. According to advocates of capitalism, success is determined by competitive excellence in the marketplace. Advocates further argue that consumers have freedom of choice under capitalism. According to critics of capitalism, success is determined by the ability of wealthy and powerful individuals and groups to control or destroy competition. Critics further contend that capitalists accumulate wealth by exploiting workers, who produce value far in excess of what they are paid.

casework   Services rendered to constituents by members of Congress and their staff.

categorical grant   Federal funds given to state and local governments for highly specific services or classes of activities, such as highway repair. Compare **block grant.**

caucus   A meeting of a special group to take positions on public policy issues or to endorse candidates. See **congressional caucus.**

certiorari, writ of   A written order by a higher court to a lower court or administrative agency to send the record of a case to the higher court for review.

checks and balances   The constitutional system of dispersing power among the three branches of the federal government and between the federal and state governments.

chief executive   The president's role as head of the executive branch.

chief of state   The president's ceremonial and symbolic role as head of the nation.

CIA (Central Intelligence Agency)   The federal agency mandated to coordinate the intelligence activities of the various services of the United States. The CIA also gathers intelligence abroad and carries out secret, special projects at the request of the president or the National Security Council.

civil case   A legal action in a court of law to resolve a noncriminal dispute between private individuals or between a private person and the government.

civil liberties   The freedoms of speech, press, association, and religion that cannot be infringed by the government unless justified by a compelling public interest.

civil rights   The rights of citizens—such as the right to vote, the right to protection against self-incrimination, and the right to a jury trial—that the government is required to protect.

civil service system   The system under which government employees are hired on the basis of merit and guaranteed their jobs as long as their performance is adequate.

Civil War amendments   The thirteenth, fourteenth, and fifteenth amendments that were ratified after the Civil War. These amendments outlawed slavery, made former slaves citizens, applied to the states the due process and equal protection requirements of the Constitution, and gave black citizens the right to vote.

class   A social or economic group having certain interests in common, such as legal standing or financial power.

class action suit   A legal action brought in a court of law by one or more persons on behalf of all persons similarly injured. Both civil rights and consumer rights have been advanced by class action suits.

classified information   Secret data, usually of a military nature.

class struggle   Conflict between economic classes for control of a society. The motor of history in Marxist theory.

"clear and present danger"   A standard for limiting free speech devised by Justice Oliver Wendell Holmes in Schenck v. United States (1919). The standard allows the government to suppress freedom of expression if it constitutes a clear and present danger to the security or other legitimate ends of government.

closed primary   A primary in which voters must be members of a particular party in order to vote for its candidates.

closed rule   A House rule that restricts floor debate on legislation by prohibiting amendments.

cloture   Senate Rule 22, requiring the approval of 60 senators before debate on legislation can be closed.

coalition   A usually temporary alliance of divergent nations, interest groups, political factions, or others for a specific purpose. Much of American politics is based on the formation of these temporary alliances, as in the shifting coalitions of Democrats and Republicans.

coattails   A presidential candidate's ability to draw votes to other party candidates.

COLA   Cost of living adjustment. An increase to fixed incomes, as in those provided by Social Security. COLAs are based on the rate of inflation.

Cold War   A state of nonmilitary hostilities between the United States and Soviet Union beginning in the late 1940s and perhaps ending in 1990. Both sides, however, supported surrogates who fought it out in "hot" shooting wars. During this period both the United States and the Soviet Union manufactured huge arsenals and were the largest arms merchants in the world.

commander-in-chief   The president's role under Article II as the supreme commander of all the armed forces.

commerce clause   Congress's Article I authority to regulate commerce among the states, which became the basis for far-reaching national power and supremacy over the states.

committee   A subdivision of Congress that considers and then reports to the full chamber that the committee belongs to. Most committees are divided into subcommittees that hold hearings and investigate proposed legislation before recommending it to their full committees.

committee of the whole   The entire House resolves itself into a committee to enable it to debate and discuss legislation informally.

common law   Judge-made law, based upon the decisions of courts, as distinguished from legislative enactments. The common law, derived from the English common law, is applied in every state except Louisiana.

commonwealth   **1.** State. Four American states are officially called commonwealths: Massachusetts, Virginia, Pennsylvania, and Kentucky.   **2.** An association of autonomous and semi-autonomous states under the leadership of Great Britain: the British Commonwealth of Nations.

communism   **1.** In Marxist theory, the final stage of economic, political, and social development of society. According to that theory, the class struggle led by an elite—the vanguard of the proletariat—culminates in a working-class revolution that overthrows the capitalist class and establishes socialism, a period when the working class, led by its elite, rules the state. After the worldwide successes of socialism, the state theoretically withers away and a classless society enters the final stage of history—communism. **2.** The official doctrine of the Soviet Union and other communist states, now very much repudiated by large numbers of citizens in those states.

concurrent jurisdiction   Under the Constitution federal and state governments have concurrent jurisdiction over certain areas of policy, such as commerce and taxation. State laws, however, are void if they conflict with federal legislation.

concurrent resolution   A resolution passed by both houses of Congress that does not have the power of law and does not require the president's signature.

concurring opinion   A written judgment by one or more justices of the Supreme Court that is in agreement with the majority but for different reasons. See **dissenting opinion.**

confederation   A league or association of independent and sovereign states that delegates extremely restricted powers to a central authority for limited purposes.

conference committee   A committee composed of members of both the House and the Senate that has the purpose of arranging a compromise between the houses when they have passed different versions of a bill.

conflict of interest   An occasion when a government official may allow his or her private interests to influence actions on matters of public interest.

congressional caucus   Caucuses that represent interests, such as the black caucus, women's caucus, and tourism caucus.

congressional district   The local district from which a representative is elected.

Congressional Record   Published daily while Congress is in session, the *Record* includes floor debate, members' remarks, and whatever material members choose to insert.

conservatism   A political ideology usually identified with the interests of the elite that stresses maintenance of the status quo and social stability. If change seems necessary, conservatives prefer that it be slow rather than rapid. One of the two main ideological positions in American politics. See **liberalism.**

constituency   **1.** A legislative district.   **2.** The residents of such a district.   **3.** Those to whom an elected or appointed official is responsible or beholden for his/her position: the constituency of representatives are the voters in their districts; of senators, the voters in their states; of presidents, the voters in the nation as a whole; and of Supreme Court justices, the presidents who nominate them and the senators who have the power to approve or disapprove of their appointment.   **4.** The body of supporters of a public official, either ideologically or financially.

constitution   **1.** Any written or unwritten framework of government that has the force of fundamental law.   **2.** The U.S. Constitution, which was written in 1787 and ratified by nine states in 1788. The fundamental law of the United States. It consists of basically two parts: one part outlines the structure of the federal government; the other limits the power of government and defines the rights of citizens.

constitutional amendment   An amendment to the U.S. Constitution, which is usually adopted after it has been proposed by a two-thirds vote of both houses of Congress and been ratified by three-fourths of the state legislatures. Another method is by calling a national convention, but this has not yet been tried in the United States.

constitutional democracy   A government of popular participation limited by law.

constitutional monarchy   A monarchy in which the powers of the government are limited by a written or unwritten constitution. Great Britain is the classic example of a constitutional monarchy. All European monarchies today are limited by national constitutions. The only absolute monarchies left are in the Arab states and the South Pacific.

contract theory   A theory, first developed in the seventeenth century, in which the state and its citizens have reached an agreement whereby the citizens have given up some rights in return for a number of benefits provided by the state. If the state fails to provide those benefits, the citizens have the right to change the government of the state. Contract theory serves as a basis for liberalism. See **social contract.**

Council of Economic Advisers (CEA)   A group of advisers to the president on economic matters. Appointed by the president with the consent of the Senate, the council consists of three professional economists. The CEA was established by the Employment Act of 1946.

de facto segregation   Segregation that exists in fact but not by law.

deficit   In government budgeting, the amount of expenses over income. When this situation extends for a prolonged period, the government covers its expenses either by printing more money or by borrowing from the public, as in issuing Treasury bills. This procedure is known as **deficit financing.**

de jure segregation   Segregation required by law.

delegated power   Legislative power delegated by Congress to the president or the bureaucracy.

democracy   A system of government in which the majority of the people rule. The word comes from the Greek meaning "rule by the people"; *demos* is "people" in Greek, and "-cracy" is from *kratia* meaning "rule" or "government" in Greek. See **constitutional democracy, direct democracy, parliamentary democracy, representative democracy,** and **republic.**

deregulation   The removal of government controls over such businesses as savings and loan institutions, airlines, and investment houses.

détente   The easing of tensions between the Soviet Union and the United States leading to summit conferences, trade agreements, scientific and cultural exchanges, and arms control treaties.

deterrence   The technique of preventing a world war between the East under Soviet leadership and the West under U.S. leadership. The assumption underlying deterrence is that the possession of massive retaliatory power will keep the "other side" from starting a war. Now applied to any set of enemies. See **MAD.**

dictatorship   **1.** A totalitarian form of government in which one person possesses absolute power and is above the law of the nation. Nazi Germany under Adolf Hitler and Fascist Italy under Benito Mussolini are classic examples of this type of dictatorship. **2. Military dictatorship:** a government in which a military leader and his senior officers hold supreme power in the nation. Chile under General Ugarte Pinochet and Libya under Colonel Muammar Quaddafi are military dictatorships.   **3. Dictatorship of the proletariat:** the socialist phase of communism in which the government is under the complete domination of the Communist Party and its leader.   **4.** In the ancient Roman republic, the office of a consul chosen in an emergency for a period of no more than six months and possessing absolute power during his tenure.

direct democracy   A government in which citizens participate directly, and in which the majority rules without constitutional restraints. The Framers of the Constitution were careful to create an indirect form of democracy in which the voice of the people would be filtered and checked. See **representative democracy** and **republic.**

direct primary   A political process that involves rank-and-file members in the nomination of candidates to run for office. Direct primaries often reduce the power of party leaders, although powerful leaders can manipulate primaries for their own ends.

dissent   To disagree, usually with a majority or established view. In the United States, the right to dissent is constitutionally guaranteed.

dissenting opinion   A written judgment by one or more justices of the Supreme Court that is in disagreement with the majority. See **concurring opinion.**

distributive justice   A term used by the ancient Greek philosopher Aristotle to refer to the form of justice in which a person receives a fair share of the resources or rewards of society. An important concept of modern liberalism. See **retributive justice.**

divine right   A theory of government holding that monarchs derive their authority as rulers directly from God and not from the consent of the people. The English Civil War was fought over this theory and King Charles I was beheaded when he lost the war. Since then Britain's monarchs have not claimed to rule by divine right. America's Founding Fathers were strongly opposed to the concept.

due process   Procedural protections afforded to individuals whose life, liberty, or property is at stake. The fifth and fourteenth amendments contain due process clauses.

Electoral College   The body that elects the president and vice-president; each state is represented by the same number of members as in its congressional delegation. Originally, the members of the Electoral College were selected in the manner prescribed by their state legislatures and had some discretion in making their choice. Now the 538 members (including, since 1961, three from the District of Columbia) have mainly a pro forma function: each state delegation is bound to vote as a bloc for the presidential candidate who received a plurality of the state's votes.

electorate   All those individuals who are entitled to vote—in the United States, the whole body of voting-age citizens. Little more than 50 percent of the American electorate votes in most recent presidential elections.

electronic media   Radio and television.

elite   A class of superior persons. Today it has come to connote a stratum of society that has excessive power stemming from personal wealth, prestige, ability, or connections.

elite model   The view that economic, political, and social elites determine public policy.

entitlements   Benefits, such as Social Security, that the U.S. government is legally bound to grant individuals and groups who meet a fixed set of criteria.

enumerated powers   The powers of Congress named in Article I of the Constitution.

equal protection   The same protection guaranteed by the Fourteenth Amendment, which prohibits states from denying equal protection to their citizens.

equality   An ideal in which all people are presumed to have the same capabilities or are treated—politically, socially, and economically—as if they have the same abilities. So far, no society has achieved absolute equality.

establishment clause   The clause in the First Amendment prohibiting Congress from setting up a state church. This is one of two clauses that guarantees freedom of religion in the United States.

exclusionary rule   The judicial ruling that evidence gained in an unconstitutional search and seizure may not be used in a criminal trial. This ruling is based on the Fourth Amendment, which prohibits unreasonable searches and seizures.

executive   1. A person or group of persons mandated to carry out policy.   2. The branch of government that has responsibility for carrying out laws and policies.

executive agreement   A presidential arrangement with a foreign nation made outside of the framework of a formal treaty and thus not subject to Senate approval.

executive department   A Cabinet department, headed by a secretary nominated by the president and approved by a majority of voting senators. See **cabinet.**

executive power   The president's authority under Article II to carry out the law.

executive privilege   The president's privilege of withholding information from Congress on the ground that disclosure would interfere with the exercise of executive power and the constitutional responsibilities of the president.

faction   1. A segment or subgroup of a political organization.   2. In the view of James Madison and other founders, a group having a special interest that is counter to the national interest. Madison argued in *Federalist* 10 that federalism and representative government would disperse and neutralize factions, enabling the national interest to prevail.

fascism   1. An extremely nationalistic ideology that placed the state above the individual, advocated total control over every aspect of life, refused to tolerate divergent beliefs, demanded that conformity be enforced by violence, and glorified *the leader,* who was above the law and possessed absolute power in every domain. Fascism also promoted an aggressive military policy that was extremely expansionist. Aspects of fascist doctrine derived from socialism and made a strong appeal to the working classes.   **2.** The official state doctrine of Italy under the Fascists. See **dictatorship** and **Nazism.**

federalism   A government system in which constitutional authority is divided between a central government and state or provincial governments.

feminism   The political and social principle that women should have full equality with men in all areas of life. For example, women managers should earn the same salary as men for the same jobs.

filibuster   The tactic of killing bills by talking them to death. Historically, both conservative and liberal senators have used filibusters to get their way.

fireside chats   Informal radio addresses from the White House by President Franklin D. Roosevelt to explain his New Deal policies.

fiscal policy   A technique of managing the national economy by raising or lowering taxes and by increasing or cutting government expenses. For example, the government will often try to control inflation by raising taxes, thereby reducing disposable income and excessive demand for goods and services, a frequent cause of inflation. On the other hand, by spending more money during a recession on economic programs, the government hopes to stimulate the economy and move the country out of its economic slump. See **monetary policy.**

floor manager   A member of Congress who attempts to steer a bill through floor debate to a final vote.

founders   The Founding Fathers. All the historical figures who had a major part in the American Revolution and the formative years of the United States. Compare **Framers.**

Four Freedoms   Freedom of speech and expression, freedom of worship, freedom from want, and freedom from fear—which President Franklin D. Roosevelt stated would assure universal peace if they prevailed ''everywhere in the world.''

fourth branch of government   The bureaucracy.

''fourth estate''   The media; the press. From the thirteenth to the eighteenth century in Europe, especially France, social and economic classes were called ''estates.'' France's national legislature was, during this period, called the Estates General, which consisted of three classes: the first estate was the clergy; the second, the nobility; and the third, the commons. The three estates were distinct centers of power. Hence, calling the press the ''fourth estate'' suggests that in America it too is a center of power along with the president, Congress, and the federal judiciary.

Framers   The Framers of the Constitution; those who met during the summer of 1787 in Philadelphia and wrote the U.S. Constitution.

franchise   The right to vote, which has been extended to more and more classes of people since the founding of the nation; suffrage.

freedom   Liberty.   **1.** A condition in which one can make a decision without being constrained or restricted—in short, **freedom of choice.**   **2.** The situation of being outside the power of another or others—in other words, **freedom from slavery** or **imprisonment.**   **3.** The legal right to believe as one wishes and to act on the basis of that belief—**freedom of conscience.**   **4.** The constitutionally guaranteed right to participate in the political life of a nation, as by voting, running for office, speaking at political meetings, and the like—the basic freedom of American citizens.   **5.** A circumstance in which one's behavior or life style is unhampered by financial worries—**economic freedom.**

Freedom of Information Act (1966)   A law that allows citizens to obtain information from government agencies.

free-exercise clause   The clause in the First Amendment that prevents the government from interfering with religious practices, except where the government can show a compelling interest.

free-rider problem   A recruiting problem faced by organizations that gain for their members benefits that also extend to nonmembers. Thus individuals can enjoy these benefits without having to pay the costs of membership.

free-speech clause   The clause in the First Amendment that guarantees the right to freedom of expression except when it threatens the state. See **clear and present danger.**

GAO (General Accounting Office)   An agency of Congress charged with the responsibility of auditing all government operations and expenditures.

gatekeeper   1. A person on a news organization who has the power to decide which story will be printed or aired and what will be included within it. 2. Any person or institution having the power to decide which political figure or cause will be advanced and which will not; political gatekeepers can range from ward captains to presidents and from individual political contributors to political action committees.

germaneness rule   A requirement that all amendments to a bill be relevant.

gerrymander   To draw the lines of political districts to favor particular groups, usually the political party in power.

GNP (Gross National Product)   This represents the money value of all the goods and services produced in the United States and is a principal measure of the growth or decline of the national economy.

GOP   Republican party, derived from "Grand Old Party," a common reference to the Republicans in the late nineteenth century.

government   The instrument or apparatus by which people within a society are ruled.

government corporation   A type of administrative unit that is analogous in its structure to a private corporation but has a public responsibility and accountability, such as the Tennessee Valley Authority.

"government of laws and not of men"   A shorthand description of constitutional government in which the rulers are bound by the higher law of a constitution.

grant-in-aid   A grant of money from the federal government to the states or local communities with strings attached, requiring grant recipients to adhere to designated national standards. Compare **block grant.**

grass roots   The base or root of political power; in a democracy, the people; in a political party, the rank-and-file members.

Great Depression   The period between the stock market crash of 1929 and the onset of World War II in 1939. During this period the capitalist economies of the United States and Europe experienced the worst economic downturn in the twentieth century. A wide variety of efforts were made to solve the difficulties of the Great Depression and all involved one degree or another of state intervention in the economy. See **New Deal.**

Great Society   President Lyndon B. Johnson's programs to eliminate poverty and achieve equality and prosperity. The Great Society programs went far beyond the New Deal in supporting federal intervention in the economic and social life of the country.

guerrilla war   A type of war in which irregular military forces battle the regular military troops of an established government; the main strategy of the guerrillas is to play hide-and-seek with the regular forces until the existing government is overthrown and the guerrillas are in power.

habeas corpus, writ of   A court order to a government official detaining a person in prison to bring the prisoner before the court and state the cause for the detention, after which judgment is rendered on whether or not the confinement violates the prisoner's due process. Habeas corpus is Latin meaning "you have the body."

hearings   Formal, judiciallike proceedings conducted by administrative agencies and congressional committees to gain information pertaining to individual cases or broader public issues.

higher law   In the Western political tradition, the law of nature from which immutable principles of government and the inalienable rights of the individual are drawn. It is also often used to refer to a moral code or rule that is supposedly of divine origin.

hopper   The box on the clerk's desk of the House of Representatives in which members deposit bills they wish to introduce.

ICBM (intercontinental ballistic missile)   A long-range nuclear missile that can be fired from the United States and hit targets in the Soviet Union or the reverse; a basic component of deterrence and MAD.

ideology   A collection of ideas, based upon the values and aspirations of those who believe in them, that often becomes the foundation of political activities and movements.

immunity   Freedom from prosecution granted to a person in return for self-incriminating testimony at a hearing or trial for the purpose of getting information that could not otherwise be obtained.

impeachment   A formal charge or accusation of "treason, bribery, or other high crimes and misdemeanors" brought by the House of Representatives against a president, vice president, federal judges, and other ranking government officials. The Senate then tries the accused, who is removed from office only if convicted by a two-thirds majority. When a president is impeached, the chief justice of the Supreme Court presides over the Senate trial.

imperialism   The extension of power beyond original legal limits, especially one nation's acquisition of territory belonging to another nation through the use of military or economic force. Both the Soviet Union and the United States have been charged with imperialism. The term ultimately derives from the Latin *imperium* meaning "supreme power," which was granted to a dictator by the senate of Republican Rome for a maximum of six months and was later taken on permanently by the emperors of Rome.

imperial presidency   Dominant presidencies built upon the use of constitutional prerogative powers by presidents of the United States. These increased powers are usually seen as at the expense of Congress.

implied powers   Powers that are not specifically enumerated in the Constitution but may be implied if they are "necessary and proper" to the exercise of enumerated powers.

impounded funds   Money appropriated by Congress for a program that the president refuses to spend, either because of opposition to the program or as a tactic to force compliance by a state. Under the Budget and Impoundment Control Act of 1974 the president can no longer permanently impound funds.

incorporation doctrine   The expansion of the Bill of Rights to limit power of the states as well as of the federal government. The expansion was made possible because of the due process clause of the Fourteenth Amendment.

incumbency effect   The tendency of incumbents to be reelected, mainly because voters generally are more comfortable with known figures than with unknown ones.

incumbent   A person holding office, particularly an elected official such as a member of Congress or the president.

independent regulatory commission   Multiheaded administrative agencies whose members are appointed by the president but are independent of direct presidential control. The Federal Communications Commission is an independent regulatory commission.

indictment   Formal accusation against a defendant, usually made by a grand jury.

INF treaty   Intermediate-Range Nuclear Force treaty. An arms control treaty between the United States and the Soviet Union that was signed in 1987 and ratified by the U.S. Senate and the Presidium of the U.S.S.R. in 1988.

inflation   Rising costs of goods and services. During the 1970s, the United States experienced double-digit inflation, ranging from 10 to 18 percent per annum. In the 80s, the rate of inflation was brought down to an average of 4 percent.

initiative   An electoral process in which citizens themselves may propose state and local laws. If the citizens have collected a specified number of signatures on a petition, their proposal is placed on a ballot for consideration by the electorate.

interest group   An organized collection of people with similar concerns who join together for the purpose of influencing government policy.

interventionist   Following a government policy of entering into economic or social affairs so as to change a situation or correct an imbalance; on an international level, interfering in a foreign conflict or the affairs of a foreign nation.

iron triangle   The mutually beneficial relationship between legislators, bureaucrats, and lobbyists.

joint committee   A congressional committee, usually investigative in nature, which includes members from both the House and Senate.

joint resolution   A resolution approved by both the House and the Senate that becomes a law upon the signature of the president.

journalism   The art and practice of gathering and reporting the news in the media.

judicial activism   The practice of making public policy through judicial decisions by substituting judicial judgments for legislative actions. The practice has been most closely associated with the Supreme Court and is an outgrowth of judicial review. Two examples of judicial activism are the *Dred Scott* decision of 1857, which held that Congress could not prohibit slavery, and the *Brown* decision of 1954, which held that states could not discriminate against blacks by having segregated schools.

judicial restraint   The belief that judges should limit their decisions to constitutional or other legal issues and not become involved in legislative or executive matters. Judges who share this belief have tried to exercise judicial self-restraint and interpret laws in the narrowest fashion possible. An example of judicial restraint would have been the refusal of the Supreme Court to hear the Dred Scott case because the Court lacked jurisdiction. This would have allowed the Congressional law restricting slavery to stand, and that in effect would have been to make policy negatively or passively.

judicial review   The authority of the higher courts to review the decisions and actions of the legislative and executive branches of the government and of the lower courts.

jurisdiction   The extent of the legal authority of a governmental body, usually used in reference to a court or administrative agency.

keynote address   A highly partisan speech given at the outset of national nominating conventions to stir up the party faithful and set the theme.

laissez-faire   Following or advocating a doctrine of minimum government interference in economic, social, or private affairs. The word comes from a French idiomatic expression meaning "let people do as they wish."

lame duck   An officeholder whose term is coming to an end.

Left   **1.** Those holding extreme liberal views, often including socialist ones, and advocating government intervention to redistribute income in favor of the lower classes and manage the economy for the benefit of all classes. The term comes from the seating arrangements of the 1789 National Assembly of France.

Those who opposed the monarchy and favored a republic of commoners sat on the left of the person who presided over the assembly, while those who supported King Louis XVI and the principle of monarchy sat on the right. The terms "Right" and "Left" are virtually meaningless today, except perhaps as a rough indication of whether one favors the upper or lower classes. Both Right and Left intervene to redistribute income in opposite directions and manage the economy for the benefit of opposite classes. The word "Left" is frequently used today to cover a hodgepodge of sometimes contradictory political ideologies: liberalism, Communism, Anarchism, socialism, pacificism, and sometimes feminism.   **2. left wing.** A faction of a political organization that is to the Left of the majority. See **Right.**

legislation   Laws that apply to all persons within the jurisdiction of the legislative body enacting them.

legislative veto   Congressional action overturning administrative decisions. The legislative veto was declared unconstitutional by the Supreme Court in 1983.

legitimacy   The legal and moral right of a government to rule.

libel   False and malicious statements—either written or spoken—that injure a person's reputation. If proven, libel is punishable by law and the injured party can receive monetary compensation.

liberalism   **1.** A contemporary political ideology advocating government support for those who are socially or economically vulnerable—the poor, the elderly, the sick, the disadvantaged, the discriminated against, and the like—and, within limits, for redistributing income from the wealthy to those less fortunate. Although most liberals believe in an interventionist government, they also generally believe the government should not intrude into the private lives of people and should not attempt to regulate personal behavior. Most liberals welcome change if it seems to increase personal freedom. One of the two main ideological positions in America. Compare **conservatism.**   **2.** Also called **classic liberalism.** A nineteenth-century belief in minimum government. Individuals were to be left alone to manage their affairs on the supposition that everything would work out for the best. A laissez-faire concept of social organization. Believers in classic liberalism are today called **libertarians.**

Library of Congress   A comprehensive library and adjunct to Congress, containing the Congressional Research Service that provides staff assistance to legislators. Thomas Jefferson's book collection launched the library.

line-item veto   Presidential authority to veto portions of legislative bills without having to veto the entire legislation. The president does not have the constitutional authority to exercise a line-item veto, which the White House has long sought.

lobby   1. To pressure members of Congress. **2.** An individual or group that seeks to influence Congress.

logrolling   The exchange of votes among legislators, which can be summed up in the statement: "You vote for my pork barrel and I'll vote for yours." See **quid pro quo.**

machine   A disciplined local party organization headed by a political boss.

MAD (Mutual Assured Destruction)   The strategic basis for deterrence.

mainstream   The political position occupied by most people, generally the center on the ideological spectrum.

Majority Leader   In the House and Senate, the leader chosen by the majority party.

majority rule   Control of government by the majority of citizens, but without the constitutional restraints that the Framers of the Constitution were so careful to provide.

mark up   To change, revise, or amend bills under consideration by a congressional committee. When a bill is in committee, it usually undergoes considerable revision and a marked-up version is submitted to the full house for a vote.

Marxism   The theoretical basis of Communism and certain aspects of socialism. Karl Marx, with the assistance of Friedrich Engels, developed a systematic philosophy that dealt with metaphysical, ethical, historical, and political issues among others. In summary, the basic premise of Marxism is that the universe is wholly materialistic and that materialistic forces alone determine all events. Under the rubric

of **dialectical materialism,** reality is conceived as moving through a process of conflict in which two opposites give rise to a third component, which creates within itself its own opposition, thus repeating the original process, and on and on. **Historical materialism** is the application of the dialectical process to the political development of the state and society. In this instance the motive force is the class struggle in which one class creates its opposing class and through their conflict both create a new class, which replaces them and repeats the process. Each class struggles for control over the means of production, which is the basis for the whole of society. The end of the process occurs when the working class (the proletariat) overturns the capitalist class and society, during the dictatorship of the proletariat, eliminating all class conflict and with it the need for the state. Society then returns to its original stateless condition of harmony.

Marxism-Leninism   A combination of the philosophy of Marxism with the theory of government and revolutionary action developed by V.I. Lenin. Basically, Lenin argued that capitalism can be changed only by a working-class revolution led by a small disciplined party. This "vanguard" of the working class would lead society through the intermediate phase of socialism to the final classless stage of communism. Marxism-Leninism is the official doctrine of the Communist Party of the Soviet Union and of all other communist parties under its influence.

managed news   Information or news released by the government to put it in a favorable light.

mass media   That part of the media that appeals to very large numbers of people.

media   Newspapers, magazines, television, and radio. The word "media" is the Latin plural for "medium," which has the sense of "instrument," "means," or "conveyance." We use the plural to mean *instruments of communication.* See **electronic media, print media.**

Medicaid   A joint federal and state program run by the states to pay for medical care for the needy.

Medicare   A federal program that pays some of the costs for health care for persons over the age of 65.

military-industrial complex   The "iron triangle" of the Defense Department, its supervisory committees on Capitol Hill, and the armaments industry that often determines defense policy.

Minority Leader   In the House and the Senate the leader elected by members of the minority party.

monetary policy   A technique of managing the economy by increasing or decreasing the amount of money that is available by raising or lowering interest rates or by requiring larger or smaller bank reserves (the amount of money a bank must keep on hand to cover deposits). For example, when the government wants to fight inflation it often adopts a "tight money" policy—which in effect means decreasing the amount of money that is available, raising interest rates, and requiring larger bank reserves. See **fiscal policy.**

multiparty system   A political system composed of more than two parties, which usually requires a coalition among parties to form a government.

nationalism   1. A belief that the inhabitants or citizens of a country constitute a single, homogeneous community. In multiethnic societies, such as the United States, differences between people are ignored in favor of elements that unite them, such as a common history or experience.   2. Concentration of power or authority in the central government of a nation.

nationalization   Government ownership of the major instruments of wealth or public service, such as banks, railroads, electric utilities, farms, retail chains, and the like. Socialism is characterized by nationalization—complete in the case of most Communist countries, existing alongside private enterprise in most social democratic ones. Today, almost all political systems have some degree of nationalization, such as Amtrak or TVA in the United States.

national supremacy   The doctrine established in *McCulloch* v. *Maryland* (1819) that the Constitution, federal laws, and treaties are the supreme law of the land and that conflicting state actions are void.

NATO (North Atlantic Treaty Organization)   The Western anticommunist alliance consisting of the United States, Canada, western European nations, and Turkey. It has an integrated military command structure. See **Warsaw Pact.**

natural law   The "higher law" derived from the relationships among persons in a state of nature.

natural rights   Rights derived from natural law, such as the right to life, liberty, and property.

Nazism   The official doctrine of the National Socialist German Workers Party under Adolf Hitler. A jumble of disconnected beliefs, Nazism is principally a variation of fascism that glorified the "Aryan" race as superior to all other races. Thus, in the Nazi view, Aryans are a master race and all other races should be subordinate to it. In pursuit of racial mastery, the Nazi leaders of Germany undertook a campaign of conquest across Europe and genocide against the Jews as well as oppression of all non-German nationalities. Nazism derived from a species of nineteenth-century Austrian socialism combined with racist doctrines of French and English writers, supranationalist and hero-worship ideas of a number of Germans, and the paranoid notions of Hitler himself. Although World War II ended with the defeat of Nazi Germany, Nazism has not come to an end. The United States, England, and Germany all have **neo-Nazi** movements. In the United States, the neo-Nazis are linked to the Ku Klux Klan, the Aryan Nation movement, and other hate groups.

necessary and proper clause   See **implied powers.**

neutrality   A government policy of not taking sides in a war or other conflict. Neutrality is usually declared so that a nation can trade with all belligerents.

New Deal   President Franklin D. Roosevelt's program, adopted in 1933 and subsequent years during the Great Depression, to bring economic prosperity and social security through government intervention.

New Federalism   First announced by President Richard M. Nixon in 1969, New Federalism encompasses programs whose purpose is to transfer responsibilities from the federal government to state and local governments.

nominating convention   The gathering of party delegates for the purpose of choosing candidates.

NRC (Nuclear Regulatory Commission)   A federal agency that is mandated to license and regulate the nuclear industry.

nuclear freeze   An ideological position that advocates stopping all nuclear weapons research, testing, production, and deployment by all nuclear powers. Freeze supporters argue that each side of the East-West rivalry has enough weapons to destroy each other and the world several times over.

OAS (Organization of American States)   An international association of Western Hemisphere states created in 1948 for mutual defense and cooperation in economic, cultural, and other fields.

off-the-record   Information given by public officials to reporters, but not for attribution.

off year   Nonpresidential election years.

oligarchy   A form of government in which a few powerful, wealthy individuals rule for their own benefit.

OMB (Office of Management and Budget)   The department of the Executive Office of the President charged with preparing the federal budget, developing fiscal policy, and overseeing the federal bureaucracy on behalf of the president.

ombudsman   An official who acts as an intermediary between citizens and the government.

one man (person), one vote   The requirement established by the Supreme Court that electoral districts be apportioned so as to be equal in population.

open convention   A national convention in which no candidate starts with a majority of the delegates.

opinion leader   A person, usually a member of the political, economic, or social elite, who can influence the views of others.

original intent   The presumption that the Framers had a unified, coherent program or set of values that was fully realized in the Constitution. Original intent is a basic element of conservative thought.

original jurisdiction   The authority to hear a case the first time it is raised, i.e., to hold the trial that determines the facts of the case.

oval office   The president's official office, used as a synonym for the president and his closest advisors.

oversight   The supervisory function of a legislature. On the federal level, Congress oversees the operations of executive agencies and departments to make certain they conform to the law. Specific congressional committees and subcommittees keep tabs on particular departments, as for example the Senate Foreign Relations Committee keeps an eye on the State Department.

parity   Equality or equivalence.   **1. nuclear parity.** The approximate equivalence of the destructive capability of U.S. and Soviet nuclear forces. **2. wage parity.** Same salary levels established for rival government agencies, such as the police and fire fighters.   **3.** In farm pricing, a guaranteed price for agricultural produce paid by the federal government to farmers to secure their income levels and thereby their continued operation. The price support is intended to assure farmers that they would continue to have the same purchasing power as at an earlier period for grain, tractors, and the like.

parliamentary democracy   A system of government in which supreme authority rests with the legislature, from within which the executive is chosen. The leading parliamentary democracy is Great Britain, although there are a good many others as well. Indeed, this form of democracy is far more common than the kind practiced in the United States.

partisan   A person who is strongly committed to a political party or ideology. American voters are becoming increasingly less partisan, so that parties are less able to count on the support of certain segments of the population.

party discipline   Voting the party line after policy positions have been taken.

party line   The official position of a political party on current issues. Party discipline usually involves enforcement of a party line.

party platform   A statement of party positions, developed by a platform committee and adopted by national nominating conventions. American party platforms reflect the diverse viewpoints within each party, which often requires that positions be stated in broad terms.

patronage   The rewards of office dispensed to loyal followers and supporters by elected officials as a means of securing political power. Although it has been under continuous attack since its origins in classical Rome, patronage has proven to be one of the most permanent instruments of power.

pigeonholing   A congressional committee's effort to kill a bill by refusing to report it to the whole chamber.

plank   Part of a party platform, stating a position on a given issue.

pluralism   The existence of a variety of groups in the political process.

plurality   A greater number of votes than those of any other candidate, but not a majority of the votes cast.

pocket veto   A presidential veto of legislation by refusing to sign it within 10 days of congressional adjournment.

police state   A form of government that denies its citizens basic civil rights, such as the right to free expression or to due process of law, and rules through the use of police terror. The arbitrary will of the state's leader is superior to the law. Totalitarian governments are necessarily police states.

policy   The goal that is to be achieved by an action or series of actions undertaken by a government, political party, interest group, or individual. For example, the tax policy of liberal governments is the redistribution of income to lower economic levels. The term *policy* is also sometimes used for the plan or program by means of which a goal is reached.

political action committee (PAC)   A fund-raising organization that makes contributions to political campaigns on behalf of corporations, unions, professional associations, interest groups, or ideological causes. The purpose of PACs, of course, is to influence legislation or executive agency activities.

political apathy   Lack of interest in politics; failure to vote and participate in the political system.

political party   A group formed to field candidates for elective office and to advance general or specific policies.

political science   The systematic study of government and politics to determine the nature of political behavior.

politics   **1.** The interaction between government and the people who are governed. In democratic societies, that interaction occurs principally during elections, as in the United States and Great Britain. In a police state, that interaction often takes the form of suppressing dissent, as in Nazi Germany and Communist China.   **2. playing politics.** The methods for gaining and using power within a community or society, as for example by currying favor with influential individuals or groups.   **3.** The process by which the rewards of society are distributed. In the words of a well-known political scientist, the means for determining "who gets what, when, and how."

polity   **1.** Participants in a political system, such as the citizens of a state.   **2.** The political organizations of a society, such as the government or political parties.   **3.** In Aristotle's thought, an acceptable form of government, one that most closely resembles what we today would call a limited or constitutional democracy.

poll tax   A tax on voters in Southern states to discourage blacks and poor whites from voting; no longer permitted.

populism   An ideological position in which appeals are made to poor farmers, workers, and others to organize against bankers, big business, and other wealthy interests who are seen as exploiting those who are weak and poor. It first arose in various parts of the United States in the late nineteenth century as a progressive movement. Somewhat later it split and one segment of the populist movement turned racist—anti-black, anti-Catholic, and anti-immigrant. Populism has retained much appeal throughout the twentieth century and has periodically found powerful spokesmen, from Huey Long to Jesse Jackson.

pork barrel   A government appropriation that benefits a particular district or state and thereby gains political credit for the member of Congress representing the district or state.

pragmatism   **1.** In politics, a practical approach to problems without regard to principles or ideologies. The basic slogan of a pragmatist might be, "if it works, it's good." American politics is often thought to be pragmatic rather than ideological. Whether this is actually possible is an open question.   **2.** A school of American philosophy that holds truth, value, and meaning are found in the practical consequences of action.

precedent   A judicial opinion that is followed in future cases of a similar nature.

president pro tempore   The presiding officer of the Senate in the absence of the vice president, elected by the body and by tradition the most senior member of the majority party.

press secretary   A person who is in charge of media relations for politicians.

print media   The press; newspapers and magazines.

private bill   See **bill.**

private calendar   A list of private bills in the House.

privatization   A program or policy of turning over public properties and functions to private entrepreneurs and other business people. A favored goal of conservatives.

procedural rights   Those amendments that protect the accused: specifically, the fourth, fifth, sixth, and eighth amendments as well as the due process clause of the fourteenth amendment.

pro-choice   Advocating the freedom to choose whether to have an abortion. Pro-choice supporters believe that the decision to give birth to a child is an extremely private one and should not be dictated by government or community rules. The Supreme Court approved the pro-choice position in *Roe* v. *Wade*.

progressive   Believing that government has the responsibility to care for those who are weak, downtrodden, or vulnerable in some way and to make the democratic system open to all segments of the population; also, a person holding such beliefs.

proletariat   The working class in Marxist vocabulary.

pro-life   Advocating government restriction of the right to choose to have an abortion. Pro-life supporters argue that a fetus is a living human being and that to have an abortion is to commit murder. They oppose *Roe* v. *Wade* and seek to have it overturned.

public bill   See **bill.**

public policy   See **policy.**

quid pro quo   Latin meaning "something for something." A basic principle of political deals. In English it can be rendered as, "I'll do this for you, if you do that for me."

quorum   The minimum number of members who must be present in a legislative or other body to conduct business. In the House and the Senate a majority of members constitutes a quorum.

quota   A fixed number of members of a particular group that is given entry to opportunities. Jews had experienced the quota system as restrictive and pro- ducing negative effects on their chances for advancement. Blacks have looked forward to quotas as a means for assuring increased opportunities, thus having a positive effect on their chances for advancement. See **affirmative action.**

racism   Hostility or antagonism based on skin color, national origin, or religious affiliation. Another aspect of racism is belief in one's own superiority and another's inferiority because of skin color, national origin, or religion.

radical   **1.** Advocating fundamental change in a social, economic, or political system, such as replacing economic competition with mutual aid. Often, radical positions call for revolutionary or other violent action to bring about change.   **2.** A person holding such views.   **3. radical Right.** An extreme fringe of the Right usually advocating the use of coercive power to impose its own views and suppress all dissenting ideas; also often called the far Right.

rank and file   The broad membership as opposed to the leaders in any group.

recess   A temporary suspension of House or Senate proceedings.

redistribution   A policy of shifting wealth and other social benefits from one segment of the population to another. The basic instrument of redistribution is taxation. The liberals are believed to favor redistributing wealth from the rich to the poor, while conservatives are believed to advocate redistributing wealth back from the poor to the rich. Some methods for redistributing social benefits are affirmative action programs, legislative redistricting, and school integration.

red tape   Formal and inefficient administrative procedures.

referendum   An electoral device for submitting a law or constitutional amendment to the citizenry for approval.

regulation   **1.** Government oversight of private business so as to achieve a social benefit, such as protecting consumers or the environment.   **2.** The rules of a federal, state, or municipal agency that private organizations are required to satisfy to either operate or do business with the government.

representative democracy   A form of government in which citizens periodically choose their representatives from among contending parties or individuals. Compare **direct democracy.**

republic   Representative government; a form of government in which authority is delegated to elected officials by those who are eligible to vote. This form of government goes back to ancient Rome and has existed in one way or another since. The Founding Fathers created a republic when they wrote the United States Constitution. See **direct democracy.**

resolution   A measure passed by the House or the Senate expressing sentiments on political issues or personal matters.

retributive justice   The process by which an accused person is found guilty of a crime and punished. The procedural rights in the Constitution address the issue of retributive justice. In the philosophy of Aristotle, one of the two forms that justice takes. Compare **distributive justice.**

rider   An amendment to a bill that may or may not relate to the subject of the bill and that would have little chance of passing on its own.

Right   Those holding conservative views, which may range from support for cutting taxes for the wealthy to opposition to government programs to help the poor. Compare **radical Right.**   **2. right wing.** A faction of a political organization that is to the Right of the majority. See **Left.**

right   A privilege or power to which a person is legitimately entitled.   **1. fundamental rights.** Basic rights that come before those granted by a government or constitution and that cannot be taken from a person, such as the right of self-defense. See **natural rights.**   **2. right to privacy.** The right to be free of government intrusion into personal matters. This right is implied by several of the amendments that make up the Bill of Rights: the first, fourth, fifth, and ninth amendments each suggest in different ways that the founders assumed a fundamental right of privacy.

Rules Committee   The legislative gatekeeper of the House that determines the procedures under which most legislation is debated and amended on the floor.

SALT (Strategic Arms Limitation Talks)   Negotiations between the United States and the Soviet Union for the purpose of limiting the production of long-range nuclear weapons. **SALT I** began in 1969 and led to the ABM treaty of 1972. **SALT II** started in 1972 and a treaty was signed in 1979 but not ratified by the Senate because of the Soviet invasion of Afghanistan.

SDI (Strategic Defense Initiative)   See **Star Wars.**

select committee   A special committee of the House or the Senate created for a specific purpose, usually investigative in nature, and for a limited period of time.

senatorial courtesy   The Senate's custom of not confirming a presidential nominee for office in a senator's state when that senator is of the president's party and disapproves of the nominee.

seniority   The custom of assigning committee chairmanships in Congress to the most senior member of the majority party on the committee.

separation of church and state   An American principle first developed by Thomas Jefferson under which the government cannot impose a religion on its citizenry and religious organizations cannot receive support from the state. Made part of the Constitution by the First Amendment.

separation of powers   The partial division of legislative, executive, and judicial authority among the three branches of the national government.

shared functions   The interlinking of powers and responsibilities among the three branches of government, so that each has some influence on the others, resulting in checks and balances.

Sherman Antitrust Act   The federal law of 1890 that makes monopolies, price fixing, and the like illegal.

social contract   A political theory holding that before governments were created individuals joined together to form states for mutual protection. In doing so they entered into implicit contracts by which they surrendered certain individual rights in return for the securities and guarantees provided by the state. The term derives from a work by the eighteenth-century French philosopher Jean-Jacques Rousseau. See **contract theory** and **state of nature.**

social democrat   A person who believes in nationalization and central planning of an economy while allowing some private enterprise. Though most social democrats believe in a single-party state, they also believe that some divergence of opinion should be tolerated and that parliamentary government should be permitted. Most social democrats also hold that significant change can be brought about only by gradual means in a democratic process, not by revolutionary ones in an authoritarian setting. Several European countries have social democratic governments.

socialism   A political ideology holding in most cases that all aspects of society must be under the control of the state. This may require that an entire economy be nationalized and that all social activity—such as religious worship, public meetings, or political discussions—be subject to government supervision. However, there are and have been many variations on the theme of socialism since its origins in the early nineteenth century. All share certain features, though. They all claim to hold the best interests of workers at the center of their form of socialism. Uncontrolled capitalism, they each argue, produces extreme economic and social dislocations. See **communism, fascism, Marxism-Leninism,** and **Nazism.** Compare **liberalism.**

Social Security Act   The 1935 law establishing the first social insurance program that provides retirement benefits, survivors' benefits, aid to disabled workers, as well as federal-state unemployment insurance.

sovereignty   Supreme authority in a political state. The possession of sovereignty determines the type of government a society has. For example, in a monarchy, a king or queen is sovereign. In a federal republic, such as the United States, sovereignty is divided between individual states and the central government.

Speaker of the House   A representative chosen by a majority of the representatives to preside over the U.S. House of Representatives. The office of Speaker is called for in the Constitution.

special interests   A code word for interest groups of which the person using the phrase disapproves. All interests are of course "special."

split ticket   A ballot cast by a voter who chooses candidates from different parties for different offices.

spoils system   Patronage. The term comes from an ancient military adage, "to the victor belong the spoils," and has had negative connotations from its first use.

standing   The legal right to start a lawsuit. To have standing a person or others bringing suit must show that they have suffered an injury.

standing committee   A permanent, major committee of the House or the Senate.

START (Strategic Arms Reduction Treaty)   An effort by the Reagan administration to achieve a treaty agreement with the Soviet Union in which long-range nuclear weapons are reduced as well as limited in quantity. See **SALT.**

Star Wars   The popular name for SDI, the Strategic Defense Initiative, which is a space-based defense system that was strongly advocated by President Reagan despite scientific skepticism about its viability. *Star Wars* is the title of a science-fiction movie.

state   An organized community occupying a geographical area and providing authority, security, rewards, a system of justice, and laws. In ancient times this community consisted of a city and the surrounding area under its control and is known as a **city-state.** Since the late Middle Ages, the geographical area has grown and has consisted of a number of communities under a central authority and is known as a **nation-state.**

state of nature   In contract theories, the original condition of humanity before the social contract. There have been a wide variety of notions of what that original condition was. Since it is an imagined state, it is always described to suit the theoretical needs of the thinker using it.

State of the Union message   The president's annual report to Congress, required by the Constitution.

statutory law   The body of law made up of all legislation enacted by Congress and state legislatures. Compare **common law.**

strict construction   A narrow and literal interpretation of the Constitution, resulting in a restrictive rather than expansive view of national power.

Succession Act (1947)   The law that established the order of succession to the presidency in the event of the president's death or disability: vice-president, Speaker of the House, president pro tempore of the Senate, and members of the Cabinet in the order of the seniority of their departments.

suffrage   The right to vote; the franchise.

supply-side economics   The theory that low tax rates encourage investment, which in turn leads to growth in productivity and increased employment, which then leads to more tax revenues than are possible with high taxes. A basic economic principle of conservatism.

supremacy clause   A clause in Article VI of the Constitution stating in effect that federal laws are superior to state and local laws.

terrorism   Random violence perpetrated against civilians and noncombatants by radical political groups in an effort to bring down a government or to change its policies; considered an especially heinous form of political activity.

theocracy   A form of government in which the clergy or those under the control of the clergy rule and which operates according to religious laws. Iran and the Vatican are theocracies.

third party   In presidential politics, a party outside of the two major political parties that fields candidates for the presidency and vice-presidency.

Third World   Underdeveloped nations, mainly former colonies lying chiefly south of the industrialized countries of the planet, that have extremely poor economies and are dependent on the wealthy nations of the world.

ticket   A slate of candidates, almost always from the same party, who run for office as a team.

totalitarianism   A form of government in which the leadership of the state has total and absolute control over its population and every aspect of society. Totalitarian systems do not allow dissent and are not bound by law. See **absolutism; dictatorship;** and **police state.**

trade balance   See **balance of payments.**

trade deficit   See **balance of payments.**

trade surplus   See **balance of payments.**

triad   The U.S. nuclear defense strategy. This consists of three parts: land-based ICBMs; submarine-launched ballistic missiles; and long-range bombers armed with nuclear bombs.

"trickle-down" theory   The belief that the wealth and prosperity of corporations and individuals inevitably "trickle down" to benefit lower-income groups.

UN (The United Nations)   An international organization founded in 1945 for the purpose of maintaining worldwide peace. It has a membership of 150 states but has so far not succeeded in its primary mission. The organization consists of the **Security Council,** which is an executive body, and the **General Assembly,** which is a deliberative body that can only recommend actions to the Security Council.

unanimous consent   A Senate procedure under which the rules are suspended and the conduct of business is facilitated.

unicameral   A one-house legislature. Nebraska is the only state with a unicameral legislature.

Union Calendar   A list of appropriations and revenue bills in the House.

U.S.S.R. (Union of Soviet Socialist Republics)   The Soviet Union, a federation of fifteen constituent republics; Russia under communist rule since 1917.

veto   Rejection by the president of congressional legislation; only a two-thirds vote by both houses of Congress can override a presidential veto.

voice vote   In the house or the Senate, when the presiding officer calls for the "ayes" and "nays," and gives the decision to the louder chorus.

War Powers Resolution   A 1973 law asserting congressional authority over the power of the president to order hostile military action.

Warsaw Pact   The alliance of East European communist nations under the leadership of the Soviet Union. Created in response to the formation of NATO.

welfare state   A system under which the government takes action to ensure the economic welfare of its citizens.

whip   A legislative party leader who ensures the party members are present to vote the party line.

women's liberation   A movement by women for the purposes of achieving full equality with men in social, political, and economic areas. See **feminism.**

zoning   A formal process by local government of restricting the types of activities and structures in a specific area. Originally devised to protect middle-class residential areas from the incursion of industrial and commercial enterprises, it has since been used to exclude low-income people and racial minorities.

INDEX